EDWIN HATCH

ESSAYS
IN BIBLICAL GREEK

STUDIES ON
THE VALUE AND USE OF THE SEPTUAGINT
ON THE MEANINGS OF WORDS
AND PSYCHOLOGICAL TERMS IN BIBLICAL GREEK
ON QUOTATIONS FROM THE SEPTUAGINT
ON ORIGEN'S REVISION OF JOB AND ON THE TEXT
OF ECCLESIASTICUS
WITH AN INDEX OF BIBLICAL PASSAGES

Wipf & Stock
PUBLISHERS
Eugene, Oregon

Wipf and Stock Publishers
199 West 8th Avenue, Suite 3
Eugene, Oregon 97401

Essays in Biblical Greek
By Hatch, Edwin
ISBN: 1-59244-467-9
Publication date 1/14/2004
Previously published by Oxford, 1889

PREFACE.

—+—

THE present work consists of the substance of the Lectures delivered by the writer during his terms of office as Grinfield Lecturer on the Septuagint. It is designed not so much to furnish a complete answer to the questions which it raises as to point out to students of sacred literature some of the rich fields which have not yet been adequately explored, and to offer suggestions for their exploration. It is almost entirely tentative in its character: and the writer has abstained from a discussion of the views which have been already advanced on some of the subjects of which it treats, because he thinks that in Biblical philology even more than in other subjects it is desirable for a student in the present generation to investigate the facts for himself, uninfluenced by the bias which necessarily arises from the study of existing opinions.

Those portions of the work which depend on the *apparatus criticus* of Holmes and Parsons must especially be regarded as provisional (see pp. 131, 132). The writer shares the gratification which all Biblical students feel at the prospect of a new critical edition of the Septuagint being undertaken by members of the great school of Cambridge scholars which has already done work of exceptional importance in the criticism of the New Testament: and he looks forward to the time when it will be possible to study the Greek text of the Old Testament with the same confidence in the data of criticism which is possessed by students of the New Testament. But instead of suspending all critical study until that time arrives, he thinks that the forming of provisional inferences, even upon imperfect data, will tend to accelerate its arrival.

It is proper to add that in his references both to the Hebrew and to the Syriac version, the writer has had the advantage of the assistance of some distinguished Oxford friends : but he refrains from mentioning their names, because he is too grateful for their help to wish to throw upon them any part of the responsibility for his shortcomings.

PURLEIGH RECTORY,
September 19, 1888.

CONTENTS.

—•◦•—

CONTENTS.

ESSAY III.

ON PSYCHOLOGICAL TERMS IN BIBLICAL GREEK.

ESSAY IV.

ON EARLY QUOTATIONS FROM THE SEPTUAGINT.

CONTENTS.

ESSAY V.

ON COMPOSITE QUOTATIONS FROM THE SEPTUAGINT.

ESSAY VI.

ON ORIGEN'S REVISION OF THE LXX TEXT OF JOB.

CONTENTS.

ESSAY VII.

ON THE TEXT OF ECCLESIASTICUS.

I. ON THE VALUE AND USE OF THE SEPTUAGINT.

THERE is a remarkable difference between the amount of
attention which has been given to the language of the Old
Testament and that which has been given to the language
of the New Testament. To the language of the Old
Testament scholars not only of eminence but of genius
have consecrated a lifelong devotion. The apparatus of
study is extensive. There are trustworthy dictionaries and
concordances. There are commentaries in which the
question of the meaning of the words is kept distinct from
that of their theological bearings. There are so many
grammars as to make it difficult for a beginner to choose
between them. In our own University the study is en-
couraged not only by the munificent endowment of the
Regius Professorship, which enables at least one good
scholar to devote his whole time to his subject, but also
by College lectureships and by several forms of rewards
for students.

The language of the New Testament, on the other hand,
has not yet attracted the special attention of any considerable scholar. There is no good lexicon. There is no
philological commentary. There is no adequate grammar.
In our own University there is no professor of it, but only
a small endowment for a terminal lecture, and four small
prizes.

The reason of this comparative neglect of a study which
should properly precede and underlie all other branches of

theological study, seems to me mainly to lie in the assumption which has been persistently made, that the language of the New Testament is identical with the language which was spoken in Athens in the days of Pericles or Plato, and which has left us the great monuments of Greek classical literature. In almost every lexicon, grammar, and commentary the words and idioms of the New Testament are explained, not indeed exclusively, but chiefly, by a reference to the words and idioms of Attic historians and philosophers. The degree of a man's knowledge of the latter is commonly taken as the degree of his right to pronounce upon the former; and almost any average scholar who can construe Thucydides is supposed to be thereby qualified to criticise a translation of the Gospels.

It would be idle to attempt to deny that the resemblances between Attic Greek and the language of the New Testament are both close and numerous : that the two languages are in fact only the same language spoken under different conditions of time and place, and by different races. But at the same time there has been, and still is, an altogether inadequate appreciation of their points of difference : and, as a result of this inadequate appreciation, those points of difference have not been methodically and exhaustively studied. Such a methodical and exhaustive study lies before the coming generation of scholars : it is impossible now, and it would under any circumstances be impossible for a single scholar. It requires an apparatus which does not yet exist, and which can only be gathered together by co-operation : it requires a discussion of some of its canons of investigation by persons not only of various acquirements but also of various habits of mind : it requires also, at least for its more difficult questions, a maturity of judgment which is the slow growth of time. All that can be here attempted is a brief description of the points to which attention must primarily be directed, of the chief means which exist for their investigation, and of the main principles upon which such an investigation should proceed.

The differences between the language of Athens in the fourth century before Christ and the language of the New Testament may be roughly described as differences of time and differences of country.

I. Many differences were the natural result of the lapse of time. For Greek was a living language, and a living language is always in movement. It was kept in motion partly by causes external to itself, and partly by the causes which are always at work in the speech of all civilized races.

The more important of the former group of causes were the rise of new ideas, philosophical and theological, the new social circumstances, the new political combinations, the changes in the arts of life, and the greater facilities of intercourse with foreign nations.

Causes of the latter kind were stronger in their operation than the attempt which was made by the literary class to give to ancient models of style and expression a factitious permanence. By the operation of an inevitable law some terms had come to have a more general, and others a more special, application : metaphors had lost their original vividness : intensive words had a weakened force, and required to be strengthened : new verbs had been formed from, substantives, and new substantives from verbs : compound words had gathered a meaning of their own which could not be resolved into the meaning of their separate parts : and the peculiar meaning which had come to attach itself to one member of a group of conjugates had passed to other members.

In a large number of cases the operation of these causes which are due to the lapse of time, forms a sufficient explanation of the differences between Classical and Biblical

Greek. The inference that this was the case is corroborated by the fact that in many cases the differences are not peculiar to Biblical Greek, but common to it and to all contemporary Greek.

The following are examples of the operation of these causes.

ἀδυνατεῖν has lost its active sense 'to be unable to . . .' and acquired the neuter sense 'to be impossible': e. g. LXX. Gen. 18. 14 μὴ ἀδυνατήσει παρὰ τῷ Θεῷ ῥῆμα ; S. Matt. 18. 20/οὐδὲν ἀδυνατήσει ὑμῖν. Aquil. Jer. 32. 17 οὐκ ἀδυνατήσει ἀπὸ σοῦ πᾶν ῥῆμα, = LXX. οὐ μὴ ἀποκρυβῇ ἀπὸ σοῦ οὐθέν.

ἀκαταστασία : the political circumstances of Greece and the Eas· after the death of Alexander had developed the idea of politica instability, and with it the word ἀκαταστασία, Polyb. 1. 70. 1 S. Luke 21. 9, which implied more than mere unsettledness : for it is used by Symm. Ezek. 12. 19 as a translation of רָאֲנָה 'dread' or 'anxious care,' and it is coupled by Clem. R. 3. 2 with διωγμός.

ἐντροπή had borrowed from a new metaphorical use of ἐντρέπεσθαι the meaning of 'shame,' 1 Cor. 6. 5 : cf. τὸ ἐντρεπτικόν Epict. 1. 5. 3, 9.

ἐπισκιάζειν had come to be used not only of a cloud which overshadows, and so obscures, but also of a light which dazzles by its brightness,/Exod. 40. 29 (35) . . . ὅτι ἐπεσκίαζεν ἐπ' αὐτὴν ἡ νεφέλη καὶ δόξης κυρίου ἐνεπλήσθη ἡ σκηνή : the current use of the word in this sense is shown by e. g. Philo, De Mundi Opif. i. p. 2, where the beauties of the Mosaic account of the Creation are spoken of as ταῖς μαρμαρυγαῖς τὰς τῶν ἐντυγχανόντων ψυχὰς ἐπισκιάζοντα : id. Quod omnis probus liber, ii. p. 446 δι' ἀσθένειαν τοῦ κατὰ ψυχὴν ὄμματος ὃ ταῖς μαρμαρυγαῖς πέφυκεν ἐπισκιάζεσθαι.

ἐπιτιμία had given up the meaning in which it is used by the Attic orators, 'possession of full political rights,' and acquired the meaning of the Attic ἐπιτίμησις or ἐπιτίμιον, 'punishment,' or 'penalty': Wisd. 3. 10; |2 Cor. 3. 6.

ἐργάζεσθαι had added?to its meaning of manual labour, in which in the LXX. it translates עָבַד, e. g. Exod. 20. 9, the meaning of moral practice, in which in the LXX. it translates פָּעַל especially in the Psalms, e. g. 5. 6 ; 6. 9 ; 13 (14). 4 ; in the N. T. e. g. S. Matt. 7. 23 ; Rom. 2. 10.

ζωοποιεῖν has lost its meaning 'to produce live offspring' (e. g. Arist. *H. A.* 5. 27. 3), and has acquired the meaning 'to preserve alive,' e. g. Judges 21. 14 τὰς γυναῖκας ἃς ἐζωοποίησαν ἀπὸ τῶν θυγατέρων Ἰαβεῖς Γαλαάδ (cf. Barnab. 6 πρῶτον τὸ παιδίον μέλιτι εἶτα γάλακτι ζωοποιεῖται), or 'to quicken,' e. g. 2 Kings 5. 7 ὁ θεὸς ἐγὼ τοῦ θανατῶσαι καὶ ζωοποιῆσαι . . . ; S. John 5. 21 οὕτως καὶ ὁ υἱὸς οὓς θέλει ζωοποιεῖ. Rom. 4. 17 . . . θεοῦ τοῦ ζωοποιοῦντος τοὺς νεκρούς. So also ζωογονεῖν, which in later non-Biblical Greek has the meaning 'to produce live offspring,' as Pallas was produced from Ζεὺς, Lucian, *Dial. Deor.* 8, is used in Biblical Greek in the same senses as ζωοποιεῖν, e. g. Judges 8. 19 εἰ ἐζωογονήκειτε αὐτούς, οὐκ ἂν ἀπέκτεινα ὑμᾶς. 1 Sam. 2. 6 κύριος θανατοῖ καὶ ζωογονεῖ. S. Luke 17. 33 ὃς ἂν ἀπολέσῃ αὐτὴν ζωογονήσει αὐτήν. Both words are in the LXX. translations of חָיָה *pi.* and *hiph.* (There is a good instance of the way in which most of the Fathers interpret specially Hellenistic phrases by the light of Classical Greek in St. Augustine's interpretation of the word, *Quaest. super Levit.* lib. iii. c. 38, 'Non enim quae vivificant, i. e. vivere faciunt, sed quae vivos foetus gignunt, i. e. non ova sed pullos, dicuntur ζωογονοῦντα).'

κειρία, which was used properly of the cord of a bedstead, e. g. Aristoph. *Av.* 816, had come to be used of bedclothes, LXX. Prov. 7. 16 (where Aquila and Theodotion have περιστρώμασι): hence, in S. John 11. 44, it is used of the swathings of a corpse.

κτίσις had come to have the meaning of κτίσμα, i. e. like *creatio*, it was used not of the act of creating, but of the thing created: Judith 9. 12 βασιλεῦ πάσης κτίσεώς σου. Wisd. 16. 24 ἡ γὰρ κτίσις σοι τῷ ποιήσαντι ὑπηρετοῦσα. Rom. 8. 20 τῇ γὰρ ματαιότητι ἡ κτίσις ὑπετάγη.

λικμᾶν had expanded its meaning of separating grain from chaff into the wider meaning of scattering as chaff is scattered by the wind, e. g. LXX. Is. 41. 15, 16 ἀλοήσεις ὄρη καὶ λεπτυνεῖς βουνοὺς καὶ ὡς χνοῦν θήσεις καὶ λικμήσεις: hence it and διασπείρειν are used interchangeably as translations of זָרָה 'to scatter,' both in the LXX. and in the other translations of the Hexapla, e. g. Ps. 43 (44). 12, LXX. διέσπειρας, Symm. ἐλίκμησας, Jer. 15. 7, LXX. διασπερῶ, Aquil. Symm. λικμήσω. Hence it came to be used as the nearest metaphorical expression for annihilation: in Dan. 2. 44 Theodotion uses λικμήσει to correct the LXX. ἀφανίσει as the translation of הָסֵף *aph.* from סוּף 'to put an end to.' Hence the antithesis between συνθλασθήσεται and λικμήσει in S. Luke 20. 18.

πάροικος had lost its meaning of 'neighbour' and had come to mean 'sojourner,' so that a clear distinction existed between παροικεῖν and κατοικεῖν, e.g. LXX. Gen. 36. 44 (37. 1) κατῴκει δὲ Ἰακὼβ ἐν τῇ γῇ οὗ παρῴκησεν ὁ πατὴρ αὐτοῦ, ἐν γῇ Χαναάν, cf. Philo *De confus. ling.* i. p. 416 . . . κατῴκησαν ὡς ἐν πατρίδι, οὐχ ὡς ἐπὶ ξένης παρῴκησαν.

πράκτωρ seems to have added to its Attic meaning 'tax-gatherer' the meaning 'jailer': since in an Egyptian inscription in the *Corp. Inscr. Graec.* No. 4957. 15 πρακτόρειον is used in the sense of a prison, εἰς τὸ πρακτόρειον καὶ εἰς τὰς ἄλλας φυλακάς. Hence τῷ πράκτορι in S. Luke 12. 58 is equivalent to τῷ ὑπηρέτῃ in S. Matt. 5. 25.

προβιβάζειν had acquired the special meaning 'to teach,' or 'to teach diligently': it occurs in LXX. Deut. 6. 7 προβιβάσεις αὐτὰ τοὺς υἱούς σου, where it is the translation of שׁנן *pi.* 'to sharpen' sc. the mind, and hence 'to inculcate.' Hence S. Matt. 14. 8 ἡ δὲ προβιβασθεῖσα ὑπὸ τῆς μητρὸς αὐτῆς.

συνοχή had acquired from the common use of συνέχεσθαι the new meaning of 'distress': S. Luke 21. 25 συνοχὴ ἐθνῶν ἐν ἀπορίᾳ. In Ps. 118 (119). 143 Aquila uses it as the translation of מצוק = LXX. ἀνάγκαι.

ὑποζύγιον had narrowed its general meaning of 'beast of burden' to the special meaning of 'ass': it is the common translation in the LXX. of חמור. Hence its use in S. Matt. 21. 5; 2 Pet. 2. 16.

It will be seen from these instances, which might be largely multiplied, that in certain respects the ordinary changes which the lapse of time causes in the use of words are sufficient to account for the differences between Classical and Biblical Greek. There are certain parts of both the LXX. and the New Testament in which no other explanation is necessary: so far as these parts are concerned the two works may be treated as monuments of post-Classical Greek, and the uses of words may be compared with similar uses in contemporary secular writers. It is probably this fact which has led many persons to overrate the extent to which those writers may be used to throw light upon Biblical Greek in general.

But the application of it without discrimination to all parts of the Greek Bible ignores the primary fact that neither the Septuagint nor the Greek Testament is a single book by a single writer. Each is a collection of books which vary largely in respect not only of literary style, but also of philological character. A proposition which may be true of one book in the collection is not necessarily true of another: and side by side with the passages for whose philological peculiarities contemporary Greek furnishes an adequate explanation, is a largely preponderating number of passages in which an altogether different explanation must be sought.

Before seeking for such an explanation, it will be advisable to establish the fact of the existence of differences; and this will be best done not by showing that different words are used, for this may almost always be argued to be a question only of literary style, but by showing that the same words are used in different parts of the New Testament in different senses—the one sense common to earlier or contemporary Greek, the other peculiar to Biblical Greek. The following few instances will probably be sufficient for the purpose.

ἀγαθοποιεῖν (1) is used in 1 Pet. 2. 15, 20 in its proper sense of doing what is morally good in contrast to doing what is morally evil: so Sext. Empir. 10. 70, 2 Clem. Rom. 10. 2. But (2) it is used in the LXX. Num. 10. 32, Jud. 17. 13 (Cod. A. and Lagarde's text, but Cod. B. and the Sixtine text ἀγαθυνεῖ), Zeph. 1. 12 as the translation of יָטַב hi. in the sense of benefiting and as opposed to doing harm. So in the Synoptic Gospels, S. Luke 6. 9, 35; S. Mark 3. 4 (Codd. A B C L, but Codd. אD ἀγαθὸν ποιῆσαι which is found in the same sense, and as a translation of יָמַב in Prov. 11. 17, where Symmachus has εὐεργετεῖ): and in Codd. D E L, etc. Acts 14. 17, where Codd. אA B C have the otherwise unknown (except to later ecclesiastical writers) ἀγαθουργῶν.

βλασφημεῖν and its conjugates (1) have in Rom. 3. 8, 1 Cor. 10. 30, 1 Pet. 4. 4, and elsewhere, the meaning which they have both in the Attic orators and in contemporary Greek, of slander or defamation of character.

But (2) in the Gospels they have the special sense of treating with scorn or contumely the name of God, as in the LXX., where (a) βλασφημεῖν translates נָּדַף *pi.* 2 Kings 19. 6, 22; in Num. 15. 30, Is. 37. 23 the same word is translated by παροξύνειν, but in the latter passage the other translators of the Hexapla revert to βλασφημεῖν; (b) βλασφημεῖν translates נָאֵץ *hithpo.* in Isa. 52. 5, and its derivative נֶאָצָה in Ezek. 35. 12; (c) βλάσφημος translates מְבָרֵךְ אָוֶן ' he blesses iniquity' (*i.e.* an idol) in Is. 66. 3.

διαλογισμός (1) is used in S. Luke 9. 46, Phil. 2. 14, and probably Rom. 14. 1, in the ordinary late Greek sense of discussion or dispute; but (2) it is used elsewhere in the Gospels, S. Matt. 15. 19 = S. Mark 7. 21; S. Luke 5. 22 (= S. Matt. 9. 4 ἐνθυμήσεις); 6. 8 of thoughts or cogitations in general. This is its meaning in the LXX., where it is used both of the thoughts or counsels of God, e. g. Ps. 39 (40). 6; 91 (92). 5, and of the (wicked) thoughts or counsels of men, e. g. Ps. 55 (56). 6; Is. 59. 7. In all these instances it is the translation of מַחֲשָׁבָה or מַחֲשֶׁבֶת.

ἐπιγινώσκειν, ἐπίγνωσις (1) are used in S. Luke 1. 4 in the Pauline Epistles, e. g. Rom. 3. 20; 1 Cor. 13. 12; Eph. 4. 13; and in Heb. 10. 26; 2 Pet. 1. 2. 8; 2. 20, in the sense of knowing fully, which is a common sense in later Greek, and became ultimately the dominant sense, so that in the second century Justin Martyr, *Tryph.* 3, defines philosophy as ἐπιστήμη τοῦ ὄντος καὶ τοῦ ἀληθοῦς ἐπίγνωσις: and still later, in Const. Apost. 7. 39, it was the second of the three stages of perfect knowledge, γνῶσις, ἐπίγνωσις, πληροφορία.

But (2) in the Synoptic Gospels ἐπιγινώσκειν is used in the sense of recognizing or being conscious of: e. g. S. Matt. 7. 16; 17. 12; S. Mark 5. 30; S. Luke 24. 16.

This variety may perhaps be partly explained by the hypothesis that some books reflect to a greater extent the literary language of the time, and others the popular language. But such an explanation covers only a small proportion of the facts. Even if it be allowed that what is peculiar to Biblical Greek reflects rather a popular than a literary use of words, the nature of that popular use requires a further investigation: and hence we pass to a different series of causes.

II. Biblical Greek belongs not only to a later period of the history of the language than Classical Greek, but also to a different country. The physical and social conditions were different. This is shown by the change in the general cast of the metaphors. The Attic metaphors of the law-courts, the gymnasia, and the sea are almost altogether absent, except so far as they had indelibly impressed themselves on certain words, and probably, in those words, lost their special reference through frequency of familiar usage. Their place is taken by metaphors which arose from the conditions of Syrian life and from the drift of Syrian ideas.

For example, whereas in Athens and Rome the bustling activity of the streets gave rise to the conception of life as a quick movement to and fro, ἀναστρέφεσθαι, ἀναστρόφη, *versari, conversatio,* the constant intercourse on foot between village and village, and the difficulties of travel on the stony tracks over the hills, gave rise in Syria to a group of metaphors in which life is conceived as a journey, and the difficulties of life as the common obstacles of a Syrian traveller. The conduct of life is the manner of walking, or the walking along a particular road, e.g. ἐπορεύθησαν ὑψηλῷ τραχήλῳ, ἐπορεύθη ἐν ὁδῷ τοῦ πατρὸς αὐτοῦ. A change in conduct is the turning of the direction of travel, ἐπιστρέφεσθαι. The hindrances to right conduct are the stones over which a traveller might stumble, or the traps or tanks into which he might fall in the darkness, σκάνδαλα, προσκόμματα, παγίδες, βόθυνοι. The troubles of life are the burdens which the peasants carried on their backs, φορτία. Again, the common employments of Syrian farmers gave rise to the frequent metaphors of sowing and reaping, of sifting the grain and gathering it into the barn, σπείρειν, θερίζειν, σινιάζειν, συνάγειν : the threshing of wheat furnished a metaphor for a devastating conquest, and the scattering of the chaff by the wind for utter annihilation, ἀλοᾶν, λικμᾶν. The pastoral life provided metaphors for both civil and moral government: sheep astray (πλανώμενοι) upon the hills, or fallen bruised down the rocky ravines (ἐσκυλμένοι καὶ ἐριμμένοι) furnished an apt symbol of a people which had wandered away from God. The simple ministries of an Eastern household (διακονεῖν, διακονία), the grinding of corn in the handmill, the leavening of bread, the earthen lamp on its lampstand which lit up the cottage room; the custom of giving of presents in return for presents (ἀνταποδιδόναι, ἀνταπόδοσις); the money-lending which, then as now, filled a large place in the rural economy of Eastern lands (δανείζειν, ὀφειλή, ὀφείλημα, ὀφειλέτης); the payment of daily wages (μισθός); the hoarding of money out of the reach alike of the robber and the tax-gatherer (θησαυρός, θησαυρίζειν); the numerous local courts with their judges and witnesses (κριτής, μάρτυρες, μαρτύριον, μαρτυρία); the capricious favouritism of Oriental potentates (προσωποληψία), all furnished metaphors which were not only expanded into apologues or parables, but also impressed themselves upon the common use of words.

But these changes in the cast and colour of metaphors, though they arise out of and indicate social circumstances to which Classical literature is for the most part a stranger, are intelligible without special study. They explain themselves. They might have taken place with a purely Greek population. The difficulty of Biblical Greek really begins when we remember that it was Greek as spoken not merely in a foreign country and under new circumstances, but also by an alien race. The disputed question of the extent to which it was so spoken does not affect the literary monuments with which we have to deal. Whether those monuments appealed immediately to a narrower or a wider circle of readers, they undoubtedly reflect current usage. They afford clear internal evidence that their writers, in most cases, were men whose thoughts were cast in a Semitic and not in a Hellenic mould. They were not only foreigners talking a language which was not their own, as an Englishman talks French : they were also men of one race speaking the language of another, as a Hindoo Mussulman talks English. This affected the language chiefly in that the race who thus spoke it had a different inheritance of religious and moral ideas from the race to which it properly belonged. The conceptions of God and goodness, the religious sanction and the moral ideal, were very different in men whose traditions came down from Moses and the prophets, from what they had been in men whose gods lived upon Olympus, and whose Pentateuch was the Iliad. The attitude of such men towards human life, towards nature, and towards God was so different that though Greek words were used they were the symbols of quite other than Greek ideas. For every race has its own mass and combinations of ideas; and when one race adopts the language of another, it cannot, from the very nature of the human mind, adopt with it the ideas of which that language is the expression. It takes the words but it cannot take their connotation : and it has ideas of its own for which it only finds in foreign phrases a rough and partial covering.

Biblical Greek is thus a language which stands by itself. What we have to find out in studying it is what meaning certain Greek words conveyed to a Semitic mind. Any induction as to such meaning must be gathered in the first instance from the materials which Biblical Greek itself affords. This may be taken as an axiom. It is too obvious to require demonstration. It is the application to these particular philological phenomena of the universal law of inductive reasoning. But at the same time it has been so generally neglected that in a not inconsiderable number of cases the meaning of New Testament words has to be ascertained afresh : nor does it seem probable that

the existing confusion will be cleared up until Biblical
Greek is treated as a newly discovered dialect would be
treated, and the meaning of all its words ascertained by
a series of new inferences from the facts which lie nearest
to them.   It will probably be found that in a majority of
cases the meaning which will result from such a new induction will not differ widely from that which has been
generally accepted: it will probably also be found that
in a majority of cases in which a new meaning is demon-
strable, the new meaning links itself to a classical use.   But
it will also be found, on the one hand, that new and
important shades of meaning attach themselves to words
which retain for the most part their classical use: and, on
the other hand, that some familiar words have in the sphere
of Biblical Greek a meaning which is almost peculiar to
that sphere.

For the purposes of such an induction the materials
which lie nearest at hand are those which are contained in
the Septuagint, including in that term the extra-canonical
books which, though they probably had Semitic originals,
exist for us only in a Greek form.

A. Even if the Septuagint were only a Greek book, the
facts that it is more cognate in character to the New Testament than any other book, that much of it is proximate in
time, and that it is of sufficient extent to afford a fair basis
for comparison, would give it a unique value in New Testament exegesis.

(1) This value consists partly in the fact that it adds to
the vocabulary of the language.   It is a contemporary
Greek book with new words, and many words which are
found in the New Testament are found for the first time in
the Septuagint :—

(a) Some of these words are expressions of specially Jewish
ideas or usages : ἀκροβυστία, ἀλισγεῖν, ἀναθεματίζειν, ἀπερίτμητος, ἀπο-

δεκατοῦν, εὐωδία, ἐφημερία, ματαιότης, πατριάρχης, περιτομή, προσήλυτος, πρωτοτόκια, ῥαντισμός.

(b) Some of them are legitimately formed, but new compounds from existing elements: ἀκρογωνιαῖος, ἀλλογενής, ἐκμυκτηρίζειν, ἐμπαίκτης, ἐνδυναμοῦν, ἐνωτίζεσθαι, ἐπισκοπή, εὐδοκία, ἥττημα, κατακαυχᾶσθαι, κατακληρονομεῖν, κατανύσσειν, κατοικητήριον, καύχησις, κλυδωνίζεσθαι, κραταιοῦν, μεγαλωσύνη, ὀρθρίζειν, παγιδεύειν, παραζηλοῦν, πεποίθησις, πληροφορεῖν, σητόβρωτος, σκανδαλίζειν, σκάνδαλον, σκληροκαρδία, σκληροτράχηλος, στυγνάζειν, ὑπακοή, ὑστέρημα, φωστήρ.

(2) The other and more important element in the value of the Septuagint viewed simply as a Greek book is that it affords a basis for an induction as to the meaning not of new but of familiar words. Very few lexicographers or commentators have gone seriously astray with new words. But the meaning of familiar words has been frequently taken for granted, when the fact of their constant occurrence in the Septuagint in the same connexion and with predicates of a particular kind, afford a strong presumption that their connotation was not the same as it had been in Classical Greek.

Instances of such words will be found among those which are examined in detail below, e. g. διάβολος, πονηρός.

These characteristics attach not only to the Septuagint proper, but also to the deutero-canonical books, or 'Apocrypha.' Those books have a singular value in regard to the syntax of the New Testament, which is beyond the range of the present subject. Some of them have also a special value in regard to some of the more abstract or philosophical terms of the New Testament, of which more will be said below. But they have also a value in the two respects which have been just mentioned:

(1) They supply early instances of New Testament words:

ἐκτένεια, Acts 26. 7, is first found in 2 Macc. 14. 38: it is also found in Judith 4. 9. Its earliest use elsewhere is Cic. *Att.* 10. 7. 1.

ἐξισχύειν, Eph. 3. 18, is first found, and with the same construction as in the N. T., in Sirach. 7. 6. Its earliest use elsewhere is Strabo 788 (but with ὥστε).

καταλαλιά, 2 Cor. 12. 20, 1 Pet. 2. 1, is first found in Wisd. 1. 11. Its earliest uses elsewhere are Clem. Rom. 30. 35; Barnab. 20.

κτίσις, Rom. 8. 19 sqq., etc., in the sense of things created and not of the act of creation, is first found in Wisd. 5. 18; 16. 24; 19. 6.

σκανδαλίζειν, Matt. 5. 29, and freq., is first found in Sir. 9. 5.

ὑπογραμμός, 1 Pet. 2. 21, is first found in 2 Macc. 2. 28: its earliest use elsewhere is Clem. Rom. 5.

φυλακίζειν, Acts 22. 19, is first found in Wisd. 18. 4: its earliest use elsewhere is Clem. Rom. 45.

χαριτοῦν, Luke 1. 28, Eph. 1. 6, is first found in Sir. 18. 17.

(2) They also supply instances of the use of familiar words in senses which are not found in earlier Greek, but which suggest or confirm inferences which are drawn from their use in the New Testament.

An instance of this will be found below in the meaning of πονηρός, which results from its use in Sirach.

B. But that which gives the Septuagint proper a value in regard to Biblical philology which attaches neither to the Apocrypha nor to any other book, is the fact that it is a translation of which we possess the original. For the meaning of the great majority of its words and phrases we are not left solely to the inferences which may be made by comparing one passage with another in either the Septuagint itself or other monuments of Hellenistic Greek. We can refer to the passages of which they are translations, and in most cases frame inductions as to their meaning which are as certain as any philological induction can be. It is a true paradox that while, historically as well as philologically, the Greek is a translation of the Hebrew, philologically, though not historically, the Hebrew may be regarded as a translation of the Greek. This apparent paradox may be illustrated by the analogous case of the Gothic translation of the Gospels : historically as well as philologically that translation is, as it professes to be, a rendering of the Greek into the Moeso-Gothic of the fourth century A.D.; but since all other monuments of Moeso-Gothic have perished, the Greek of the Gospels becomes for philological purposes, that is to say, for the understanding of Moeso-Gothic words, a key to, or translation of, the Gothic.

But that which makes the possession of this key to its meaning of singular value in the case of the Septuagint, is the fact that to a considerable extent it is not a literal translation but a Targum or paraphrase. For the tendency of almost all students of an ancient book is to lay too great a stress upon the meaning of single words, to draw too subtle distinctions between synonyms, to press unduly the force of metaphors, and to estimate the weight of compound words in current use by weighing separately the elements of which they are compounded. Whereas in the ordinary speech of men, and with all but a narrow, however admirable, school of writers in a literary age, distinctions between synonyms tend to fade away, the original force of metaphors becomes so weakened by familiarity as to be rarely present to the mind of the speaker, and compound words acquire a meaning of their own which cannot be resolved into the separate meanings of their component parts. But the fact that the Septuagint does not, in a large proportion of cases, follow the Hebrew as a modern translation would do, but gives a free and varying rendering, enables us to check this common tendency of students both by showing us not only in another language, but also in another form, the precise extent of meaning which a word or a sentence was intended to cover, and also by showing us how many different Greek words express the shades of meaning of a single Hebrew word, and conversely how many different Hebrew words explain to us the meaning of a single Greek word.

These special characteristics of the Septuagint may
be grouped under three heads : (1) it gives glosses and
paraphrases instead of literal and word for word renderings : (2) it does not adhere to the metaphors of the
Hebrew, but sometimes adds to them and sometimes
subtracts from them : (3) it varies its renderings of
particular words and phrases.   Of each of these characteristics the following examples are given by way of
illustration.

1. *Glosses and paraphrases :*

(*a*) Sometimes designations of purely Jewish customs are glossed :
e. g. שָׁנָה בֶּן 'the son of the year,' Num. 7. 15, etc., i. e. a male of
the first year which was required in certain sacrifices, is rendered by
(ἀμνός) ἐνιαύσιος : הַמָּרִים מֵי 'bitter waters,' Num. 5. 18, etc., is
rendered by τὸ ὕδωρ τοῦ ἐλεγμοῦ ; נֵזֶר the 'separation' or 'conse-
cration' of the Nazarite, Num. 6. 4, and even נִזְרוֹ רֹאשׁ 'the head
of his separation,' ib. v. 9, are rendered simply by εὐχή ; נִיחֹחַ רֵיחַ
'a savour of quietness,' Lev. 1. 9, etc., is rendered by ὀσμὴ
εὐωδίας.

. (*b*) Sometimes ordinary Hebraisms are glossed : e.g. נֵכָר בֶּן 'the
son of the foreigner,' Ex. 12. 43, etc., is rendered simply by ἀλλογενής ; אֱלִילִם 'things of nought,' Lev. 19. 4, etc., is rendered by
εἴδωλα ; פָּקַד 'to visit' (used of God), is rendered in Jeremiah and
several of the minor prophets by ἐκδικεῖν : שְׂפָתַיִם עֲרַל 'of uncircumcised lips,' Ex. 6. 12, is rendered by ἄλογός εἰμι.

(*c*) More commonly, an interpreting word, or paraphrase, is substituted for a literal rendering : similar examples to the following
can be found in almost every book.   Gen. 12. 9, etc., נֶגֶב 'the
South' is interpreted by ἡ ἔρημος : Gen. 27. 16 חֶלְקָה 'the smooth-
ness,' sc. of Jacob's neck, is interpreted by τὰ γυμνά : Gen. 50. 3
חֲנֻטִים 'the embalming' is rendered by the more familiar τῆς ταφῆς,
'the burial,' and in the following verse, בַּיִת the 'house' of Pharaoh
is interpreted by τοὺς δυνάστας, 'the mighty men' of Pharaoh : Num.
31. 5 וַיִּמָּסְרוּ 'were handed over,' sc. to Moses, = ἐξηρίθμησαν, 'were
counted out': 1 Sam. 6. 10 אֲנָשִׁים 'the men' is interpreted by οἱ
ἀλλόφυλοι, 'the Philistines': Job 2. 8 הָאֵפֶר בְּתוֹךְ 'among the
ashes' is interpreted by ἐπὶ τῆς κοπρίας, 'on the midden': Job 31.

32 לָאֹרַח 'to the way' (possibly reading לְאֹרֵחַ 'to a traveller') is interpreted by παντὶ ἐλθόντι: in Ps. 3. 4; 118 (119). 114 מָגֵן 'a shield' (used of God) is interpreted by ἀντιλήπτωρ: in Ps. 17 (18). 3; 18 (19). 15; 77 (78). 35; 93 (94). 22 צוּר 'a rock' is interpreted by βοηθός, and in Ps. 117 (118). 6 the same Greek word is added as a paraphrase of the personal pronoun לִ, κύριος ἐμοὶ βοηθός: in Ps. 15 (16). 9 כְּבוֹדִי 'my glory' is interpreted by ἡ γλῶσσά μου: in Ps. 38 (39). 2 מַחְסוֹם 'a bridle' is interpreted by φυλακήν: in Ps. 33 (34). 11 כְּפִירִים 'young lions' is interpreted by πλούσιοι: in Ps. 126 (127). 5 אַשְׁפָּתוֹ 'a quiver' is interpreted by τὴν ἐπιθυμίαν.

(d) In some cases instead of the interpretation of a single word by its supposed equivalent, there is a paraphrase or free translation of a clause: for example, Ex. 24. 11 'upon the nobles of the children of Israel he laid not his hand': LXX. τῶν ἐπιλέκτων τοῦ 'Ισραὴλ οὐ διεφώνησεν οὐδὲ εἷς, 'of the chosen men of Israel not one perished': 1 Sam. 6. 4 'What shall be the trespass-offering which we shall return to him': LXX. τί τὸ τῆς βασάνου ἀποδώσομεν αὐτῇ; 'what is the [offering for] the plague that we shall render to it' (sc. to the ark): 1 Kings 21 (20). 39 'if by any means he be missing' (פָּקַד niph.): LXX. ἐὰν δὲ ἐκπηδῶν ἐκπηδήσῃ, 'if escaping he escape': Ps. 22 (23). 4 'through the valley (בְּגֵיא) of the shadow of death': LXX. ἐν μέσῳ σκιᾶς θανάτου: Ps. 34 (35). 14 'I bowed down heavily as one that mourneth for his mother' (כַּאֲבֶל אֵם): LXX. ὡς πενθῶν καὶ σκυθρωπάζων οὕτως ἐταπεινούμην: Ps. 43 (44). 20 'that thou shouldest have sore broken us in the place of jackals' (תַנִּים): LXX. ὅτι ἐταπείνωσας ἡμᾶς ἐν τόπῳ κακώσεως: Is. 60. 19 'neither for brightness shall the moon give light unto thee': LXX. οὐδὲ ἀνατολὴ σελήνης φωτιεῖ σου [Cod. A. σοι] τὴν νύκτα, 'neither shall the rising of the moon give light to thy night' (or 'give light for thee at night').

2. Metaphors:

(a) Sometimes there is a change of metaphor, e. g. in Amos 5. 24 נַחַל אֵיתָן 'a mighty,' or 'perennial stream,' is rendered by χειμάρρους ἄβατος, 'an impassable torrent': Micah 3. 2 אָהֵב 'to love' is rendered by ζητεῖν, 'to seek.'

(b) Sometimes a metaphor is dropped: e. g. Is. 6. 6 'then *flew* (וַיָּעָף) one of the seraphim unto me,' LXX. ἀπεστάλη πρὸς μὲ ἓν τῶν Σεραφίμ: Ps. 5. 13, and elsewhere, חָסָה 'to fly for refuge' is rendered by ἐλπίζειν: Job 13. 27 אָרְחוֹת 'ways' is rendered ἔργα, 'deeds.'

C

(c) Sometimes a metaphor appears to be added, i. e. the Greek word contains a metaphor where the corresponding Hebrew word is neutral : e. g. Jer. 5. 17 רָשַׁשׁ *po.* 'to destroy' is rendered by ἀλοᾶν, 'to thresh': Ezek. 21. 11 הָרַג 'to kill' is rendered by ἀποκεντεῖν, and Num. 22. 29 by ἐκκεντεῖν, 'to pierce through' (so as to kill): Deut. 7. 20 אָבַד *hiph.* 'to destroy' is rendered by ἐκτρίβεσθαι, 'to be rubbed out': שָׁכַן 'to dwell' is frequently rendered by κατασκηνοῦν, 'to dwell in a tent.'

These tendencies both to the glossing and paraphrasing of the Hebrew, and to the changing or apparent adding of metaphors, will be best seen by analysing the translations of some typical word. The following is such an analysis of the translations of נָתַן 'to give.'

(a) In the following cases there is a paraphrase.

Jos. 14. 12 'Give me this mountain,' LXX. αἰτοῦμαί σε τὸ ὄρος τοῦτο.

Deut. 21. 8 'Lay not innocent blood unto My people of Israel's charge,' LXX. ἵνα μὴ γένηται αἷμα ἀναίτιον ἐν τῷ λαῷ σου 'Ισραήλ.

Esther 3. 11 'The silver is given to thee,' LXX. τὸ μὲν ἀργύριον ἔχε.

Ezek. 45. 8 'They shall give the land to the house of Israel according to their tribes,' LXX. τὴν γῆν κατακληρονομήσουσιν οἶκος 'Ισραὴλ κατὰ φυλὰς αὐτῶν.

(β) In the following cases a local colouring is given to the translation, so that the translation of the verb must be taken in its relation to the translation of the whole passage.

Gen. 20. 6 'therefore suffered I thee not to touch her,' ἕνεκα τούτου οὐκ ἀφῆκά σε ἅψασθαι αὐτῆς.

Gen. 38. 28 'the one put out his hand,' ὁ εἷς προεξήνεγκε τὴν χεῖρα.

Gen. 39. 20 'Joseph's master . . . put him into the prison,' ἐνέβαλεν αὐτὸν εἰς τὸ ὀχύρωμα.

Gen. 41. 41 'I have set thee over all the land of Egypt,' καθίστημι σε σήμερον ἐπὶ πάσῃ γῇ Αἰγύπτου.

Gen. 43. 23 'the man . . . gave them water and they washed their feet,' ἤνεγκεν ὕδωρ νίψαι τοὺς πόδας αὐτῶν.

Exodus 3. 19 'I am sure that the king of Egypt will not let you go,' οἶδα ὅτι οὐ προήσεται ὑμᾶς Φαραώ.

Exodus 7. 4 'I will lay my hand upon Egypt,' ἐπιβαλῶ τὴν χεῖρά μου ἐπ' Αἴγυπτον.

Exodus 18. 25 'Moses . . . made them heads over the people, rulers of thousands . . .,' ἐποίησεν αὐτοὺς ἐπ' αὐτῶν χιλιάρχους.

Exodus 21. 19 'he shall pay for the loss of his time,' τῆς ἀργείας αὐτοῦ ἀποτίσει.

Exodus 27. 5 'thou shalt put it under the ledge of the altar beneath,' ὑποθήσεις αὐτοὺς (sc. τοὺς δακτυλίους) ὑπὸ τὴν ἐσχάραν τοῦ θυσιαστηρίου κάτωθεν.

Exodus 30. 19 'thou shalt put water therein,' ἐκχεεῖς εἰς αὐτὸν ὕδωρ.

Lev. 2. 15 'thou shalt put oil upon it,' ἐπιχεεῖς ἐπ' αὐτὴν ἔλαιον.

Lev. 19. 14 'Thou shalt not . . . put a stumbling block before the blind,' ἀπέναντι τυφλοῦ οὐ προσθήσεις σκάνδαλον.

Deut. 15. 17 'Thou shalt take an aul and thrust it through his ear unto the door,' λήψῃ τὸ ὀπήτιον καὶ τρυπήσεις τὸ ὠτίον αὐτοῦ πρὸς τὴν θύραν.

2 *Sam.* 18. 9 'he was taken up between the heaven and the earth,' ἐκρεμάσθη ἀνὰ μέσον τοῦ οὐρανοῦ καὶ ἀνὰ μέσον τῆς γῆς.

2 *Kings* 16. 14 '. . . and put it on the north side of the altar,' ἔδειξεν αὐτὸ ἐπὶ μηρὸν τοῦ θυσιαστηρίου.

1 *Chron.* 16. 4 'he appointed certain of the Levites to minister,' ἔταξε . . . ἐκ τῶν Λευιτῶν λειτουργοῦντας.

2 *Chron.* 16. 10 '. . . and put him in the stocks,' παρέθετο αὐτὸν εἰς φυλακήν.

Esth. 1. 20 'all the wives shall give to their husbands honour,' πᾶσαι αἱ γυναῖκες περιθήσουσι τιμὴν τοῖς ἀνδράσιν ἑαυτῶν.

Job 2. 4 'all that a man hath will he give for his life,' ὅσα ὑπάρχει ἀνθρώπῳ ὑπὲρ τῆς ψυχῆς αὐτοῦ ἐκτίσει.

Job 9. 18 'He will not suffer me to take my breath,' οὐκ ἐᾷ γάρ με ἀναπνεῦσαι.

Job 35. 10 'who giveth songs in the night,' ὁ κατατάσσων φυλακὰς νυκτερίνας.

Job 36. 3 'For truly my words are not false,' ἔργοις δέ μου δίκαια ἐρῶ ἐπ' ἀληθείας.

Prov. 10. 10 'He that winketh with the eye causeth sorrow,' ὁ ἐννεύων ὀφθαλμοῖς μετὰ δόλου συνάγει ἀνδράσι λύπας.

Prov. 21. 26 'but the righteous giveth and spareth not,' ὁ δὲ δίκαιος ἐλεᾷ καὶ οἰκτείρει ἀφειδῶς.

Is. 3. 4 'I will give children to be their princes,' ἐπιστήσω νεανίσκους ἄρχοντας αὐτῶν.

Is. 43. 9 'let them bring forth their witnesses,' ἀγαγέτωσαν τοὺς μάρτυρας αὐτῶν.

Jer. 44 (37). 15 'the princes . . . put him in prison in the house of Jonathan,' ἀπέστειλαν αὐτὸν εἰς τὴν οἰκίαν 'Ιωνάθαν.

Ezek. 14. 8 'I will set my face against that man,' στηριῶ τὸ πρόσωπόν μου ἐπὶ τὸν ἄνθρωπον ἐκεῖνον.

3. Variations of rendering.

(*a*) In a comparatively small number of cases a single Greek word corresponds to a single Hebrew word, with such accidental exceptions as may be accounted for by a variation in the text: it is legitimate to infer that, in such cases, there was in the minds of the translators, and since the translators were not all of one time or locality, presumably in current usage, an absolute identity of meaning between the Hebrew and the Greek: e.g. δοῦλος = עֶבֶד (or עָבַד).

(*b*) In certain cases in which a single Greek word stands for two or more different Hebrew words, the absence of distinction of rendering may be accounted for by the paraphrastic character of the whole translation, and will not of itself give trustworthy inferences as to the identity in each case of the meaning of the Greek and the Hebrew words.

e.g. εἴδωλον, εἴδωλα stands for (1) אֱלֹהִים 'gods,' (2) אֱלִילִים 'things of nought' (=τὰ μάταια Zach. 11. 17, βδελύγματα Is. 2. 8, 20, χειροποιητά Lev. 26. 1, Is. 2. 18, etc.), (3) אֵילִים 'terebinth-trees,' (4) בָּמוֹת 'high-places' (more commonly=τὰ ὑψηλά), (5) בְּעָלִים 'Baalim,' (6) גִּלּוּלִים 'idol-blocks,' (7) הֲבָלִים 'vanities,' (8) חַמָּנִים 'sun-pillars,' (9) עֲצַבִּים 'idols,' (10) פְּסִילִים 'graven images' (also=τὰ γλυπτά), (11) צֶלֶם 'images' (also=εἰκών), (12) שִׁקֻּץ 'abomination,' (13) תְּרָפִים 'teraphim.'

It is clear that in the majority of these cases εἴδωλα is a paraphrastic or generic term, and not the exact equivalent of the Hebrew.

(c) In certain cases a single Hebrew word is represented by two or more Greek words, not in single but in repeated instances, and not in different but in the same books or group of books; it is reasonable to infer in such cases, unless a close examination of each instance reveals a marked difference of usage, that in the minds of the translators the Greek words were practically synonymous:

e. g. in Psalm 36 (37) רָשָׁע occurs 13 times: in vv. 10, 12, 14, 17, 18, 20, 21, 32, 40 it is rendered by ἁμαρτωλός, in vv. 28, 35, 38 by ἀσεβής: it is difficult to account for this except by the hypothesis that the two words were regarded as identical in meaning.

(d) In certain cases in which a single Hebrew word is repeatedly represented by two or more Greek words, the variation exists only, or almost only, in different books, and may therefore be mainly attributed to a difference in the time or place of translation, or in the person of the translator: but at the same time such a repeated rendering of a single Hebrew word by two or more Greek words argues a close similarity of meaning between the Greek words which are so used:

e. g. in Genesis, Exodus, Leviticus, Numbers קָהָל is translated by συναγωγή; in Deuteronomy and the following books to Nehemiah inclusive (56 times in all), with only the exception of Deut. 5. 22, it is translated by ἐκκλησία.

In Exodus, Deuteronomy, Joshua, Judges, but elsewhere only 2 Sam. 15. 8, עָבַד is generally translated by λατρεύειν: in Numbers by λειτουργεῖν: in Genesis, the historical books, and the prophets by δουλεύειν.

In Exodus, Leviticus, and Numbers מִנְחָה is ordinarily, and frequently, translated by θυσία: in Genesis (except 4. 3, 5) by δῶρον: in other books, e. g. Isaiah, by both words.

It is reasonable in these cases to infer a close similarity of meaning between συναγωγή and ἐκκλησία; λατρεύειν, λειτουργεῖν, and δουλεύειν; and δῶρον and θυσία, respectively.

(*e*) But in many cases it is found that a single Hebrew word is represented by two or more different Greek words not only in various books of the Septuagint but sometimes also in the same book, and with sufficient frequency to preclude the hypothesis of accidental coincidence. It is also found that another Hebrew word, of similar meaning, is represented, under the same conditions, by the same two or more Greek words as the preceding. Consequently each of a small group of Hebrew words is represented by one or other of a corresponding group of Greek words, and, conversely, each of the small group of Greek words stands for one or other of a small group of Hebrew words. It is reasonable to infer in such cases that the Greek words so used are practically synonymous : i.e. that whatever distinctions may have been drawn between them by the literary class, they were used indifferently in current speech. For example,

גָאַל is rendered in Isaiah by (1) ἐξαιρεῖν c. 60. 16, (2) λυτροῦν c. 35. 9 : 41. 14 : 43. 1. 14 : 44. 22, 23, 24 : 52. 3 : 62. 12 : 63. 9, (3) ῥύεσθαι c. 44. 6 : 47. 4 : 48. 17, 20 : 51. 10 : 52. 9 : 54. 5, 8 : 59. 20 : 63. 16.

יָשַׁע *hiph.* is rendered by (1) ἐξαιρεῖν Jer. 49 (42). 11, (2) ῥύεσθαι Is. 5. 29 : 36. 14, 15, 18, 19, 20 : 37. 11, 12 : 38. 6 : 50. 2, (3) σώζειν Is. 19. 20 : 25. 9 : 30. 15 : 33. 22 : 35. 4 : 37. 20, 35 : 43. 3, 11, 12 : 45. 17, 20, 22 : 46. 7 : 49. 25 : 59. 1 : 60. 16 : 63. 9.

כָּלַט *pi.* is rendered by (1) ἐξαιρεῖν 2 Sam. 19. 5, 9, 1 Kings 1 12, (2) ῥύεσθαι Ps. 40 (41). 2 : 88 (89). 49 : 106 (107). 20 : 114 (116). 4 : 123 (124). 7, (3) σώζειν 1 Sam. 19. 11, 12 : 27. 1, 1 Kings 18. 40 : 19. 17 : 21 (20). 20, 2 Kings 19. 37.

נָצַל *hiph.* is rendered in Isaiah by (1) ἐξαιρεῖν c. 31. 5 : 42. 22 : 43. 13 : 44. 17, 20 : 47. 14 : 57. 13, (2) ῥύεσθαι c. 44. 6 : 47. 4 : 48. 17, 20 : 49. 7, 26 : 51. 10 : 52. 9 : 54. 5, 8 : 59. 20 : 63. 16, (3) σώζειν c. 19. 20 : 20. 6.

פָּדָה is rendered by (1) λυτροῦν Ps. 24 (25). 22 : 25 (26). 11 : 30 (31). 6 : 33 (34). 23 : 43 (44). 27 : 48 (49). 8, 16 : 54 (55). 19 : 70 (71). 23 : 77 (78). 42 : 118 (119). 134 : 129 (130). 8, (2) ῥύεσθαι Job 5. 20 : 6. 23, Ps. 68 (69). 19, (3) σώζειν Job 33. 28.

פָּלַט *pi.* is rendered by (1) ἐξαιρεῖν Ps. 36 (37). 40: 70 (71). 2 : 81 (82). 4, (2) λυτροῦν Ps. 31 (32). 7, (3) ῥύεσθαι Ps. 16 (17). 13 : 17 (18). 44, 49 : 21 (22). 5, 9 : 30 (31). 2 : 36 (37). 40 : 42 (43). 1 : 70 (71). 4 : 90 (91). 14, (4) σώζειν (for the derivatives פָּלִים, פְּלֵיטָה) Is. 10. 20: 37. 32 : 45. 20 : 66. 19: so also ἀνασώζειν Jer. 51 (44). 14, etc., διασώζειν Job 21. 10, etc.

Conversely, ἐξαιρεῖν is used to translate (1) גָּאַל Is. 60. 16, (2) יָשַׁע *hi.* Jer. 49 (42). 11, (3) מָלַט 2 Sam. 19. 5, 9, 1 Kings 1. 12, Ezek. 33. 5, (4) נָצַל twelve times in the Pentateuch, thirty-three times in the historical books, thirty-two times in the poetical books, (5) פָּלַט *pi.* 2 Sam. 22. 2, Ps. 36 (37). 40 : 70 (71). 2 : 81 (82). 4.

λυτροῦν is used to translate (1) גָּאַל twenty times in Exodus and Leviticus, twenty-four times in the poetical books, (2) פָּדָה fifteen times in the Pentateuch, seven times in the historical books, nineteen times in the poetical books, (3) פָּלַט *pi.* Ps. 31 (32). 7.

ῥύεσθαι is used to translate (1) גָּאַל Gen. 48. 16 and twelve times in Isaiah, (2) יָשַׁע *hiph.* Ex. 2. 17 : 14. 30, Jos. 22. 22, Is. 49. 26 : 63. 5, Ezek. 37. 23, (3) מָלַט *pi.* Job 22. 30, and in the above-mentioned five passages of the Psalms, (4) נָצַל Exod. 2. 19 : 5. 23 : 6. 6 : 12. 27, fourteen times in the historical books, sixty times in the poetical books, (5) פָּדָה Job 5. 20 : 6. 23, Ps. 68 (69). 19, Hos. 13. 14, (6) פָּלַט *pi.* 2 Sam. 22. 44, and in the above-mentioned ten passages of the Psalms.

σώζειν is used to translate (1) יָשַׁע *hiph.* Deut. 33. 29, fifty-six times in the historical books, nearly a hundred times in the poetical books, (2) מָלַט *pi.* Gen. 19. 17, 22, ten times in the historical books, twenty-seven times in the poetical books, (3) נָצַל Gen. 32. 30, eight times in the historical books, fourteen times in the poetical books, (4) פָּדָה Job 33. 28, (5) פָּלַט or one of its derivatives, Gen. 32. 8, 2 Chron. 20. 24, Neh. 1. 2, Is. 10. 20 : 37. 32 : 45. 20 : 66. 19, Jer. 51 (44). 28.

It is reasonable to infer that, in their Hellenistic use, the Greek words which are thus used interchangeably for the same Hebrew words did not differ, at least materially, from each other in meaning, and that no substantial argument can be founded upon the meaning of any one of them unless that meaning be common to it with the other members of the group.

III. There is a further circumstance in relation to the

Septuagint which requires to be taken into account to a much greater extent than has usually been done. It is that in addition to the Septuagint we possess fragments of other translations of the Hebrew, those of Aquila, Symmachus, Theodotion, and of two anonymous translators, who are generally referred to as the Fifth and Sixth.

Part of the value of these translations lies in the fact that they belong to the period when the right interpretation of the Old Testament had become a matter of controversy between Jews and Christians: but very little is positively known about their authors or their approximate dates.

Accounts of *Aquila* are given by Irenaeus 3. 21. 1 (=Eus. *H. E.* 5. 8. 10), Origen *Epist. ad African.* 2 (i. p. 13), Eusebius *Dem. Ev.* 7. 1. 32, Epiphanius *de Mens. et pond.* 14, Jerome *Ep.* 57 *ad Pammach.* (i. p. 314), *Cata.* 54 (ii. p. 879), *Praef. in lib. Job* (ix. p. 1100), *Comm. in Jes.* 8. 11 (iv. p. 122), *Comm. in Abac.* III (vi. p. 656), and in the Jerusalem Talmud *Megilla* i. 11, p. 71, *Kiddush.* i. 1, p. 59. Accounts of *Symmachus* are given by Eusebius *H. E.* 6. 17, *Dem. Ev. l. c.*, Jerome, and Epiphanius *ll. cc.* Accounts of Theodotion are given by Irenaeus and Epiphanius *ll. cc.*, Jerome *ll. cc.*, and Praef. in Dan. (v. p. 619).

But these accounts vary widely, and, especially those of Epiphanius, appear to be in a large degree conjectural.

In regard to their dates, Aquila is placed by the Talmud *ll. cc.* in the time of R. Akiba, R. Eliezer, and R. Joshua, i.e. early in the second century A.D.: but it has been inferred from the fact of his being mentioned by Irenaeus and not by Justin Martyr that he flourished in the interval between those two writers. The date of Symmachus may be inferred from the fact that he is not mentioned by Irenaeus to have been near the end of the second century, a view which is in harmony with the account of Eusebius *H. E.* 6. 17, which places him a generation before the time of Origen. The date of Theodotion is more uncertain than that of the other two: he certainly lived before the time of Irenaeus, and, if the view be correct that his translation is quoted in Hermas, he may even have preceded Aquila.

But the chief part of their value lies in the contributions which they make to the vocabulary of Biblical Greek. Some words which are found in the New Testament are not found elsewhere within the range of Biblical Greek except in these translations.

ἀποκαραδοκία, Rom. 8. 19, Phil. 1. 20 (most Codd.), is interpreted by the verb ἀποκαραδοκεῖν, which is used by Aquila in Ps. 36 (37). 7 as the translation of הִתְחוֹלֵל (*hithpa.* of חוּל), for which the LXX. ἱκέτευσον and *Symm.* ἱκέτευε are less accurate renderings. The reading of Codd. FG. in Phil. 1. 20, καραδοκία, is known only from its use by Aquila in Prov. 10. 28 as the translation of תּוֹחֶלֶת 'expectation,' = *Symm.* ὑπομόνη, *Theod.* προσδοκία.

ἐγκακεῖν, in the sense of 'to be weary or faint,' is first found outside the N. T. as Symmachus's translation of קַצְתִּי in Gen. 27. 46, = LXX. προσώχθικα, *Aquil.* ἐσίκχανα, E. V. 'I am weary of my life because of the daughters of Heth.'

ἐμβριμᾶσθαι, Matt. 9. 30, Mark 1. 43: 14. 5, John 11, 33, 38, which in Classical Greek is found only in Aesch. *Septem c. Theb.* 461, of the snorting of horses in their harness, is best explained by its use (1) as the translation of זָעַם 'to be angry' in *Aquil.* Ps. 7. 12 ἐμβριμώμενος = LXX. ὀργὴν ἐπάγων, *Alius* ἀπειλούμενος : so ἐμβρίμησις = the derivative זַעַם in *Aquil. Symm.* Ps. 37 (38). 4 = LXX. ὀργῆς : in *Theod.* Is. 30. 27 = LXX. ὀργῆς : and in *Theod. Symm.* Ezek. 21. 31 (36) = LXX. ὀργήν, *Aquil.* ἀπειλήν : (2) as the translation of גָּעַר 'to rebuke,' in *Symm.* Is. 17. 13 ἐμβριμήσεται αὐτῷ = LXX. ἀποσκορακιεῖ αὐτόν, *Aquil.* ἐπιτιμήσει ἐν αὐτῷ : so ἐμβρίμησις translates the derivative גְּעָרָה in *Symm.* Ps. 75 (76). 7 = LXX. *Aquil.* ἐπιτιμήσεως.

ἐνθύμησις, Matt. 9. 4 : 12. 25, Heb. 4. 12 finds its only parallel in the sense of 'thoughts,' or 'cogitations,' in *Symm.* Job 21. 27 (in the same collocation with ἐννοιῶν as in Hebrews 4. 12, Clem. Rom. 21. 9), where it translates מַחְשָׁבוֹת, which, like ἐνθύμησις in S. Matthew, is used of malicious thoughts (e. g. Esth. 8. 3, 5).

ἐπίβλημα, in the sense of a 'patch,' Matt. 9. 16 (= Mark 2. 21, Luke 5. 36), is found only in *Symm.* Jos. 9. 11 (5).

καταφέρεσθαι, the expressive word which is used for 'dropping fast asleep' in Acts 20. 9, finds its only parallel in this sense in Biblical Greek (elsewhere, Arist. *De Gen. Anim.* 5. 1, p. 779 *a*) in *Aquil.* Ps. 75 (76). 7, where it translates נִרְדָּם = LXX. ἐνύσταξαν.

θεομάχος, Acts 5. 39, occurs elsewhere in Biblical Greek only in

Symm. Job 26. 5 (= *Theod.* γίγαντες), Prov. 9. 18 (=LXX. γηγενεῖς, *Theod.* γίγαντες), Prov. 21. 16 (=LXX. γιγάντων): in each case it translates רְפָאִים.

ὁροθεσία, Acts 17. 26, is not found elsewhere, but the verb ὁροθετεῖν (many MSS. ὁριοθετεῖν) is found in *Aquil.* Deut. 19. 14, Zach. 9. 2, and in *Symm.* Exod. 19. 12.

σπλαγχνίζεσθαι, which is found 12 times in the Synoptic Gospels (not elsewhere in the N. T.) in the sense 'to feel compassion,' is found as the translation of חֲמַלְתֶּם in *Symm.* 1. Sam. 23. 21, ἐσπλαγ-χνίσθητε=LXX. ἐπονέσατε, *Theod.* ἐφείσασθε (which is the LXX. translation of the same verb in Ex. 2. 6). The compound ἐπι-σπλαγχνίζεσθαι is found in *Symm.* Deut. 13. 8 (9). as the translation of the same verb, =LXX. οὐκ ἐπιποθήσεις ἐπ' αὐτῷ. The active σπλαγ-χνίζειν occurs in 2 Macc. 6. 8, but in the sense of the Classical σπλαγχνεύειν=to eat the entrails of an animal after a sacrifice (Aristoph. *Av.* 984).

Another element in the value of these translations consists in the corrections which they make in the LXX. rendering, sometimes substituting a literal translation for a gloss, and sometimes a gloss for a literal translation.

(1) Sometimes a gloss or paraphrase of the LXX. is replaced by a literal or nearly literal rendering: this is the case chiefly, though not exclusively, with Aquila: for example,

Gen. 24. 67 אֹהֶל 'tent': LXX. (as frequently) οἶκος, *Aquil.* σκηνήν.

Ex. 6. 12 עֲרַל שְׂפָתָיִם 'uncircumcised in lips': LXX. ἄλογός εἰμι, *Aquil.* ἀκρόβυστος χείλεσι.

Ex. 21. 6 אֶל הָאֱלֹהִים 'to the gods' (sc. probably the judges): LXX. πρὸς τὸ κριτήριον τοῦ θεοῦ, *Aquil. Symm.* πρὸς τοὺς θεούς.

Lev. 4. 2, 22: 5. 15 בִּשְׁגָגָה 'through error': LXX. ἀκουσίως, *Aquil. Symm.* ἐν ἀγνοίᾳ.

Lev. 26. 13 קוֹמְמִיּוּת 'standing upright': LXX. μετὰ παρρησίας, *Alius* ἀνισταμένους.

Num. 21. 25 וּבְכָל בְּנֹתֶיהָ ' and in all its daughters' (i. e. dependent villages): LXX. καὶ ἐν πάσαις ταῖς συγκυρούσαις αὐτῇ, *Aquil. Symm. Theod.* θυγατράσιν αὐτῆς.

Num. 23. 21 תְּרוּעַת מֶלֶךְ 'the shout of a king': LXX. τὰ ἔνδοξα ἀρχόντων, *Aquil.* ἀλαλαγμὸς βασιλέως, *Symm.* σημασία, *Theod.* σαλπισμός.

Deut. 10. 16 אֵת עָרְלַת לְבַבְכֶם 'the foreskin of your heart': LXX. τὴν σκληροκαρδίαν ὑμῶν, *Aquil.* ἀκροβυστίαν καρδίας.

Deut. 32. 10 יִמְצָאֵהוּ 'found him': LXX. αὐτάρκησεν αὐτόν, *Aquil. Theod.* ηὗρεν αὐτόν.

Job 1. 6: 2. 1 בְּנֵי הָאֱלֹהִים 'sons of God': LXX. οἱ ἄγγελοι τοῦ θεοῦ, *Alius* οἱ υἱοὶ θεοῦ.

Ps. 15 (16). 9 כְּבוֹדִי 'my glory': LXX. ἡ γλῶσσά μου, *Aquil. Symm. Theod.* δόξα μου.

Ps. 30 (31). 11 עָשֵׁשׁוּ 'have waxed old': LXX. ἐταράχθησαν, *Aquil.* ηὐχμώθη, *Symm.* εὐρωτίασαν.

Ps. 31 (32). 6 לְעֵת מְצֹא 'in a time of finding': LXX. ἐν καιρῷ εὐθέτῳ, *Aquil.* εἰς καιρὸν εὑρέσεως αὐτοῦ.

Ps. 34 (35). 15 בְּצַלְעִי שָׂמֵחוּ 'in my halting they rejoice': LXX. κατ' ἐμοῦ εὐφράνθησαν, *Aquil.* ἐν σκασμῷ μου ηὐφράνθησαν, *Symm.* σκάζοντος δέ μου ηὐφραίνοντο.

Ps. 40 (41). 3 בְּנֶפֶשׁ אֹיְבָיו 'unto the soul (i. e. will) of his enemies': LXX. εἰς χεῖρας ἐχθροῦ αὐτοῦ, *Aquil.* ἐν ψυχῇ ἐχθροῦ, *Symm.* εἰς ψυχὰς ἐχθρῶν.

(2) Sometimes, on the other hand, a literal rendering of the LXX. is replaced by a gloss or paraphrase in one or the other translation: this is the case chiefly, though not exclusively, with Symmachus: e. g.

Judges 8. 21 אֶת־הַשַּׂהֲרֹנִים 'the little moons' (ornaments): LXX. τοὺς μηνίσκους, *Symm.* τὰ κόσμια.

1 *Sam.* 20. 30 עֶרְוַת 'uncovering': LXX. ἀποκαλύψεως, *Symm.* ἀσχημοσύνης.

1 *Sam.* 22. 8 גֹּלֶה אֶת־אָזְנִי 'uncovering the ear': LXX. ἀποκαλύπτων τὸ ὠτίον, *Alius* φανερὸν ποιεῖ.

Job 1. 16 תֹּאכְלֵם 'devoured': LXX. κατέφαγεν, *Symm.* ἀπέκτεινεν.

Ps. 21 (22). 17 כְּלָבִים 'dogs': LXX. κύνες, *Symm.* θηραταί.

Ps. 37 (38). 4 מִפְּנֵי חַטָּאתִי 'from the face of my sins': LXX. ἀπὸ προσώπου τῶν ἁμαρτιῶν μου, *Symm.* διὰ τὰς ἁμαρτίας μου.

Ps. 40 (41). 9 לֹא־יוֹסִיף לָקוּם 'will not add to rise up': LXX. οὐ προσθήσει τοῦ ἀναστῆναι, *Symm.* οὐκέτι ἀναστήσεται.

(3) But the chief contribution which these translations make to Biblical philology is that they enable us to correct

or corroborate the inferences which are drawn from the
relation of the Septuagint to the Hebrew, by supplying us
with a number of new and analogous data for determining
the meaning of words. It is found in a large number of
instances that the word which one or other of the translators substitutes for the LXX. word is itself used in other
passages of the LXX. as the translation of the same
Hebrew word: it is also found that, conversely, the LXX.
word is used elsewhere by the other translators for the
same Hebrew word. The inference to be drawn in such
cases is that the words which are so interchanged are
practically synonymous.

Gen. 8. 13 מִכְסֵה, LXX. στέγην, *Aquil. Symm.* καλύμμα, which is
the LXX. rendering of the same word in Num. 8. 10, 11, 12, 25.

Gen. 24. 61 נַעֲרֹת, LXX. ἅβραι, *Aquil.* παιδίσκαι, which is the LXX.
rendering of the same word in Ruth. 4. 12, Amos 2. 7 : *Symm.*
κοράσια, which is the LXX. rendering of the same word in Ruth 2.
8, *et al.*

Ex. 2. 22 גֵּר, LXX. πάροικος, *Aquil.* προσήλυτος, which is much
the more frequent translation of the same word in the LXX.

Ex. 3. 16 אֶת־זִקְנֵי, LXX. τὴν γερουσίαν, *Aquil.* τοὺς πρεσβυτέρους,
which is the ordinary translation of the same word in the LXX.
outside the Pentateuch.

Ex. 23. 16 הָאָסִף, LXX. συντελείας, *Aquil.* συλλογῆς, *Symm.* συγ-
κομιδῆς : the word occurs elsewhere only in Ex. 34. 22, where the
LXX. renders it by συναγωγῆς. (The use of συντέλεια in the sense of
harvest is noteworthy in its bearing upon S. Matt. 13. 39.)

Lev. 2. 6 פִּתִּים, LXX. κλάσματα, *Aquil. Symm. Theod.* ψωμούς :
but in Judges 19. 5 the MSS. of the LXX. vary between ψωμῷ
and κλάσματι as the translation of the same word.

Lev. 3. 9 תְּמִימָה, LXX. ἄμωμον, *Aquil.* τελείαν, which is the LXX.
rendering of the same word in Ex. 12. 5 *et al. Symm.* ὁλόκληρον,
which is the LXX. rendering in Lev. 23. 15.

Lev. 6. 2 (5. 22) עָשַׁק, LXX. ἠδίκησέ τι, *Aquil. Symm. Theod.* ἐσυκοφάντησε, which is the LXX. rendering of the same word in Job
35. 9, etc.

Num. 25. 4 הוֹקַע, LXX. παραδειγμάτισον, *Aquil.* ἀνάπηξον, *Symm.*
κρέμασον.

Deut. 7. 2 הַחֲרֵם תַּחֲרִים, LXX. ἀφανισμῷ ἀφανιεῖς, *Aquil. Symm. Theod.* ἀναθεματίσεις, which is the rendering of the LXX. in Deut. 13. 15: 20. 17.

Deut. 30. 9 וְהוֹתִירְךָ, LXX. καὶ εὐλογήσει (so Codd. B., etc., but Codd. A., etc., πολυωρήσει) σε, *Aquil. Theod.* περισσεύσει, *Symm.* αὐξήσει.

1 *Sam.* 6. 9 מִקְרֶה, LXX. σύμπτωμα, (*Aquil.*) συνάντημα, which is the LXX. rendering in Ecclesiastes 2. 14. 15: 3. 19: 9. 2, 3, *Symm.* συγκυρία (cf. S. Luke 10. 31).

1 *Sam.* 9. 22 לִשְׁכָּתָה, LXX. εἰς τὸ κατάλυμα, *Aquil.* γαζοφυλάκιον, which is the ordinary LXX. rendering in Nehemiah, *Symm.* ἐξέδραν, which is the ordinary LXX. rendering in Ezekiel.

1 *Sam.* 19. 14 חֹלֶה, LXX. ἐνοχλεῖσθαι, *Aquil.* ἀρρωστεῖν, which is a common LXX. rendering of the word.

1 *Sam.* 21. 4 (5) לֶחֶם חֹל, LXX. ἄρτοι βέβηλοι, *Aquil. Symm. Theod.* λαϊκοί.

1 *Sam.* 22. 15 חָלִילָה לִּי, LXX. μηδαμῶς, *Aquil.* βεβηλόν, *Symm. Theod.* ἵλεως, which is the LXX. rendering of the same word in 2 Sam. 20. 20.

2 *Sam.* 2. 26 לָנֶצַח, LXX. εἰς νῖκος, *Alius* ἕως ἐσχάτου. The phrase is important in its bearing upon Matt. 12. 20: the same Hebrew phrase is rendered εἰς νῖκος in *Aquil.* and *Quintus,* Ps. 48 (49). 9 = LXX. εἰς τέλος, *Symm.* εἰς αἰῶνα; in *Aquil. Theod.* Is. 33. 20 = LXX. εἰς τὸν αἰῶνα χρόνον, *Symm.* εἰς τέλος; and in *Aquil.* Is. 57. 16 = LXX. διαπαντός, *Symm.* εἰς τέλος. So also in Is. 34. 10 לָנֶצַח נְצָחִים = LXX. εἰς χρόνον πολύν, *Aquil.* εἰς νῖκος νικέων, *Theod.* εἰς ἔσχατα ἐσχάτων.

Job 6. 8 תִּקְוָתִי, LXX. τὴν ἐλπίδα μου, *Aquil.* ὑπομονήν (so also 4. 16: 17. 15). which is the LXX. rendering of the same word in 14. 19.

Ps. 10 (11). 4, 5 יִבְחָנוּ, LXX. ἐξετάζει, *Aquil.* δοκιμάζει, which elsewhere in the Psalms, viz. 16 (17). 3 : 25 (26). 2 : 65 (66). 10 : 80 (81). 8 : 94 (95). 9 is the constant LXX. rendering of the same word.

It follows from this relation of the other translators to the Septuagint that they afford a test of the inferences which are derived from the Septuagint itself. Since the Septuagint is presumably, it may almost be said demonstrably, the work of different persons and different periods, it is natural to expect that a new group of translators, working under analogous conditions, although at a different period of time, should stand in the same relative position to the several groups of translation of the Septuagint in which those groups stand to one another. If, for example, it is found that certain words are used interchangeably to translate the same Hebrew word by different groups of translators of the Septuagint, it must be presumed that a new group of translators will also use those words interchangeably. Their not doing so would raise a presumption that the variations in the Septuagint were due to personal or local peculiarities, and that no general inference could be drawn from them. Their doing so affords an evidence which almost amounts to proof, that the words were in common use as synonyms. This evidence is the more important because of the fact that the translators of the Hexapla lived after New Testament times. It consequently shows that, in the case of the words to which it applies, the meaning which is gathered from the Septuagint lasted through New Testament times.

This evidence is sometimes of a negative and sometimes of a positive kind : it is negative, when the absence of any record of corrections of the LXX. by the other translators makes it probable that the latter accepted the translations of the former; it is positive, when such corrections are recorded.

The following is an example of the application of this test to a group of words of which the LXX. uses have been given fully above. It has been shown that the Hebrew words גָּאַל, יָשַׁע, מָלַט, נָצַל, פָּדָה, פָּלַט are translated to a great extent interchangeably by the Greek words ἐξαιρεῖν, λυτροῦν, ῥύεσθαι, σώζειν. The negative evidence which the other translators afford that the Greek words were regarded as practically identical in meaning is that they rarely disturb the LXX. rendering : the positive evidence which they afford to the same effect is that wherever they do amend that rendering they do so, with the exception mentioned below, by using another member of the same group.

(1) In Is. 35. 9 גְּאוּלִים is translated by the LXX. λελυτρωμένοι, by Theodotion ἐρρυσμένοι: (2) in Ps. 114 (116). 4 מַלְּטָה is translated by the LXX. ῥῦσαι, by Aquila περίσωσον, by Symmachus ἐξελοῦ: in Jer. 46 (39). 18 מַלֵּט אֲמַלֵּם is translated by the LXX. σώζων σώσω σε, by Aquila ῥυόμενος ῥύσομαί σε: (3) in 1 Sam. 30. 22 הִצַּלְנוּ is translated by the LXX. ἐξειλόμεθα, by Aquila ἐρρυσάμεθα: in Job 5. 19 יַצִּיל is translated by the LXX. ἐξελεῖται, by Aquila ῥύσεται: in Ps. 30 (31). 3 הַצִּיל is translated by the LXX. τοῦ ἐξελέσθαι, by Symmachus ἐξελοῦ: in Ps. 32 (33). 16 יִנָּצֵל is translated by the LXX. σωθήσεται, by Aquila ῥυσθήσεται, by Symmachus διαφεύξεται: in Ps. 33 (34). 5 הִצִּיל is translated by the LXX. ἐρρύσατο, by Symmachus ἐξείλετο: in Ps. 38 (39) הַצִּיל is translated by the LXX. ῥῦσαι, by Symmachus ἐξελοῦ: in Ps. 71 (72). 12 יַצִּיל is translated by the LXX. ἐρρύσατο, by Symmachus ἐξελεῖται: in Prov. 24. 11 הַצֵּל is translated by the LXX. ῥῦσαι, by Symmachus σῶσον: in Is. 38. 6 אַצִּיל is translated by the LXX. and Aquila ῥύσομαι, by Symmachus ἐξελοῦμαι, by Theodotion σώσω: (4) in 2 Sam. 4. 9 פָּדָה is translated by the LXX. ἐλυτρώσατο, by Symmachus ῥυσάμενος: in Ps. 43 (44.) 27 וּפְדֵנוּ is translated by the LXX. καὶ λύτρωσαι ἡμᾶς, by another translator (Ἄλλος, ap. Chrysost. ad loc.) καὶ ῥῦσαι ἡμᾶς: (5) in Ps. 17 (18). 44 תְּפַלְּטֵם is translated by the LXX. and Symmachus ῥῦσαι (ῥύσῃ), by Aquila διασώσεις: in Ps. 31 (32). 7 פַּלֵּט is translated by the LXX. λύτρωσαι, by Aquila διασώζων.

The exception mentioned above is that the translators of the Hexapla introduce into the group of Greek words another word which is not found in the N. T., and which is found in the LXX. in other senses, viz. ἀγχιστεύειν. The use of this word helps to confirm the general inference as to the practical identity of meaning of the other members of the group, and the word itself affords an interesting illustration of the light which the fragments of the Hexapla throw upon later Greek philology.

ἀγχιστεύειν occurs in the LXX. in the active, in Leviticus, Numbers, Deuteronomy, Joshua, and Ruth: in all cases as the translation of גָּאַל kal, or גֹּאֵל; and in the passive, in 2 Esdr. 2. 62,

Neh. 7. 64 as the translation of another word גאל *pu.* The meaning 'to be next of kin' had evidently passed into the meaning 'to act as next of kin,' with especial reference to the buying back of a kinsman's possession (Lev. 25. 25), and exacting the penalty of a kinsman's blood (Num. 35. 19, etc.), and 'purchasing,' i. e. marrying a kinsman's widow, 'to raise up the name of the dead upon his inheritance' (Ruth 3. 12: 4. 5). These derived meanings had become so thoroughly identified with the word in Hellenistic Greek that in time they lost their specific reference, and passed into the general meaning 'to redeem' or 'set free.' Hence it is used commonly by Aquila, and occasionally by Symmachus and Theodotion, where the LXX. uses ἐξαιρεῖν, λυτροῦν, ῥύεσθαι: Gen. 48. 16 LXX. ὁ ῥυόμενος, Aquila ὁ ἀγχιστεύων: Ps. 118 (119). 153 LXX. λύτρωσαί με, Aquila ἀγχίστευσόν με: Prov. 23. 11 LXX. ὁ λυτρούμενος, Aquila, Symmachus and Theodotion ἀγχιστεύς: Is. 35. 9 LXX. λελυτρωμένοι, Aquila and Symmachus ἀγχιστευμένοι, Theodotion ἐρρυσμένοι: Is. 47. 4 and 54. 5 LXX. ὁ ῥυσάμενος, Aquila ἀγχιστεύων: Is. 60. 16 LXX. ἐξαιρούμενος, Aquila ἀγχιστεύς: Is. 63. 16 LXX. ῥῦσαι, Aquila ἀγχιστεῦσαι.

The application of this test seems to show clearly that the inference which was derived from the interchange of the words in the LXX. is valid: its validity is rather strengthened than weakened by the admission of a new member into the group of virtual synonyms.

IV. Inferences which are drawn from the LXX. in regard to the meaning, and especially in regard to the equivalence in meaning, of certain words may sometimes be further checked and tested by an examination of the various readings of the MSS. of the LXX. For in those MSS. it is not unfrequently found that a word is replaced by another of similar meaning: e. g. in Prov. 8. 20, Codd. A B have τρίβων, Cod. S[1] has ὁδῶν, in Prov. 11. 9, Codd. A B have ἀσεβῶν, Cod. S[1] has ἁμαρτωλῶν. These phenomena may be explained on more than one hypothesis: they may be survivals of other translations: or they may be signs of successive revisions: or they may be indications that the copyists dealt more freely with a translation than they would have dealt with an original work, and that they took upon themselves to displace a word for another which they thought more appropriate. But whatever be the origin of the phenomena, they afford additional data for determining the meanings of words, if not in the time of the original translators, at least in that of early revisers and copyists. They consequently may be used in the same way as the fragments of the Hexapla to test inferences as to the equivalence of words.

The following is an example of a partial application of the test to the same group of words which has been already discussed in its use both in the LXX. and the Hexapla. It will be noted that only the historical books have been examined.

In Judges 6. 9, Codd. IV, 54, 58, 108 *al.* read ἐρρυσάμην, Codd. X, XI, 15, 18, 19 *al.* read ἐξειλάμην (ἐξειλόμην) as the translation of נצל: in Judges 9. 17 the same two groups of MSS. vary between ἐρρύσατο and ἐξείλατο, and in Judges 18. 28 between ὁ ῥυόμενος and ὁ ἐξαιρούμενος: in 2 Sam. 12. 7 Codd. X, XI, 15, 18, 85 have ἐρρυσάμην, Codd. 82, 93 ἐξειλάμην: in 2 Sam. 14, 16 Codd. X. 92, 108, 242 have ῥυσάσθω, Codd. XI, 29, 44, 52, 56 *al.* ἐξελεῖται: in 2 Sam. 19. 9 Codd. X, XI, 29, 44, 55 *al.* have ἐρρύσατο, Codd. 19, 82, 93, 108 ἐξείλετο: in 2 Sam. 22. 18 Codd. X, XI, 29, 44, 55 have ἐρρύσατο, Codd. 19, 82, 93, 108 ἐξείλετο: in 2 Sam. 22. 44 Codd. X, XI, 29, 44, 55 have ῥύσῃ, Codd. 19, 82, 93, 108 have ἐξείλου.

These instances are sufficient to show that the general inference as to the identity in meaning of ἐξαιρεῖν and ῥύεσθαι is supported by their interchange in the MSS., as it was also supported by their interchange in the Hexapla.

If we now put together the several groups of facts to which attention has been directed, it will be possible to draw some general inferences, and to frame some general rules, for the investigation of the meanings of words in the New Testament.

There are two great classes of such words, one of which may be subdivided:

D

I. (*a*) There are some words which are common to Biblical Greek and contemporary secular Greek, and which, since they are designations of concrete ideas, are not appreciably affected by the fact that Biblical Greek is the Greek of a Semitic race. The evidence as to the meaning of such words may be sought in any contemporary records, but especially in records which reflect the ordinary vernacular rather than the artificial literary Greek of the time.

Instances of such words will be found below in ἀγγαρεύειν, γλωσσόκομον, συκοφαντεῖν.

(*b*) There are some words which are common to Biblical Greek and to contemporary secular Greek, in regard to which, though they express not concrete but abstract ideas, there is a presumption that their Biblical use does not vary to any appreciable extent from their secular use, from the fact that they are found only in those parts of the New Testament whose style is least affected by Semitic conceptions and forms of speech. The evidence as to the meaning of such words may be gathered from any contemporary records, whether Biblical or secular.

An instance of such words will be found below in δεισιδαιμονία.

II. The great majority of New Testament words are words which, though for the most part common to Biblical and to contemporary secular Greek, express in their Biblical use the conceptions of a Semitic race, and which must consequently be examined by the light of the cognate documents which form the LXX.

These words are so numerous, and a student is so frequently misled by his familiarity with their classical use, that it is a safe rule to let no word, even the simplest, in the N. T. pass unchallenged. The process of enquiry is (1) to ascertain the Classical use of a word, (2) to ascertain whether there are any facts in relation to its Biblical use which raise a presumption that its Classical use had been altered. Such facts are afforded partly by the context in which the word is found, but mainly by its relation to the Hebrew words which it is used to translate.

It is obvious that the determination of this relation is a task of considerable difficulty. The extent and variety of the LXX., the freedom which its authors allowed themselves, the existence of several revisions of it, necessitate the employment of careful and cautious methods in the study of it. As yet, no canons have been formulated for the study of it; and the final formulating of canons must from the nature of the case rather follow than precede the investigations which these essays are designed to stimulate.

But two such canons will be almost self-evident :—

(1) A word which is used uniformly, or with few and intelligible exceptions, as the translation of the same Hebrew word, must be held to have in Biblical Greek the same meaning as that Hebrew word.

(2) Words which are used interchangeably as translations of the same Hebrew word, or group of cognate words, must be held to have in Biblical Greek an allied or virtually identical meaning.

II. SHORT STUDIES OF THE MEANINGS OF WORDS IN BIBLICAL GREEK.

OF the application of the principles and methods which have been described in the preceding essay the following short studies are examples.

Some of the words have been selected on account of the interest or importance which attaches to their use in the New Testament, some on account of their being clear instances of contrast between Classical and Biblical Greek, and some also to illustrate the variety of the evidence which is available. They fall into two groups, corresponding to the two great classes into which all words in Biblical Greek may be divided, some of them having meanings which are common to Biblical Greek and to contemporary secular Greek, and some of them having meanings which are peculiar to the former, and which, even if suspected, could not be proved without the evidence which is afforded by the versions of the Old Testament. There has been an endeavour in regard to both groups of words to exclude evidence which is not strictly germane to the chief object of enquiry; but it will be noted that in some instances evidence of the special use of words in Biblical Greek has been gathered from sources which have not been described in the preceding essay, and which require a more elaborate discussion than can be attempted in the present work, viz. from writers of the sub-Apostolic age who had presumably not lost the traditions of Biblical Greek, and who confirm certain inferences as to the meanings of New Testament words by showing that those meanings lasted on until the second century A. D.

ἀγγαρεύειν.

1. Classical use.

In Classical Greek this word and its paronyms were used with strict reference to the Persian system of mounted couriers which is described in Herod. 8. 98, Xen. *Cyr.* 8. 6. 17.

2. Post-Classical use.

Under the successors of the Persians in the East, and under the Roman Empire, the earlier system had developed into a system not of postal service, but of the forced transport of military baggage by the inhabitants of a country through which troops, whether on a campaign or otherwise, were passing.

The earliest indication of this system is a letter of Demetrius Soter to the high priest Jonathan and the Jewish nation (Jos. *Ant.* 13. 2. 3), in which among other privileges which he concedes to them he exempts their baggage animals from forced service, κελεύω δὲ μηδὲ ἀγγαρεύεσθαι τὰ Ἰουδαίων ὑποζύγια.

In the important inscription of A.D. 49, *Corp. Inscr. Gr.* No. 4956, A 21, found in the gateway of the temple in the Great Oasis, there is a decree of Capito, prefect of Egypt, which, after reciting that many exactions had been made, goes on to order that soldiers of any degree when passing through the several districts are not to make any requisitions or to employ forced transport unless they have the prefect's written authorization (μηδὲν λαμβάνειν μηδὲ ἀγγαρεύειν εἰ μή τινες ἐμὰ διπλώματα ἔχωσι).

Epictetus, *Diss.* 4. 1. 79, arguing that a man is not master of his body, but holds it subject to any one who is stronger than it, takes the case of a man's pack-ass being seized by a soldier for forced service : 'don't resist,' he says, 'nay, don't even grumble. If you do, you'll not only be beaten, but lose your ass as well, all the same ' (ἂν δ' ἀγγαρεία ᾖ καὶ στρατιώτης ἐπιλάβηται, ἄφες μὴ ἀντίτεινε μηδὲ γόγγυζε· εἰ δὲ μὴ πληγὰς λαβὼν οὐδὲν ἧττον ἀπολεῖς καὶ τὸ ὀνάριον).

The extent to which this system prevailed is seen in the elaborate provisions of the later Roman law: *angariae* came to be one of those modes of taxing property which under the vicious system of the Empire ruined both individuals and communities. A title of the Theodosian Code, lib. 8, tit. 5, is devoted to various provisions respecting it, limiting the number of horses to be employed and the weights which were to be carried in the carts.

3. Use in the N. T.

Hence ἀγγαρεύειν is used in S. Matt. 27. 32, S. Mark 15. 31 in reference to Simon the Cyrenian, who was pressed by the Roman soldiers who were escorting our Lord not merely to accompany them but also to carry a load.

Hence also in S. Matt. 5. 41 the meaning is probably not merely ' whosoever shall compel thee to *go* one mile,' but ' whosoever shall compel thee to *carry his baggage* one mile': and there may be a reference, as in S. Luke 3. 14, to the oppressive conduct of the Roman soldiers.

ἀναγινώσκειν.

1. Post-Classical use.

That the word was sometimes used in post-Classical Greek of reading aloud with comments is shown by its use in Epictetus.

In Epictet. *Diss.* 3. 23. 20, there is a scene from the student-life of Nicopolis. A student is supposed to be ' reading' the *Memorabilia* of Xenophon : it is clear that he not merely reads but comments.

Πολλάκις ἐθαύμασα τίσι ποτὲ λόγοις . . . ' I have often wondered on what grounds . . . ' (these are the words of Xenophon, *Mem.* 1. 1, upon which the ' Reader' comments).

οὔ· ἀλλὰ τίνι ποτὲ λόγῳ, 'No : rather, On what ground: this is a more finished expression than the other' (this is the comment of the Reader).

μὴ γὰρ ἄλλως αὐτὰ ἀνεγνώκατε ἢ ὡς ᾠδάρια ; ' Why, you do not lecture upon it any differently than you would upon a poem, do you ?' (these are the words of Epictetus, finding fault with this way of lecturing upon the words of a *philosopher*).

The students appear to have 'read' or lectured in the presence of the professor, who made remarks upon their reading : for which the technical word was ἐπαναγινώσκειν, Epict. *Diss.* 1. 10. 8.

2. Use in the N. T.

It is probable that this practice of reading with comments explains the parenthesis in S. Matt. 24. 15, S. Mark 13. 14 ὁ ἀναγινώσκων νοείτω, 'let him who reads, and comments upon, these words in the assembly take especial care to understand them.' It may also account for the co-ordination of 'reading' with exhortation and teaching in S. Paul's charge to Timothy, 1 Tim. 4. 13.

ἀποστοματίζειν.

1. Classical use.

In its Classical use the word is used of a master dictating to a pupil a passage to be learnt by heart and afterwards recited : Plat. *Euthyd.* 276 c ὅταν οὖν τις ἀποστοματίζει ὁτιοῦν, οὐ γράμματα ἀποστοματίζει ; 'when, then, any one dictates a passage to be learnt, is it not letters that he dictates?'

2. Post-Classical use.

But in its later use the meaning of the word widened from the recitation of a lesson which had been dictated to the answering of any question which a teacher put in regard to what he had taught : Pollux 2. 102 defines it as ὑπὸ τοῦ διδασκάλου ἐρωτᾶσθαι τὰ μαθήματα.

3. Use in the N. T.

Hence its use in S. Luke 11. 53 ἤρξαντο οἱ γραμματεῖς καὶ οἱ Φαρισαῖοι ... ἀποστοματίζειν αὐτὸν περὶ πλειόνων, 'they began to put questions to him as if they were questioning a pupil on points of theology.'

ἀρετή.

1. Use in the LXX.

The word occurs in the following passages of the canonical books:

(1) In the two following passages it is the translation of הוֹד 'glory.'

Hab. 3. 3 ἐκάλυψεν οὐρανοὺς ἡ ἀρετὴ αὐτοῦ, 'his glory covered the heavens': another translator in the Hexapla renders הוד by τὴν εὐπρέπειαν τῆς δόξης αὐτοῦ.

Zach. 6. 13 καὶ αὐτὸς λήψεται ἀρετήν (of the Branch), 'and he shall bear the glory': other translators in the Hexapla render הוד by ἐπιδοξότητα, εὐπρέπειαν, δόξαν.

(2) In the four following passages it is the translation of תְּהִלָּה 'praise.'

Is. 42. 8 τὴν δόξαν μου ἑτέρῳ οὐ δώσω οὐδὲ τὰς ἀρετάς μου τοῖς γλυπτοῖς, 'my glory will I not give to another, neither my praise to graven images': τὰς ἀρετάς is corrected by Aquila to τὴν ὕμνησιν, by Symmachus to τὸν ἔπαινον.

Is. 42. 12 δώσουσι τῷ θεῷ δόξαν, τὰς ἀρετὰς αὐτοῦ ἐν ταῖς νήσοις ἀναγγελοῦσι, 'they shall give glory to God, His praises shall they declare in the islands.'

Is. 43. 21 λαόν μου ὃν περιεποιησάμην τὰς ἀρετάς μου διηγεῖσθαι, 'my people which I acquired for myself to show forth my praises': Symmachus corrects τὰς ἀρετάς to τὸν ὕμνον.

Is. 63. 7 τὸν ἔλεον κυρίου ἐμνήσθην, τὰς ἀρετὰς κυρίου, 'I will mention the lovingkindness of the Lord, the praises of the Lord': another translator in the Hexapla corrects τὰς ἀρετάς to αἴνεσιν.

Outside the canonical books the word occurs once in an apocryphal addition to the book of Esther, and three times in the Wisdom of Solomon.

Esth. 4. 17, line 33, ed. Tisch. (Esther prays God for help against the efforts which the heathen were making) : ἀνοῖξαι στόμα ἐθνῶν εἰς ἀρετὰς ματαίων, 'to open the mouth of the Gentiles for the praises of vain idols.' The translation of ἀρετάς by 'praises' is supported by the Vulgate 'laudent.'

Wisd. 4. 1; 5. 13; 8. 7: there can be no doubt that in these passages ἀρετή has its ordinary Classical meaning, and not the meaning which it has in the LXX.: in 8. 7 the ἀρεταί are enumerated, viz. σωφροσύνη, φρόνησις, δικαιοσύνη, ἀνδρεία.

2. Use in the N. T.

In the N. T. the word occurs in the Epistle to the Philippians, and in the two Epistles of St. Peter.

Phil. 4. 8 τὸ λοιπόν, ἀδελφοί, ὅσα ἐστὶν ἀληθῆ, ὅσα σεμνά, ὅσα δίκαια, ὅσα ἁγνά, ὅσα προσφιλῆ, ὅσα εὔφημα, εἴ τις ἀρετὴ καὶ εἴ τις ἔπαινος, ταῦτα λογίζεσθε : since ἀρετή is here coordinated with ἔπαινος and follows immediately after εὔφημα, its most appropriate meaning will be that which it has in the canonical books of the O. T. as a translation of הוֹד or תְּהִלָּה, viz. 'glory' or 'praise.'

1 *Pet.* 2. 9 ὅπως τὰς ἀρετὰς ἐξαγγείλητε τοῦ ἐκ σκότους ὑμᾶς καλέσαντος.

It seems most appropriate, especially when the general philological character of the Epistle is taken into consideration, to give the word the LXX. meaning of 'praises.'

2 *Pet.* 1. 3 διὰ τῆς ἐπιγνώσεως τοῦ καλέσαντος ἡμᾶς ἰδίᾳ δόξῃ καὶ ἀρετῇ.

Here also the coordination with δόξα, as in Is. 42. 8, 12, seems to make the meaning 'praise' more appropriate than any other : the use of the singular has its parallels in Hab. 3. 3, Zach. 6. 13.

2 *Pet.* 1. 5 ἐπιχορηγήσατε ἐν τῇ πίστει ὑμῶν τὴν ἀρετήν, ἐν δὲ τῇ ἀρετῇ τὴν γνῶσιν.

This is the most obscure use of the word in the N. T. : nor, in the absence of philological indications, can its meaning be determined without a discussion of the general scope both of the passage and of the whole Epistle, which belongs rather to exegesis than to philology.

γλωσσόκομυν.

1. Classical use.

The word, in the form γλωσσοκομεῖον, is very rare in Attic Greek, being chiefly known to us from a quotation by Pollux 10. 154 of a fragment of the *Bacchae* of Lysippus, a poet of the Old Comedy, which however is sufficient to show its derivation from γλῶσσα in the sense of the tongue or reed of a musical pipe or clarionet : αὐτοῖς αὐλοῖς ὁρμᾷ [so Bentley, *Ad Hemsterh.* p. 69, for ὁρμαί] καὶ γλωττοκομείῳ '(the piper) rushes in with his pipes and tongue-case.'

2. Use in later Greek.

But of this first and literal use there is no trace in later Greek. In the LXX. it is used (1) in 2 Sam. 6. 11, Codd. A. 247, and Aquila, of the Ark of the Lord, = Cod. B. and most cursives ἡ κιβωτός, (2) in 2 Chron. 24. 8, 10, 11 of the chest which was placed by order of Joash at the gate of the temple to receive contributions for its repair, = in the corresponding passages of 2 Kings 12 ἡ κιβωτός.   It is also used for the Ark of the Covenant by Aquila in Exod. 25. 10 : 38 (37). 1 : and Josephus, *Ant.* 6. 1, 2, uses it for the 'coffer' into which were put 'the jewels of gold' 'for a trespass-offering' when the Ark was sent back (1 Sam. 6. 8 = LXX. θέμα).

In a long inscription from one of the Sporades, probably Thera, known as the *Testamentum Epictetae,* and now at Verona, which contains the regulations of an association founded by one Epicteta, γλωσσόκομον is the 'strong-box' or muniment-chest of the association, and is in the special custody of the γραμματοφύλαξ or 'registrar.'

This wider meaning is recognized by the later Atticists : for Phrynichus, § 79 (ed. Rutherford, p. 18) defines it as βιβλίων ἢ ἱματίων ἢ ἀργύρου ἢ ὁτιοῦν ἄλλου.

3. Use in the N. T.

It is found in the N. T. only in S. John 12. 6 : 13. 29, where it is appropriately used of the common chest of our Lord and His disciples, out of which were not only their own wants provided but also the poor relieved.

In still later Greek this wide use of it was again narrowed : it was used, at last exclusively, of a wooden coffin, σορός having apparently come to be used only of a stone-coffin or sarcophagus. The earliest instance of this use is probably in Aquila's version of Gen. 50. 26. In modern Greek it means a purse or bag.

δεισιδαίμων, δεισιδαιμονία.

1. Classical use.

It is clear that the dominant if not the only sense of these words in Classical Greek is a good one, 'religious,' 'religion': e. g.

Xenophon, *Cyrop*. 3. 3. 58, tells the story of Cyrus, before attacking the Assyrians, beginning the accustomed battle-hymn and of the soldiers piously (θεοσεβῶς) taking up the strain with a loud voice: 'for it is under circumstances such as these that those who fear the gods (οἱ δεισιδαίμονες) are less afraid of men.'

Aristotle, *Pol*. 5. 11, p. 1315 a, says that rulers should be conspicuously observant of their duties to the gods: 'for men are less afraid of being unjustly treated by them if they see a ruler religious (δεισιδαίμονα) and observant of the gods, and they plot against him less because they consider that he has the gods also as his allies.'

In this last instance the reference is probably to the outward observance of religion: and that this was implied in the words is shown by a senatus consultum of B. C. 38, which is preserved in an inscription at Aphrodisias in Caria (*Corp. Inscr. Gr.*, No. 2737 *b*). The senatus consultum decrees that the precinct (τέμενος) of Aphrodite shall be held as consecrated, 'with the same rights and the same religious observances, ταὐτῷ δικαίῳ ταὐτῇ τε δεισιδαιμονίᾳ (eodem jure eademque religione), as the precinct of the Ephesian goddess at Ephesus.'

2. Post-Classical use.

In later Greek the words have a meaning which is probably first found in Theophrast. *Charact.* 16, ἀμέλει ἡ δεισιδαιμονία δόξειεν ἂν εἶναι δειλία πρὸς τοὺς θεούς : ' no doubt δεισιδαιμονία will be thought to be a feeling of cowardice in relation to the gods :' they are used not of the due reverence of the gods, which is religion, but of the excessive fear of them, which constitutes superstition. Of this there are several proofs :—

(1) Philo repeatedly distinguishes δεισιδαιμονία from εὐσεβεία : e.g. *De Sacrif. Abel et Cain*, c. 4 (i. 166), where he speaks of the way in which nurses foster fear and cowardice and other mischiefs in the minds of young children ' by means of habits and usages which drive away piety, and produce superstition—a thing akin to impiety,' δι' ἐθῶν καὶ νομίμων εὐσεβείαν μὲν ἐλαυνόντων δεισιδαιμονίαν δὲ πρᾶγμα ἀδελφὸν ἀσεβείᾳ κατασκευαζόντων. Again, in *Quod Deus immut.* c. 35 (i. 297), he defines it more precisely in Aristotelian language as the ' excess' of which impiety is the corresponding ' defect' and piety (εὐσεβεία) the ' mean' : cf. *De Gigantibus*, c. 4 (i. 264): *De Plantat. Noe*, c. 25 (i. 345): *De Justitia*, c. 2 (ii. 360).

(2) Josephus, *Ant.* 15. 8, 2, relates that, among the other means which Herod adopted for adorning the amphitheatre which he had built at Jerusalem, he erected trophies in the Roman fashion with the spoils of the tribes whom he had conquered. The Jews thought that they were men clad in armour, and that they came within the prohibition of the divine law against images. A popular tumult was threatened. Herod, wishing to avoid the use of force, talked to some of the people, trying to draw them away from their superstition (τῆς δεισιδαιμονίας ἀφαιρούμενος), but without success, until he took some of them into the theatre and showed them that the armour was fixed on bare pieces of wood.

(3) Plutarch has a treatise Περὶ δεισιδαιμονίας (*Moral.* vol. ii. pp. 165 sqq.), which begins by saying that the stream of ignorance about divine things divides at its source into two channels, becoming in the harder natures atheism (ἀθεότης), in the softer, superstition (δεισιδαιμονία).

(4) M. Aurelius, 6. 30, in painting the almost ideal character of his adopted father, speaks of him as ' god-fearing without being superstitious ' (θεοσεβὴς χωρὶς δεισιδαιμονίας).

It seems clear from these facts that in the first century and a half of the Christian era the words had come to have in ordinary Greek a bad or at least a depreciatory sense. That it had this sense in Christian circles as well as outside them is clear from its use in Justin M. *Apol.* 1. 2, where it is part of his complimentary introduction to those to whom his Apology is addressed that they are ' not men who are under the dominion of prejudice or a desire to gratify superstitious persons ' (μὴ προλήψει μηδ᾽ ἀνθρωπαρεσκείᾳ τῇ δεισιδαιμόνων κατεχομένους), but that they can form a candid judgment on the arguments which are addressed to them.

3. Use in the N. T.

This having been the current meaning, it is improbable that the words can be taken in any other sense in the two passages in which they occur in the Acts of the Apostles : in 17. 22 S. Paul tells the Athenians that they are δεισιδαιμονεστέρους, 'rather inclined to superstition' : and in 25. 19 Festus tells Agrippa that the charges which Paul's accusers bring against him are questions περὶ τῆς ἰδίας δεισιδαιμονίας, 'concerning their own superstition.'

διάβολος, διαβάλλω.

1. Classical use.

These words were ordinarily used in reference to slanderous, or at least malicious, accusation : διαβάλλω is sometimes found in the probably earlier sense of setting at variance, e.g. Plat. *Rep.* 6. p. 498 d μὴ διάβαλλε ἐμὲ καὶ Θρασύμαχον ἄρτι φίλους γεγονότας, and, in the passive, of being at variance, e.g. Thucyd. 8. 83 καὶ πρότερον τῷ Τισσα-φέρνει ἀπιστοῦντες πολλῷ δὴ μᾶλλον ἔτι διεβέβληντο : but διάβολος, whether as substantive or as adjective, seems invariably to have connoted malice. Hence the Atticists, e.g. Pollux 5. 18, coordinate λοίδορος, βλάσφημος, διάβολος, and Lucian's treatise, Περὶ τοῦ μὴ ῥᾳδίως πιστεύειν διαβολῇ, gives no trace of any other meaning.

2. Use in the LXX.

In Job and Zechariah, and also in Wisd. 2. 24, ὁ διάβολος is clearly used of a single person, שָׂטָן, the 'enemy' of mankind. In the other passages in which it occurs it is used to translate either the same word or its equivalent in meaning, צָר, but without the same reference to that single person. The passages are the following:—

1 *Chron.* 21. 1 ἀνέστη διάβολος ἐν τῷ Ἰσραήλ, of the 'enemy' who stirred up David to number Israel (the E. V., following Codd. 19, 93, 108, transliterates the Hebrew, ' Satan ').

Esth. 7. 4 οὐ γὰρ ἄξιος ὁ διάβολος τῆς αὐλῆς τοῦ βασιλέως.

Esth. 8. 1 ὅσα ὑπῆρχεν Ἀμὰν τῷ διαβόλῳ (Cod. S′ omits τῷ δ. but Codd. S² 249 add τῶν Ἰουδαίων).

In both these passages the Hebrew has צָר or צֹרֵר, which have no other connotation than that of hostility, and of which the former is ordinarily translated by ἐχθρός.

Ps. 108 (109). 5 καὶ διάβολος στήτω ἐκ δεξιῶν αὐτοῦ.

In *Numb.* 22. 22 where the LXX. translates by ἀνέστη ὁ ἄγγελος τοῦ θεοῦ ἐνδιαβάλλειν (so Codd. A B and most cursives, Ed. Sixt. διαβαλεῖν) αὐτόν, Aquila transliterates the Hebrew (εἰς) σατάν, Theodotion translates by ἀντικεῖσθαι: so in Job 1. 6, where the LXX. have ὁ διάβολος, Aquila has σατάν, Theodotion ἀντικείμενος. Conversely in 1 Kings 11. 14, where the LXX. transliterates σατάν, Aquila agrees with Theodotion in translating by ἀντικείμενος.

In *Numb.* 22. 32 where the LXX. has καὶ ἰδοὺ ἐγὼ ἐξῆλθον εἰς διαβολήν σου, Symmachus translates by ἐναντιοῦσθαι, Theodotion by ἀντικεῖσθαι.

The Hebrew word in both passages is שָׂטָן.

It seems to be clear that the LXX. used διάβολος and its

paronyms with the general connotation of enmity, and without implying accusation whether true or false.

3. Use in the N. T.

In the New Testament διάβολος is invariably used as a proper name, except in the Pastoral Epistles, where it is also used as an adjective, and when so used has its ordinary meaning of 'slanderous' (1 Tim. 3. 11; 2 Tim. 3. 3; Tit. 2. 3). But when used as a proper name there is no reason for supposing that it is used in any other sense than that which it has in the LXX., viz. as the equivalent of שָׂטָן and as meaning 'enemy.'

διαβάλλω occurs only once, viz. S. Luke 16. 1 of the 'unjust steward': the accusation was presumably true, and hence the meaning of slander would be inappropriate; so Euseb. *H. E.* 3. 39. 16, referring to Papias and possibly using his words, speaks of the woman who was taken in adultery 'in the very act' as γυναικὸς . . . διαβληθείσης ἐπὶ τοῦ κυρίου.

διαθήκη.

1. Classical use.

The word has at least two meanings, (1) a 'disposition' of property by will, which is its most ordinary use, (2) a 'covenant,' which is a rare meaning, but clearly established e.g. by Aristoph. *Av.* 439.

2. Use in the LXX.

It occurs nearly 280 times in the LXX. proper, i. e. in the parts which have a Hebrew original, and in all but four passages it is the translation of בְּרִית 'covenant': in those passages it is the translation respectively of אַחֲוָה 'brotherhood,' Zech. 11. 14, דָּבָר 'word,' Deut. 9. 5, and דִּבְרֵי הַבְּרִית 'words of the covenant,' Jer. 41 (34). 18; in

Ex. 31. 7 τὴν κιβωτὸν τῆς διαθήκης takes the place of the more usual τὴν κιβωτὸν τοῦ μαρτυρίου.

In the Apocryphal books, which do not admit of being tested by the Hebrew, it occurs frequently and always in the same sense of 'covenant.'

3. Use in the Hexapla.

The Hexapla Revisers sometimes change it to that which is the more usual Greek word for 'covenant,' viz. συνθήκη : e.g. *Aquil. Symm.* Gen. 6. 18 : *Aquil. Theod.* 1 Sam. 6. 19 : *Aquil. Symm.* Ps. 24 (25). 10. This fact accentuates and proves the peculiarity of its use in the LXX.

4. Use in Philo.

In Philo it has the same sense as in the LXX. : e.g. *De Somniis* 2. 33, vol. i. p. 688, where he speaks of God's covenant as Law and Reason, νόμος δέ ἐστι καὶ λόγος: cf. Justin M. *Tryph.* c. 43, where he speaks of Christ as being the αἰώνιος νόμος καὶ καινὴ διαθήκη.

5. Use in the N. T.

There can be little doubt that the word must be invariably taken in this sense of 'covenant' in the N. T., and especially in a book which is so impregnated with the language of the LXX. as the Epistle to the Hebrews. The attempt to give it in certain passages its Classical meaning of 'testament' is not only at variance with its use in Hellenistic Greek, but probably also the survival of a mistake : in ignorance of the philology of later and vulgar Latin, it was formerly supposed that 'testamentum,' by which the word is rendered in the early Latin versions as well as in the Vulgate, meant 'testament' or 'will,' whereas in fact it meant also, if not exclusively, 'covenant.'

δίκαιος, δικαιοσύνη.

1. Use in the LXX. and Hexapla.

Into the Classical meaning of these words it is hardly necessary to enter.; that meaning is found also in both the LXX. and the N. T.: but intertwined with it is another meaning which is peculiar to Hellenistic Greek. The existence of this meaning is established partly by the meaning of the Hebrew words which δίκαιος, δικαιοσύνη are used to translate, and partly by the meaning of the Greek words with which they are interchanged.

(1) חֶסֶד 'kindness' is usually (i. e. more than 100 times) translated by ἔλεος, sometimes by ἐλεημοσύνη, ἐλεήμων: but nine times (Gen., Ex., Prov., Is.) it is translated by δικαιοσύνη, and once by δίκαιος.

Conversely, צְדָקָה 'justice,' which is usually translated by δικαιοσύνη, is nine times translated by ἐλεημοσύνη, and three times by ἔλεος.

(2) Sometimes the LXX. δικαιοσύνη is changed by the Hexapla Revisers into ἐλεημοσύνη, and sometimes the reverse: apparently with the view of rendering חֶסֶד uniformly by ἐλεημοσύνη, and צְדָקָה by δικαιοσύνη: for example—

Exod. 15. 13 LXX. δικαιοσύνη, Aquil. ἐλεημοσύνη.

Deut. 24. 13 LXX. ἐλεημοσύνη, Aquil. δικαιοσύνη.

1 *Sam.* 12. 7 LXX. δικαιοσύνη, Symm. ἐλεημοσύνη. So also Ps. 30 (31). 2: 35 (36). 11: 105 (106). 3.

Ps. 32 (33). 5 LXX. ἐλεημοσύνην, Aquil., Int. Quint. δικαιοσύνην.

Is. 1. 27 LXX. ἐλεημοσύνης, Aquil., Symm., Theod. δικαιοσύνης. So also 28. 17.

Is. 56. 1 LXX. ἔλεος, Aquil., Symm., Theod. δικαιοσύνη.

Is. 59. 16 LXX. ἐλεημοσύνη, Theod. δικαιοσύνη.

Dan. 9. 16 LXX. δικαιοσύνην, Theod. ἐλεημοσύνη.

This revision seems to show that the sense in which δικαιοσύνη is used in the LXX. was not universally accepted, but was a local peculiarity of the country in which that

E

translation was made.   The same tendency to the revision
of the word is seen in some MSS.: e. g. in Ps. 34 (35). 24,
where all MSS. (except one cursive, which has ἔλεος) read
δικαιοσύνην, Cod. S reads ἐλεημοσύνην, and in Ps. 37 (38). 21,
where Codd. A B and many cursives read δικαιοσύνην, Cod.
S² and many other cursives read ἀγαθωσύνην (-οσύνην).

The context of many of these passages shows that the
meanings of the two words δικαιοσύνη and ἐλεημοσύνη had
interpenetrated each other :

(a) Sometimes, where ἐλεημοσύνη is used to translate צְדָקָה, no
other meaning than ' righteousness' is possible : e. g.

Deut. 6. 25 ἐλεημοσύνη ἔσται ἡμῖν ἐὰν φυλασσώμεθα ποιεῖν πάσας τὰς
ἐντολὰς ταύτας . . . 'It shall be our righteousness if we observe to
do all these commandments . . .'

Deut. 24. 13 (15) . . . καὶ ἔσται σοι ἐλεημοσύνη ἐναντίον κυρίου τοῦ
θεοῦ σου.

('In any case thou shalt deliver him his pledge again when the
sun goeth down) . . . and it shall be righteousness unto thee
before the Lord thy God.'

(b) Conversely, sometimes, where δικαιοσύνη is used to render
חֶסֶד, no other meaning than 'kindness' or 'mercy' is possible :
e. g.

Gen. 19. 19 (Lot said after having been brought out of Sodom)
ἐπειδὴ εὗρεν ὁ παῖς σου ἔλεος ἐναντίον σου καὶ ἐμεγάλυνας τὴν δικαιοσύνην
σου . . .

'Since thy servant hath found grace in thy sight, and thou hast
magnified thy *mercy* which thou showest unto me in saving my
life . . .'

Gen. 24. 27 (when Eliezer is told that the damsel is the daughter
of Bethuel, he blesses God) ὃς οὐκ ἐγκατέλιπε τὴν δικαιοσύνην αὐτοῦ
καὶ τὴν ἀλήθειαν ἀπὸ τοῦ κυρίου μου.

'Who hath not left destitute my master of his mercy and his
truth.'

2. Use in the N. T.

There is one passage of the N. T. in which this meaning
of δικαιοσύνη is so clear that scribes who were unaware of
its existence altered the text: in S. Matt. 6. 1 the estab-

lished reading is undoubtedly δικαιοσύνην, for which the later uncials and most cursives have ἐλεημοσύνην, and for which also an early reviser of Cod. ℵ, as in some similar cases in the LXX., substituted δόσιν.

There is no other passage of the N. T. in which it is clear that this meaning attaches to either δίκαιος or δικαιοσύνη : but at the same time it gives a better sense than any other to the difficult statement about Joseph in S. Matt. i. 19 Ἰωσὴφ δὲ ὁ ἀνὴρ αὐτῆς δίκαιος ὢν καὶ μὴ θέλων αὐτὴν δειγματίσαι, 'Joseph her husband, *being a kindly man*, and since he was not willing to make her a public example . . .'

ἑτοιμάζειν, ἑτοιμασία, ἕτοιμος.

1. Use in the LXX.

In the great majority of instances ἑτοιμάζειν, ἑτοιμασία, ἕτοιμος are used in the LXX. to translate כוּן or one of its derivatives. That word, which properly means 'to stand upright,' was used in the meanings 'to set upright,' 'to make firm' (e.g. 2 Sam. 7. 13 'I will *stablish* the throne of his kingdom for ever'), and hence in the more general meanings 'to make ready,' 'to prepare' (e.g. Job 29. 7 'when I *prepared* my seat in the street,' Deut. 19. 3 thou shalt *prepare* thee the way'). This latter use being the more common use of the word, it was ordinarily translated by ἑτοιμάζειν, which in Classical Greek has no other mean- ing. But the use of this Greek word in the Septuagint affords an interesting illustration of the manner in which the meaning of the Hebrew acted upon the Greek; for it is clear that it came to have some of the special meanings of the Hebrew 'to set upright,' 'to establish,' 'to make firm.'

(1) The existence of that meaning when the Septuagint versions were made is shown by the use of words which undoubtedly express it : that is to say, כוּן is translated by

(*a*) ἀνορθοῦν 2 Sam. 7. 13, 16, 26, Prov. 24. 3, Jer. 10. 12 : 40 (33). 2.

(*b*) ἐπιστηρίζειν Cod. A, Judges 16. 26, 30 (=Cod. B ἱστάναι).

(*c*) θεμελιοῦν Ps. 8. 4 : 47 (48). 9 : 86 (87). 5 : 118 (119). 90.

(*d*) κατορθοῦν 1 Chron. 16. 30, Ps. 95 (96). 10.

(*e*) στερεοῦν Ps. 92 (93). 2.

(2) In similar passages, and sometimes in the same books, the same Hebrew word is translated by ἑτοιμάζειν,

e. g. (*a*) 2 Sam. 7. 13 ἀνορθώσω τὸν θρόνον αὐτοῦ, but *ib*. v. 12 ἑτοιμάσω τὴν βασιλείαν αὐτοῦ : *ib*. v. 24 ἡτοίμασας σεαυτῷ τὸν λαόν σου Ἰσραὴλ εἰς λαὸν ἕως τοῦ αἰῶνος : *ib*. v. 26 (Cod. A) ὁ οἶκος τοῦ δούλου σου Δαυὶδ ἔσται ἀνωρθωμένος ἐνώπιόν σου.

(*b*) Ps. 64 (65). 7 ἑτοιμάζων ὄρη ἐν τῇ ἰσχύϊ σου : Ps. 47 (48). 9 ὁ θεὸς ἐθεμελίωσεν αὐτὴν εἰς τὸν αἰῶνα : Ps. 8. 4 σελήνην καὶ ἀστέρας ἃ σὺ ἐθεμελίωσας : Prov. 3. 19 ἡτοίμασε δὲ οὐράνους ἐν φρονήσει.

(*c*) Ps. 23 (24). 2 ἐπὶ ποταμῶν ἡτοίμασεν αὐτήν (*sc.* τὴν οἰκουμένην) : Ps. 95 (96). 10 κατώρθωσε τὴν οἰκουμένην ἥτις οὐ σαλευθήσεται : Ps. 92 (93). 2 ἐστερέωσε τὴν οἰκουμένην ἥτις οὐ σαλευθήσεται.

In other words, ἑτοιμάζειν is used interchangeably with ἀνορθοῦν, θεμελιοῦν, κατορθοῦν, στερεοῦν as the translation of כון.

In the same way ἑτοιμασία is used to translate both the verb and its derivatives מָכוֹן, מְכוֹנָה, 'base,' or 'foundation,' or 'fixed seat'; and ἕτοιμος is used to translate both מָכוֹן and נָכוֹן (*part. niph.*) : e. g.

1 *Kings* 2. 45 ὁ θρόνος Δαυὶδ ἔσται ἕτοιμος ἐνώπιον κυρίου εἰς τὸν αἰῶνα.

1 *Kings* 8. 39, 43, 49, 2 *Chron.* 6. 30, 33, 39, *Ps.* 32 (33). 14 מִמְּכוֹן־שִׁבְתּוֹ ἐξ ἑτοίμου κατοικητηρίου σου.

2 *Esdr.* 2. 68 τοῦ στῆναι αὐτὸν ἐπὶ τὴν ἑτοιμασίαν αὐτοῦ.

Ps. 56 (57). 8 : 107 (108). 1 : 111 (112). 7 ἑτοίμη ἡ καρδία μου.

Ps. 88 (89). 15 δικαιοσύνη καὶ κρίμα ἑτοιμασία τοῦ θρόνου σου.

Ps. 92 (93). 3 ἕτοιμος ὁ θρόνος σου ἀπὸ τότε.

Zach. 5. 11 θήσουσιν αὐτὸ ἐκεῖ ἐπὶ τὴν ἑτοιμασίαν αὐτοῦ.

It seems clear from these passages that, like ἑτοιμάζειν,

ἐτοιμασία and ἕτοιμος had come to have the meaning of the Hebrew words which they were used to translate.

2. Use in the Hexapla.

This inference that the three Greek words are used in the LXX. in the proper sense of כוּן and its derivatives, is strongly confirmed by their use in the Hexapla.

(1) Sometimes they are replaced by words of whose use in the proper sense of כוּן there is no doubt :

Ex. 15. 17 LXX. εἰς ἕτοιμον κατοικητήριόν σου, *Aquil., Symm.* ἕδρασμα εἰς καθέδραν σου.

Ibid. LXX. ἡτοίμασαν, *Aquil.* ἥδρασαν.

1 *Sam.* 20. 31 LXX. ἐτοιμασθήσεται, *Symm.* ἑδρασθήσεται, *Alius* κατορθώσεις.

1 *Sam.* 23. 33 LXX. εἰς ἕτοιμον, *Symm.* ἐπὶ βεβαίῳ.

2 *Sam.* 5. 12 LXX. ἡτοίμασεν, *Symm.* ἥδρασεν.

2 *Sam.* 7. 12 LXX. ἑτοιμάσω, *Symm.* ἑδράσω.

2 *Sam.* 7. 24 LXX. ἡτοίμασας, *Symm.* ἥδρασας.

Ps. 9. 8 LXX. ἡτοίμασεν ἐν κρίσει τὸν θρόνον, *Symm.* ἥδρασεν.

Ps. 9. 39 (10. 18) LXX. τὴν ἑτοιμασίαν τῆς καρδίας, *Symm.* πρόθεσιν.

Ps. 10 (11). 2 LXX. ἡτοίμασαν, *Aquil., Symm.* ἥδρασαν.

Ps. 20 (21). 13 LXX. ἑτοιμάσεις, *Aquil., Symm.* ἑδράσεις.

Ps. 23 (24). 2 LXX. ἡτοίμασεν, *Aquil., Symm.* ἥδρασεν.

Ps. 32 (33). 14 LXX. ἐξ ἑτοίμου κατοικητηρίου σου, *Aquil.* ἀπὸ ἑδράσματος καθέδρας αὐτοῦ, *Symm.* ἀπὸ ἑδραίας (s. ἕδρας) κατοικίας αὐτοῦ.

Ps. 56 (57). 8 LXX. ἑτοίμη ἡ καρδία μου, *Symm.* ἑδραία ἡ κ. μου.

Ps. 64 (65). 7 LXX. ἑτοιμάζων ὄρη, *Symm.* ἥδρασας ὄρη.

Ib. v. 10 LXX. ὅτι οὕτως ἡ ἑτοιμασία, *Symm.* ὅτι οὕτως ἥδρασας αὐτήν.

Ps. 88 (89). 3 LXX. ἐτοιμασθήσεται, *Symm.* ἑδρασθήσεται (but *ib.* v. 4 Symmachus retains ἑτοιμάσω).

Ib. v. 15 LXX. ἑτοιμασία τοῦ θρόνου σου, *Aquil.* τὸ ἕδρασμα, *Symm.* βάσις.

Prov. 8. 27 LXX. ἡτοίμαζε, *Symm.* ἥδραζε.

Prov. 16. 12 LXX. ἑτοιμάζεται, *Symm. Theod.* ἑδρασθήσεται.

(2) Sometimes, on the contrary, they are substituted for

other words which had been used in the Septuagint as translations of כון :

Gen. 41. 32 LXX. ἀληθὲς ἔσται τὸ ῥῆμα, *Aquil.* ἕτοιμον, *Symm.* βέβαιος.

Ps. 8. 4 LXX. ἐθεμελίωσας, *Aquil. Theod.* ἡτοίμασας, *Int. Sextus* ἤδρασας.

Ps. 86 (87). 5 LXX. καὶ αὐτὸς ἐθεμελίωσεν αὐτὴν ὁ ὕψιστος, *Aquil.* ἔδρασει, *Symm.* ἤδρασεν, *Theod.* ἡτοίμασεν.

Prov. 4. 18 LXX. ἕως κατορθώσῃ ἡ ἡμέρα, *Aquil.* (ἕως) ἑτοίμης ἡμέρας, *Symm.* (ἕως) ἑδραίας ἡμέρας, *Theod.* ἕως ἑτοιμασίας ἡμέρας, *Int. Quintus* ἑτοιμασίας.

Prov. 12. 3 LXX. κατορθώσει, *Aquil.*, *Symm.* ἑτοιμασθήσεται.

Prov. 12. 20 LXX. κατορθοῖ, *Aquil.*, *Symm.*, *Theod.* ἑτοιμασθήσεται.

Prov. 25. 5 LXX. κατορθώσει, *Aquil.*, *Symm.* ἑδρασθήσεται, *Theod.* ἑτοιμασθήσεται.

This latter group of facts makes the inference certain that in the latter part of the second century ἑτοιμάζειν was sometimes used in Hellenistic Greek in the sense of 'to set upright,' 'to establish,' 'to make firm,' ἕτοιμος in that of 'established,' 'made firm,' and ἑτοιμασία in that of 'establishment,' 'firm foundation.'

3. Use in the N. T.

In the majority of passages in which the words ἑτοιμάζειν, ἕτοιμος occur in the N. T., their ordinary meanings are sufficient to cover the obvious sense which is required by the context. There are some passages in which the secondary meaning which they bear in the LXX. and Hexapla is appropriate, if not necessary: for example,

S. Matt. 20. 23, *S. Mark* 10. 40 οἷς ἡτοίμασται: *S. Matt.* 25. 34 τὴν ἡτοιμασμένην ὑμῖν βασιλείαν ἀπὸ καταβολῆς κόσμου: *ib.* v. 41 τὸ πῦρ τὸ αἰώνιον, τὸ ἡτοιμασμένον [Cod. D et al. ὃ ἡτοίμασεν ὁ πατήρ μου] τῷ διαβόλῳ καὶ τοῖς ἀγγέλοις αὐτοῦ: 1 *Cor.* 2. 9 ἃ ἡτοίμασεν ὁ θεὸς τοῖς ἀγαπῶσιν αὐτόν: *Heb.* 11. 16 ἡτοίμασε γὰρ αὐτοῖς πόλιν. The nearest English equivalent in each of these passages would probably be 'destined,' as in 2 Sam. 5. 12 (= 1 Chron. 14. 2) ἔγνω Δαυὶδ ὅτι ἡτοίμασεν αὐτὸν Κύριος εἰς βασιλέα ἐπὶ Ἰσραήλ, Tobit 6. 18 μὴ φοβοῦ ὅτι σοὶ αὕτη ἡτοιμασμένη ἦν ἀπὸ τοῦ αἰῶνος.

Ephes. 6. 15 ὑποδησάμενοι τοὺς πόδας ἐν ἐτοιμασίᾳ τοῦ εὐαγγελίου τῆς εἰρήνης. In this, which is the only instance of the use of ἐτοιμασία in the N. T., it seems most appropriate to take it in the sense which it has been shown to have elsewhere in Biblical Greek of 'firm foundation,' or 'firm footing.' This view is confirmed by the use of the instrumental ἐν which, though not without Classical parallels (e. g. Hom. *Il.* 5. 368 δῆσαν κρατερῷ ἐνὶ δεσμῷ), gives to the passage a strong Hellenistic colouring.

θρησκεία.

1. Classical use.

The word is used by Herodotus 2. 37 of the ceremonial observances of the Egyptian priests: it does not appear to occur in Attic Greek.

2. Use in the LXX.

In the LXX. it is found in Wisdom 14. 18, 27 of the worship of idols, ἡ τῶν ἀνωνύμων εἰδώλων θρησκεία : and in 4 Macc. 5. 6 of the religion of the Jews, in relation to its prohibition of the eating of swine's flesh, as τῇ Ἰουδαίων θρησκείᾳ. Symmachus uses it in Dan. 2. 46 of the worship paid to Daniel by Nebuchadnezzar's orders (LXX. ἐπέταξε θυσίας καὶ σπονδὰς ποιῆσαι αὐτῷ), and in Jer. 3. 19, Ezek. 20. 6, 15 as a translation of צְבִי.

3. Use in Philo and Josephus.

Its use is equally clear in Philo and Josephus, both of whom distinguish it from εὐσεβεία, which = religion in its deeper sense, or piety.

Philo *Quod det. potiori insid.* c. 7 (i. 195), in substance: 'Nor if anyone uses lustrations or purifications and makes his body clean, but soils the purity of his mind—nor again, if out of his abundance he builds a temple or offers ceaseless hecatombs of sacrifices, is he to be reckoned among pious men (εὐσεβῶν): nay rather he has altogether wandered from the path that leads to piety, with heart set on external observances instead of on holiness (θρησκείαν ἀντὶ ὁσιότητος ἡγούμενος), offering gifts to Him who cannot be bribed, and flattering Him who cannot be flattered.'

Josephus *Ant.* 9. 13. 3 (Solomon restored the decaying practice of giving tithes and firstfruits to the priests and levites) ἵνα ἀεὶ τῇ θρησκείᾳ παραμένωσι καὶ τῆς θεραπείας ὦσιν ἀχώριστοι τοῦ Θεοῦ, 'that they may always remain in attendance on public worship, and might not be separated from the service of God.'

Ib. 12. 5. 4 ἠνάγκασε δ᾽ αὐτοὺς ἀφιεμένους τῆς περὶ τὸν αὐτῶν Θεὸν θρησκείας τοὺς ὑπ᾽ αὐτοῦ νομιζομένους σέβεσθαι, '(Antiochus Epiphanes) compelled them to abandon their worship of their own God, and to pay honour to the gods in whom he believed.'

Ib. 5. 10. 1 γυναῖκας τὰς ἐπὶ θρησκείᾳ παραγινομένας, of the women who went to worship and offer sacrifices at the Tabernacle.

Ib. 4. 4. 4 (of those who sacrifice at home) εὐωχίας ἕνεκα τῆς αὐτῶν ἀλλὰ μὴ θρησκείας, 'for the sake of their own private enjoyment rather than of public worship.'

Ib. 12. 6. 2 (When a Jew offered sacrifice on an idol altar, Mattathias rushed upon him and slew him, and having overthrown the altar cried out) εἴ τις ζηλωτής ἐστι τῶν πατρίων ἐθῶν καὶ τῆς τοῦ Θεοῦ θρησκείας ἐπέσθω ἐμοί, 'whoever is zealous for his fathers' customs and for the worship of God, let him follow me.'

4. Use in sub-Apostolic writers:—

Clem. R. i. 45. 7 τῶν θρησκευόντων τὴν μεγαλοπρεπῆ καὶ ἔνδοξον θρησκείαν τοῦ ὑψίστου, 'those who practised the magnificent and glorious worship of the Most High.'

Ib. 62. 1 περὶ μὲν τῶν ἀνηκόντων τῇ θρησκείᾳ ἡμῶν, τῶν ὠφελιμωτάτων εἰς ἐνάρετον βίον τοῖς θέλουσιν εὐσεβῶς καὶ δικαίως διευθύνειν, 'of the things which pertain to our religion, things that are most useful to those who wish to guide their life piously and righteously into the way of virtue (we have given you sufficient injunctions, brethren).'

5. Use in the N. T.

This contemporary use of θρησκεία for religion in its

external aspect as worship, or as one mode of worship contrasted with another, must be held to be its meaning in the N. T. It occurs in the following passages :

Acts 26. 5 (in St. Paul's address to Agrippa) κατὰ τὴν ἀκριβεστάτην αἵρεσιν τῆς ἡμετέρας θρησκείας ἔζησα Φαρισαῖος, 'after the straitest sect of our religion I lived a Pharisee.'

Col. 2. 18 ἐν ταπεινοφροσύνῃ καὶ θρησκείᾳ τῶν ἀγγέλων, 'by humility and worshipping of the angels.'

James 1. 26, 27 . . . . θρησκεία καθαρὰ καὶ ἀμίαντος, 'worship pure and undefiled in the sight of our God and Father is to visit orphans and widows in their affliction, to keep oneself unspotted from the world.'

μυστήριον.

1. Use in the LXX. and Hexapla.

The only canonical book of the O. T. in which μυστήριον is used by the LXX. is Daniel, where it occurs several times in c. 2 as the translation of רָז 'a secret,' which is used of the king's dream, i. e. of the king's 'secret' which had gone from him and which was revealed to Daniel.

The other Greek translators of the O. T. use it in the following passages :—

Job 15. 8 Theodotion μυστήριον, = LXX. σύνταγμα, Aquila ἀπόρρητα, Symm. ὁμιλία, Heb. סוֹד.

Ps. 24 (25). 14 Theodotion and the *Interpres Quintus* μυστήριον, = LXX. and the *Interpres Sextus* κραταίωμα, Aquila ἀπόρρητον, Symm. ὁμιλία, Heb. סוֹד.

Prov. 20. 19 Theodotion uses it to translate סוֹד in a passage which the LXX. omit.

Is. 24. 16 Theodotion and Symmachus use it as a translation of רָזִי in a passage which the LXX. omit (but which has found its way into some cursive MSS. from Theodotion).

It is frequently used in the Apocryphal books. In Sirach 22. 22 ; 27. 16, 17, 21 of the secrets of private life, especially between friends : in Wisd. 14. 15, 23, in connexion with τελεταί, of heathen sacrifices and ceremonies: but in a majority of passages of secrets of state, or the plans which a king kept in his own mind. This was a strictly Oriental conception. A king's 'counsel' was his 'secret,' which was known only to himself and his trusted friends. It was natural to extend the conception to the secret plans of God.

Tob. 12. 7, 11 μυστήριον βασιλέως, 'It is good to keep close the secret of a king, but it is honourable to reveal the works of God.'

Judith 2. 2 Nabuchodonosor called all his officers unto him and communicated to them τὸ μυστήριον τῆς βουλῆς, 'his secret plan.'

2 Macc. 13. 21 of one who disclosed τὰ μυστήρια, 'the secret plans' of the Jews to their enemies.

Wisd. 2. 22 of the wicked who knew not μυστήρια Θεοῦ, 'the secret counsels of God,' and especially that He created man to be immortal.

Ib. 6. 24 of the 'secrets' of wisdom.

2. Use in the N. T.

This meaning of μυστήριον in the Apocryphal books throws considerable light upon its meaning in the N. T.

Matt. 13. 11 (=Mark 4. 11, Luke 8. 10) ὑμῖν δέδοται γνῶναι τὰ μυστήρια τῆς βασιλείας τῶν οὐρανῶν: the word implies not merely 'secrets,' but rather the secret purposes or counsels which God intended to carry into effect in His kingdom. The contrast with ἐν παραβολαῖς which immediately follows is interesting when viewed in the light of the further meaning of μυστήριον, which will be mentioned below.

Rom. 11. 25 τὸ μυστήριον τοῦτο .... ὅτι πώρωσις ἀπὸ μέρους τῷ Ἰσραὴλ γέγονεν, the secret purpose or counsel of God, by which 'a hardening in part hath befallen Israel until the fulness of the Gentiles be come in.'

Rom. 16. 25 κατὰ ἀποκάλυψιν μυστηρίου χρόνοις αἰωνίοις σεσιγημένου φανερωθέντος δὲ νῦν, of the secret purpose or counsel 'which hath been kept in silence through times eternal but now is manifested'—that the Gentiles were to be fellow-heirs with the seed of

Abraham : and in the same sense 1 Cor. 2. 1 (unless μαρτύριον be there read with Codd. B D etc.).

1 *Cor.* 15. 51 ἰδοὺ μυστήριον ὑμῖν λέγω, 'I tell you a secret counsel of God' for the time that is coming.

Ephes. 1. 9 τὸ μυστήριον τοῦ θελήματος, 'the secret counsel of His will' : 3. 3, 4 ἐν τῷ μυστηρίῳ τοῦ Χριστοῦ: 3. 9 τίς ἡ οἰκονομία τοῦ μυστηρίου : 6. 19 τὸ μυστήριον τοῦ εὐαγγελίου; all in reference to the 'secret counsel' of God in regard to the admission of the Gentiles. So also Col. 1. 26, 27 : 2. 2 : 4. 3.

1 *Tim.* 3. 9 τὸ μυστήριον τῆς πίστεως, probably the secret counsel of God which is expressed in the Christian creed: hence *ib.* 3. 16 τὸ τῆς εὐσεβείας μυστήριον is expressed in detail in the earliest and shortest form of creed which has come down to us.

Rev. 10. 7 (In the days of the voice of the seventh angel, when he is about to sound) καὶ ἐτελέσθη τὸ μυστήριον τοῦ Θεοῦ ὡς εὐηγγέλισε τοὺς ἑαυτοῦ δούλους τοὺς προφήτας, 'then is finished the secret counsel which God purposed to fulfil according to the good tidings which He declared to His servants the prophets.'

2 *Thess.* 2. 7 τὸ γὰρ μυστήριον ἤδη ἐνεργεῖται τῆς ἀνομίας. In this passage the meaning which has hitherto seemed appropriate is less obvious in its application : but nevertheless it seems to me to be more probable than any other. The passage and its context seem to be best paraphrased thus : ' The secret purpose or counsel of lawlessness is already working: lawlessness is already in process of effecting that which it proposed to effect. But it is not yet fully revealed: there is he who restraineth, but he who now restraineth will be put out of the way; and then shall that lawless one be fully revealed whom the Lord shall consume with the breath of His mouth . . . .'

3. Use in the Apologists.

But there are two passages in the Apocalypse, and probably one in the Epistle to the Ephesians, for which this meaning of μυστήριον does not seem to afford a sufficient or appropriate explanation, and for which we have to depend on the light which is thrown backwards on the N. T. by Christian writers of the second century.

The word is used several times by Justin Martyr, and in almost every case it is in connexion with σύμβολον, τύπος, or παραβολή: and it is used in a similar connexion in a fragment of Melito.

Justin M. *Apol.* i. 27: in all the false religions the serpent is pictured as σύμβολον μέγα καὶ μυστήριον.

Id. *Tryph.* c. 40, with reference to the paschal lamb, τὸ μυστήριον οὖν τοῦ προβάτου . . . . τύπος ἦν τοῦ Χριστοῦ.

Id. *Tryph.* c. 44 (some of the commandments of the Law were given with a view to righteous conduct and godliness : others were given) ἢ εἰς μυστήριον τοῦ Χριστοῦ ἢ διὰ τὸ σκληροκάρδιον τοῦ λαοῦ ὑμῶν.

Id. *Tryph.* c. 68 (with reference to Ps. 132. 11 'of the fruit of thy body will I set upon thy throne,' and Is. 7. 14 'Behold a virgin shall conceive . . .') . . . τὸ εἰρημένον πρὸς Δαυὶδ ὑπὸ Θεοῦ ἐν μυστηρίῳ διὰ Ἡσαΐου ὡς ἔμελλε γίνεσθαι ἐξηγήθη· εἰ μήτι τοῦτο ἐπίστασθε, ὦ φίλοι, ἔφην, ὅτι πολλοὺς λόγους, τοὺς ἐπικεκαλυμμένως καὶ ἐν παραβολαῖς ἢ μυστηρίοις ἢ ἐν συμβόλοις ἔργων λελεγμένους οἱ . . . . προφῆται ἐξηγήσαντο, ' that which God said to David symbolically was interpreted by Isaiah as to how it would actually come to pass : unless you do not know this, my friends, I said, that many things which had been said obscurely and in similitudes or figures or symbolical actions were interpreted by the prophets.'

Id. *Tryph.* c. 78 (commenting on Is. 8. 4 'he shall take away the riches of Damascus and the spoil of Samaria'), Justin interprets it in reference to the Magi, who by worshipping Christ revolted from the power of the evil demon which had taken them captive) ἦν ἐν μυστηρίῳ ἐσήμαινεν ὁ λόγος οἰκεῖν ἐν Δαμασκῷ· ἁμαρτωλὸν δὲ καὶ ἄδικον οὖσαν ἐν παραβολῇ τὴν δύναμιν ἐκείνην καλῶς Σαμάρειαν καλεῖ, 'which power, as the passage indicated symbolically, lived at Samaria : and since that power was sinful and unrighteous he properly calls it by a figurative expression Samaria.' (The equivalence of ἐν μυστηρίῳ and ἐν παραβολῇ is evident.)

Melito *frag.* ix. (ap. Otto *Corpus Apolog.* vol. ix. p. 417) (Isaac is said to be ὁ τύπος τοῦ Χριστοῦ, 'a type of the Messiah,' and one which caused astonishment to men), ἦν γὰρ θεάσασθαι μυστήριον καινόν . . . ' for one might see a strange symbolical representation, a son led by a father to a mountain to be sacrificed.'

It is evident that μυστήριον was closely related in meaning to the words which are interchanged with it, τύπος, σύμβολον, παραβολή: and if with this fact in our minds we turn again to the N. T. there will be some instances in which the appropriateness of this meaning will be clear.

Rev. I. 20 τὸ μυστήριον τῶν ἐπτὰ ἀστέρων, 'the symbol of the seven stars,' which is immediately explained to refer to the 'angels' of the seven churches.

Ib. 17. 7 τὸ μυστήριον τῆς γυναικός, 'the symbolical representation of the woman,' is in a similar way explained to refer to 'the great city which reigneth over the kings of the earth.'

It is probable that the same meaning is to be given in *Ephes.* 5. 32 τὸ μυστήριον τοῦτο μέγα ἐστίν· ἐγὼ δὲ λέγω εἰς Χριστὸν καὶ εἰς τὴν ἐκκλησίαν, 'this symbol (sc. of the joining of husband and wife into one flesh) is a great one: I interpret it as referring to Christ and to the Church.'

The connexion of this meaning with the previous one is not far to seek. A secret purpose or counsel was intimated enigmatically by a symbolical representation in words, or in pictures, or in action. Such symbolical representations played a much more important part in the world in early times than they play now: the expression of ideas by means of pictures only passed by gradual and slow transitions into the use of written signs, in which the original picture was lost: and every written word was once a μυστήριον. It was by a natural process that the sign and the thing signified came to be identified, and that the word which was used for the one came also to be used for the other.

The meaning of μυστήριον was expressed in early ecclesiastical Latin by *sacramentum*. It has hence resulted that the meaning which came to be attached to *sacramentum*, and which has passed with the word into most European tongues, is the meaning which is proper not to the word itself but to its Greek original, μυστήριον. (The instances of the early use of *sacramentum* in this sense are given in detail by Rönsch, *Itala und Vulgata*, p. 323, and

Das Neue Testament Tertullian's, p. 585.) And although it is true that Tertullian, as was natural to one who had been educated in the rhetorical schools and had there dabbled in etymologies, does connect the theological use of *sacramentum* with its Classical use to designate a military oath (*Ad Mart.* c. 19, 24), yet that reference to Classical use is probably as misleading as it is insufficient to cover the facts which have to be explained: and just as the theological use of *persona* must be explained simply with reference to ὑπόστασις, so the theological use of *sacramentum* must be explained simply with reference to μυστήριον.

οἰκονόμος.

The word was used in later Greek in two special senses, each of which appears in the N. T.

1. It was used of the *dispensator* or slave who was employed to give the other slaves of a household their proper rations: it is found in this sense in *Corp. Inscr. Gr.* 1247, 1498.

Hence in *S. Luke* 12. 42 ὁ πιστὸς οἰκονόμος ὁ φρόνιμος, ὃν καταστήσει ὁ κύριος ἐπὶ τῆς θεραπείας αὐτοῦ, τοῦ διδόναι ἐν καιρῷ τὸ σιτομέτριον, 'the faithful and wise steward whom his lord shall set over his household to give them their portion of food in due season.'

2. It was used of the *villicus* or land-steward: it is found in this sense in an inscription at Mylasa (Le Bas et Waddington, vol. iii, No. 404), in which οἰκονόμοι and ταμίαι are mentioned together, the former being in all probability the administrators of the domain, the latter the treasurers.

Hence, in *S. Luke* 16. 1, the οἰκονόμος is in direct relations with the tenants of the lord's farms: and hence the point of his remark, σκάπτειν οὐκ ἰσχύω, 'I have no strength to dig,' since a degraded bailiff might be reduced to the status of a farm-labourer.

Hence also in *Rom.* 16. 23 ὁ οἰκονόμος τῆς πόλεως is probably the administrator of the city lands.

ὁμοθυμαδόν.

1. Classical use.

The uses of the word in Classical Greek seem to imply that the connotation which is suggested by its etymology was never wholly absent : it can always be translated 'with one accord.'

2. Use in the LXX.

In the LXX. (*a*) it is used to translate Hebrew words which mean simply 'together,' (*b*) it is interchanged with other Greek words or phrases which mean simply 'together,' (*c*) it occurs in contexts in which the strict etymological meaning is impossible.

(*a*) Its Hebrew originals are either יַחַד, e.g. in Job 3. 18, or יַחְדָּו, e. g. in Job 2. 11.

(*b*) The same Hebrew words are more commonly rendered by ἅμα e. g. in Gen. 13. 6 : 22. 6, ἐπὶ τὸ αὐτό e. g. in Deut. 22. 10, Jos. 9. 2, κατὰ τὸ αὐτό e. g. in Ex. 26. 24, 1 Sam. 30. 24 (by ὁμοῦ only in a passage which is inserted from Theodotion, Job 34. 29) : the other translators and revisers sometimes substitute one of these phrases for it, and *vice versa*, e. g. Job 2. 11 : 3. 18 LXX. ὁμοθυμαδόν, Symm. ὁμοῦ, Ps. 2. 2 LXX. ἐπὶ τὸ αὐτό, Symm. ὁμοθυμαδόν, Ps. 33 (34). 4 LXX. ἐπὶ τὸ αὐτό, Aquil. ὁμοθυμαδόν.

(*c*) *Num.* 24. 24 αὐτοὶ ὁμοθυμαδὸν ἀπολοῦνται, 1 Chron. 10. 6 καὶ ὅλος ὁ οἶκος αὐτοῦ ὁμοθυμαδὸν ἀπέθανε.

Job 38. 33 ἐπίστασαι δὲ τροπὰς οὐρανοῦ ἢ τὰ ὑπ' οὐρανὸν ὁμοθυμαδὸν γινόμενα.

In these and similar passages any such meaning as 'with one accord' is excluded by the nature of the case.

3. Use in the N. T.

In the N. T. the word occurs in Acts 1. 14 [some Codd., not ℵ A B C, of 2. 1], 2. 46, 4. 24, 5. 12, 7. 57, 8. 6, 12. 20, 15. 25, 18. 12, 19. 29, Rom. 15. 6. In none of these

passages is there any reason for assuming that the word
has any other meaning than that which it has in the Greek
versions of the O. T., viz. 'together.'

παραβολή, παροιμία.

1. Classical use.

(a) παραβολή :

Aristotle, *Rhet.* 2. 20, p. 1393 *b*, defines it as one of the
subdivisions of παράδειγμα, 'example,' and coordinates it
with λόγοι : as an instance of it he gives τὰ Σωκρατικά : as
when Socrates showed that it is not right for rulers to
be chosen by lot by using the illustration or analogous case
that no one would choose by lot those who should run
in a race or steer a ship. Quintilian, 5. 11. 1, follows
Aristotle in making παραβολή a kind of παράδειγμα, and says
that its Latin name is *similitudo :* elsewhere, 5. 11. 22, he
says that Cicero called it *conlatio :* he gives an instance
of it, the passage from the *Pro Murena*, about those who
return into port from a dangerous voyage, telling those who
are setting out of the dangers and how to avoid them.

(b) παροιμία :

Aristotle, *Rhet.* 3. 11, p. 1413 *a*, defines παροιμίαι as
μεταφοραὶ ἀπ' εἴδους ἐπ' εἶδος ; and, *ib.* 1. 11, p. 1371 *b*, he
gives as instances the sayings ἧλιξ ἥλικα τέρπει, ἀεὶ κολοιὸς
παρὰ κολοιόν : in a fragment preserved in Synes. *Calvit.
Encom.* c. 22, p. 234 (Bekker's Aristotle, p. 1474 *b*), he says
of them παλαιᾶς εἰσὶ φιλοσοφίας … ἐγκαταλείμματα περισωθέντα
διὰ συντομίαν καὶ δεξιότητα. Quintilian, 5. 11. 21, says of
παροιμία that it is 'Velut fabella brevior, et per allegoriam
accipitur : non nostrum, inquit, onus : bos clitellas.'

2. Use in the LXX. and Hexapla.

παραβολή occurs about thirty times in the Canonical books
as the translation of מָשָׁל, and of no other word (in Eccles.

1. 17, where all the MSS. have it as a translation of הֹלֵלוֹת 'madness,' it is an obvious mistake of an early transcriber for παραφοράς, which is found in Theodotion).

The passages in which מָשָׁל is not rendered by παραβολή are the following :—

1 *Kings* 9. 7, and *Ezek.* 14. 8; the Targum ἔσται (θήσομαι) εἰς ἀφανισμόν, 'shall be for a desolation,' is substituted for the literal translation ἔσται (θήσομαι) εἰς παραβολήν, 'shall be for a byword.'

Job 13. 12 ἀποβήσεται δὲ ὑμῶν τὸ γαυρίαμα ἴσα σποδῷ, is so far from the Hebrew as to afford no evidence.

Ib. 27. 1 and 29. 1: it is rendered by προοίμιον, which may be only a transcriber's error for παροιμία: in 27. 1 Aquila has παραβολήν.

Prov. 1. 1: the LXX. have παροιμίαι, Aquila παραβολαί.

Is. 14. 4 LXX. λήψει τὸν θρῆνον τοῦτον ἐπὶ τὸν βασιλέα Βαβ. Aquil., Symm., Theod. παραβολήν: cf. Ezek. 19. 14, where the LXX. combine the two words in the expression εἰς παραβολὴν θρήνου, and Mic. 2. 4 where they are coordinated.

It will be seen then in a majority of the cases in which παραβολή was not used to translate מָשָׁל, παροιμία was used instead of it :ᐧ this is also the case with the following passages, in which the LXX. used παραβολή but the Hexapla revisers substituted παροιμία :—

1 *Sam.* 10. 12 LXX. παραβολήν, Ἄλλος· παροιμίαν.

Ib. 24. 14 LXX. παραβολή, *Symm.* παροιμία.

Ps. 77 (78). 2 LXX. and *Aquil.* ἐν παραβολαῖς, *Symm.* διὰ παροιμίας.

Eccles. 12. 9 LXX. παραβολῶν, *Aquil.* παροιμίας.

Ezek. 12. 22 LXX. *Aquil.*, *Theod.* παραβολή, *Symm.* παροιμία.

Ib. 18. 3 LXX. παραβολή, *Aquil.* παροιμία.

Prov. 25. 1: Codd. AS² of the LXX. have παροιμίαι, Codd. BS¹ and most cursives παιδεῖαι: Aquila, Symmachus, and Theodotion παραβολαί.

Ib. 26. 7, 9: in the first of these verses most MSS. of the LXX.

F

have παρανομίαν (παρανομίας), a transcriber's error for παροιμίαν (παρανομίας), which is found in Codd. 68, 248, 253; Symmachus has παραβολή. In v. 9 the LXX. have, without variant, the impossible translation δουλεία (possibly the original translation was παιδεία, as in I. 1, and this being misunderstood, the gloss δουλεία was substituted for it) : there is a trace of the earlier reading in S. Ambrose's quotation of the passage in his *Comment. in Ps.* 35, p. 768 *d*, 'ita et injusti sermone nascuntur quae compungant loquentem': but in Epist. 37, p. 939, he seems to follow the current Greek.

These facts that παραβολή and παροιμία are used by the LXX. to translate the same Hebrew word, and that the other translators and revisers frequently substitute the one for the other, show that between the two words there existed a close relationship, and that the sharp distinction which has been sometimes drawn between them does not hold in the Greek versions of the O. T. If we look at some of the sayings to which the word παραβολή is applied, we shall better see the kind of meaning which was attached to it :—

1 *Sam.* 10. 12 of the 'proverb' 'Is Saul also among the prophets'?

Ib. 24. 14 of the 'proverb of the ancients,' 'Wickedness proceedeth from the wicked.'

Ezek. 12. 22 of the 'proverb that ye have in the land of Israel, saying, The days are prolonged, and every vision faileth.'

Ezek. 16. 44 of the 'proverb' 'As is the mother, so is her daughter.'

Ib. 18. 2 of the 'proverb' 'The fathers have eaten sour grapes, and the children's teeth are set on edge.'

Deut. 38. 37, 2 *Chron.* 7. 20, *Ps.* 43 (44). 15 : 68 (69). 12, *Jer.* 24. 9, *Wisd.* 5. 3, of men or a nation being made a byword and a reproach.

Intertwined with and growing out of this dominant sense of παραβολή and παροιμία as a 'common saying' or 'proverb,' is their use of sayings which were expressed more or less

symbolically and which required explanation. The clearest
instance of this in the canonical books is probably Ezek.
20. 47–49, where after the prophet has been told to speak
of the kindling of a fire in the 'forest of the south field,' he
replies μηδαμῶς, κύριε κύριε· αὐτοὶ λέγουσι πρὸς μέ Οὐχὶ παραβολή ἐστι λεγομένη αὕτη; hence παραβολή and παροιμία are
sometimes associated with αἴνιγμα: e.g. Sir. 39. 2, 3 (quoted
below) ἐν αἰνίγμασι παραβολῶν, and in Num. 21. 27 the
LXX. have οἱ αἰνιγματισταί, where a reviser (Ἄλλος) in the
Hexapla has οἱ παροιμιαζόμενοι as a translation of הַמֹּשְׁלִים.
It appears even more distinctly in Sirach.

Sir. 13. 26 εὕρεσις παραβολῶν διαλογισμοὶ μετὰ κόπου, E. V. 'the
finding out of parables is a wearisome labour of the mind.'

Sir. 39. 2, 3 (of the man 'that giveth his mind to the law of the
Most High') ἐν στροφαῖς παραβολῶν συνεισελεύσεται· ἀπόκρυφα παροιμιῶν
ἐκζητήσει, καὶ ἐν αἰνίγμασι παραβολῶν ἀναστραφήσεται, E. V. 'where
subtil parables are he will be there also, he will sell out the secrets
of grave sentences, and be conversant in dark parables.'

Sir. 47. 17 (of Solomon) ἐν ᾠδαῖς καὶ παροιμίαις καὶ παραβολαῖς καὶ
ἐν ἑρμηνείαις ἀπεθαύμασάν σε χῶραι, E. V. 'the countries marvelled
at thee for thy songs and proverbs and parables and interpreta-
tions.'

The reference in this last passage to 1 Kings 4. 29 (33) may be
supplemented by the similar reference to it in Josephus Ant. 8. 2,
5: and it is interesting to note that the words of the LXX.
ἐλάλησεν ὑπὲρ τῶν ξύλων ἀπὸ τῆς κέδρου ... are paraphrased by
Josephus καθ᾽ ἕκαστον γὰρ εἶδος δένδρου παραβολὴν εἶπεν ἀπὸ ὑσσώπου
ἕως κέδρου.

A review of the whole evidence which the LXX. offers
as to the meaning of παραβολή and παροιμία seems to show

(1) that they were convertible terms, or at least that
their meanings were so closely allied that one could be
substituted for the other ;

(2) that they both referred (a) to 'common sayings' or
'proverbs,' and (b) to sayings which had a meaning below
the surface, and which required explanation.

3. Use in sub-apostolic writers.

These inferences are supported by the use of the word in sub-apostolic writers and in Justin Martyr :—

Barnabas 6. 10 (quotes the words 'into a good land, a land flowing with milk and honey,' and then proceeds) εὐλογητὸς ὁ κύριος ἡμῶν, ἀδελφοί, ὁ σοφίαν καὶ νοῦν θέμενος ἐν ἡμῖν τῶν κρυφίων αὐτοῦ· λέγει γὰρ ὁ προφήτης παραβολὴν κυρίου· τίς νοήσει εἰ μὴ σοφὸς καὶ ἐπιστήμων καὶ ἀγαπῶν τὸν κύριον αὐτοῦ, ' Blessed be our Lord, brethren, who hath put into us wisdom and understanding of His secrets : for what the prophet says is a parable of the Lord,' i. e. evidently, a saying which has a hidden meaning and requires explanation: ' who will understand it but he who is wise and knowing, and who loves his Lord.'

Id. 17. 2 (' If I tell you about things present or things to come, ye will not understand) διὰ τὸ ἐν παραβολαῖς κεῖσθαι, ' because they lie hid in symbols.'

The Shepherd of Hermas consists to a great extent of παραβολαί, Vet. Lat. ' similitudines '; they are symbols or figures of earthly things, which are conceived as having an inner or mystical meaning : e. g. in the second ' similitude ' the writer pictures himself as walking in the country, and seeing an elm-tree round which a vine is twined.   The Shepherd tells him αὕτη ἡ παραβολὴ εἰς τοὺς δούλους τοῦ Θεοῦ κεῖται, ' this figure is applied to the servants of God ': and he proceeds to explain that the elm-tree is like a man who is rich but unfruitful, the vine like one who is fruitful but poor, and that each helps the other.

Justin M. *Tryph.* c. 36 says that he will show, in opposition to the contention of the Jews, that Christ is called by the Holy Spirit both God and Lord of Hosts, ἐν παραβολῇ, i. e. in a figurative expression : he then quotes Psalm 24, the Messianic application of which was admitted.

Id. *Tryph.* c. 52 (It was predicted through Jacob that there would be two Advents of Christ, and that believers in Christ would wait for Him): ἐν παραβολῇ δὲ καὶ παρακεκαλυμμένως τὸ πνεῦμα τὸ ἅγιον διὰ τοῦτο αὐτὰ ἐλελαλήκει, ' But the Holy Spirit had said this in a figure and concealedly, for the reason which I mentioned,' viz. because, if it had been said openly, the Jews would have erased the passage from their sacred books.

Id. *Tryph.* c. 63 : the words of the same last speech of Jacob, 'he shall wash his clothes in the blood of grapes,' were said ἐν παραβολῇ, 'figuratively,' signifying that Christ's blood was not of human generation.

Id. *Tryph.* c. 113, 114, Christ is spoken of ἐν παραβολαῖς by the prophets as a stone or a rock.

So *Tryph.* c. 68, 90, 97, 115, 123.

4. Use in the N. T.

In the N. T. παραβολή is used only in the Synoptic Gospels and in Heb. 9. 9, 11. 19 : παροιμία is used only in the Fourth Gospel and in 2 Pet. 2. 22. If we apply to these passages the general conclusions which are derived from the LXX. and confirmed by the usage of sub-apostolic writers, their appropriateness will be evident : nor is it necessary in any instance to go outside the current contemporary use to either the etymological sense or the usage of the rhetorical schools. The majority of passages in which παραβολή is used belong to the common foundation of the Synoptic Gospels, and refer to the great symbolical illustrations by which Christ declared the nature of the kingdom of heaven. They are Matt. 13. 3 = Mk. 4. 2, Luke 8. 4; Matt. 13. 10 = Mk. 4. 10, Luke 8. 9; Matt. 13. 13 = Mk. 4. 11, Luke 8. 10; Matt. 13. 18 = Mk. 4. 13, Luke 8. 11; Matt. 13. 24, Matt. 13. 31 = Mk. 4. 30; Matt. 13. 33, Matt. 13. 34, 35 = Mk. 4. 33, 34; Matt. 13. 36, 53, Matt. 21. 33 = Mk. 12. 1, Luke 20. 9; Matt. 21. 45 = Mk. 12. 12, Luke 20. 19; Matt. 22. 1, Matt. 24. 32 = Mk. 13. 28, Luke 21. 29, Luke 19. 11. It is also used of the similar illustrations which are peculiar to S. Luke, and which do not all illustrate the nature of the kingdom of heaven in its larger sense, Luke 12. 16, 41; 13. 6; 14. 7; 15. 3; 18. 1, 9. In all these instances the requirements of the context are fully satisfied by taking it to mean a story with a hidden meaning, without pressing in every detail the idea of a 'comparison.'

In S. Luke 4. 23 it is used in a sense of which the LXX. affords many instances : πάντως ἐρεῖτέ μοι τὴν παραβολὴν ταύτην· ἰατρέ, θεράπευσον σεαυτόν, 'doubtless ye will say to me this *proverb*' [so e. g. 1 Sam. 10. 12; 24. 14], 'Physician, heal thyself.'

In S. Luke 6. 39 it is used of the illustration of the blind leading the blind : and in S. Mark 3. 23 of that of Satan casting out Satan, neither of which had so far passed into popular language as to be what is commonly called a 'proverb,' but which partook of the nature of proverbs, inasmuch as they were symbolical expressions which were capable of application to many instances.

The other passages in which παραβολή occurs in the N. T. are—(1) Heb. 9. 9 ἥτις παραβολὴ εἰς τὸν καιρὸν τὸν ἐνεστηκότα, 'which' [i. e. the first tabernacle] 'is a symbol for the present time'; (2) Heb. 11. 19 ὅθεν [sc. ἐκ νεκρῶν] αὐτὸν καὶ ἐν παραβολῇ ἐκομίσατο, 'from whence he did also in a figure receive him back.' In both passages the meaning of παραβολή, 'a symbol,' is one of which many instances, some of which have been given above, are found in Justin Martyr.

2 *Pet.* 2. 22 τὸ τῆς ἀληθοῦς παροιμίας· κύων ἐπιστρέψας ἐπὶ τὸ ἴδιον ἐξέραμα . . . . 'the (words) of the true proverb, The dog turning to his own vomit.' . . . . Here παροιμίας is an application of the title of the book Παροιμίαι, from which (26. 11) the quotation is taken.

S. *John* 10. 6 ταύτην τὴν παροιμίαν εἶπεν αὐτοῖς ὁ Ἰησοῦς· ἐκεῖνοι δὲ οὐκ ἔγνωσαν τίνα ἦν ἃ ἐλάλει αὐτοῖς, 'this parable said Jesus to them ; but they did not understand what it was that He spake to them': the reference is to the illustration of the sheep and the shepherd, for which the other Evangelists would doubtless have used the word παραβολή : with the substitution of παροιμία for it in S. John may be compared the similar substitution of it as a translation of לָשָׁל by the Hexapla revisers of the LXX., which has been mentioned above.

S. *John* 16. 25, 29 οὐκέτι ἐν παροιμίαις λαλήσω, παροιμίαν οὐδεμίαν λέγεις are contrasted with παρρησίᾳ [Codd. B D ἐν παρρησίᾳ] ἀπαγ-

γελῶ, ἐν παρρησίᾳ λαλεῖς: the contrast makes the meaning clear: ἐν
παροιμίαις λαλεῖν is equivalent to the ἐν παραβολῇ καὶ παρακεκαλυμμένως
of Justin Martyr (quoted above), the substitution of παροιμίαις for
παραβολαῖς having its exact parallel in Ps. 77 (78). 2, where Symmachus substitutes διὰ παροιμίας for the ἐν παραβολαῖς of the LXX.
(and of S. Matt. 13. 35).

πειράζειν, πειρασμός.

1. Use in the LXX.

The words are used sometimes of the trying or proving
of God by men, e. g. Ex. 17. 2, 7, Num. 14. 22 : but more
commonly of the trying or proving of men by God. The
purpose of this trying or proving is sometimes expressly
stated : e. g. Ex. 16. 4 πειράσω αὐτοὺς εἰ πορεύσονται τῷ νόμῳ
μου ἢ οὔ; Judges 2. 22 τοῦ πειράσαι τὸν Ἰσραὴλ εἰ φυλάσσονται
τὴν ὁδὸν Κυρίου. The mode in which God tried or proved
men was almost always that of sending them some affliction
or disaster: and consequently 'trial' (as not unfrequently
in English) came to connote affliction or disaster : hence
πειρασμός is used, e. g. with reference to the plagues of
Egypt, Deut. 7. 19 τοὺς πειρασμοὺς τοὺς μεγάλους οὓς ἴδοσαν
οἱ ὀφθαλμοί σου, τὰ σημεῖα καὶ τὰ τέρατα τὰ μεγάλα ἐκεῖνα, τὴν
χεῖρα τὴν κραταιὰν καὶ τὸν βραχίονα τὸν ὑψηλόν, 'the great
trials which thine eyes saw, the signs and those great
wonders, the mighty hand and the uplifted arm': so also
29. 3. In the Apocryphal books this new connotation
supersedes the original connotation, and is linked with the
cognate idea of 'chastisement.'

Wisd. 3. 5 καὶ ὀλίγα παιδευθέντες μεγάλα εὐεργετηθήσονται· ὅτι ὁ θεὸς
ἐπείρασεν αὐτοὺς καὶ εὗρεν αὐτοὺς ἀξίους ἑαυτοῦ, 'And having been a
little chastised, they shall be greatly benefited: for God proved
them and found them worthy of Himself.'

Ib. 11. 10 (the Israelites are contrasted with the Egyptians) ὅτε
γὰρ ἐπειράσθησαν καίπερ ἐν ἐλέει παιδευόμενοι ἔγνωσαν πῶς ἐν ὀργῇ κρινό-
μενοι ἀσεβεῖς ἐβασανίζοντο, E. V. 'For when they were tried, albeit

but in mercy chastised, they knew how the ungodly were judged in wrath and tormented . . .'

Sir. 2. 1 τέκνον εἰ προσέρχῃ δουλεύειν κυρίῳ θεῷ ἑτοίμασον τὴν ψυχήν σου εἰς πειρασμόν, 'My son, if thou come near to serve the Lord God, prepare thy soul for trial.'

Judith 8. 24–27 εὐχαριστήσωμεν κυρίῳ τῷ θεῷ ἡμῶν ὃς πειράζει ἡμᾶς καθὰ καὶ τοὺς πατέρας ἡμῶν, 'let us give thanks to the Lord our God, who trieth us as He did also our fathers' (sc. by sending an army to afflict us) . . . . . . ὅτι οὐ καθὼς ἐκείνους ἐπύρωσεν εἰς ἐτασμὸν τῆς καρδίας αὐτῶν καὶ ἡμᾶς οὐκ ἐξεδίκησεν ἀλλ᾽ εἰς νουθέτησιν μαστιγοῖ κύριος τοὺς ἐγγίζοντας αὐτῷ, 'for He hath not tried us in the fire as He did them for the examination of their hearts, neither hath He taken vengeance on us: but the Lord doth scourge them that come near unto Him to admonish them.'

2. Use in the N. T.

There are some passages of the N. T. in which the meaning which the words have in the later books of the LXX. seems to be established:—

S. Luke 8. 13 ἐν καιρῷ πειρασμοῦ has for its equivalent in S. Matt. 13. 21, S. Mark 4. 17 γενομένης θλίψεως ἢ διωγμοῦ, so that 'in time of trial' may properly be taken to mean 'in time of tribulation' or 'persecution.'

Acts 20. 19 πειρασμῶν τῶν συμβάντων μοι ἐν ταῖς ἐπιβουλαῖς τῶν Ἰουδαίων. S. Paul is evidently speaking of the 'perils by mine own countrymen' of 2 Cor. 11. 26, the hardships that befel him through the plots of the Jews against him.

Heb. 2. 18 ἐν ᾧ γὰρ πέπονθεν αὐτὸς **πειρασθείς**, δύναται τοῖς **πειρα-ζομένοις** βοηθῆσαι, 'for in that He Himself suffered, having been tried, He is able to succour them that are being tried.'

1 Pet. 1. 6 ὀλίγον ἄρτι εἰδέον λυπηθέντες ἐν ποικίλοις πειρασμοῖς, 'though now for a little while, if need be, ye have been put to grief by manifold trials,' with evident reference to the persecutions to which those to whom the epistle was addressed were subjected (so 4. 12).

Rev. 3. 10 κἀγώ σε τηρήσω ἐκ τῆς ὥρας τοῦ πειρασμοῦ τῆς μελλούσης ἔρχεσθαι ἐπὶ τῆς οἰκουμένης ὅλης, πειράσαι τοὺς κατοικοῦντας ἐπὶ τῆς γῆς, 'I also will keep thee from the hour of trial, the hour that is about to come upon the whole world to try them that dwell upon the earth,' with evident reference to the tribulations which are prophesied later on in the book.

This meaning, the existence of which is thus established by evident instances, will be found to be more appropriate than any other in instances where the meaning does not lie upon the surface:—

S. Matt. 6. 13 = S. Luke 11. 4 μὴ εἰσενέγκῃς ἡμᾶς εἰς πειρασμόν, 'bring us not into trial,' i.e. into tribulation or persecution ; but, on the contrary, ' deliver us from him who—or that which—does us mischief' (see below, p. 79): cf. 2 Pet. 2. 9 οἶδεν κύριος εὐσεβεῖς ἐκ πειρασμοῦ ῥύεσθαι ἀδίκους δὲ εἰς ἡμέραν κρίσεως κολαζομένους τηρεῖν, ' the Lord knoweth how to deliver the godly out of trial, but to keep the unrighteous under punishment unto the day of judgment.'

S. Matt. 4. 1 = S. Mark 1. 13, S. Luke 4. 2 πειρασθῆναι ὑπὸ τοῦ διαβόλου, ' to be tried,' i.e. afflicted ' by the devil,' with reference to the physical as well as the spiritual distresses of our Lord in the desert: cf. *Heb.* 4 15 πεπειρασμένον δὲ κατὰ πάντα καθ᾽ ὁμοιότητα χωρὶς ἁμαρτίας, 'tried,' i.e. afflicted 'in all points like as we are, yet without sin': this interpretation is strongly confirmed by Irenaeus 3. 19. 3, who says of our Lord ὥσπερ ἦν ἄνθρωπος ἵνα πειρασθῇ οὕτως καὶ Λόγος ἵνα δοξασθῇ, ' as He was man that He might be afflicted, so also was He Logos that He might be glorified.'

πένης, πραΰς, πτωχός, ταπεινός.

1. Classical use.

In Classical Greek these words are clearly distinguished from each other. πένης is 'poor' as opposed to rich, πτωχός is ' destitute ' and in want : cf. Aristoph. *Plut.* 552 :

πτωχοῦ μὲν γὰρ βίος, ὃν σὺ λέγεις, ζῆν ἐστιν μηδὲν ἔχοντα·
τοῦ δὲ πένητος ζῆν φειδόμενον καὶ τοῖς ἔργοις προσέχοντα,
περιγίγνεσθαι δ᾽ αὐτῷ μηδέν, μὴ μέντοι μηδ᾽ ἐπιλείπειν.

πραΰς (πρᾶος) is 'easy-tempered' as distinguished from

ὀργίλος, 'passionate' (Arist. *Eth. N.* 2. 7, p. 1108 *a*, 4. 11,
p. 1125 *a*), and πικρός, 'sour-tempered' (*Rhet. ad Alex.* 38):
ταπεινός is not only 'lowly' but almost always also 'dejected'
(e.g. Arist. *Pol.* 4. 11, p. 1295 *b*, of οἱ καθ᾽ ὑπερβολὴν ἐν
ἐνδείᾳ τούτων, sc. ἰσχύος καὶ πλούτου καὶ φίλων, who consequently submit to be governed like slaves, ἄρχεσθαι δουλικὴν
ἀρχήν) and 'mean-spirited' (e.g. Arist. *Rhet.* 2. 7, p. 1384 *a*,
who says that to submit to receive services from another, and
to do so frequently, and to disparage whatever he himself
has done well, are μικροψυχίας καὶ ταπεινότητος σημεῖα).

2. Use in the LXX.

In the LXX., on the contrary, the words are so constantly
interchanged as to exclude the possibility of any sharp distinction between them: nor can any of them connote, as in
Classical Greek, moral inferiority.

(1) They are all four (but πραΰς less than the other
three) used interchangeably to translate the same Hebrew
words:—

עָנִי, 'afflicted,' is rendered by πένης in Deut. 15. 11 : 24. 14 (16),
15 (17). Ps. 9. 13, 19 : 71 (72). 12 : 73 (74). 19 : 108 (109). 16.
Prov. 24. 77 (31. 9) : 29. 38 (31. 20). Eccles. 6. 8. Is. 10. 2 : by
πτωχός in Lev. 19. 10 : 23. 22. 2 Sam. 22. 28. Job 29. 12 : 34.
28 : 36. 6. Ps. 9. 23 (10. 2) : 9. 30 (10. 9) : 11 (12). 6 : 13 (14).
6 : 21 (22). 25 : 24 (25). 16 : 33 (34). 6 : 34 (35). 10 : 36 (37).
15 : 39 (40). 18 : 67 (68). 11 : 68 (69). 30 : 69 (70). 6 : 71 (72).
2, 4 : 73 (74). 21 : 85 (86). 1 : 87 (88). 16 : 101 *tit.* : 108 (109).
22 : 139 (140). 13. Amos 8. 4. Hab. 3. 14. Is. 3. 14, 15 : 41.
17 : 58. 7. Ezek. 16. 49 : 18. 12 : 22. 29 : by ταπεινός in Ps. 17
(18). 28 : 81 (82). 3. Amos 2. 7. Is. 14. 32 : 32. 7 : 49. 13 :
54. 11 : 66. 2. Jer. 22. 16 : by πραΰς in Job 24. 4. Zach. 9. 9.
Is. 26. 6.

עָנָו, 'meek,' is rendered by πένης in Ps. 9. 38 (10. 17) : 21. 27 :
by πτωχός in Ps. 68 (69). 33. Prov. 14. 21. Is. 29. 19 : 61. 1 :
by ταπεινός in Prov. 3. 34. Zeph. 2. 3. Is. 11. 4 : by πραΰς in
Num. 12. 3. Ps. 24 (25). 9 : 33. 3 : 36 (37). 11 : 75 (76). 10 :
146 (147). 6 : 149. 4.

אֶבְיוֹן, 'needy,' is rendered by πένης in Ex. 23. 6.   Ps. 11 (12).
6 : 34 (35). 10 : 36 (37). 15 : 39 (40). 18 : 48 (49). 2 : 68 (69).
34 : 71 (72). 4, 13 : 73 (74). 21 : 85 (86). 1 : 106 (107). 41 : 108
(109). 22, 31 : 111 (112). 9 : 112 (113). 7 : 139 (140). 13. Prov.
24. 37 (30. 14).   Amos 2. 6 : 4. 1 : 5. 12 : 8. 4, 6.   Jer. 20. 13 :
22. 16.   Ezek. 16. 49 : 18. 12 : 22. 29 : by πτωχός in Ex. 23. 11.
1 Sam. 2. 8.   Esth. 9. 22.   Ps. 9. 19 : 71 (72). 12 : 81 (82). 4 :
108 (109). 16 : 131 (132). 15.   Prov. 14. 31 : 29. 38 (31. 20).
Is. 14. 30 : by ταπεινός in Is. 32. 7.

דַּל, 'weak,' is rendered by πένης in Ex. 23. 3.   1 Sam. 2. 8.
Ps. 81 (82). 4.   Prov. 14. 33 : 22. 16, 22 : 28. 11 : by πτωχός in
Lev. 19. 15.   Ruth 3. 10.   2 Kings 24. 14.   Job 34. 28.   Ps. 71
(72). 13 : 112 (113). 6.   Prov. 19. 4, 17 : 22. 9, 22 : 28. 3, 8 :
29. 14.   Amos 2. 7 : 4. 1 : 5. 11 : 8. 6.   Is. 10. 2 : 14. 30.   Jer.
5. 4 : by ταπεινός in Zeph. 3. 12.   Is. 11. 4 : 25. 4 : 26. 6.

רוּשׁ, 'poor,' is rendered by πένης in 2 Sam. 12. 1, 3, 4.   Ps. 81
(82). 3.   Eccles. 4. 14 : 5. 7 : by πτωχός in Prov. 13. 8 : 14. 20 :
17. 5 : 19. 1, 7, 22 : 22. 2, 7 : 28. 6, 27 : by ταπεινός in 1 Sam.
18. 23.

(2) They are used interchangeably by different translators
to translate the same Hebrew word : e. g.

Ps. 11 (12). 5 עֲנִיִּים is translated by the LXX. and Symmachus
πτωχῶν; by Aquila πενήτων: conversely, אֶבְיוֹנִים is translated by
Aquila πενήτων, and by the LXX. and Symmachus πτωχῶν.

Ps. 17 (18). 28 עָנִי is translated by the LXX. ταπεινόν, by Aquila
πένητα, and by Symmachus πρᾶον.

Is. 11. 4 עֲנָוֵי is translated by the LXX. and Theodotion ταπει-
νούς, by Aquila πραέσι, by Symmachus πτωχούς.

Is. 66. 2 עָנִי is translated by the LXX. ταπεινόν, by Aquila
πραΰν, by Symmachus πτωχόν, by Theodotion συντετριμμένον.

(3) In a large proportion of cases the context shows that,
though the words vary in both Hebrew and Greek, the
same class of persons is referred to : the reference
ordinarily being either (a) to those who are oppressed,
in contrast to the rich and powerful who oppress them ;
or (b) to those who are quiet, in contrast to lawless wrong-
doers : e. g.

(a) *Ps.* 9. 31 (10. 9):

'He lieth in wait secretly as a lion in his den:
He lieth in wait to catch the poor (πτωχόν);
He doth catch the poor, dragging him with his net.
And being crushed, he sinketh down and falleth;
Yea, through his mighty ones the helpless fall.'

(LXX. ἐν τῷ αὐτὸν κατακυριεῦσαι τῶν πενήτων,
Symm. ἐπιπεσόντος αὐτοῦ μετὰ τῶν ἰσχυρῶν αὐτοῦ τοῖς ἀσθενέσιν.)

Ps. 34 (35). 10:

'All my bones shall say, Lord, who is like unto thee,
Which deliverest the poor (πτωχόν) from him that is too
strong for him,
Yea, the poor and the needy (πτωχὸν καὶ πένητα) from him
that spoileth him.'

So also, and with especial reference to God as the deliverer of the
oppressed, Ps. 11 (12). 6 : 33 (34). 6 : 36 (37). 14 : 39 (40). 18 :
71 (72). 4, 13 : 75 (76). 10.

(b) *Ps.* 36 (37). 10, 11:

'Yet a little while and the wicked shall not be,
Yea, thou shalt diligently consider his place, and it shall
not be:
But the meek (οἱ πραεῖς) shall inherit the earth;
And shall delight themselves in the abundance of peace.'

Ps. 146 (147). 6:

'The Lord lifteth up the meek (πραεῖς):
He casteth the wicked down to the ground.'

The inference to which these comparisons lead is that
the πτωχοί, πένητες, πραεῖς, ταπεινοί are all names for one
and the same class, the poor of an oppressed country, the
peasantry or *fellahin* who, then as now, for the most part
lived quiet and religious lives, but who were the victims of
constant ill-treatment and plunder at the hands not only
of tyrannical rulers, but also of powerful and lawless
neighbours.

3. Use in the N. T.

It is probable that this special meaning underlies the use
of the words in the Sermon on the Mount. This is in-

dicated partly by the coordination of subjects, which in the
LXX. are used interchangeably, οἱ πτωχοί, οἱ πραεῖς, and
which are in harmony with the following subjects—οἱ
πενθοῦντες, οἱ πεινῶντες καὶ διψῶντες, οἱ δεδιωγμένοι; and
partly by the fact that at least one of the predicates comes
from a psalm in which the contrast between οἱ πονηρευόμενοι,
οἱ ἁμαρτωλοί, and οἱ δίκαιοι, οἱ πραεῖς is strongly marked, viz.
Ps. 36 (37). 11 οἱ δὲ πραεῖς κληρονομήσουσι γῆν. The addition
in S. Matthew of the modifying phrases οἱ πτωχοὶ τῷ πνεύματι,
οἱ πεινῶντες καὶ διψῶντες τὴν δικαιοσύνην, οἱ δεδιωγμένοι ἕνεκεν
δικαιοσύνης, shows that the reference was not simply to the
Syrian peasantry, as such; but the fact that those modifying
phrases are omitted by S. Luke helps to confirm the view
that the words themselves have the connotation which they
have in the LXX.

πονηρός, πονηρία.

I.

1. Classical use.

The connotation of πονηρός in Classical Greek is probably best shown by Arist. *Eth. N.* 7. 11, p. 1152 *a*, where
Aristotle, speaking of the ἀκρατής, says that what he does
is wrong, and that he acts as a free agent, but that he is
not wicked in himself, ἑκὼν μέν . . . . πονηρὸς δ᾽ οὔ· ἡ γὰρ
προαίρεσις ἐπιεικής· ὥσθ᾽ ἡμιπόνηρος. καὶ οὐκ ἄδικος· οὐ γὰρ
ἐπίβουλος, 'He (i. e. the weak man), though he is a free
agent . . . . yet is not wicked: for his will is good: he
may consequently be called "half-wicked." And he is
not unrighteous: for what he does is not done afore-
thought.'

2. Use in the LXX.

Πονηρός, πονηρία are used frequently, and in various
relations, to translate רַע, רָעָה,

Of wild or ravenous beasts,

Gen. 37. 20 καὶ ἐροῦμεν, θηρίον **πονηρὸν** κατέφαγεν αὐτόν.   So *ib.*
v. 33 ; Lev. 26. 6.

Ezek. 14. 15 ἐὰν καὶ θηρία **πονηρὰ** ἐπάγω ἐπὶ τὴν γῆν καὶ τιμωρή-
σομαι αὐτήν.   So *ib.* v. 21 : 5. 17 : 34. 25.

Of the plagues of Egypt,

Deut. 7. 15 πάσας νόσους Αἰγύπτου τὰς **πονηρὰς** ἃς ἑώρακας.   So
28. 60.

Of Divine plagues in general, and their ministers,

Jos. 23. 15 ἐπάξει κύριος ὁ θεὸς ἐφ' ὑμᾶς πάντα τὰ ῥήματα τὰ **πονηρά**,
ἕως ἂν ἐξολοθρεύσῃ ὑμᾶς ἀπὸ τῆς γῆς . . . .

Ps. 77 (78). 49 ἐξαπέστειλεν εἰς αὐτοὺς ὀργὴν θυμοῦ αὐτοῦ . . . .
ἀποστολὴν δι' ἀγγέλων **πονηρῶν** (*Symm.* κακούντων).

Of unwholesome water or food,

2 *Kings* 2. 19 τὰ ὕδατα **πόνηρα** (the water which Elisha healed).

Jer. 24. 2 σύκων **πονηρῶν** σφόδρα ἃ οὐ βρωθήσεται ἀπὸ πονηρίας
αὐτῶν.

In connexion with blood-shedding,

Is. 59. 7 οἱ δὲ πόδες αὐτῶν ἐπὶ **πονηρίαν** τρέχουσι, ταχινοὶ ἐκχέαι
αἷμα.

Of the malice or mischievousness of an enemy,

Sir. 12. 10 μὴ πιστεύσῃς τῷ ἐχθρῷ σου εἰς τὸν αἰῶνα· ὡς γὰρ ὁ
χαλκὸς ἰοῦται οὕτως ἡ **πονηρία** αὐτοῦ.

Esth. 7. 6 ἄνθρωπος ἐχθρὸς [Cod. א ἐπίβουλος καὶ ἐχθρὸς] 'Αμὰν
ὁ **πονηρὸς** οὗτος.

They are used in similar relations and with equivalent
meanings to translate other Hebrew words,

Is. 35. 9 οὐκ ἔσται λέων οὐδὲ τῶν **πονηρῶν** θηρίων οὐ μὴ ἀναβῇ εἰς
αὐτήν: Heb. פָּרִיץ 'violent.'

Is. 10. 1 γράφοντες γὰρ **πονηρίαν** γράφουσι : Heb. עָמָל 'mischief.'

In all these cases it seems clear that the words connote
not so much passive badness as active harmfulness or
mischief.

3. Use in the N. T.

There are several passages in the Synoptic Gospels
in which this meaning of 'mischievous' seems to be
appropriate :

S. Matt. 5. 39 (' Ye have heard that it was said, An eye for an eye, and a tooth for a tooth') ἐγὼ δὲ λέγω ὑμῖν μὴ ἀντιστῆναι τῷ πονηρῷ· ἀλλ' ὅστις σε ῥαπίζει εἰς τὴν δεξιὰν σιαγόνα, στρέψον αὐτῷ καὶ τὴν ἄλλην. Whether τῷ πονηρῷ be masculine or neuter, the appropriate meaning seems to be, 'Resist not him who—or, that which—does thee mischief,' and an instance of the kind of mischief referred to is at once given, viz. that of a blow on the cheek.

Ib. 6. 13 ῥῦσαι ἡμᾶς ἀπὸ τοῦ πονηροῦ. Here also, whether τοῦ πονηροῦ be masculine or neuter, the appropriate meaning seems to be, 'Deliver us from him who—or, that which—does us mischief.' This meaning will be confirmed by the antithetical clause μὴ εἰσενέγκῃς ἡμᾶς εἰς πειρασμόν, if it be assumed that the meaning which is assigned above to εἰς πειρασμόν is correct (see p. 71): the two clauses are probably two modes of stating that which is in effect the same prayer, ' Bring us not into affliction, but on the contrary, deliver us from him who—or, that which—is mischievous to us:' hence in the shorter form of the prayer which is given by S. Luke, the second of the two clauses is omitted (in Codd. ℵ B L, etc.: cf. Origen *De Orat.* c. 30, vol. i. p. 265, ed. Delarue, δοκεῖ δέ μοι ὁ Λουκᾶς διὰ τοῦ μὴ εἰσενέγκῃς ἡμᾶς εἰς πειρασμὸν δυνάμει δεδιδαχέναι καὶ τὸ ῥῦσαι ἡμᾶς ἀπὸ τοῦ πονηροῦ)[1].

S. Mark 12. 45 (= S. Luke 11. 26) πνεύματα πονηρότερα ἑαυτοῦ. S. Luke 7. 21 : 8. 2 πνεύματα πονηρά. Probably rather ' *mischievous*' or ' *baneful spirits*,' i. e. spirits who do harm to men, than spirits who are bad in themselves: so in Tob. 3. 8 of Asmodaeus τὸ πονηρὸν δαιμόνιον, who killed the seven husbands of Sara.

S. Matt. 5. 11 μακάριοί ἐστε ὅταν ὀνειδίσωσιν ὑμᾶς καὶ διώξωσιν καὶ εἴπωσιν πᾶν πονηρὸν καθ' ὑμῶν ψευδόμενοι ἕνεκεν ἐμοῦ. Probably, though less clearly than in the previous instances, the meaning is ' *mischievous*' or ' *malicious accusation.*'

S. Matt. 22. 18 γνοὺς δὲ ὁ Ἰησοῦς τὴν πονηρίαν αὐτῶν, ' *their malice*' or ' *evil intent*' (= S. Mark 12. 15 τὴν ὑπόκρισιν, S. Luke 20. 23 τὴν πανουργίαν).

II.

Another meaning of the words, though of less frequent

---

[1] The important questions of the gender of τοῦ πονηροῦ and, if it be masculine, of the identification of ὁ πονηρός with ὁ διάβολος, involving as it does theological as well as philological considerations, cannot conveniently be discussed here.

occurrence, is clearly established, and helps to explain some otherwise obscure passages of the Synoptic Gospels :

Sir. 14. 4, 5 has the following pair of antithetical verses,—

ὁ συνάγων ἀπὸ τῆς ψυχῆς αὐτου συνάγει ἄλλοις
καὶ ἐν τοῖς ἀγαθοῖς αὐτοῦ τρυφήσουσιν ἄλλοι·
ὁ πονηρὸς ἑαυτῷ τίνι ἀγαθὸς ἔσται;
καὶ οὐ μὴ εὐφρανθήσεται ἐν τοῖς χρήμασιν αὐτοῦ.

'He that gathereth by defrauding his own soul gathereth for others,
And in his goods shall others run riot:
He that is niggardly to himself to whom shall he be liberal?
And he shall not take pleasure in his goods.'

Then follow five verses, each containing two antithetical clauses, and each dealing with some form of niggardliness: the first clauses of vv. 8, 9, 10 are strictly parallel to each other,

πονηρὸς ὁ βασκαίνων ὀφθαλμῷ . . . .
πλεονέκτου ὀφθαλμὸς οὐκ ἐμπίπλατο μερίδι . . . . .
ὀφθαλμὸς πονηρὸς φθονερὸς ἐπ' ἄρτῳ . . . . . .

'the grudging eye,' 'the eye of the miser,' 'the niggardly eye,' being evidently different names for the same thing.

Sir. 34 (31). 23,

λαμπρὸν ἐπ' ἄρτοις εὐλογήσει χείλη,
καὶ μαρτυρία τῆς καλλονῆς αὐτοῦ πιστή·
πονηρῷ ἐπ' ἄρτῳ διαγογγύσει πόλις,
καὶ ἡ μαρτυρία τῆς πονηρίας αὐτοῦ ἀκριβής.

E. V. 'Whoso is liberal of his meat men shall speak well of him,
And the report of his good housekeeping will be believed.
But against him that is a niggard of his meat the whole city shall murmur,
And the testimonies of his niggardness shall not be doubted of.'

The Hebrew word רַע, which is usually translated by πονηρός, is also sometimes translated by βάσκανος, with a distinct reference, as in Sirach, to the 'evil' or 'grudging eye': e. g.

Prov. 23. 6,

μὴ συνδείπνει ἀνδρὶ βασκάνῳ
μηδὲ ἐπιθύμει τῶν βρωμάτων αὐτοῦ.

(For βασκάνῳ Schol. ap. Nobil. and Cod. 161 in marg. have πονηροφθάλμῳ).

'Feast not with him that hath an evil eye,
Neither desire thou his dainty meats,
(For he is as though he had a divided soul, [so Ewald]
Eat and drink, saith he to thee,
But his heart is not with thee).'

So Deut. 28. 56 רַע LXX. βασκανεῖ, *Aquil.* πονηρεύεται.

This use of πονηρός in the sense of 'niggardly' or 'grudging,' especially in connexion with the idea of the 'evil eye,' throws a clear light upon a well-known passage of the Sermon on the Mount, which, if taken in its context, will be seen to refer not to goodness or badness in general, but specially to the use of money:

S. Matt. 6. 19 Lay not up for yourselves treasures upon the earth . . .

20 But lay up for yourselves treasures in heaven. . . .

21 For where thy treasure is,
There will thy heart be also.

22 The lamp of the body is the eye,
If therefore thine eye be liberal,
Thy whole body shall be full of light:

23 But if thine eye be grudging (πονηρός),
Thy whole body shall be full of darkness.

. . . . .

24 Ye cannot serve God and mammon.

If this meaning does not wholly remove the difficulties of the passage, it at least contains elements which any exegesis of it must recognize. The same meaning appears to be appropriate in two other passages of S. Matthew:

S. Matt. 7. 11 (=S. Luke 11. 13) εἰ οὖν ὑμεῖς πονηροὶ ὄντες οἴδατε δόματα ἀγαθὰ διδόναι τοῖς τέκνοις ὑμῶν . . . (which may be paraphrased thus): 'If ye then, whose own nature is rather to keep what you

G

have than to bestow it on others, are still able to give good gifts to
your children, how much more shall your Father in heaven, who is
always bestowing and never keeping back, give good things to
them that ask Him'?

S. *Matt.* 20. 15 ἢ ὁ ὀφθαλμός σου πονηρός ἐστιν ὅτι ἐγὼ ἀγαθός εἰμι,
'Art thou envious at my being liberal'?

παράκλητος.

This word is found in the N. T. only in the Gospel and
first Epistle of S. John.   The facts upon which any induction as to its meaning there must be sought in the first
instance in contemporary writings cognate in character to
those of S. John.   They are found in Philo in sufficient
numbers and in a sufficiently clear connexion to render
the induction from them free from doubt: they show that
Philo used the word (*a*) in a sense closely akin to its Attic
sense of one who helps or pleads for another in a court
of law, and hence (*b*) in the wider sense of helper in
general.

(*a*) Philo *De Josepho* c. 40, vol. ii. p. 75 (Joseph after discovering
himself to his brethren says to them) ἀμνηστίαν ἁπάντων παρέχω τῶν
εἰς ἐμὲ πεπραγμένων· μηδενὸς ἑτέρου δεῖσθε παρακλήτου, 'I grant you free
forgiveness for all that you have done to me: you need no one else
to intercede for you.'

Vit. Mos. iii. 14, vol. ii. p. 155 (Philo gives the reason why the
High Priest in going into the Holy of Holies wore the symbol of
the Logos) ἀναγκαῖον γὰρ ἦν τὸν ἱερωμένον τῷ τοῦ κόσμου πατρὶ παρακλήτῳ
χρῆσθαι τελειοτάτῳ τὴν ἀρετὴν υἱῷ πρός τε ἀμνηστείαν ἁμαρτημάτων καὶ
χορηγίαν ἀφθονωτάτων ἀγαθῶν, 'it was necessary that he who was
consecrated to the Father of the world should employ as his inter-
cessor the Son who is most perfect in virtue, for both the forgiveness of sins and the supply of boundless goods.'

So *De Exsecrat.* c. 9, vol. ii. p. 436: *in Flacc.* c. 3, vol. ii. p.
519, *ib.* c. 4, p. 520.

(*b*) *De Mund. Opif.* c. 6, vol. i. p. 5 οὐδενὶ δὲ παρακλήτῳ, τίς γὰρ ἦν
ἕτερος, μόνῳ δὲ ἑαυτῷ χρησάμενος ὁ θεὸς ἔγνω δεῖν εὐεργετεῖν . . . τὴν

φύσιν, 'employing not any helper—for who else was there?—but only Himself, did God resolve that He ought to bless the world with His benefits.'

The meaning which is thus established in Philo must be held to be that which underlies its use by S. John. The meaning 'consoler' or 'comforter' is foreign to Philo, and is not required by any passage in S. John: it may, indeed, be supposed that 'comforter' in its modern sense represents the form only and not the meaning of *confortator*.

πίστις.

In philosophical and later Greek πίστις may be said to have three meanings,—a psychological, a rhetorical, and a moral meaning. In Biblical Greek it adds to these a theological meaning.

(1) Its psychological meaning appears in Aristotle: it is 'conviction,' and as such is distinguished from ὑπόληψις or 'impression,' for a man may have an 'impression' and not be sure of it, *Top.* 4. 5, p. 125 *b* κατὰ ταῦτα δ' οὐδ' ἡ πίστις ὑπόληψις· ἐνδέχεται γὰρ τὴν αὐτὴν ὑπόληψιν καὶ μὴ πιστεύοντα ἔχειν: it is used both of the conviction which comes through the senses and of that which comes through reasoning, *Phys. Auscult.* 8. 8, p. 262 *a* ἡ πίστις οὐ μόνον ἐπὶ τῆς αἰσθήσεως ἀλλὰ καὶ ἐπὶ τοῦ λόγου, 'the conviction (of a particular fact which is mentioned) lies not only in the sensible perception of it but also in the reason': hence it may come either mediately or immediately, *Top.* 1. 1, p. 100 *b* τὰ μὴ δι' ἑτέρων ἀλλὰ δι' αὐτῶν ἔχοντα τὴν πίστιν, (of primary truths) 'which force their conviction not mediately through other truths but immediately of themselves.'

(2) Its rhetorical meaning also appears in Aristotle. It is not conviction but that which causes conviction in

the mind of a hearer. It is the 'proof' of a case as distinguished from 'statement' of it (which is πρόθεσις or διήγησις, the latter word being limited by Aristotle to judicial speeches), the relation being similar to that of ἀπόδειξις to a πρόβλημα: *Rhet.* 3. 13, p. 1414 *a* τούτων δὲ [i. e. of the two parts of a speech] τὸ μὲν πρόθεσίς ἐστι τὸ δὲ πίστις ὥσπερ ἂν εἴ τις διέλοι ὅτι τὸ μὲν πρόβλημα τὸ δὲ ἀπόδειξις.

(3) Its moral meaning is also found in Aristotle: it is good faith or mutual trust: e.g. *Pol.* 5. 11, p. 1313 *b* ἡ γὰρ γνῶσις πίστιν ποιεῖ μᾶλλον πρὸς ἀλλήλους, 'mutual knowledge tends rather to produce mutual trust.' It is found more frequently in the later Greek philosophy: e.g. pseudo-Aristot. *De Virtut. et Vit.* c. 5, p. 1250 *b* ἀκολουθεῖ δὲ τῇ δικαιοσύνῃ . . . . ἡ πίστις καὶ ἡ μισοπονηρία, 'justice is accompanied by . . . . good faith and the hatred of wrong-doing,' and *Ethic. Eudem.* 5. 2, p. 1237 *b* οὐκ ἔστι δ' ἄνευ πίστεως φιλία βέβαιος, 'there is no firm friendship without mutual trust.'

(4) In Biblical Greek it has another or theological meaning which we shall best understand by first examining its use in Philo, who furnishes a connecting link between its philosophical and its biblical use, and who, while using it in the main in its biblical sense, adds explanations which make its meaning clear.

He sometimes uses it in its rhetorical sense of 'proof' or 'evidence': e.g. *De Mundi Opif.* c. 28, vol. i. p. 20 πίστις τῆς ἀρχῆς ἐναργεστάτη τὰ φαινόμενα, 'the actual facts (of man's relation to animals) are the clearest proof that God gave him dominion over them.' But he more commonly uses it in a sense in which the intellectual state of mind which is called 'conviction' is blended with the moral state of mind which is called 'trust.' It is transferred alike from the conviction which results from sensible perception and from that which results from reasoning to that which is based on a conception of the nature of God. The mass of men trust their senses or their reason: in a similar way the good man trusts God. Just as the former believe that their senses and their reason do not deceive them, so the latter believes that God does not deceive him: and the conviction of the latter has a firmer ground than that of the former, inasmuch as both the senses and the reason do deceive men, whereas God never deceives.

This use of the word will be made clear by the following passages.

De Mundi Opif. c. 14, vol. i. p. 10 (God anticipated, before ever men were created, that they would be guessers of probabilities and plausibilities) καὶ ὅτι πιστεύσουσι τοῖς φαινομένοις μᾶλλον ἢ Θεῷ, 'and that they would trust things apparent rather than God.'

Legis Alleg. iii. 81, vol. i. p. 132 ἄριστον οὖν τῷ Θεῷ πεπιστευκέναι καὶ μὴ τοῖς ἀσαφέσι λογισμοῖς καὶ ταῖς ἀβεβαίοις εἰκασίαις, 'it is best, then, to trust God and not uncertain reasonings and unstable conjectures.'

Quis rer. div. heres c. 18, vol. i. pp. 485-6 (the trust in God with which Abraham is credited is not so easy as you may think, because of our close kindness with this mortal part of us which persuades us to trust many other things rather than God) τὸ δὲ ἐκνίψασθαι τούτων ἕκαστον καὶ ἀπιστῆσαι γενέσει τῇ πάντα ἐξ ἑαυτῆς ἀπίστῳ, μόνῳ δὲ πιστεῦσαι Θεῷ τῷ καὶ πρὸς ἀλήθειαν μόνῳ πιστῷ, μεγάλης καὶ ὀλυμπίου διανοίας ἔργον ἐστί, πρὸς οὐδενὸς οὐκέτι δελεαζομένης τῶν παρ' ἡμῖν, 'to wash ourselves thoroughly from each one of these things, and to distrust the visible creation which is of itself in every way to be distrusted, and to trust God who is indeed in reality the only object of trust, requires a great and Olympian mind—a mind that is no longer caught in the toils of any of the things that surround us.'

De Migrat. Abraham. c. 9, vol. i. p. 442 (commenting on Genesis 12. 1 '.... into a land that I *will* shew thee,' he says that the future tense is used rather than the present in testimony of the faith which the soul had in God: for the soul) ἀνενδοίαστα νομίσασα ἤδη παρεῖναι τὰ μὴ παρόντα διὰ τὴν τοῦ ὑποσχομένου βεβαιοτάτην πίστιν, ἀγαθὸν τέλειον ἆθλον εὕρηται, 'believing without a wavering of doubt that the things which were not present were actually present because of its sure trust in him who had promised, has obtained a perfect good for its reward': (this 'perfect good' is probably faith itself: cp. *De praemiis et poenis* c. 4, vol. ii. p. 412 ἆθλον αἱρεῖται τὴν πρὸς τὸν Θεὸν πίστιν).

De praemiis et poenis c. 5, vol. ii. pp. 412–13 (A man who has sincere trust in God has conceived a distrust of all things that are begotten and corruptible, beginning with the two things that give themselves the greatest airs, sense and reason. For sense results in opinion, which is the sport of plausibilities: and reason, though it fancies that its judgments depend on unchanging truths, is found to be disquieted at many things: for when it tries to deal with the ten thousand particular facts which encounter it, it feels its want of power and gives up, like an athlete thrown by a stronger wrestler) ὅτῳ δὲ ἐξεγένετο πάντα μὲν σώματα πάντα δὲ ἀσώματα ὑπεριδεῖν καὶ ὑπερκῦψαι μόνῳ δὲ ἐπερείσασθαι καὶ στηρίσασθαι Θεῷ μετ᾽ ἰσχυρογνώμονος λογισμοῦ καὶ ἀκλινοῦς καὶ βεβαιοτάτης πίστεως, εὐδαίμων καὶ τρισμακάριος οὗτος ἀληθῶς, 'but he to whom it is granted to look beyond and transcend all things corporeal and incorporeal (objects of sense and objects of reason alike), and to rest and fix himself firmly upon God alone with obstinate reasoning and unwavering and settled faith, that man is happy and truly thrice blessed.'

It will be seen from these passages that faith is regarded as something which transcends reason in certainty, and that when spoken of without further definition its object is God. It is consequently natural to find that it is not only ranked as a virtue, but regarded as the chief of virtues, τὴν τελειοτάτην ἀρετῶν *Quis rer. div. heres* c. 18, vol. i. p. 485, the queen of virtues, τὴν βασιλίδα τῶν ἀρετῶν *De Abraham.* c. 46, vol. ii. p. 39: in having it a man offers to God the fairest of sacrifices and one that has no blemish, ἄμωμον καὶ κάλλιστον ἱερεῖον οἴσει Θεῷ, πίστιν *De Cherubim* c. 25, vol. i. p. 154. And in one passage he sings its praises in the following remarkable enconium:

De Abraham. c. 46, vol. ii. p. 39 μόνον οὖν ἀψευδὲς καὶ βέβαιον ἀγαθὸν ἡ πρὸς τὸν Θεὸν πίστις, παρηγόρημα βίου, πλήρωμα χρηστῶν ἐλπίδων, ἀφορία μὲν κακῶν, ἀγαθῶν δὲ φορά, κακοδαιμονίας ἀπόγνωσις, εὐσεβίας γνῶσις, εὐδαιμονίας κλῆρος, ψυχῆς ἐν ἅπασι βελτίωσις, ἐπερηρεισμένης τῷ πάντων αἰτίῳ, καὶ δυναμένῳ μὲν πάντα βουλομένῳ δὲ τὰ ἄριστα, 'Faith towards God [i.e. trust which has God for its object] is the only undeceiving and certain good, the consolation of life, the fulness of good hopes, the banishment of evils, the bringing of blessings, the renunciation of misfortune, the knowledge of piety, the possession of happiness, the bettering in all things of the soul which rests for its support upon Him who is the Cause of all things, and who though He can do all things wills only to do what is best.'

It will be clear from this use of the word in Philo that its use in the N. T. was not a wholly new application of it: 'trust,' or 'faith,' had already become in the Alexandrian schools an ideal virtue. It will also be clear that, assuming it to be used by S. Paul in the sense which it bore in the philosophical language with which he was familiar, it is not used of a vague and mystical sentiment, the hazy state of mind which precedes knowledge, like a nebula which has not yet taken a definite outline or become condensed into a star, but that it is a state of firm mental conviction, based upon a certain conception of the nature of God; hence it is used in close connexion with the strongest word for full assurance, viz. πληροφορεῖσθαι: Rom. 4. 20, 21 ἐνεδυναμώθη τῇ πίστει, δοὺς δόξαν τῷ Θεῷ καὶ πληροφορηθεὶς ὅτι ὃ ἐπήγγελται δυνατός ἐστι καὶ ποιῆσαι, 'he waxed strong through faith, giving glory to God, and being fully assured that what He had promised He is able also to perform.'

Hence in the Epistle to the Hebrews it is used, as Philo used it, to designate a state of mind which transcends ordinary knowledge, the conviction that the words or promises of God have a firmer basis of certainty than either phenomena of sense or judgments of reason; it believes that certain things exist because God has said so, and in spite of the absence of other evidence of their existence: and since it believes also that what God has promised will certainly come to pass, its objects are also objects of hope: hence it is described (11. 1) as ἐλπιζομένων ὑπόστασις, πραγμάτων ἔλεγχος οὐ βλεπομένων, 'the ground of things hoped for, the evidence of things not seen.'

ὑπόστασις.

The word is used by the LXX. only 18 times in the canonical books, but it represents 15 different Hebrew words: in some cases it is difficult to avoid the conclusion that the LXX. misunderstood the Hebrew words, in other cases it must be admitted that the Hebrew text is itself both obscure and uncertain.

In some passages it appears to be the translation of מַצָּב 'outpost' or 'garrison,' viz. 1 Sam. 13. 23 (= Theod. στάσις): 14. 4. That it can bear this meaning is shown by its use in a fragment of the *Phoenix* of Sophocles in the sense of ἐνέδρα (Iren. ap. Socrat. *H. E.* 3. 7 παρὰ Σοφο-κλεῖ ἐν τῷ Φοίνικι ἐνέδραν σημαίνειν τὴν ὑπόστασιν: and Pollux, *Hist. Phys.* p. 376).

The consideration of some of the other passages seems to belong rather to Hebrew than to Hellenistic philology: but there is a small group of passages which furnish a well-established meaning and which throw a clear light upon some instances of the use of the word in the N. T.

Ruth 1. 12 ὅτι εἶπα ὅτι ἔστι μοι ὑπόστασις τοῦ γενηθῆναί με ἀνδρὶ καὶ τέξομαι υἱούς ... 'for my saying (i. e. if I said) that there is ground of hope of my having a husband and I shall bring forth sons ...': ὑπόστασις = תִּקְוָה 'hope.'

Ps. 38 (39). 8 ἡ ὑπόστασίς μου παρὰ σοί ἐστιν, 'my ground of hope is in thee': ὑπόστασις = תּוֹחֶלֶת 'expectation,' which Aquila renders by καραδοκία, Symmachus by ἀναμονή.

Ezek. 19. 5 ἀπώλετο ἡ ὑπόστασις αὐτῆς, 'her ground of hope was lost': ὑπόστασις = תִּקְוָה, which Symmachus renders by προσδοκία, Theodotion by ἐλπίς.

This meaning 'ground of hope' probably follows from the Classical use of ὑπόστασις for the 'ground' or 'foundation' of anything: and it passes by a natural transition into the meaning of 'hope' itself. Hence its use in several passages of the N. T.

2 *Cor.* 9. 4 μήπως .... καταισχυνθῶμεν ἡμεῖς ... ἐν τῇ ὑποστάσει ταύτῃ, 'lest by any means ... we should be put to shame ... in this ground' (sc. of our glorying on your behalf: Codd. אᶜ. Dᶜ. and others add τῆς καυχήσεως, from the following passage).

2 *Cor.* 11. 17 ὁ λαλῶ οὐ κατὰ κύριον λαλῶ ἀλλ᾽ ὡς ἐν ἀφροσύνῃ, ἐν ταύτῃ τῇ ὑποστάσει τῆς καυχήσεως, 'that which I speak I speak not after the Lord but as in foolishness, in this ground of my glorying.'

Heb. 3. 14 ἐάνπερ τὴν ἀρχὴν τῆς ὑποστάσεως μέχρι τέλους βεβαίαν κατάσχωμεν, 'we have become partakers of Christ, if, that is to say, we continue to hold the beginning of our hope firm until the end': cf. v. 6 ἐὰν τὴν παρρησίαν καὶ τὸ καύχημα τῆς ἐλπίδος μέχρι τέλους βεβαίαν κατάσχωμεν.

Heb. 11. 1 ἔστιν δὲ πίστις ἐλπιζομένων ὑπόστασις, 'Faith is the ground of things hoped for,' i.e. trust in God, or the conviction that God is good and that He will perform His promises, is the ground for confident hope that the things hoped for will come to pass.

(In the same passage ἔλεγχος appears to be used in its Hellenistic sense of a fact which serves as the clear proof of another fact: e.g. Jos. *Ant.* 16. 8. 1 Herod's slaves stated that he had dyed his hair, thereby κλέπτοντα τὸν ἔλεγχον τῆς ἡλικίας, 'concealing the clear proof of his age': Epict. *Diss.* 4. 146 speaks of the fears of the Emperor's favour or disfavour which were ἐλέγχους, 'clear proofs,' that though the professors of philosophy said that they were free, they were in reality slaves: so trust in God furnishes to the mind which has it a clear proof that things to which God has testified exist, though they are not visible to the senses).

συκοφαντεῖν.

1. Classical use.

In Classical Greek the word and its paronyms are used exclusively of calumnious accusations, especially of such as were intended to extort money: e.g. Xen. *Mem.* 2. 9. 1, where it is used of those who brought suits against Crito,

who was known to be rich, because, as he says, νομίζουσιν
ἤδιον ἄν με ἀργύριον τελέσαι ἢ πράγματα ἔχειν, 'they think
that I would a good deal rather pay money than have
trouble.'

2. Use in the LXX.

Its wider range of meaning in the LXX. is made clear
by several kinds of proof: (*a*) it is used to translate
Hebrew words which mean simply either 'to oppress' or
'to deceive': (*b*) it is interchanged with other Greek words
or phrases which mean simply 'to oppress': (*c*) it occurs
in contexts in which its Classical meaning is impossible.

(*a*) In Job 35. 9. Ps. 71 (72). 4: 118 (119). 122, 134. Prov.
14. 31: 22. 16: 28. 3, 16. Eccles. 4. 1: 5. 7: 7. 8, they are
translations of עָשׁק 'to oppress,' or of one of its derivatives: in
Lev. 19. 11 of שׁקר 'to lie.'

(*b*) In Gen. 26. 20 LXX. ἀδικία· ἠδίκησαν γὰρ αὐτόν = Aquil. συκο-
φαντία· ἐσυκοφάντησαν γὰρ αὐτόν. Lev. 6. 2 LXX. ἠδίκησε = Aquil.
Symm. Theod. ἐσυκοφάντησε. Deut. 24. 14 LXX. οὐκ ἀπαδικήσεις =
Aquil. Symm. Theod. οὐ συκοφαντήσεις. Job 10. 3 LXX. ἐὰν ἀδι-
κήσω = Ἄλλος· ὅταν συκοφαντήσῃς. Ezek. 22. 29 LXX. ἐκπιεζοῦντες
ἀδικίᾳ = Aquil. Symm. ἐσυκοφάντησαν συκοφαντίαν. Ezek. 22. 12 LXX.
καταδυναστεία, Symm. συκοφαντία, and so also Aquil. in *Jer.* 6. 6.·

(*c*) It is used especially in reference to the poor, whereas the
Classical use related especially to the rich: Ps. 71 (72). 4 'he shall
save the children of the needy and shall break in pieces the oppressor
(συκοφάντην): Prov. 14. 31: 22. 16 'he that oppresseth (συκοφαντῶν)
the poor': id. 28. 3 'a poor man (so E. V. but LXX. ἀνδρεῖος ἐν
ἀσεβέσι) that oppresseth (συκοφαντῶν) the poor': Eccles. 4. 1 'so I
returned and considered all the oppressions (συκοφαντίας) that are
done under the sun: and behold the tears of such as were oppressed
(τῶν συκοφαντουμένων), and they had no comforter; and on the side
of their oppressors (συκοφαντούντων) there was power; but they had
no comforter.'

3. Other Hellenistic uses.

The meaning of the word which appears in the LXX.
appears also in some Egyptian documents, which are the

more valuable for comparison because the social state of
Egypt under the Ptolemies and afterwards under Roman
rule was in many respects closely similar to the state of
Palestine in the corresponding period of its history.

In Brunet de Presle *Notices et textes du Musée du Louvre* in the
Notices et extraits des manuscrits de la Bibliothèque Impériale, Tom.
xviii. 2de partie, Paris 1865, papyrus No. 61, p. 351, consists of a
letter of B.C. 145 from Dioscorides, a chief officer of finance, to
Dorion, a local subordinate. After reciting the strong desire of
the king and queen (Ptolemy Physcon and Cleopatra) that there
even justice should be dealt (δικαιοδοτεῖσθαι) to all classes of their
subjects, the document proceeds περὶ δὲ **διασεισμῶν** καὶ **παραλειῶν**
ἐνίων δὲ καὶ **συκοφαντεῖσθαι** προφερομένων βουλόμεθ᾽ ὑμᾶς μὴ διαλανθάνειν
ὅτι [ταῦτα] πάντα ἐστὶν ἀλλότρια τῆς τε ἡμῶν ἀγωγῆς οὐχ ἧσσον δὲ καὶ τῆς
ὑμετέρας σωτηρίας ἐπάν τις ἐξελεγχθῇ λελυπηκώς τινα τῶν κατὰ μέρος, 'in
the matter of fictitious legal proceedings and plunderings, some
persons being moreover alleged to be even made the victims of
false accusations, we wish you to be aware that all these things are
at variance not only with our administration but also and still more
with your safety when any one is convicted of having injured anyone in his district.'

The offences διασεισμός, παραλεία, συκοφαντία, are evidently all offences committed by taxgatherers.

In the *Corpus Inscr. Graec.*, N°. 4957 consists of a decree of
Julius Alexander, prefect of Egypt in A. D. 68, and is almost
entirely concerned with the wrongs done by local authorities, especially in the matter of the revenue.

ὑπόκρισις, ὑποκριτής.

In the Old Testament ὑποκριτής is found in two passages
of Theodotion's translation of Job which have been incorporated into the LXX. text, and in each case it is the
translation of חָנֵף 'impious': Job 34. 30 βασιλεύων ἄνθρωπον ὑποκριτὴν ἀπὸ δυσκολίας λαοῦ, 'making an impious
man king on account of the discontent of the people':

Job 36. 13 καὶ ὑποκριταὶ καρδίᾳ τάξουσι θυμόν, 'and the impious in heart shall ordain (for themselves) wrath.' The word חָנֵף is also translated by ὑποκριτής by Aquila and Theodotion in Job 15. 34, where the LXX. have ἀσεβοῦς; by Aquila in Job 20. 5, where the LXX. have παρανόμων; by Aquila, Symmachus, and Theodotion in Prov. 11. 9, where the LXX have ἀσεβῶν: and by the same three translators in Is. 33. 14, where the LXX. have ἀσεβεῖς. Similarly חֹנֶף, which only occurs in Is. 32. 6, is there translated by the LXX. ἄνομα, and by Aquila, Symmachus, and Theodotion ὑπόκρισιν.

These facts seem to shew that early in the second century, and among Greek-speaking Jews, ὑποκριτής had come to mean more than merely 'the actor of a false part in life.' It connoted positive badness. The inference is corroborated by its use in the 'Two Ways,' especially in the form in which that treatise is appended to the Epistle of Barnabas, c. 19. 2 οὐ κολληθήσῃ μετὰ πορευομένων ἐν ὁδῷ θανάτου, μισήσεις πᾶν ὃ οὐκ ἔστιν ἀρεστὸν τῷ Θεῷ, μισήσεις πᾶσαν ὑπόκρισιν οὐ μὴ ἐγκαταλίπῃς ἐντολὰς κυρίου, 'thou shalt not join thyself with those who go in the way of death, thou shalt hate whatever is not pleasing to God, thou shalt hate all ὑπόκρισιν, thou shalt not abandon the commandments of the Lord.' The collocation and emphasis can hardly be accounted for unless ὑπόκρισιν has a stronger meaning than that of 'false pretence.'

The meaning which is evident in the Hexapla seems more appropriate than any other in the Synoptic Gospels:

S. Matt. 24. 51 (of the master returning suddenly and finding the slave whom he had set over his household beating his fellow slaves) διχοτομήσει αὐτὸν καὶ τὸ μέρος αὐτοῦ μετὰ τῶν ὑποκριτῶν θήσει, 'he will surely scourge him, and will appoint his portion with the impious': it would be mere bathos to render ὑποκριτῶν by 'false pretenders.'

S. Matt. 23. 28 ἔσωθεν δέ ἐστε μεστοὶ ὑποκρίσεως καὶ ἀνομίας,

'within they are full of impiety and wickedness': and in the
denunciations of the Scribes and Pharisees which both precede
and follow this verse the point seems to be not merely that they
were false pretenders but that they were positively irreligious.

S. Mark 12. 15 εἰδὼς αὐτῶν τὴν ὑπόκρισιν = S. Matt. 22. 18 γνοὺς
δὲ ὁ Ἰησοῦς τὴν πονηρίαν αὐτῶν, S. Luke 20. 23 κατανοήσας δὲ αὐτῶν τὴν
πανουργίαν: the three words ὑπόκρισιν, πονηρίαν, πανουργίαν are of
equivalent meaning: and in S. Mark as in the two other Evangelists that which our Lord is said to have known was not their
'false pretence' but their 'wickedness' or 'malice.'

III. ON PSYCHOLOGICAL TERMS IN BIBLICAL GREEK.

IN examining any philosophical terms which are found in Hellenistic Greek it is necessary to observe to an increased degree the caution with which all Hellenistic words must be treated. At every step the student is haunted by their Classical meanings, and at every step the ghosts of their Classical meanings must be exorcised. For Greece and the Greek world had come not only under a different political rule, and into new social circumstances, but also into a new atmosphere of thought and to a new attitude of mind towards the questions with which philosophy deals. Those questions were, almost of necessity, stated in their ancient form: the technical terms remained the same: but by the operation of those silent changes by which all thinking races are constantly elaborating new meanings, and finding new points of view, the connotation of those terms and the answers to those questions had undergone more than one complete transformation. The philosophical words of Hellenistic Greek must be viewed in relation not to past but to contemporary philosophy. Nor can that contemporary philosophy be taken as an undivided whole. It is as various in its character as the philosophy of our own time, with which it is the more interesting to compare it because, as in our modern philosophy, a large part of it was syncretistic.

For the investigation of such philosophical terms as are found in the New Testament we possess a mass of material of unique value in the writings which are com-

monly gathered together under the name of Philo. Except
in relation to the doctrine of the Λόγος, which is itself
often misunderstood because it is isolated from the rest
of the philosophy, those writings are an almost wholly
unworked mine. Many of the MSS. which contain them
remain uncollated : no attempt has been made to differen-
tiate the characteristics of the main group of writings so
as to afford a criterion for distinguishing between the
writings of Philo himself and those of his school : the
philosophy itself, which is more like a mosaic than an
organic unity, has for the most part not been resolved
into its elements. But although whatever is now said
about Philo must be regarded as subject to correction
in the future when the writings which bear his name have
been more critically investigated, the study of those writings is indispensable for the determination of the meanings
of Hellenistic words which even touch the circumference
of the philosophical sphere. It would be unwarrantable
to assert that the meaning of such words in Philo deter-
mines their meaning in the New Testament : but at the
same time no inference as to their meaning in the New
Testament can be regarded as even approximately certain
if it leaves out of sight the evidence which Philo affords.

But the number of words in the New Testament which
can be regarded simply as philosophical terms with an
added theological connotation is very small. An instance
has been given in the preceding chapter in πίστις. The
majority of terms which appear to be philosophical require
a different kind of caution in their treatment. For Biblical
Greek is with comparatively rare exceptions not a philosophical but a popular language. It is not, that is to
say, the language of men who were writing with scientific
precision to an inner circle of students, but that which
was addressed to, and therefore reflected from, the mass
of the people, to whom, then as now, the minute distinc-

tions of philosophy are unfamiliar, and to a great extent incomprehensible. The tendency of many commentators and lexicographers has been to assume the existence in Biblical Greek of the distinctions which are found in philosophical writers, and to attach to words in their popular use meanings which belong to them only in their philosophical use. The presumption is that in the majority of cases those distinctions and meanings are inapplicable: and the presumption is sometimes raised to proof by the evidence which the LXX. affords.

I propose to deal with a special group of philosophical terms, viz. psychological terms, partly because of their importance in themselves, and partly because they furnish a good illustration of the general principle which has been stated. In dealing with them I propose to investigate (1) their use in the LXX. and Hexapla, (2) their use in Philo.

I. Psychological terms in the LXX. and Hexapla.

In the case of all but concrete terms, such as horse, fire, wood, used in their primary sense, it must be borne in mind that a general equivalence of connotation between two words in two different languages must not be held to imply an exact coincidence of such connotation. The dominant meaning of a word in one language must no doubt be held to form at least an integral part of the meaning of the word by which it is translated in another language: but it is only by adding together all the predicates of the two words in their respective languages that an inference becomes possible as to the extent to which the spheres of their connotation coincide.

When the two terms are each of them so far isolated in their respective languages that the one is uniformly the translation of the other, this addition of predicates is the only method by which the extent of the coincidence of their connotation can be determined. But in dealing with groups of allied terms, for example, psychological terms, this method may be supplemented by others. If it be found that each member of the group in one language is rendered uniformly by one and only one member of the corresponding group in the other language, it must no doubt be inferred that each term had in its own language a distinct and isolated meaning, and no other method than that of the addition of predicates will be applicable. But if it be found, as it is found in the case of the terms with which we are about to deal, that the members of the group in the one language are each rendered by more than one of the members of the group in the other language, it must be inferred that while the group as a whole in the one language corresponded as a whole to the group in the other, the individual members of the two groups did not so correspond.

The question which lies immediately before us is that of the precise extent of the correspondence or non-correspondence between the respective members of the two groups, and of the light which that correspondence or non-correspondence throws upon the meaning of the Greek terms. In other words, given a group of Hebrew terms *ABC*, and a corresponding group of Greek terms *abc*, since it is found that *a* is used to translate not only *A* but also sometimes *B* and *C*, and that *b* is used to translate not only *B* but also sometimes *A* and *C*, and that *c* is used to translate not only *C* but also sometimes *A* and *B*, and conversely that *A* and *B* and *C* are each of them translated, though in varying degrees, by *a* and *b* and *c*, what may we infer as to the relations of the Greek terms *a* and *b* and *c* to each other?

It will thus be found necessary to ascertain

    (i) of what Hebrew words each member of the Greek group is the translation :

(ii) what corrections of and additions to the translations of the words in the LXX. are found in
the Hexapla.

(iii) by what Greek words each member of the Hebrew
group is translated :

When these questions have received provisional answers,
it will be found necessary to ascertain further how far
those provisional answers are confirmed by (1) the combinations and interchanges of the several words in the
same or similar passages, (2) the predicates which are
attached to the several words.

1. *Translations.*

I. καρδία.

It is ordinarily the translation of לֵב or לֵבָב.

i. The other words which it is used to translate are—

(1) בֶּטֶן 'the belly': Prov. 22. 18, Hab. 3. 15.

(2) מֵעַי 'my bowels': Thren. 2. 11, where the MSS. vary
between κοιλία and καρδία.

(3) קֶרֶב 'the inward parts': Ps. 5. 10: 61 (62). 5: 93 (94).
19, Prov. 14. 33: 26. 24.

(4) רוּחַ 'the spirit': Ezek. 13. 3.

In several passages the Hebrew is paraphrased rather
than translated : e. g. Ps. 31 (32). 5: 84 (85). 9, Prov. 15.
22; and in one instance, Ps. 36 (37). 14 τοὺς εὐθεῖς τῇ καρδίᾳ
is a mistake of either the translator or the transcriber for
the less familiar τοὺς εὐθεῖς τῇ ὁδῷ.

ii. The translation of לֵב by καρδία is almost always accepted by the translators of the Hexapla, and the MSS.
of the LXX. do not greatly vary: the corrections and
variations are the following :

Deut. 6. 5: 28. 47, Jos. 22. 5 MSS. vary between καρδίας
(καρδίᾳ) and διανοίας (διανοίᾳ).

2 *Sam.* 7. 27 LXX. καρδίαν, *Symm.* διάνοιαν.

Ps. 36 (37). 15 Codd. A. B. καρδίαν, Cod. S¹. ψυχήν, S². ψυχάς.

Ps. 72 (73). 13 LXX. *Aquil.* καρδίαν, *Symm. Theod.* ψυχήν.

Prov. 7. 3 LXX. καρδίας, *Symm.* στήθους.

Eccles. 7. 3 LXX. εἰς καρδίαν, *Symm.* τῇ διανοίᾳ.

Eccles. 10. 3 לִבּוֹ חָסֵר 'his heart faileth him': LXX. καρδία αὐτοῦ ὑστερήσει, *Symm.* ἀνόητος.

Jer. 5. 21 וְאֵין לֵב 'without heart' : LXX. καὶ ἀκάρδιος, *Symm.* καὶ ἀδιανόητος.

Jer. 38 (31). 33 LXX. καρδίας, *Theod.* στήθους.

iii. The other words by which לֵבָב, לֵב are translated are :

(1) νοῦς, Jos. 14. 7, Is. 10. 7, 12 : and in the phrase νοῦν ἐφιστάνειν for שִׁית לֵב 'to apply the heart to . . .'=καρδίαν ἐφιστάνειν Prov. 22. 17 : 27. 23, καρδίαν τιθέναι 1 Sam. 13. 20, Ps. 47 (48). 14: so *Symm.* Job 7. 17 νοῦν προσέχειν: and for שׂוֹם לֵב Is. 41. 22=*Aquil. Symm. Theod.* καρδίαν ἐφιστάνειν.

(2), (3) διάνοια, ψυχή : see below.

(4) σάρξ, Ps. 27 (28). 7 ἀνέθαλεν ἡ σάρξ μου, *Aquil. Symm. Theod.* ἡ καρδία.

II. πνεῦμα.

It is ordinarily the translation of רוּחַ.

i. The other words which it translates are—

(1) חַיִּים 'life' : Is. 38. 12=*Aquil. Symm.* ζωή, as usually in LXX.

(2) נְשָׁמָה 'breath' : 1 Kings 17. 17.

ii. The translation of רוּחַ by πνεῦμα is almost always accepted by the other translators who are included in the Hexapla, and the MSS. of the LXX. do not greatly vary : but several of the instances of revision and variation are important.

Job 1. 19 LXX. πνεῦμα, *Aquil.* ἄνεμος: so *ib.* 30. 15 *Symm.*

Ps. 32 (33). 6 LXX. τῷ πνεύματι, *Symm.* τῇ πνοῇ.

Ps. 142 (143). 4 LXX. πνεῦμα, *Aquil.* ψυχή.

Ps. 148. 8 LXX. πνεῦμα, *Alius* ἄνεμος.

Eccles. 1. 14 LXX. προαίρεσις πνεύματος, *Aquil.* νομὴ ἀνέμου (so *Aquil. Theod. ib.* 2. 11), *Symm.* βόσκησις ἀνέμου (so also *ib.* 4. 16).

Eccles. 3. 19 LXX. πνεῦμα, *Symm.* ἀναπνοή.

Eccles. 6. 9 LXX. προαίρεσις πνεύματος, *Aquil. Theod.* νομὴ ἀνέμου, *Symm.* κάκωσις πνεύματος.

Eccles. 7, 8 (9). LXX. ὑψηλὸν πνεύματι, *Symm.* ὑψηλοκάρδιον.

Is. 7. 2 LXX. πνεύματος, *Symm.* ὁ ἄνεμος.

Is. 32. 15 LXX. πνεῦμα, *Symm.* ἀνάψυξις, *Theod.* ἄνεμος.

iii. The other words by which רוּחַ is translated are the following:

(1) ἄνεμος, Prov. 30. 4, so also *Symm.*, but *Aquil.* πνεῦμα.

(2) θυμός, Job 15. 13, Prov. 18. 14 (*Aquil.* πνεῦμα): 29. 11, Ezek. 39. 29, Zach. 6. 8.

(3) καρδία, Ezek. 13. 3.

(4) νοῦς, Is. 40. 13 τίς γὰρ ἔγνω νοῦν κυρίου, *Aquil.* πνεῦμα: the passage is important on account of its quotation by S. Paul in Rom. 11. 34, 1 Cor. 2. 16: the use of νοῦς rather than πνεῦμα in the latter passage is especially noteworthy because πνεῦμα would have followed more naturally from the preceding verses: and since this is the only passage in the LXX. in which רוּחַ is translated by νοῦς, the presumption is very strong that S. Paul had the LXX. in mind.

(5) ὀργή, Prov. 16. 32, Is. 59. 19, *Aquil. Symm. Theod.* πνεῦμα (which is used, without any qualifying word, to denote anger in LXX. Judges 8. 3).

(6) πνοή, Gen. 7. 22 πνοὴν ζωῆς: Prov. 1. 23 ἐμῆς πνοῆς ῥῆσιν, *Aquil. Theod.* πνεῦμά μου: *ib.* 11. 13 πιστὸς δὲ πνοῇ, *Aquil. Symm.* πνεύματι: Is. 38. 16 ἐξήγειράς μου τὴν πνοήν, *Aquil.* ζωὴ πνεύματός μου.

(7) ψυχή, Gen. 41. 8, Ex. 35. 21.

(8) φρόνησις, Jos. 5. 1.

In Job 6. 4, Prov. 17. 23: 25. 28, Is. 32. 2 the LXX. translation is not literal, and the Greek and Hebrew cannot be balanced word for word.

There are some noteworthy compound phrases into which רוּחַ enters, which in the LXX. are rendered by ὀλιγόψυχος, ὀλιγοψυχία:

Ex. 6. 9 קֹצֶר רוּחַ 'shortness of spirit': LXX. ὀλιγοψυχία, *Aquil.* κολοβότης πνεύματος.

Ps. 54 (55). 9 מֵרוּחַ סֹעָה 'from the stormy wind' is rendered in the LXX. by the gloss ἀπὸ ὀλιγοψυχίας, *Aquil. Theod.* ἀπὸ πνεύματος λαιλαπώδους.

Prov. 14. 29 קְצַר רוּחַ 'hasty of spirit': LXX. ὀλιγόψυχος, *Alius* μικρόψυχος.

Prov. 18. 14 רוּחַ נְכֵאָה 'a broken spirit': LXX. ὀλιγόψυχον ἄνδρα, *Theod.* πνεῦμα πεπληγμένον.

Is. 54. 6 עֲצוּבַת רוּחַ 'pained in spirit': LXX. ὀλιγόψυχος, *Aquil. Symm. Theod.* κατώδυνος πνεύματι.

III. ψυχή.

It is ordinarily the translation of נֶפֶשׁ.

i. The other words of which it is the translation are the following:

(1) אִישׁ 'man': Lev. 17. 9, where the MSS. vary between ψυχή and ἄνθρωπος.

(2) חַיָּה, חַיִּים 'life': Job 38. 39, Ps. 63 (64). 1 (*Symm.* ζωήν): 73 (74). 20.

(3) לֵב, לֵבָב 'heart': 2 Kings 6. 11, 1 Chron. 12. 38 : 15. 29 : 17. 2 : 22. 9, 2 Chron. 7. 11 : 9. 1 : 15. 15 : 31. 21, Ps. 68 (69). 21 (*Aquil. Symm.* καρδίαν), Prov. 6. 21 : 16. 1 (15. 32), Is. 7. 2, 4 : 10. 7 : 13. 7 : 24. 7 : 33. 18 : 42. 25 : 44. 19. In Ps. 20 (21). 2 : 36 (37). 15, Prov. 26. 25 the MSS. vary between ψυχή and καρδία.

(4) מֵת 'a dead body': Ezek. 44. 25, *Symm.* νεκρῷ: in Num. 23. 10 ἀποθάνοι ἡ ψυχή μου ἐν ψυχαῖς δικαίων, ψυχαῖς must be considered to be part of a paraphrase rather than a literal translation of מָוֶת 'death': but in Num. 9. 6 ἐπὶ ψυχῇ (לְנֶפֶשׁ) no doubt means 'by the dead body.'

(5) פְּנֵי 'look': Prov. 27. 23 (perhaps like the English 'person').

(6) רוּחַ 'spirit': Gen. 41. 8, Ex. 35. 21 (*Aquil.* πνεῦμα).

In Ps. 38 (39). 12 τὴν ψυχήν is a free gloss for that which is more literally rendered by Symmachus τὸ ἐπιθυμητόν.

ii. The variations in the translation of נֶפֶשׁ by ψυχή in the Hexapla and in MSS. of the LXX. are the following:

Ex. 23. 9 LXX. τὴν ψυχήν, *Aquil.* (τὴν) θλίψιν.

Num. 9. 6 LXX. ἐπὶ ψυχῇ, *Alius* ἐπὶ νεκρῷ.

1 *Sam.* 24. 10 LXX. τὴν ψυχήν, *Aquil. Symm. Theod.* τὴν κακίαν.

Job 6. 11 ὅτι ἀνέχεταί μου ἡ ψυχή, *Aquil.* ὅτι μακροθυμήσω.

Ps. 87 (88). 15 Codd. AS. ἵνατι ἀπωθεῖς τὴν ψυχήν μου, so *Aquil. Symm.*: Cod. B., ed. Rom., τὴν προσευχήν μου.

Prov. 24. 12 ὁ πλάσας πνοὴν πᾶσιν, *Aquil. Symm.* διατηρῶν ψυχήν σου.

Prov. 28. 26 רְחַב־נֶפֶשׁ literally as in *Aquila* πλατὺς ψυχῇ = *Symm.* πλατύψυχος : the LXX. drops נֶפֶשׁ and has *Cod. A.* ἄπληστος, *Cod. B.* ἄπιστος.

In *Prov.* 13. 25 δίκαιος ἔσθων ἐμπιπλᾷ τὴν ψυχὴν αὐτοῦ, ψυχαὶ δὲ ἀσεβῶν ἐνδεεῖς, it is possible that there is some confusion in the text : ψυχήν, as usual, translates נַפְשׁוֹ, but is wrongly amended by a reviser (Ἄλλος) to κοιλίαν, but ψυχαί translates בֶּטֶן 'belly,' and is rightly amended to κοιλίαι (*Aquil. Symm. Theod. Quint.* in Syriac, κοιλία).

iii. The other words by which נֶפֶשׁ is translated are the following :

(1) ἀνήρ, Gen. 14. 21, Prov. 16. 26, = *Aquil. Symm.* ψυχή.

(2) *Jos.* 10. 28, 30, 35, 39 כָּל־הַנֶּפֶשׁ is translated by πᾶν ἐμπνέον.

(3) *Is.* 43. 4 ἄρχοντας ὑπὲρ τῆς κεφαλῆς σου.

(4) *Gen.* 36. 6 πάντα τὰ σώματα, i. e. slaves, as probably πᾶσαν ψυχήν in Gen. 12. 5.

In Is. 29. 8 μάταιον τὸ ἐνύπνιον is a free gloss for that which Aquila, Symmachus, and Theodotion render literally by κενὴ ἡ ψυχὴ αὐτοῦ.

In Jer. 28 (51). 14 ὤμοσε Κύριος κατὰ τοῦ βραχιόνος αὐτοῦ is a characteristic periphrasis for τῆς ψυχῆς, which is not amended in the existing fragments of the Hexapla.

IV. διάνοια.

It is ordinarily the translation of לֵב.

i. The other words which it translates are—

(1) מַחֲשָׁבָה 'thoughts' : Is. 55. 9.

(2) קֶרֶב 'inward parts' : Jer. 38 (31). 33.

ii. The variations of the LXX. translation of לֵב by διάνοια in the Hexapla are—

Gen. 34. 3 LXX. κατὰ τὴν διάνοιαν, *Aquil.* ἐπὶ καρδίαν, *Symm.* καταθύμια.

Ex. 35. 22 LXX. *Symm.* τῇ διανοίᾳ, *Aquil.* καρδίᾳ.

Lev. 19. 17 LXX. τῇ διανοίᾳ, *Alius* ἐν τῇ καρδίᾳ.

Job 1. 5 LXX. ἐν τῇ διανοίᾳ, *Aquil.* ἐπὶ καρδίας.

Is. 35. 4 LXX. οἱ ὀλιγόψυχοι τῇ διανοίᾳ, *Aquil.* τοῖς ταπεινοῖς τῇ καρδίᾳ, *Symm.* τοῖς ἀνοήτοις, *Theod.* ταχυκαρδίοις.

iii. The other words by which לֵב is translated have been given above, under καρδία.

2. *Combinations and interchanges in the same or similar passages.*

(1) **καρδία** and **πνεῦμα**: Ex. 9. 13 etc. ἐσκλήρυνε δὲ κύριος τὴν καρδίαν Φαραώ, but Deut. 2. 30 ἐσκλήρυνε κύριος ὁ Θεὸς τὸ πνεῦμα αὐτοῦ : Jos. 2. 11 ἐξέστημεν τῇ καρδίᾳ ἡμῶν καὶ οὐκ ἔστη ἔτι πνεῦμα ἐν οὐδένι ἡμῶν : Ps. 50 (51). 19 θυσία τῷ θεῷ πνεῦμα συντετριμμένον, καρδίαν συντετριμμένην καὶ τεταπεινωμένην ὁ θεὸς οὐκ ἐξουδενώσει : Ps. 76 (77). 7 νυκτὸς μετὰ τῆς καρδίας μου ἠδολέσχουν καὶ ἔσκαλλον τὸ πνεῦμά μου : Ps. 77 (78). 8 γενεὰ ἥτις οὐ κατεύθυνεν ἐν τῇ καρδίᾳ αὐτῆς καὶ οὐκ ἐπιστώθη μετὰ τοῦ θεοῦ τὸ πνεῦμα αὐτῆς : Ps. 142 (143). 4 ἠκηδίασεν ἐπ' ἐμὲ τὸ πνεῦμά μου, ἐν ἐμοὶ ἐταράχθη ἡ καρδία μου : Ezek. 11. 19 δώσω αὐτοῖς καρδίαν ἑτέραν καὶ πνεῦμα καινὸν δώσω ἐν αὐτοῖς, so *ib.* 36. 26. In one instance the words are interchanged between the LXX. and the Hexapla, Eccles. 7. 8 LXX. ὑψηλὸν πνεύματι, *Symm.* ὑψηλοκάρδιον.

(2) **καρδία** and **ψυχή**: (*a*) Sometimes they are combined: Deut. 6. 5 ἔσται τὰ ῥήματα ταῦτα .... ἐν τῇ καρδίᾳ σου καὶ ἐν τῇ ψυχῇ σου : so *ib.* 11. 18, Jos. 23. 14, 1 Sam. 2. 35, 1 Chron. 22. 19. (*b*) Sometimes they have the same or analogous predicates: Judges 19. 5 στήρισον τὴν καρδίαν σου ψωμῷ ἄρτου: Ps. 103 (104). 15 ἄρτος καρδίαν ἀνθρώπου στηρίζει: Ps. 34 (35). 13 ἐταπείνουν ἐν νηστείᾳ τὴν ψυχήν μου, so Ps. 68 (69). 11: Ps. 77 (78). 18 βρώματα ταῖς ψυχαῖς αὐτῶν : Jer. 4. 10 ἥψατο ἡ μάχαιρα ἕως τῆς ψυχῆς αὐτῶν, *ib.* v. 18 ἥψατο ἕως τῆς καρδίας σου. (*c*) Sometimes they are interchanged in the MSS. of the LXX., or in the Hexapla: e. g. Ps. 20 (21). 2, Codd. A. B. ψυχῆς, Cod. S². καρδίας : Ps. 36 (37). 15, Codd. A. B. καρδίαν, Cod. S. ψυχήν (ψυχάς): Ps. 72 (72). 13 LXX. *Aquil.* καρδίαν, *Symm. Theod.* ψυχήν: so 2 Kings 6. 11, Ps. 68 (69). 21, Prov. 6. 21: 16. : (15. 32). The most important instance of the combination of the two words is in the phrase ἐξ ὅλης τῆς καρδίας σου καὶ ἐξ ὅλης τῆς

ψυχῆς σου: Deut. 4. 29: 10. 12: 11. 13: 13. 3: 26. 16: 30. 2, 6, 10, Jos. 22. 5 [Cod. B.], 2 Chron. 15. 12. The variations of this phrase are significant: (a) Deut. 6. 5, Jos. 22. 5 [Cod. A.] substitute διανοίας for καρδίας: (b) 1 Sam. 12. 24, 1 Kings 2. 4 omit the mention of ψυχή and substitute ἐν ἀληθείᾳ, the force of the phrase being shown in Jer. 3. 10 by a contrast with its opposite, οὐκ ἐπεστράφη πρὸς μὲ . . . . ἐξ ὅλης τῆς καρδίας αὐτῆς ἀλλ' ἐπὶ ψεύδει: so Jer. 39 (32). 41 ἐν πίστει καὶ ἐν πάσῃ καρδίᾳ μου καὶ ἐν πάσῃ ψυχῇ.

(3) πνεῦμα and ψυχή: (a) of the principle of life, Gen. 1. 30 ψυχὴν ζωῆς, ib. 6. 17 πνεῦμα ζωῆς (חַיִּים רוּחַ), and Ezek. 1. 20, 21: 10. 17 (הַחַיָּה רוּחַ): (b) of fainting, i. e. the apparent suspension of life, Ps. 106 (107). 5 ἡ ψυχὴ αὐτῶν ἐν αὐτοῖς ἐξέλιπεν, ib. 142 (143). 7 ἐξέλιπε τὸ πνεῦμά μου: (c) of dying, Gen. 35. 18 ἐν τῷ ἀφιέναι αὐτὴν τὴν ψυχήν, 1 Kings 17. 21 ἐπιστραφήτω δὴ ἡ ψυχὴ τοῦ παιδαρίου τούτου εἰς αὐτόν, Is. 53. 12 παρεδόθη εἰς θάνατον ἡ ψυχὴ αὐτοῦ, Thren. 2. 12 ἐν τῷ ἐκχεῖσθαι ψυχὰς αὐτῶν, Ps. 103 (104). 29 ἀντανελεῖς τὸ πνεῦμα αὐτῶν καὶ ἐκλείψουσι, ib. 145 (146). 4 ἐξελεύσεται τὸ πνεῦμα αὐτοῦ, Eccles. 12. 7 τὸ πνεῦμα ἐπιστρέψῃ πρὸς τὸν θεὸν ὃς ἔδωκεν αὐτό.

In only one instance are the words interchanged between the LXX. and the Hexapla, Ps. 142 (143). 4 LXX. πνεῦμα, Aquil. ψυχή.

The elements of the two words are sometimes combined in a single phrase: Judges 15. 19 (Cod. A.) ἐπέστρεψε τὸ πνεῦμα αὐτοῦ καὶ ἀνέψυξεν, Ps. 76 (77). 4 ὠλιγοψύχησε τὸ πνεῦμα αὐτοῦ, Jer. 2. 24 ἐν ἐπιθυμίαις ψυχῆς αὐτοῦ ἐπνευματοφορεῖτο, Ezek. 21. 7 ἐκψύξει πᾶσα σὰρξ καὶ πᾶν πνεῦμα.

Cf. 1 Sam. 16. 23 רָוַח, LXX. ἀνέψυχε, Aquil. ἀνέπνεε.

(4) καρδία and διάνοια: (a) they are sometimes interchanged, Ex. 25. 2 οἷς ἂν δόξῃ τῇ καρδίᾳ αὐτοῦ=ib. 35. 22 ᾧ ἔδοξε τῇ διανοίᾳ: ib. 28. 3: 35. 9: 36. 1 πᾶσι τοῖς σοφοῖς τῇ διανοίᾳ=ib. 31. 6 παντὶ συνετῷ καρδίᾳ: so in Deut. 6. 5: 28. 47, Jos. 22. 5, Prov. 27. 19 the MSS. vary between καρδία and διάνοια: (b) they are sometimes combined, Gen. 6. 5 πᾶς τις διανοεῖται ἐν τῇ καρδίᾳ αὐτοῦ, 1 Chron. 29. 18 φύλαξον ταῦτα ἐν διανοίᾳ καρδίας.

3. Predicates of the several words.

(i) *Strong emotion* is expressed by ταράσσειν with each of the three words:

(1) *Job* 36. 34 (37. 1) ἐταράχθη ἡ καρδία μου: so Ps. 37 (38). 10:
54 (55). 3: 142 (143). 4, Thren. 2. 11.

(2) 1 *Kings* 20 (21). 5 τί τὸ πνεῦμά σου τεταραγμένον; so Is.
19. 3.

(3) *Gen.* 41. 8 ἐταράχθη ἡ ψυχὴ αὐτοῦ (where, as noted above, the
Hebrew word is not נֶפֶשׁ but רוּחַ): so also Ps. 6. 4: 41 (42). 7.

(ii) *Pride* is expressed by ὑψοῦν, ὑψηλός, with each of
the three words:

(1) *Deut.* 17. 20 ἵνα μὴ ὑψωθῇ ἡ καρδία αὐτοῦ: so 2 Chron. 32. 25,
Ps. 130 (131). 1, Jer. 31 (48). 29, Ezek. 28. 2, 5, 17: so also Is.
9. 9 ἐφ' ὕβρει καὶ ὑψηλῇ καρδίᾳ.

(2) *Eccles.* 7. 8 ὑπὲρ ὑψηλὸν πνεύματι.

(3) *Ps.* 130 (131). 2 εἰ μὴ ἐταπεινοφρόνουν ἀλλὰ ὕψωσα τὴν ψυχήν
μου.

(iii) *Humility*, with ταπεινός and cognate words:

(1) καρδία:
Ps. 108 (109). 16 ἄνθρωπον πένητα καὶ πτωχὸν καὶ κατανενυγμένον τῇ
καρδίᾳ.

(2) πνεῦμα:
Ps. 33 (34). 19 τοὺς ταπεινοὺς τῷ πνεύματι.

(3) ψυχή:
Is. 58. 3 ἐταπεινώσαμεν τὰς ψυχὰς ἡμῶν.

(iv) *Dejection* is expressed by ἀκηδιᾶν with each of the
three words:

(1) *Ps.* 60 (61). 3 ἐν τῷ ἀκηδιάσαι τὴν καρδίαν μου.

(2) *Ps.* 142 (143). 4 ἠκηδίασεν ἐπ' ἐμὲ τὸ πνεῦμά μου, Is. 61. 3
πνεῦμα ἀκηδίας.

(3) *Ps.* 118 (119). 28 ἐνύσταξεν ἡ ψυχή μου ὑπὸ ἀκηδίας.

(v) *Contrition and distress* are expressed by συντρίβεσθαι
and cognate words with each of the three words:

(1) 1 *Sam.* 1. 8 ἱνατί τύπτει σε ἡ καρδία σου; Ps. 50 (51). 11 καρδίαν
συντετριμμένην καὶ τεταπεινωμένην, ib. 146 (147). 3, Is. 57. 13, Jer.
23. 9.

(2) *Ps.* 50 (51). 19 πνεῦμα συντετριμμένον, Is. 65. 14 ἀπὸ συντριβῆς
πνεύματος ὑμῶν.

(3) *Gen.* 43. 21 τὴν θλίψιν τῆς ψυχῆς αὐτοῦ.

(vi) *Sorrow and anguish* are expressed by each of the three words:

(1) *Deut.* 15. 10 οὐ λυπηθήσῃ τῇ καρδίᾳ σου, Is. 65. 14 διὰ τὸν πόνον τῆς καρδίας ὑμῶν.

(2) *Ps.* 76 (77). 4 ὠλιγοψύχησε τὸ πνεῦμά μου: *ib.* 105 (106). 33 παρεπίκραναν τὸ πνεῦμα αὐτοῦ.

(3) 1 *Sam.* 1. 10 κατώδυνος ψυχῇ: so *ib.* 22. 2 : 30. 6, 2 Kings 4. 27 : Is. 38. 15 τὴν ὀδύνην τῆς ψυχῆς: 2 Sam. 17. 8 κατάπικροι τῇ ψυχῇ: Job 7. 11: 10. 1: 21. 25 πικρία ψυχῆς: Job 14. 22 ἡ δὲ ψυχὴ αὐτοῦ ἐπένθησεν.

(vii) The predicates which are found with καρδία and ψυχή, but not with πνεῦμα, are those of *fear and cowardice.*

(*a*) With τήκεσθαι:

(1) 2 *Sam.* 17. 10 ἡ καρδία καθὼς ἡ καρδία τοῦ λέοντος τηκομένη τακήσεται: Ps. 21 (22). 15 ἐνενήθη ἡ καρδία μου ὡσεὶ κηρὸς τηκόμενος.

(2) *Deut.* 28. 65 δώσω σοι . . . τηκομένην ψυχήν: so Ps. 106 (107). 26.

(*b*) With φόβος, φοβεῖσθαι.

(1) *Deut.* 20. 8 ὁ φοβούμενος καὶ δειλὸς τῇ καρδίᾳ: *ib.* 28. 67, Jos. 7. 15, 2 Chron. 13. 7, Ps. 26 (27). 3, 1 Sam. 28. 5 ἐφοβήθη καὶ ἐξέστη ἡ καρδία αὐτοῦ σφόδρα.

(2) *Is.* 21. 4 ἡ ψυχή μου ἐφέστηκεν εἰς φόβον.

(viii) *Of affection* with ἀγαπᾶν and cognate phrases:

(1) *Judges* 16. 15 ἠγάπηκά σε καὶ ἡ καρδία σου οὐκ ἔστι μετ᾽ ἐμοῦ: 2 Sam. 14. 1 ἡ καρδία τοῦ βασιλέως ἐπὶ ᾽Αβεσσαλώμ: *ib.* 15. 13 ἐγενήθη ἡ καρδία ἀνδρῶν ᾽Ισραὴλ ὀπίσω ᾽Αβεσσαλώμ.

(2) 1 *Sam.* 18. 1, 3 ἠγάπησεν αὐτὸν ᾽Ιωνάθαν κατὰ τὴν ψυχὴν αὐτοῦ. Cant. 3. 1, 2, 3, 4 ὃν ἠγάπησεν ἡ ψυχή μου.

(ix) *Of gladness* with ἀγαθύνειν, ἀγαλλιᾶσθαι, and cognate words:

(1) *Judges* 16. 25 ὅτι ἠγαθύνθη ἡ καρδία αὐτῶν: *ib.* 18. 20, 1 Kings 8. 66, 1 Chron. 16. 10, Is. 66. 14, Zach. 10. 7, Ps. 12 (13). 6 ἀγαλλιάσεται ἡ καρδία μου: *ib.* 118 (119). 111 ἀγαλλίαμα τῆς καρδίας μου: *ib.* 85 (86). 11 εὐφρανθήτω ἡ καρδία μου.

(2) *Ps.* 34 (35). 9 ἡ δὲ ψυχή μου ἀγαλλιάσεται ἐπὶ τῷ κυρίῳ: so Is. 61. 10, Prov. 23. 24 ἐπὶ δὲ υἱῷ σοφῷ εὐφραίνεται ἡ ψυχὴ αὐτοῦ.

(x) *Of hope*, with ἐλπίζειν:

(1) *Ps.* 27 (28). 7 ἐπ᾽ αὐτῷ ἤλπισεν ἡ καρδία μου.
(2) *Ps.* 129 (130). 6 ἤλπισεν ἡ ψυχή μου ἐπὶ τὸν κύριον.

(xi) Those which apply to the moral nature as a whole:

(1) *Deut.* 9. 5 διὰ τὴν ὁσιότητα τῆς καρδίας σου, 1 Kings 9. 4 ἐν ὁσιότητι καρδίας, Prov. 22. 11 ἀγαπᾷ κύριος ὁσίας καρδίας, Neh. 2. 2 πονηρία καρδίας.

(2) *Prov.* 26. 25 ἑπτὰ γάρ εἰσι πονηρίαι ἐν τῇ ψυχῇ αὐτοῦ, Is. 1. 16 ἀφέλετε τὰς πονηρίας ἀπὸ τῶν ψυχῶν ὑμῶν.

(xii) *Will and intention* are expressed by (1) καρδία, (2) πνεῦμα, especially by καρδία:

(1) In the phrase πάντα τὰ ἐν τῇ καρδίᾳ (τινὸς) ποιεῖν, 1 Sam. 9. 19, 2 Sam. 7. 3, 2 Kings 10. 20: the more complete phrase πάντα τὰ ἐν τῇ καρδίᾳ μου καὶ τὰ ἐν τῇ ψυχῇ μου ποιήσει is probably equivalent to 'all that I intend and that I desire.' So in the phrases βεβάρηται ἡ καρδία Φαραὼ του μὴ ... Ex. 7. 14, ἐσκληρύνθη ἡ καρδία αὐτοῦ Ex. 8. 19, and frequently in Exodus, ἀπέστησαν τὴν καρδίαν ... ὅπως μὴ εἰσέλθωσιν Num. 32. 9, Deut. 1. 28: and in the phrases ἐγένετο ἐπὶ τῆς καρδίας ... οἰκοδομῆσαι 1 Kings 8. 17, ἐγένετο ἐπὶ καρδίαν οἰκοδο-μῆσαι 1 Chron. 28. 2, 2 Chron. 6. 7, 8: so also τὰ ἀρεστὰ τῆς καρδίας Jer. 9. 13: 16. 11: 18. 12.

(2) *Deut.* 2. 30 ἐσκλήρυνεν ... τὸ πνεῦμα αὐτοῦ: 2 Chron. 36. 22, 2 Esdr. 1. 1 ἐξήγειρε Κύριος τὸ πνεῦμα Κύρου βασιλέως Περσῶν καὶ παρήγγειλε κηρῦξαι.

(xiii) *Desire* is expressed, perhaps exclusively, by ψυχή:

(*a*) Of food, Deut. 12. 21 φαγῇ ἐν ταῖς πόλεσί σου κατὰ τὴν ἐπιθυμίαν τῆς ψυχῆς σου: so *ib.* 14. 26, 1 Sam. 2. 16: 20. 4, 2 Sam. 3. 21, 1 Kings 11. 37, Job 33. 20, Ps. 68 (69). 11: 106 (107). 18, Prov. 6. 30: 10. 3: 13. 25: 19. 15: 25. 25, Is. 32. 6: 58. 11, Jer. 38 (31). 25: so ἐταπείνουν ἐν νηστείᾳ τὴν ψυχήν μου Ps. 34 (35). 13, τοῦ αἰτῆσαι βρώματα ταῖς ψυχαῖς αὐτῶν Ps. 77 (78). 18, ἡ δὲ ψυχὴ ὑμῶν προσώχθισεν ἐν τῷ ἄρτῳ Num. 21. 5.

(*b*) Of spiritual desire, Ps. 41 (42). 2 ἐπιποθεῖ ἡ ψυχή μου πρὸς σέ, ὁ θεός: *ib.* 62 (63). 2 : 83 (84). 3 : 118 (119). 20.

(xiv) *Mental* powers and operations are predicated of all three words:

(1) Of καρδία: (ἐπιστήμη), Ex. 36. 2 ᾧ θεὸς ἔδωκεν ἐπιστήμην ἐν τῇ καρδίᾳ: (εἰδέναι) Deut. 29. 4 ὁ θεὸς ἔδωκεν ὑμῖν καρδίαν εἰδέναι καὶ ὀφθαλμοὺς βλέπειν καὶ ὦτα ἀκούειν: 1 Kings 2. 44 τὴν κακίαν σου οὐ οἶδεν ἡ καρδία σου: (νοεῖν, διανοεῖσθαι) 1 Sam. 4. 20 οὐκ ἐνόησεν ἡ καρδία αὐτῆς: Is. 32. 6 ἡ καρδία αὐτοῦ μάταια νοήσει, Jer. 7. 31 : 19. 5 ὃ . . . οὐ διενοήθην ἐν τῇ καρδίᾳ μου: cf. Hos. 7. 11 ὡς περιστερὰ ἄνους οὐκ ἔχουσα καρδίαν (φρόνιμος, φρόνησις: σοφός, σοφία): 1 Kings 3. 12 δέδωκά σοι καρδίαν φρονίμην καὶ σοφήν: *ib.* 10. 24 τῆς φρονήσεως αὐτοῦ ἧς ἔδωκε κύριος τῇ καρδίᾳ αὐτοῦ: 2 Chron. 9. 23 τῆς σοφίας αὐτοῦ ἧς ἔδωκεν ὁ θεὸς ἐν καρδίᾳ αὐτοῦ: Job 17. 4 καρδίαν αὐτῶν ἔκρυψας ἀπὸ φρονήσεως: (συνιέναι, συνετός) Job 34. 10, 34 συνετοὶ καρδίας [Cod. A. καρδίᾳ]: Is. 6. 10 μή ποτε . . . τῇ καρδίᾳ συνῶσι: (βουλεύεσθαι) Neh. 5. 7 ἐβουλεύσατο καρδία μου ἐπ' ἐμέ.

(2) Of πνεῦμα: Ex. 28. 3 πνεῦμα σοφίας καὶ αἰσθήσεως: Deut. 34. 9, Job 15. 2 πνεῦμα συνέσεως: 1 Chron. 28. 12 τὸ παράδειγμα ὃ εἶχεν ἐν πνεύματι αὐτοῦ: Ps. 76 (77). 7 ἔσκαλλον τὸ πνεῦμά μου.

(3) Of ψυχή: Jos. 23. 14 γνώσεσθε τῇ καρδίᾳ ὑμῶν καὶ τῇ ψυχῇ ὑμῶν: Ps. 12 (13). 2 ἕως τίνος θήσομαι βουλὰς ἐν ψυχῇ μου: Ps. 138 (139). 14 ἡ ψυχή μου γινώσκει σφόδρα: Prov. 24. 14 αἴσθησῃ σοφίαν τῇ σῇ ψυχῇ: Cant. 6. 11 οὐκ ἔγνω ἡ ψυχή μου: Is. 44. 19 οὐκ ἐλογίσατο τῇ ψυχῇ αὐτοῦ.

Results.

If we gather together the results, it will be seen that in the LXX.

(1) καρδία, πνεῦμα, ψυχή are capable of being interchanged as translations of the same Hebrew words:

(2) consequently, the lines of distinction between them, whatever they may be, are not sharply drawn:

(3) a survey of the predicates which are attached to each of them shows a similar impossibility of limiting them to special groups of mental phenomena, with the exceptions that (*a*) καρδία

is most commonly used of will and intention,
(*b*) ψυχή of appetite and desire.

But this general inference as to Greek words does not of necessity apply also to their Hebrew originals. A student of the Hebrew terms must no doubt take into account the fact that at a certain time those terms conveyed to Greek minds a certain meaning, and that a certain group of them was to some extent treated as synonymous. But this fact is only one of many data for the determination of the meaning of the Hebrew terms themselves: and it must be carefully borne in mind that the study of the words by which Greek translators expressed Hebrew psychological terms is not identical with the study of Hebrew psychology.

II. Psychological terms in Philo.

The use of psychological terms, such as πνεῦμα and ψυχή, in Philo can only be understood when viewed in relation to his psychology as a whole. But that psychology is of great complexity. The complexity arises partly from the fact that he uses the same terms to designate different groups of phenomena, partly from the fact that he uses different terms to designate the same phenomena, and partly from the fact that he regards the phenomena from different points of view, sometimes using the terms or conceptions of one system of philosophy and sometimes those of another, and sometimes borrowing both terms and conceptions not from philosophy but from the Old Testament. There is in some cases the additional element of uncertainty which arises from the uncertain authorship of some of the writings which are attributed to him.

It would be beyond my present purpose to discuss that psychology in detail, or to endeavour to resolve it into the elements from which it was formed. I must be content to gather together the more important of the predicates which he attaches to the chief psychological terms, and to add to them only such brief explanations as may be necessary to develop their meaning.

I. σῶμα and ψυχή.

The conception of the duality of human nature runs through all Philo's writings. (1) We are compounded of two elements, body and soul, which are (2) allied during life, but (3) separated at death.

(1) *Leg. Alleg.* iii. 55 (i. 119) δύο ἐστὶν ἐξ ὧν συνέσταμεν ψυχή τε καὶ σῶμα.

De Ebriet. 26 (i. 372) (ἄνθρωπον) τὸ ψυχῆς καὶ σώματος ὕφασμα ἢ πλέγμα ἢ κρᾶμα ἢ ὅ τί ποτε χρὴ καλεῖν τουτὶ τὸ σύνθετον ζῶον.

De Cherubim 32 (i. 159) ἔγωγ' οὖν ἐκ ψυχῆς καὶ σώματος συνεστώς.

De Mundi Opif. 46 (i. 32) ἐκ σώματος καὶ ψυχῆς συνεστώς.

(2) *Quod det. pot. insid.* 6 (i. 194) συζυγὴ δὲ καὶ συνεταιρὶς καλεῖται Χεβρών, συμβολικῶς ἡμῶν τὸ σῶμα ὅτι συνέζευκται καὶ ὥσπερ ἑταιρίαν καὶ φιλίαν πρὸς ψυχὴν τέθειται.

(3) *Leg. Alleg.* i. 33 (i. 65) ὁ μὲν οὖν ἀνθρώπου (*sc.* θάνατος) χωρισμός ἐστι ψυχῆς καὶ σώματος.

II. σῶμα, σάρξ.

If we gather together the predicates of σῶμα, we find that the word is sometimes used in a narrower, sometimes in a wider sense.

i. The body in its strict sense is (1) a compound of earth and other elements: (2) it is the passive receptacle of soul, its dwelling-place, its temple, its prison, its tomb: (3) it is dead, and we carry about, as it were, a corpse with us.

(1) *Leg. Alleg.* iii. 55 (i. 119) τὸ μὲν οὖν σῶμα ἐκ γῆς δεδημιούργηται.

Ibid. τὸ μὲν ἐκ γῆς διαπλασθὲν σῶμα.

De Migrat. Abraham. 1 (i. 436) τὸ μὲν σῶμα καὶ ἐκ γῆς ἔλαβε τὴν σύστασιν καὶ ἀναλύεται πάλιν εἰς γῆν.

De Sacrificant. 2 (ii. 252) ἔστιν οὖν ἡμῶν ἡ κατὰ τὸ σῶμα οὐσία ἡ γῆ καὶ ὕδωρ: (and earth and water are conceived as saying to men) ἡμεῖς ἐσμὲν ἡ τοῦ σώματος ὑμῶν οὐσία· ἡμᾶς ἡ φύσις κερασαμένη, ἡ θεία τέχνη, διέπλασεν εἰς ἀνθρωπόμορφον ἰδέαν.

De Mundi Opif. 51 (i. 35). (In respect of his body man is akin to the whole visible world) συγκέκριται γὰρ ἐκ τῶν αὐτῶν, γῆς καὶ ὕδατος καὶ ἀέρος καὶ πυρός, ἑκάστου τῶν στοιχείων εἰσενεγκόντος τὸ ἐπιβάλλον μέρος πρὸς ἐκπλήρωσιν αὐταρκεστάτης ὕλης, ἣν ἔδει λαβεῖν τὸν δημιουργόν ἵνα τεχνιτεύσηται τὴν ὁρατὴν ταύτην εἰκόνα.

(2) *De Somniis* i. 5 (i. 624) ἀλλὰ καὶ ὅτι ψυχῆς ἐστιν ἀγγεῖον (sc. τὸ σῶμα) οὐκ ἀγνοοῦμεν.

Ibid. i. 20 (i. 639) τὸν συμφυᾶ τῆς ψυχῆς οἶκον, τὸ σῶμα.

De Migrat. Abraham. 5 (i. 439) τὸν σωματικὸν οἶκον: *ibid.* 2 (i. 438) ἐκφυγὼν δεσμωτήριον, τὸ σῶμα.

Quod Deus immut. 33 (i. 295) ὁ τῆς ψυχῆς οἶκος ἢ τύμβος ἢ ὁτιοῦν χρὴ καλεῖν.

De Mundi Opif. 47 (i. 33) οἶκος γάρ τις ἢ νεὼς ἱερὸς ἐτεκταίνετο ψυχῆς λογικῆς ἣν ἔμελλεν ἀγαλματοφορήσειν ἀγαλμάτων τὸ θεοειδέστατον.

Quis rer. divin. heres 14 (i. 482) ὁ μένων ἐν τῇ σώματος εἱρκτῇ λογισμός.

De agricult. 5 (i. 304) τὸν σύνθετον χοῦν, τὸν πεπλασμένον ἀνδριάντα, τὸν ψυχῆς ἔγγιστα οἶκον, ὃν ἀπὸ γενέσεως ἄχρι τελευτῆς, ἄχθος τοσοῦτον, οὐκ ἀποτίθεται νεκροφοροῦσα.

Leg. Alleg. iii. 22 (i. 100, 101) μὴ γὰρ ἄλλο τι ποιήσειε ἕκαστον ἡμῶν ποιεῖν ἢ νεκροφορεῖν, τὸ νεκρὸν ἐξ ἑαυτοῦ σῶμα ἐγειρούσης καὶ ἀμοχθὶ φερούσης τῆς ψυχῆς: *ibid.* τοῦ νεκροῦ ὄντος σώματος ἀλογεῖ.

De Gigant. 3 (i. 264) τὸν συμφυᾶ νεκρὸν ἡμῶν, τὸ σῶμα.

ii. The term body is sometimes used in an extended sense : (1) it includes the senses and desires : (2) the passions grow out of it : (3) hence it is regarded as evil, the seat of the vices, and the enemy of the higher life.

(1) *Leg. Alleg.* i. 32 (i. 64) αἰσθήσεσι σώματος.

Quod det. pot. insid. 29 (i. 212) τὸ γεῶδες σῶμα καὶ τὰς συγγενεῖς αἰσθήσεις.

Leg. Alleg. i. 32 (i. 64) τὸ σῶμα καὶ τὰς ἐπιθυμίας αὐτοῦ.

(2) *Quis rerum divin. heres* 54 (i. 511) νόθα γὰρ καὶ ξένα διανοίας τὰ σώματος ὡς ἀληθῶς πάθη, σαρκὸς ἐκπεφυκότα, ᾗ προσερρίζωνται.

De Somniis ii. 39 (i. 692) τὸ ἡμέτερον σῶμα καὶ τὰ ἐν αὐτῷ καὶ δι' αὐτὸ ἐγγινόμενα πάθη.

(3) *Leg. Alleg.* iii. 22 (i. 100) τὸν γὰρ δερμάτινον ὄγκον ἡμῶν τὸ σῶμα . . . . πονηρόν τε καὶ ἐπίβουλον τῆς ψυχῆς, οὐκ ἀγνοεῖ, καὶ νεκρὸν καὶ τεθνηκὸς ἀεί.

Leg. Alleg. i. 32 (i. 64) τὸ δὲ σῶμα οὐκ οἷον οὐ συνεργεῖ πρὸς τοῦτο (*sc.* the attainment of virtue) ἀλλὰ καὶ κωλυσιεργεῖ.

De Somniis ii. 39 (i. 693) τὰς σώματος καὶ διὰ σώματος κακίας.

In this extended sense the terms 'flesh' (σάρξ) and 'sense' (αἴσθησις) are sometimes substituted for body, and in addition to the constant antithesis between body and soul (σῶμα and ψυχή) as different physical elements, an antithesis is sometimes made not only (1) between the same terms, but also between (2) flesh and soul (σάρξ and ψυχή), (3) flesh and the divine spirit (σάρξ and τὸ θεῖον πνεῦμα), as representing different elements of consciousness and different aims of human action.

(1) *Quod Deus immut.* 11 (i. 281) τῶν γὰρ ἀνθρώπων οἱ μὲν ψυχῆς οἱ δὲ σώματος γεγόνασι φίλοι.

De Somniis ii. 39 (i. 692) ὁ σπουδαῖος κλῆρον ἔλαχε ψυχὴν καὶ τὰς ψυχῆς ἀρετάς, ὥσπερ ὁ φαῦλος ἔμπαλιν σῶμα καὶ τὰς σώματος καὶ διὰ σώματος κακίας.

De Abraham. 41 (ii. 34) οἱ ψυχῇ μᾶλλον ἢ σώματι ζῶντες.

(2) *De Gigantibus* 10 (i. 268) ἀντίθες γάρ, φησίν, ὦ γενναῖε, τὸ σαρκὸς ἀγαθὸν τῷ τῆς ψυχῆς καὶ τῷ τοῦ παντὸς ἀγαθῷ· οὐκοῦν τὸ μὲν σαρκός ἐστιν ἄλογος ἡδονή, τὸ δὲ ψυχῆς καὶ τοῦ παντὸς ὁ νοῦς τῶν ὅλων, θεός.

(3) *De Gigantibus* 7 (i. 266) αἴτιον δὲ τῆς ἀνεπιστημοσύνης μέγιστον ἡ σὰρξ καὶ ἡ πρὸς σάρκα οἰκείωσις· καὶ αὐτὸς δὲ ὁμολογεῖ φάσκων διὰ τὸ εἶναι αὐτοὺς σάρκας μὴ δύνασθαι τὸ θεῖον πνεῦμα καταμεῖναι.

Quis rer. divin. heres 12 (i. 481) ὥστε διττὸν εἶναι γένος ἀνθρώπων τὸ μὲν θείῳ πνεύματι καὶ λογισμῷ βιούντων τὸ δὲ αἵματι καὶ σαρκὸς ἡδονῇ ζώντων.

III. ψυχή.

i. The term ψυχή is used sometimes, though rarely, (1) in a very wide sense, to designate all life whether conscious or unconscious, (2) in a special sense, to designate the highest form of mind, that is, the intuitive reason as distinguished from apprehension by the senses.

(1) *De Mundi Opif.* 22 (i. 15) Nature fashions τὴν μὲν ὑγρὰν οὐσίαν (i.e. the element water, cf. infra c. 45, i. 31) εἰς τὰ τοῦ σώματος μέλη καὶ μέρη διανέμουσα τὴν δὲ πνευματικὴν (i.e. the element air) εἰς τὰς τῆς ψυχῆς δυνάμεις, τήν τε θρεπτικὴν καὶ τὴν αἰσθητικήν. But

elsewhere he distinguishes between ἕξις the power of cohesion which holds material bodies together, φύσις the power of growth, ψυχή animal life, λογικὴ ψυχή rational life: *Quod Deus immut.* 7 (i. 277) τῶν γὰρ σωμάτων τὰ μὲν ἐνεδύσατο ἕξει, τὰ δὲ φύσει, τὰ δὲ ψυχῇ, τὰ δὲ καὶ λογικῇ ψυχῇ : *De Somniis* i. 22 (i. 641) ἐποίει γὰρ αὐτὸν ὁ τεχνίτης ἀκινήτων μὲν σωμάτων ἕξιν κινουμένων δὲ ἀφαντάστως (i. e. without power of perception) φύσιν, ἤδη δὲ ὁρμῇ καὶ φαντασίᾳ χρῆσθαι δυναμένων ψυχήν.

(2) *Quis rer. divin. heres* 22 (i. 487) αἴσθησις, which is usually included in ψυχή, is made coordinate with it, thus limiting ψυχή to reason as distinguished from sensation: so *De gigant.* 3 (i. 264) ψυχὴν ἢ νοῦν· τὸ κράτιστον τῶν ἐν ἡμῖν.

But in its ordinary use ψυχή, though limited to *conscious* life, is made to cover all the phenomena of conscious life, sensations, emotions, and thoughts. These phenomena are commonly grouped into the two divisions which, in the language of the Peripatetics, he calls the irrational and rational parts of the soul, or, in language which is probably that of the Stoics, sense and mind. Hence ψυχή is said to have two meanings, or to be divided into two parts.

Quis rer. divin. heres 11 (i. 480) ψυχὴ διχῶς λέγεται, ἥ τε ὅλη καὶ τὸ ἡγεμονικὸν αὐτῆς μέρος ὅ, κυρίως εἰπεῖν, ψυχὴ ψυχῆς ἐστί.

De Migrat. Abraham. 1 (i. 436) αἴσθησις δὲ συγγενὲς καὶ ἀδελφόν ἐστι διανοίας, ἄλογον λογικῆς, ἐπειδὴ μιᾶς ἄμφω μέρη ψυχῆς ταῦτα.

De Agricult. 7 (i. 304) τῆς ψυχῆς ὥσπερ ἀπὸ μιᾶς ῥίζης ἔρνη διττὰ ἀναβλαστούσης ὧν τὸ μὲν ἄτμητον ὅλον δι᾽ ὅλων ἐαθὲν ἐπεφημίσθη νοῦς, τὸ δ᾽ ἑξαχῇ σχισθὲν εἰς ἑπτὰ φύσεις πέντε τῶν αἰσθήσεων καὶ δυοῖν ἄλλων ὀργάνων φωνητηρίου τε καὶ γονίμου.

In some passages Philo substitutes the threefold division of Plato for this Aristotelian dichotomy:

Leg. Alleg. i. 22 (i. 57) νοητέον οὖν ὅτι ἐστὶν ἡμῶν ἡ ψυχὴ τριμερὴς καὶ ἔχει μέρος τὸ μὲν λογικὸν τὸ δὲ θυμικὸν τὸ δὲ ἐπιθυμητικόν.

Ibid. iii. 38 (i. 110) τριμερῆ συμβέβηκε τὴν ψυχὴν ἡμῶν εἶναι καὶ ἔχειν μέρος μὲν ἓν λογιστικὸν δεύτερον δὲ θυμικὸν τρίτον δὲ ἐπιθυμητικόν.

De confus. ling. 7 (i. 408) τριμεροῦς ἡμῶν τῆς ψυχῆς ὑπαρχούσης τὸ μὲν νοῦς καὶ λόγος τὸ δὲ θυμὸς τὸ δὲ ἐπιθυμία κεκληρῶσθαι λέγεται.

I

Quis rer. divin. heres 45 (i. 504) ψυχὴ γὰρ τριμερής ἐστι δίχα δὲ ἕκαστον τῶν μερῶν ὡς ἐδείχθη (SC. *ante*, c. 26, i. 491) τέμνεται· μοιρῶν δὴ γενομένων ἐξ ἕβδομος εἰκότως τομεὺς ἦν ἁπάντων, ὁ ἱερὸς καὶ θεῖος λόγος.

In other passages he adopts in whole or in part the Stoical division into sense (or the five senses enumerated separately), speech, the reproductive faculty, and the governing faculty: in some of these passages he combines the Stoical and the Aristotelian divisions: in others, though he preserves the coordination of speech with sense and reason, he omits the reproductive faculty.

De mundi opific. 40 (i. 28) τῆς ἡμετέρας ψυχῆς τὸ δίχα τοῦ ἡγεμονικοῦ μέρος ἑπταχῇ σχίζεται, πρὸς πέντε αἰσθήσεις καὶ τὸ φωνητήριον ὄργανον καὶ ἐπὶ πᾶσι τὸ γόνιμον.

Leg. Alleg. i. 13 (i. 51) τούτῳ (SC. τῷ νῷ) μόνῳ ἐμπνεῖ ὁ θεὸς τοῖς δὲ ἄλλοις μέρεσι οὐκ ἀξιοῦ ταῖς τε αἰσθήσεσι καὶ τῷ λόγῳ καὶ τῷ γονίμῳ: (but immediately afterwards all these are grouped together as τὸ ἄλογον μέρος τῆς ψυχῆς).

Quis rer. div. heres 48 (i. 505) τὸ μὲν γὰρ ἄλογον ψυχῆς μέρος ἑξαχῇ διελὼν ὁ δημιουργὸς ἐξ μοίρας εἰργασάτο, ὅρασιν, γεῦσιν, ἀκοήν, ὄσφρησιν, ἀφήν, γόνιμον, φωνήν· τὸ δὲ λογικόν, ὃ δὴ νοῦς ὠνομάσθη ἄσχιστον εἴασε κατὰ τὴν τοῦ παντὸς ὁμοιότητα οὐρανοῦ.

Ibid. 22 (i. 487) παρακατέθετο δὲ σοὶ αὐτῷ ψυχήν, λόγον, αἴσθησιν ὁ ζωοπλάστης.

De congr. erud. grat. 18 (i. 533) ἐν ἡμῖν γὰρ αὐτοῖς τρία μέτρα εἶναι δοκεῖ, αἴσθησις, λόγος, νοῦς.

De Somniis i. 5 (i. 624) οὐκοῦν τέτταρα τὰ ἀνωτάτω τῶν περὶ ἡμᾶς ἐστι, σῶμα, αἴσθησις, λόγος, νοῦς.

But neither the Platonic nor the Stoical psychology penetrates his system, or forms to any appreciable extent the basis of other parts of his teaching: he adheres in the main, with whatever inconsistencies, to the division of the phenomena of consciousness into rational and irrational, or mind and sense.

ii. To each of these parts of ψυχή he assigns (1) a different essence, the one blood, the other spirit: (2) a different origin, which is expressed in theological language in the assertions that the one is of the earth, and the other breathed into man by God, or that the one was made by God's ministers and the other by God himself: (3) a different destiny, the one being mortal, the other immortal.

(1) *Quis rer. divin. heres* 11 (i. 481) ἔδοξε τῷ νομοθέτῃ διπλῆν εἶναι καὶ τὴν οὐσίαν τῆς ψυχῆς, αἷμα μὲν τὸ τῆς ὅλης τοῦ δὲ ἡγεμονικωτάτου πνεῦμα θεῖον.

Quod Deus immut. 10 (i. 279) τοῦτο τῆς ψυχῆς τὸ εἶδος [sc. ὁ νοῦς] οὐκ ἐκ τῶν αὐτῶν στοιχείων ἐξ ὧν τὰ ἄλλα ἀπετελεῖτο διεπλάσθη, καθαρωτέρας δὲ καὶ ἀμείνονος ἔλαχε τῆς οὐσίας.

De Concupiscent. 10 (ii. 356) τὸ μὲν αἷμα . . . . οὐσία ψυχῆς ἐστιν οὐχὶ τῆς νοερᾶς καὶ λογικῆς ἀλλὰ τῆς αἰσθητικῆς . . . . ἐκείνης [sc. τῆς νοερᾶς] γὰρ οὐσία πνεῦμα θεῖον.

(2) *Leg. Alleg.* i. 13 (i. 51) τῶν γὰρ γινομένων τὰ μὲν καὶ ὑπὸ θεοῦ γέγονεν καὶ δι᾽ αὐτοῦ, τὰ δὲ ὑπὸ θεοῦ μὲν οὔ, δι᾽ αὐτοῦ δέ· τὰ μὲν ἄριστα καὶ ὑπὸ θεοῦ γέγονε καὶ δι᾽ αὐτοῦ . . . . τούτων καὶ ὁ νοῦς ἐστι· τὸ δὲ ἄλογον ὑπὸ θεοῦ μὲν γέγονεν οὐ διὰ θεοῦ δέ, ἀλλὰ διὰ τοῦ λογικοῦ τοῦ ἄρχοντός τε καὶ βασιλεύοντος ἐν ψυχῇ.

De profugis 13 (i. 556) διαλέγεται μὲν οὖν [referring to the words ποιήσωμεν ἄνθρωπον in Gen. i. 26] ὁ τῶν ὅλων πατὴρ ταῖς ἑαυτοῦ δυνάμεσιν αἷς τὸ θνητὸν ἡμῶν τῆς ψυχῆς μέρος ἔδωκε διαπλάττειν, μιμουμέναις τὴν αὐτοῦ τέχνην, ἡνίκα τὸ λογικὸν ἐν ἡμῖν ἐμόρφου, δικαιῶν ὑπὸ μὲν ἡγεμόνος τὸ ἡγεμονικὸν ἐν ψυχῇ, τὸ δὲ ὑπήκοον πρὸς ὑπηκόων δημιουργεῖσθαι.

De Confus. ling. 35 (i. 432) τὴν τούτου (sc. of the irrational part of the soul) ὁ θεὸς περιῆψε καὶ τοῖς ὑπαρχοῖς αὐτοῦ λέγων 'ποιήσωμεν ἄνθρωπον,' ἵνα αἱ μὲν τοῦ νοῦ κατορθώσεις ἐπ᾽ αὐτὸν ἀναφέρωνται μόνον ἐπ᾽ ἄλλους δὲ αἱ ἁμαρτίαι. (He goes on, as in the preceding passage and elsewhere, to account thus for the presence of evil and sin among men: God Himself is the direct author only of good).

(3) *Leg. Alleg.* ii. 24 (i. 83) δύο γένη φορεῖ ἡ ψυχὴ τὸ μὲν θεῖον τὸ δὲ φθαρτόν.

Quod Deus immut. 10 (i. 279) μόνον τῶν ἐν ἡμῖν ἄφθαρτον ἔδοξεν εἶναι τὴν διάνοιαν.

IV. *The lower manifestations of* ψυχή.

The lower or irrational part of ψυχή, of which the essence is blood, consists of those phenomena of consciousness which are common to man with the brutes, and which may consequently be regarded as phenomena simply of physical life. It is admitted, in language which will be quoted below, that those phenomena as they actually occur in man are interpenetrated with mind, and could not be what they are without mind. At the same time a real as well as a logical distinction is drawn between the functions and phenomena of sense and those of mind.

i. The senses have, as mere functions of the animal life, (1) a certain dull power of feeling, i. e. of acquiring knowledge of external things: (2) their precise function is to present to the mind images of present objects. (3) To such objects they are limited : for they neither remember the past nor anticipate the future. (4) They are cognizant of the presence of objects, but cannot form judgments upon them : in Philo's phraseology they know σώματα but not πράγματα. (5) They are so far independent of mind that if the mind were to tell them not to act, they would refuse to obey.

(1) In *De congr. erud. grat.* 25 (i. 539, 540) he uses the difference between the senses in themselves, and the senses acting concurrently with mind, as an illustration of the difference between arts and sciences : of which he says that the former ἀμυδρῶς ὁρῶσιν, the latter τηλαυγῶς καὶ σφόδρα ἐναργῶς καταλαμβάνουσιν.

ὥσπερ γὰρ ὀφθαλμοὶ μὲν ὁρῶσιν, ὁ δὲ νοῦς δι' ὀφθαλμῶν τηλαυγέστερον καὶ ἀκούει μὲν ὦτα, ὁ δὲ νοῦς δι' ὤτων ἄμεινον καὶ ὀσφραίνονται μὲν οἱ μυκτῆρες, ἡ δὲ ψυχὴ διὰ ῥινῶν ἐναργέστερον καὶ αἱ ἄλλαι αἰσθήσεις τῶν καθ' αὑτὰς ἀντιλαμβάνονται καθαρώτερον δὲ καὶ εἰλικρινέστερον ἡ διάνοια, κυρίως γὰρ εἰπεῖν ἥδ' ἐστὶν ὀφθαλμὸς μὲν ὀφθαλμῶν ἀκοὴ δ' ἀκοῆς καὶ ἑκάστης τῶν αἰσθήσεων αἴσθησις εἰλικρινεστέρα, χρωμένη μὲν ἐκείναις ὡς ἐν δικαστηρίῳ ὑπηρέτισι δικάζουσα δὲ αὐτὴ τὰς φύσεις τῶν ὑποκειμένων ὡς τοῖς μὲν συναινεῖν τὰ δὲ ἀποστρέφεσθαι, οὕτως αἱ μὲν λεγόμεναι μέσαι τέχναι ταῖς κατὰ τὸ σῶμα δυνάμεσιν ἐοικυῖαι τοῖς θεωρήμασιν ἐντυγχάνουσι κατά τινας ἁπλᾶς ἐπιβολὰς ἀκριβέστερον δὲ ἐπιστῆμαι καὶ σὺν ἐξετάσει περιττῇ.

De mundi opif. 59 (i. 40) . . . . τὸν νοῦν ᾧ τὰ φανέντα ἐκτὸς εἴσω κομίζουσαι διαγγέλλουσι καὶ ἐπιδεικνύνται τοὺς τέπους ἑκάστων, ἐνσφραγιζόμεναι τὸ ὅμοιον πάθος.

(2) *De Somniis* i. 5 (i. 624) (αἱ αἰσθήσεις) ἄγγελοι διανοίας εἰσὶν

διαγγέλλουσαι χρώματα, σχήματα, φώνας, ἀτμῶν καὶ χυλῶν ἰδιότητας, συνόλως σώματα καὶ ὅσαι ποιότητες ἐν τούτοις.

Leg. Alleg. iii. 19 (i. 99) ὅταν γὰρ ἡ αἴσθησις ἐπιβάλλουσα τῷ αἰσθητῷ πληρωθῇ τῆς αὐτοῦ φαντασίας εὐθὺς καὶ ὁ νοῦς συμβέβληκε καὶ ἀντελάβετο καὶ τρόπον τινὰ τροφῆς τῆς ἀπ' ἐκείνου πεπλήρωται.

(3) *Ibid.* ii. 12 (i. 74) ἡ αἴσθησις φύσει νῦν ἐστί, κατὰ τὸν ἐνεστῶτα χρόνον ὑφισταμένη μόνον, ὁ μὲν γὰρ νοῦς τῶν τριῶν ἐφάπτεται χρόνων· καὶ γὰρ τὰ πάροντα νοεῖ καὶ τῶν παρεληλυθότων μέμνηται καὶ τὰ μέλλοντα προσδοκᾷ· ἡ δὲ αἴσθησις οὔτε μελλόντων ἀντιλαμβάνεται οὐδ' ἀνάλογόν τι πάσχει προσδοκίᾳ ἢ ἐλπίδι οὔτε παρεληλυθότων μέμνηται ἀλλ' ὑπὸ τοῦ ἤδη κινοῦντος καὶ πάροντος μόνον πάσχειν πέφυκεν, οἷον ὀφθαλμὸς λευκαίνεται νῦν ὑπὸ τοῦ παρόντος λευκοῦ ὑπὸ δὲ τοῦ μὴ παρόντος οὐδὲν πάσχει.

Ibid. iii. 16 (i. 97) οὔτε γὰρ ἡ ὅρασις οὔθ' ἡ ἀκοὴ οὔτε τις τῶν ἄλλων αἰσθήσεων διδακτή, ὥστε οὐ δύναται κατάληψιν πραγμάτων ποιήσασθαι· μόνων γὰρ σωμάτων διακριτικὴν εἰργάσατο αὐτὴν ὁ ἐργασάμενος : cf. infra c. 18.

(4) *Ibid.* iii. 35 (i. 109) τυφλὸν γὰρ φύσει ἡ αἴσθησις ἅτε ἄλογος οὖσα ἐπεὶ τὸ λογικὸν ἐξομματοῦται· παρ' ὃ καὶ μόνῳ τούτῳ τὰ πράγματα καταλαμβάνομεν αἰσθήσει δὲ οὐκέτι· μόνα γὰρ τὰ σώματα φαντασιούμεθα δι' αἰσθήσεως.

(5) *Ibid.* iii. 18 (i. 98) ἐὰν γοῦν βουληθῇ ὁ νοῦς προστάξαι τῇ ὁράσει μὴ ἰδεῖν, οὐδὲν ἧττον αὕτη τὸ ὑποκείμενον ὄψεται.

ii. On the other hand there is in sensation a mental element : the senses, even as powers of the physical organism, are set in motion by mind, and cannot act without it.

Leg. Alleg. ii. 12 (i. 74) πάντα γὰρ ὅσα πάσχει ἡ αἴσθησις οὐκ ἄνευ νοῦ ὑπομένει.

Ibid. iii. 65 (i. 124) ἀπὸ γὰρ τούτου (sc. τοῦ νοῦ) καθάπερ τινὸς πηγῆς αἱ αἰσθητικαὶ τείνονται δυνάμεις, μάλιστα κατὰ τὸν ἱερώτατον Μωϋσῆν ὃς ἐκ τοῦ Ἀδὰμ πεπλάσθαι φησὶ τὴν γυναῖκα, τὴν αἴσθησιν ἐκ τοῦ νοῦ.

Ibid. c. 67 ἀρχὴ δὲ ἦν αἰσθήσεως ὁ νοῦς.

De posterit. Cain. 36 (i. 249) ἢ οὐκ ἂν εἴποι τις τῶν αἰσθήσεων ἑκάστην ὥσπερ ἀπὸ πηγῆς τοῦ νοῦ ποτίζεσθαι . . . . ; οὐδεὶς γ' οὖν εὐφρονῶν εἴποι ἂν ὀφθαλμοὺς ὁρᾶν ἀλλὰ νοῦν δι' ὀφθαλμῶν οὐδ' ὦτα ἀκούειν ἀλλὰ δι' ὤτων ἐκεῖνον οὐδὲ μυκτῆρας ὀσφραίνεσθαι ἀλλὰ διὰ μυκτήρων τὸ ἡγεμονικόν.

Leg. Alleg. i. 11 (i. 49) God 'rains' the objects of sense upon the senses, i. e. He causes images from those objects to fall upon the senses; but there would be no use in His doing this, i. e. the senses would not act ἐὰν μὴ πηγῆς τρόπον ὁ νοῦς τείνας ἑαυτὸν ἄχρι τῆς αἰσθήσεως κινήσῃ τε αὐτὴν ἠρεμοῦσαν καὶ ἀναγάγῃ πρὸς ἀντίληψιν τοῦ ὑποκειμένου.

De profugis 32 (i. 573) τὸ ἡγεμονικὸν ἡμῶν, ἐοικὸς πηγῇ, δυνάμεις πολλὰς οἷα διὰ γῆς φλεβῶν ἄχρι τῶν αἰσθήσεων ὀργάνων ἀνομβροῦν, τὰς δυνάμεις ταύτας ὀφθαλμῶν, ὤτων, ῥινῶν, τῶν ἄλλων ἀποστέλλει.

This relation of subordination between the physical and the mental elements is expressed by several metaphors: the senses are described as marionettes moved by mind, as its messengers, its handmaidens, its helpmates, its satellites, the purveyors of its food: in one passage νοῦς is spoken of as being a God to the senses, as Moses was to Pharaoh.

De mundi opif. 40 (i. 28) ἃ δὴ πάντα (sc. the senses and speech) καθάπερ ἐν τοῖς θαύμασιν (i. e. in puppet-shows) ὑπὸ τοῦ ἡγεμονικοῦ νευροσπαστούμενα (i.e. worked by strings, like puppets or marionettes) τότε μὲν ἠρεμεῖ τότε δὲ κινεῖται.

Ibid. 59 (i. 40) The senses offer their gifts to their master, reason, θεραπαινίδων τρόπον.

Leg. Alleg. ii. 3 (i. 68) πῶς ἡμῶν ὁ νοῦς καταλαμβάνει ὅτι τουτὶ λευκὸν ἢ μέλαν ἐστὶν εἰ μὴ βοηθῷ χρησάμενος ὁράσει;

De plantat. Noe 32 (i. 349) τὸ τρέφον τὸν νοῦν ἡμῶν ἐστιν αἴσθησις.

Quod det. pot. insid. 23 (i. 207) τὰς δὲ νοῦ δορυφόρους αἰσθήσεις.

De Somniis i. 5 (i. 624) καὶ ὅτι ἄγγελοι διανοίας εἰσὶν διαγγέλλουσαι χρώματα .... καὶ ὅτι δορυφόροι ψυχῆς εἰσιν ὅσα ἂν ἴδωσι καὶ ἀκούσωσι δηλοῦσαι ....

Leg. Alleg. i. 13 (i. 51) ὡσανεὶ γὰρ θεός ἐστι τοῦ ἀλόγου ὁ νοῦς, παρ' ὃ καὶ Μωϋσῆν οὐκ ὤκνησεν εἰπεῖν θεὸν τοῦ Φαραώ.

But there is a metaphor sometimes used which seems to express more exactly than the preceding the relation in which the physical and mental elements stand to each other. It is that of a marriage: and it is interwoven with an allegorical interpretation of the history of Adam and Eve. Mind is represented as leaving its father, the God of the Universe, and its mother, the virtue and wisdom of God, and, joining itself to the body, becomes one flesh with it.

Leg. Alleg. ii. 14 (i. 75) ἕνεκα τῆς αἰσθήσεως ὁ νοῦς ὅταν αὐτῇ δουλωθῇ καταλείπει καὶ τὸν πατέρα, τὸν ὅλων θεόν, καὶ τὴν μητέρα τῶν συμπάντων τὴν ἀρετὴν καὶ σοφίαν τοῦ θεοῦ καὶ προσκολλᾶται καὶ ἐνοῦται τῇ αἰσθήσει καὶ ἀναλύεται εἰς αἴσθησιν ἵνα γίνωνται μία σὰρξ καὶ ἓν πάθος οἱ δύο.

iii. In itself sensation, whether acting alone or with mind, is neither good nor bad.

Leg. Alleg. iii. 21 (i. 100) λεκτέον οὖν ὅτι ἡ αἴσθησις οὔτε τῶν φαύλων οὔτε τῶν σπουδαίων ἐστὶν ἀλλὰ μέσον τι αὕτη καὶ κοινὸν σοφοῦ τε καὶ ἄφρονος καὶ γενομένη μὲν ἐν ἄφρονι γίνεται φαύλη ἐν ἀστείῳ δὲ σπουδαία.

But sensation gives not only knowledge but also pleasure and pain. Out of it the passions grow: the statement that the passions are rooted in the body and spring out of it (above p. 111) is modified into the statement that they are the products of irrational consciousness.

Leg. Alleg. ii. 3 (i. 67) τὸ δὲ ἄλογον (sc. μέρος τῆς ψυχῆς) αἴσθησίς ἐστι καὶ τὰ ταύτης ἔκγονα πάθη.

Ibid. p. 68 μιᾶς γάρ ἐστι ψυχῆς μέρη καὶ γεννήματα ἥ τε αἴσθησις καὶ τὰ πάθη.

Quod Deus immut. 11 (i. 28) τὰ ψυχῆς ἄλογα πάθη.

Quis rer. divin. heres 13 (i. 482) .... ἑτέρου ψυχῆς τμήματος ὅπερ ἄλογον ὑπάρχον αἵματι πεφύραται, θυμοὺς ζέοντας καὶ πεπυρωμένας ἐπιθυμίας ἀναφλέγον.

Hence the sense, 'the more corporeal element of the soul' (τὸ σωματοειδέστερον ψυχῆς μέρος, *De congr. erud. grat.* 5, i. 522) may become the same as 'flesh,' σάρξ (*Leg. Alleg.* ii. 14, i. 75), and is in one passage described by the phrase 'the soul of the flesh' (σαρκὸς ψυχή *Quod det. pot. insid.* 23, i. 207).

Leg. Alleg. ii. 14. (i. 75) ὅταν γὰρ τὸ κρεῖττον, ὁ νοῦς, ἐνωθῇ τῷ χείρονι, τῇ αἰσθήσει, ἀναλύεται εἰς τὸ χεῖρον τὸ σαρκὸς γένος, τὴν παθῶν αἰτίαν αἴσθησιν· ὅταν δὲ τὸ χεῖρον, ἡ αἴσθησις, ἀκολουθήσῃ τῷ κρείττονι, τῷ νῷ, οὐκέτι ἔσται σὰρξ ἀλλὰ ἀμφότερα νοῦς.

The sense is not merely logically and physically distinct from mind but at constant variance with it. Sometimes the mind wins the battle, and then sense is merged in mind : more frequently the flesh proves the stronger, and mind is lost in sense. This latter contingency is sometimes described by the expressive phrase 'the death of the soul': for there are two kinds of death, he says, the death of a man, which is the separation of soul and body, and the death of the soul, which is the loss of virtue and the acquisition of vice.

Leg. Alleg. ii. 14 (i. 75) ὅταν γὰρ τὸ κρεῖττον, ὁ νοῦς, ἐνωθῇ τῷ χείρονι, τῇ αἰσθήσει, ἀναλύεται εἰς τὸ χεῖρον, τὸ σαρκὸς γένος, τὴν παθῶν αἰτίαν αἴσθησιν· ὅταν δὲ τὸ χεῖρον, ἡ αἴσθησις, ἀκολουθήσῃ τῷ κρείττονι, τῷ νῷ, οὐκέτι ἔσται σὰρξ ἀλλὰ ἀμφότερα νοῦς.

Leg. Alleg. i. 33 (i. 64, 65) διττός ἐστι θάνατος ὁ μὲν ἀνθρώπου ὁ δὲ ψυχῆς ἴδιος· ὁ μὲν οὖν ἀνθρώπου χωρισμός ἐστι ψυχῆς ἀπὸ σώματος, ὁ δὲ ψυχῆς θάνατος ἀρετῆς μὲν φθορά ἐστι, κακίας δὲ ἀνάληψις· παρ' ὃ καί φησιν οὐκ ἀποθανεῖν αὐτὸ μόνον ἀλλὰ ' θανάτῳ ἀποθανεῖν ' (Gen. 2. 17), δηλῶν οὐ τὸν κοινόν, ἀλλὰ τὸν ἴδιον καὶ κατ' ἐξοχὴν θάνατον ὅς ἐστι ψυχῆς ἐντυμβενομένης πάθεσι καὶ κακίαις ἁπάσαις.

De poster. Caini 21 (i. 239) ψυχῆς θάνατος ὃς κατὰ πάθους ἀλόγου ἐστὶν αὐτῆς μεταβολή.

Quod det. pot. insid. 20 (i. 205) τέθνηκε δὲ . . . . τὸν ψυχικὸν θάνατον, ἀρετῆς καθ' ἣν ἄξιος μόνην ἐστὶ ζῆν ἀποσχοινισθείς.

Fragm. ap. Joh. Damasc. sacr. parall. p. 748 a (ii. 653) ἐπειδὴ δὲ ἡδονὴν ἐζήτησε δι' ἧς ψυχικὸς θάνατος ἐπιγίνεται τῇ γῇ προσενεμήθη (with reference to Gen. 3. 19).

Quis rer. divin. heres 11 (i. 480) . . . . αἴσθησιν ἦν καὶ ὁ γήινος νοῦς, ὄνομα Ἀδάμ, ἰδὼν διαπλασθεῖσαν τὸν ἑαυτοῦ θάνατον ζωὴν ἐκείνης ὠνόμασεν ' ἐκάλεσε ' γάρ, φησιν, ''Ἀδὰμ ὄνομα γυναικὸς αὐτοῦ Ζωήν, ὅτι αὕτη μήτηρ πάντων τῶν ζώντων ' τῶν πρὸς ἀλήθειαν τὸν ψυχῆς δήπου τεθνηκότων βίον.

V. *The higher manifestations of* ψυχή.

But although the higher elements of consciousness are usually so blended with the lower as to be sometimes overpowered by them, they are in their essence independent of them. It is a cardinal point of Philo's psychology that pure intelligence, ψυχή or νοῦς in its highest form, is not a phase or development of animal life, but an element infused into animal life from above and separable from it.

The nature of this higher element is expressed sometimes in the terms of physical philosophy and sometimes in the terms of theology. It is described sometimes as a part of the 'quinta essentia,' the purest of all modes of existence: and sometimes as a part of the divine nature. The terms which are used to describe its relation to God are derived from several sources: some of them come from Greek philosophy, for the belief that the mind is a part of God was not peculiar to Judaism; but the majority of them embody and combine the statements of the book of Genesis, that man was made 'in the image of God,' and that God breathed into man 'the breath of life.' Sometimes Philo himself expressly distinguishes between the philosophical and the theological modes of stating the same facts (e. g. De plantat. Noe 5, i. 332, see below): and sometimes also in adopting a philosophical term he attaches to it a theological sense, e. g. in adopting the Stoical term ἀπόσπασμα he guards himself against the inference which might be drawn from it that the essence of man is separate from that of God, τέμνεται γὰρ οὐδὲν τοῦ θείου κατ' ἀπάρτησιν (i.e. so as to be detached) ἀλλὰ μόνον ἐκτείνεται Quod det. pot. insid. 24 (i. 209).

(1) In the following passages he speaks of it in the terms of philosophy:

Quis rer. divin. heres 57 (i. 514) τὸ δὲ νοερὸν καὶ οὐράνιον τῆς ψυχῆς γένος πρὸς αἰθέρα τὸν καθαρώτατον ὡς πρὸς πατέρα ἀφίξεται· πέμπτη γάρ, ὡς ὁ τῶν ἀρχαίων λόγος, ἔστω τις οὐσία κυκλοφορητικὴ τῶν τεσσάρων κατὰ τὸ κρεῖττον διαφέρουσα, ἐξ ἧς οἵ τε ἀστέρες καὶ ὁ σύμπας οὐρανὸς ἔδοξε γεγενῆσθαι ἧς κατὰ τὸ ἀκόλουθον θετέον καὶ τὴν ἀνθρωπίνην ψυχὴν ἀπόσπασμα.

Quod Deus immut. 10 (i. 279) τοῦτο τῆς ψυχῆς τὸ εἶδος οὐκ ἐκ τῶν αὐτῶν στοιχείων ἐξ ὧν τὰ ἄλλα ἀπετελεῖτο διεπλάσθη, καθαρωτέρας δὲ καὶ ἀμείνονος ἔλαχε τῆς οὐσίας ἐξ ἧς αἱ θεῖαι φύσεις ἐδημιουργοῦντο.

De profugis 24 (i. 565) ἰδοὺ ὁ νοῦς, ἔνθερμον καὶ πεπυρωμένον πνεῦμα.

De decem orac. 25 (ii. 202) ἄνθρωπος δὲ ζῷον ἄριστον κατὰ τὸ κρεῖττον τῶν ἐν αὐτῷ, τὴν ψυχήν, συγγενέστατος τῷ καθαρωτάτῳ τῆς οὐσίας οὐρανῷ, ὡς δὲ ὁ πλεῖστων λόγος, καὶ τῷ τοῦ κόσμου πατρί, τῶν ἐπὶ γῆς ἁπάντων οἰκειότατον ἀπεικόνισμα καὶ μίμημα τῆς ἀϊδίου καὶ εὐδαίμονος ἰδέας τὸν νοῦν λαβών.

(2) In the following passages he speaks of it in the terms of theology, or in the terms of philosophy and theology combined.

De mundi opif. 46 (i. 32) τὸ γὰρ 'ἐνεφύσησεν' οὐδὲν ἦν ἕτερον ἢ πνεῦμα θεῖον ἀπὸ τῆς μακαρίας καὶ εὐδαίμονος ἐκείνης φύσεως ἀποικίαν τὴν ἐνθάδε στειλάμενον ἐπ' ὠφελείᾳ τοῦ γένους ἡμῶν.

Ibid. 51 (i. 35) πᾶς ἄνθρωπος κατὰ μὲν τὴν διάνοιαν ᾠκείωται θείῳ λόγῳ τῆς μακαρίας φύσεως ἐκμαγεῖον ἢ ἀπόσπασμα ἢ ἀπαύγασμα γεγονώς.

Quod det. pot. insid. 23 (i. 207) ἡ μὲν οὖν κοινὴ πρὸς τὰ ἄλογα δύναμις οὐσίαν ἔλαχεν αἷμα ἡ δὲ ἐκ λογικῆς ἀπορρυεῖσα πηγῆς τὸ πνεῦμα, οὐκ ἀέρα κινούμενον ἀλλὰ τύπον τινὰ καὶ χαρακτῆρα θείας δυνάμεως ἣν ὀνόματι κυρίῳ Μωϋσῆς 'εἰκόνα' καλεῖ, δηλῶν ὅτι ἀρχέτυπον μὲν φύσεως λογικῆς ὁ θεός ἐστι μίμημα δὲ καὶ ἀπεικόνισμα ἄνθρωπος.

Ibid. 24 (i. 208) ψυχὴν οὐδεμίαν τῷ σώματι ὁ ποιῶν εἰργάζετο ἱκανὴν ἐξ ἑαυτῆς τὸν ποιητὴν ἰδεῖν· λογισάμενος δὲ μεγάλα ὀνήσειν τὸ δημιούργημα εἰ λάβοι τοῦ δημιουργήσαντος ἔννοιαν, εὐδαιμονίας γὰρ καὶ μακαριότητος ὅρος οὗτος, ἄνωθεν ἐπέπνει τῆς ἰδίου θειότητος.

De plantat. Noe 5 (i. 332) οἱ μὲν ἄλλοι τῆς αἰθερίου φύσεως τὸν ἡμέτερον νοῦν μοῖραν εἰπόντες εἶναι, συγγένειαν ἀνθρώπῳ πρὸς αἰθέρα ἀνῆψαν· ὁ δὲ μέγας Μωϋσῆς οὐδένι τῶν γεγονότων τῆς λογικῆς ψυχῆς τὸ εἶδος ὁμοίως ὠνόμασεν, ἀλλ' εἶπεν αὐτὴν τοῦ θείου καὶ ἀοράτου εἰκόνα.

Quis rer. divin. heres 12 (i. 481) θείας εἰκόνος ἐμφερὲς ἐκμαγεῖον.

Ibid. 13 (i. 482) ὁ καταπνευσθεὶς ἄνωθεν οὐρανίου τε καὶ θείας μοίρας ἐπιλαχών, ὁ καθαρώτατος νοῦς.

Ibid. 38 (i. 498) [νοῦς] ἀπ' οὐρανοῦ καταπνευσθεὶς ἄνωθεν.

De mutat. nomin. 39 (i. 612) λογισμὸς .... τῆς τοῦ παντὸς ψυχῆς ἀπόσπασμα ἢ ὅπερ ὁσιώτερον εἰπεῖν τοῖς κατὰ Μωϋσὴν φιλοσοφοῦσιν, εἰκόνος θείας ἐκμαγεῖον ἐμφερές.

Vita Mosis iii. 36 (ii. 176) ὁ γὰρ νοῦς οὐκ ἂν οὕτως εὐσκόπως εὐθυβόλησεν εἰ μὴ καὶ θεῖον ἦν πνεῦμα τὸ ποδηγετοῦν πρὸς αὐτὴν τὴν ἀλήθειαν.

De Concupiscent. 11 (ii. 356) τὸ δὲ ἐμφυσώμενον δῆλον ὡς αἰθέριον ἦν πνεῦμα καὶ εἰ δή τι αἰθερίου πνεύματος κρεῖττον ἄτε τῆς μακαρίας καὶ τρισμακαρίας φύσεως ἀπαύγασμα.

This divine and immortal part of us is not only separable in its nature from the fleshly and mortal part, but it sometimes even in life disentangles itself from the body, sense, and speech, and contemplates the realities to which it is akin. The mist is dispersed and it sees clearly (*De migrat. Abraham.* 36, i. 467). The mind is constantly emancipating us from our captivity (*Quod Deus immut.* 10, i. 279 τὸ ἐξαιρούμενον εἰς ἐλευθερίαν, νοῦς). Its life in the body is but a temporary sojourn. The true home and fatherland of the soul is not the body but heaven: and to that home and fatherland the philosopher is always trying to return.

De Somniis i. 8 (i. 627) κινεῖται γὰρ ἡμῶν ἡ ψυχὴ πολλάκις μὲν ἐφ᾽ ἑαυτῆς, ὅλον τὸν σωματικὸν ὄγκον ἐκδῦσα καὶ τὸν τῶν αἰσθήσεων ὄχλον ἀποδρᾶσα.

De migrat. Abraham. 35 (i. 466). The power of our mind to rid itself of the senses, whether in sleep or when awake, is an argument for the separate personality of the Creator: εἰ μὴ νομίζετε τὸν μὲν ἡμέτερον νοῦν ἀποδυσάμενον σῶμα, αἴσθησιν, λόγον, δίχα τούτων γυμνὸν δύνασθαι τὰ ὄντα ὁρᾶν, τὸν δὲ τῶν ὅλων νοῦν τὸν θεὸν οὐκ ἔξω τῆς ὑλικῆς φύσεως πάσης ἑστάναι, περιέχοντα οὐ περιεχόμενον.

De Gigantibus 4 (i. 264) αὗται μὲν οὖν εἰσι ψυχαὶ τῶν ἄνωθέν πως φιλοσοφησάντων, ἐξ ἀρχῆς ἄχρι τέλους μελετῶσαι τὸν μετὰ σωμάτων ἀποθνήσκειν βίον ἵνα τῆς ἀσωμάτου καὶ ἀφθάρτου παρὰ τῷ ἀγεννήτῳ καὶ ἀφθάρτῳ ζωῆς μεταλάχωσιν.

De agricull. 14 (i. 310) τῷ γὰρ ὄντι πᾶσα μὲν ψυχὴ σοφοῦ πατρίδα μὲν οὐρανὸν ξένην δὲ γῆν ἔλαχε.

De confus. ling. 17 (i. 416) ἐπειδὰν οὖν ἐνδιατρίψασαι σώμασι τὰ αἰσθητὰ καὶ θνητὰ δι᾽ αὐτῶν πάντα κατίδωσιν, ἐπανέρχονται ἐκεῖσε πάλιν ὅθεν ὡρμήθησαν τὸ πρῶτον, πατρίδα μὲν τὸν οὐράνιον χῶρον ἐν ᾧ πολιτεύονται ξένον δὲ τὸν περίγειον ἐν ᾧ παρῴκησαν νομίζουσαι.

Quis rer. divin. heres 57 (i. 514). The bodily parts of us are resolved into the four elements, τὸ δὲ νοερὸν καὶ οὐράνιον τῆς ψυχῆς γένος πρὸς αἰθέρα τὸν καθαρώτατον ὡς πρὸς πατέρα ἀφίξεται.

VI. ψυχικός.

It is so reasonable to expect that the adjective ψυχικὸς should follow in Philo the varieties of meaning of its substantive, that the word would not need a separate notice if it were not for the special senses in which it is found in both the New Testament and later Greek. It is clear that although those special senses of ψυχικὸς are not inconsistent with its use in Philo, the word had not yet become narrowed to them: it is used, as ψυχὴ is used, in reference (1) sometimes to animal life, (2) sometimes to the common human life of feeling and passion, (3) sometimes to spiritual life or the highest activity of thought.

(1) *Leg. Alleg.* ii. 7 (i. 71) ὁ γυμνὸς καὶ ἀνενδέτος σώματι νοῦς . . . . πολλὰς ἔχει δυνάμεις, ἑκτικήν [*i. e.* the power of cohesion], φυτικήν, ψυχικήν, λογικήν, διανοητικήν, ἄλλας μυρίας κατά τε εἴδη καὶ γένη.

Ibid. 13 (i. 74) ὁ γὰρ νοῦς καθάπερ ἐδήλωσα, ὅτε ἐγεννᾶτο, σὺν πολλαῖς δυνάμεσι καὶ ἕξεσιν ἐγεννᾶτο, λογικῇ, ψυχικῇ, φυτικῇ, ὥστε καὶ αἰσθητικῇ.

(2) *Leg. Alleg.* ii. 21 (i. 81, 82). Solitude does not necessarily give a man freedom from the stings of sense and passion, and, on the other hand, ἔστι δὲ ὅτε καὶ ἐν πλήθει μυριάνδρῳ ἐρημῶ τὴν διάνοιαν, τὸν ψυχικὸν ὄχλον [the crowd of sensations and passions] σκεδάσαντος θεοῦ καὶ διδάξαντός με ὅτι οὐ τόπων διαφοραὶ τό τε εὖ καὶ χεῖρον ἐργάζονται ἀλλ᾽ ὁ κινῶν θεὸς καὶ ἄγων ᾗ ἂν προαιρῆται τὸ τῆς ψυχῆς ὄχημα.

Ibid. iii. 17 (i. 98) οἱ φοβούμενοι καὶ τρέμοντες ὑπ᾽ ἀνανδρίας καὶ δειλίας ψυχικῆς.

De Cherubim 24 (i. 154) of effeminate men whose strength is broken before its proper time, μετ᾽ ἐκλύσεως ψυχικῶν δυνάμεων.

Ibid. 30 (i. 158) as frescoes and pictures and mosaics adorn a house, and minister delight to its inmates, οὕτως ἡ τῶν ἐγκυκλίων ἐπιστήμη τὸν ψυχικὸν οἶκον ἅπαντα διακοσμεῖ, each kind of knowledge having some peculiar charm.

(3) *Leg. Alleg.* ii. 15 (i. 75) of the soul which, putting off the sights and sounds of sense, εἰσελεύσεται σπεῖσαι τὸ ψυχικὸν αἷμα καὶ θυμιᾶσαι ὅλον τὸν νοῦν τῷ σωτῆρι καὶ εὐεργέτῃ θεῷ.

De congr. erud. grat. 19 (i. 534) τοῦτ᾽ ἔστι, κυρίως εἰπεῖν, τὸ ψυχικὸν Πάσχα, ἡ παντὸς πάθους καὶ παντὸς αἰσθητοῦ διάβασις πρὸς τὸ δέκατον ὃ δὴ νοητόν ἐστι καὶ θεῖον.

VII. νοῦς.

For the term ψυχή, in all its senses, Philo sometimes substitutes the term νοῦς. The distinctions which exist between the terms in both earlier and later philosophy sometimes wholly disappear: and although νοῦς is used for the highest manifestations of thought, it is also used, as both ψυχή and πνεῦμα are used, for purely physical forces.

(1) It is simply convertible with ψυχή: e.g.—

De Gigant. 3 (i. 264) ψυχὴν ἢ νοῦν τὸ κράτιστον τῶν ἐν ἡμῖν.

Quis rer. divin. heres 22 (i. 487): Philo enumerates ψυχήν, αἴσθησιν, λόγον, and immediately afterwards substitutes τοῦ νοῦ where τῆς ψυχῆς would be expected.

De congr. erud. grat. 25 (i. 540) in a co-ordinate enumeration we find ὁ δὲ νοῦς .... ὁ δὲ νοῦς .... ἡ δὲ ψυχή.

(2) It is used, like ψυχή, of the highest powers of thought, those by which we have cognizance of τὰ νοητὰ and of God.

Quis rer. divin. heres 22 (i. 488) νῷ γὰρ ὁ θεὸς καταλαμβάνειν τὸν μὲν νοητὸν κόσμον δι' ἑαυτοῦ τὸν δὲ ὁρατὸν δι' αἰσθήσεως ἐφῆκεν: but immediately below he substitutes ψυχή for νοῦς, διὰ μὲν αἰσθήσεων εἰς τὰ αἰσθητὰ διακύψας ἕνεκα τοῦ τὸ ἀληθὲς εὑρεῖν διὰ δὲ τῆς ψυχῆς τὰ νοητὰ καὶ ὄντα οὕτως φιλοσοφήσας.

(3) It is used, like ψυχή, of the cognizance of the sensible world.

Quod det. pot. insid. 26 (i. 210), φαντασία, *i.e.* perception, is a function of νοῦς: but in *Quod Deus immut.* 9 (i. 278, 279) it is a function of ψυχή.

Leg. Alleg. ii. 10 (i. 73) sensation is one of the powers of νοῦς: *ibid.* iii. 90 (i. 137), and elsewhere, the senses are collectively a part of ψυχή.

(4) It is used, like ψυχή, not only for all the forces or powers of both animal and vegetable life, but also for the force of cohesion.

The two passages in *Leg. Alleg.* ii. 7, 13, which show this most clearly, are quoted above under § VI (1), p. 124.

VIII. πνεῦμα.

It will have appeared from several passages which have been already quoted that πνεῦμα is used with no less a width of meaning than ψυχὴ or νοῦς. There is the broad general distinction between the terms that πνεῦμα is regarded as the underlying cause which gives to the several forms of ψυχὴ not their capacity but their energy. The conception of πνεῦμα may be regarded as being closely analogous to the modern conception of 'force,' and especially to that form of the conception which makes no distinction of essence between 'mind-force' and other kinds of force, such as light or electricity. It is analogous but not identical: for force is conceived to be immaterial, whereas πνεῦμα, however subtle, is still material.

(1) It is used, like ψυχὴ and νοῦς, of the force which holds solid bodies together: cohesion is a 'force which returns upon itself.'

Quod Deus immut. 7 (i. 277, 278) λίθων μὲν οὖν καὶ ξυλῶν . . . . δεσμὸν κραταιότατον ἕξιν εἰργάσατο· ἡ δέ ἐστι πνεῦμα ἀναστρέφον ἐφ' ἑαυτῷ.

(2) It is used of the physical basis (οὐσία) of growth and sensation.

De mundi opif. 22 (i. 15) ἡ δὲ (*sc.* φύσις) . . . . ζωοπλαστεῖ τὴν μὲν ὑγρὰν οὐσίαν εἰς τὰ τοῦ σώματος μέλη καὶ μέρη διανέμουσα, τὴν πνευματικὴν εἰς τὰς τῆς ψυχῆς δυνάμεις τήν τε θρεπτικὴν καὶ τὴν αἰσθητικήν.

(3) It is used of both (*a*) reason and (*b*) sensation.

(*a*) *Quod det. pot. insid.* 23 (i. 207) ἀνθρώπου δὲ ψυχὴν ὀνομάζει πνεῦμα, ἄνθρωπον οὐ τὸ σύγκριμα καλῶν ὡς ἔφην ἀλλὰ τὸ θεοειδὲς ἐκεῖνο δημιούργημα ᾧ λογίζομεθα.

(*b*) *De profugis* 32 (i. 573). Each of the senses owes its activity to the πνεῦμα which the mind infuses into it, τὸ μὲν ὁρατικὸν πνεῦμα τείνοντος εἰς ὄμματα, τὸ δὲ ἀκουστικὸν εἰς οὖς, εἰς δὲ μυκτῆρας τὸ ὀσφρήσεως, τὸ δὲ αὖ γεύσεως εἰς στόμα καὶ τὸ ἁφῆς εἰς ἅπασαν τὴν ἐπιφάνειαν.

Leg. Alleg. i. 13 (i. 51) God Himself breathes only into the highest part of man, and not into the second rank of human faculties: ὑπὸ τίνος οὖν καὶ ταῦτα ἐνεπνεύσθη ; ὑπὸ τοῦ νοῦ δηλονότι· οὐ γὰρ μέτεσχεν ὁ νοῦς παρὰ τοῦ θεοῦ τούτου μεταδίδωσι τῷ ἀλόγῳ μέρει τῆς ψυχῆς, ὥστε τὸν μὲν νοῦν ἐψυχῶσθαι ὑπὸ θεοῦ, τὸ δὲ ἄλογον ὑπὸ τοῦ νοῦ.

(4) So far, the senses in which Philo uses πνεῦμα are senses in which it was also found in current Greek philosophy. To these senses he added another which comes not from philosophy but from theology, and is expressly based on the statement of Moses that God breathed into man the 'breath' of life. So that while, in some passages, by using the current philosophical language which spoke of πνεῦμα as the essence of mind, he implies that mind could not exist without it, he elsewhere implies that mind existed anterior to it and may now exist without it. He speaks of πνεῦμα being infused into mind by a special act of God, or, by another metaphor, of mind being drawn up to God so as to be in direct contact with Him and moulded by Him.

Leg. Alleg. i. 13 (i. 50) τρία γὰρ εἶναι δεῖ, τὸ ἐμπνέον, τὸ δεχόμενον, τὸ ἐμπνεόμενον· τὸ μὲν ἐμπνέον ἐστὶν ὁ θεός, τὸ δὲ δεχόμενον ὁ νοῦς, τὸ δὲ ἐμπνεόμενον τὸ πνεῦμα. τί οὖν ἐκ τούτων συνάγεται· ἔνωσις γίνεται τῶν τριῶν, τείνοντος τοῦ θεοῦ τὴν ἀφ' ἑαυτοῦ δύναμιν διὰ τοῦ μέσου πνεύματος ἄχρι τοῦ ὑποκειμένου, τίνος ἕνεκα ἢ ὅπως ἔννοιαν αὐτοῦ λαβώμεν ; ἐπεὶ πῶς ἂν ἐνόησεν ἡ ψυχὴ θεὸν εἰ μὴ ἐνέπνευσε καὶ ἥψατο αὐτῆς κατὰ δύναμιν ; οὐ γὰρ ἂν ἐπετόλμησε τοσοῦτον ἀναδραμεῖν ὁ ἀνθρώπινος νοῦς ὡς ἀντιλαβέσθαι θεοῦ φύσεως εἰ μὴ αὐτὸς ὁ θεὸς ἀνέσπασεν αὐτὸν πρὸς ἑαυτόν, ὡς ἐνῆν ἀνθρώπινον νοῦν ἀνασπασθῆναι καὶ ἐτύπωσε κατὰ τὰς ἐφικτὰς νοηθῆναι δυνάμεις.

(5) The conception of this special form of πνεῦμα seems to be required on the one hand by philosophy in order to account for the fact that some men have a knowledge or intellectual power which others have not, and on the other hand by theology, since the Pentateuch speaks of men being filled, in some special sense, by a divine spirit. The word is therefore used for 'the pure science of which every wise man is a partaker,' and especially for the knowledge of

God : and it is sometimes regarded, especially in treatises which probably belong to a generation subsequent to Philo, as an external force acting upon men and leading them to the knowledge of God.

(*a*) *De Gigant.* 5 (i. 265) λέγεται δὲ θεοῦ πνεῦμα .... καθ᾽ ἕτερον δὲ τρόπον ἡ ἀκήρατος ἐπιστήμη ἧς πᾶς ὁ σοφὸς εἰκότως μετέχει (the instance given is that of Bezalel, who was filled πνεύματος θείου, σοφίας, συνέσεως, ἐπιστήμης, Exod. 31. 3).

Vita Mosis 3. 36 (ii. 176) ὁ γὰρ νοῦς οὐκ ἂν οὕτως εὐσκόπως εὐθυβόλησεν εἰ μὴ καὶ θεῖον ἦν πνεῦμα τὸ ποδηγετοῦν πρὸς αὐτὴν τὴν ἀλήθειαν.

De Somniis 2. 38 (i. 692) ὑπηχεῖ δέ μοι πάλιν τὸ εἰωθὸς ἀφανῶς ἐνομιλεῖν πνεῦμα ἀόρατον καί φησιν· ὦ οὗτος, ἔοικας ἀνεπιστήμων εἶναι καὶ μεγάλου καὶ περιμαχήτου πράγματος .... ἴσθι δή, γενναῖε, ὅτι θεὸς μόνος ἡ ἀψευδεστάτη καὶ πρὸς ἀλήθειάν ἐστιν εἰρήνη ἡ δὲ γεννητὴ καὶ φθαρτὴ οὐσία πᾶσα συνεχὴς πόλεμος.

It follows that πνεῦμα in its theological as well as in its philosophical sense, is not a part of human nature but a force that acts upon it and within it. The dichotomy of human nature remains. There is a single body with many members; there is a single mind with many functions. But the mind may be drawn in either of two ways, yielding to the allurements of pleasure or to the special force of the divine spirit. There are thus two kinds of men. (*a*) On the one hand, though all men have mind and, so far, have an element within them which is not merely spirit but divine spirit, yet in another sense there are men in whom the divine spirit does not abide. (*b*) On the other hand there are the prophets, men in whom the manifestation of the special force of the divine spirit is so strong that the human mind for a time migrates from them, 'the sun of the reason sets,' and in the darkness of the reason the divine spirit carries them whither he wills. In other words, just as, though the material world is held together, and animals live, by virtue of a πνεῦμα, and yet men are differentiated from animals by the presence of a higher degree or special form of πνεῦμα: so men are differentiated from one another by the presence of a still higher degree or more special form of it. The conception becomes more intelligible if it be remembered that all the forms of πνεῦμα are regarded as being material, being in fact different degrees of the purity or rarefaction of the air. The lowest form is moist air near the surface of the earth, the highest is the clear ether beyond the starry firmament. (*c*) It must also be noted that Philo does not confine the expression πνεῦμα θεοῦ to the highest form, but, following Genesis 1. 2, applies it to the lowest.

(*a*) *De Gigant.* 5 (i. 265) ἐν δὴ τοῖς τοιούτοις (*i.e.* in men of pleasure) ἀμήχανον τὸ τοῦ θεοῦ καταμεῖναι καὶ διαιωνίσαι πνεῦμα ὡς δηλοῖ καὶ αὐτὸς ὁ νομοθέτης· εἶπε, γάρ, φησί, κύριος ὁ θεός· οὐ καταμενεῖ τὸ πνεῦμά μου ἐν τοῖς ἀνθρώποις εἰς τὸν αἰῶνα διὰ τὸ εἶναι αὐτοὺς σάρκας. μένει μὲν γάρ ἔστιν ὅτε καταμένει δὲ οὐδ' εἰς ἅπαν παρὰ τοῖς πολλοῖς ἡμῖν.

(*b*) *Quis rer. divin. heres* 53 (i. 511) τῷ δὲ προφητικῷ γένει φιλεῖ τοῦτο συμβαίνειν· ἐξοικίζεται μὲν γὰρ ἐν ἡμῖν ὁ νοῦς κατὰ τὴν τοῦ θείου πνεύματος ἄφιξιν, κατὰ δὲ μετανάστασιν αὐτοῦ πάλιν εἰσοικίζεται· θέμις γὰρ οὐκ ἔστι θνητὸν ἀθανάτῳ συνοικῆσαι. διὰ τοῦτο ἡ δύσις τοῦ λογισμοῦ καὶ τὸ περὶ αὐτὸν σκότος ἔκστασιν καὶ θεοφόρητον μανίαν ἐγέννησε.

(*c*) *De Gigant.* 5 (i. 265) λέγεται δὲ θεοῦ πνεῦμα καθ' ἕνα μὲν τρόπον ὁ ῥέων ἀὴρ ἐπὶ γῆς, τρίτον στοιχεῖον ἐποιχούμενον ὕδατι, παρ' ὃ φησιν ἐν τῇ κοσμοποιίᾳ πνεῦμα θεοῦ ἐπεφέρετο ἐπάνω τοῦ ὕδατος.

General Results.

The chief importance of this discussion of the psychological terms of the Septuagint and Philo is in relation to the New Testament. It will be clear that the fine distinctions which are sometimes drawn between them in New Testament exegesis are not supported by their use in contemporary Greek. Into the large subject of the psychological ideas of the several writers of the New Testament as indicated by the use of psychological terms

I do not propose now to enter: but I believe that two points may be clearly gathered from the facts which have been mentioned,—

(1) That the use of such terms in the Synoptic Gospels is closely allied to their use in the Septuagint.

(2) That the use of such terms in S. Paul differs in essential respects from the use of them in Philo, and that consequently the endeavour to interpret Pauline by Philonean psychology falls to the ground.

IV. ON EARLY QUOTATIONS FROM THE SEPTUAGINT.

THE textual criticism of the LXX. is a subject which has hitherto received but slight attention from scholars. It has naturally been postponed to that of the New Testament: and on even the textual criticism of the New Testament it is probable that by no means the last word has been said. The materials have been collected, and are being collected, with singular care: but, so far from the final inductions having been made, the principles on which they should be made have not yet been finally determined.

In the case of the LXX. we are at least one step further back. The materials have yet to be collected. They are of three kinds (i) Greek MSS., (ii) Versions, (iii) Quotations.

i. The MSS. of the whole or parts of the LXX. enumerated by Holmes and Parsons, and wholly or partially collated for their great Thesaurus[1], amount to 313, of which 13 are uncials. Since the publication of that work many additional MSS. have come to light, and among them several uncials of great importance: of the 29 MSS., including fragments, in Lagarde's list of MSS. written before A.D. 1000[2], 13 were unknown to Holmes and Parsons. The addition of this new material to the *apparatus criticus* would be a work of moderate compass, if

---

[1] *Vetus Testamentum Graecum cum variis lectionibus: Editionem a Roberto Holmes inchoatam continuavit Jacobus Parsons:* Oxonii, MDCCXCVIII–MDCCCXXVII.

[2] Lagarde, *Genesis Graece* (Lipsiae, 1868), pp. 10–16.

the existing basis were trustworthy : but it is unfortunately
the case that Holmes and Parsons entrusted no small part
of the task of collation to careless or incompetent hands :
consequently before any final inductions can be made the
whole of the MSS. must be collated afresh.

The extent and nature of the deficiencies in Holmes and Parsons
will be seen from the following comparison of a few verses, chosen
at random, of the collations made for Holmes and Parsons with
the collations made by Lagarde.

The passage chosen is Gen. xxvii. 1–20 : in it Holmes and
Parsons mention various readings from, and must therefore be
presumed to have collated, 36 cursives : of these Lagarde has
collated three, viz. a Munich MS., H. and P. No. 25 ; a Venice
MS., H. and P., No. 122 ; and a Vienna MS., H. and P., No. 130.
This more accurate collation requires the following additions to be
made to the *apparatus criticus* of the Oxford edition.

v. 1 : Cod. 130 reads 'Ισαὰκ for 'Εσαῦ, and omits υἱέ μου καὶ εἶπεν
ἰδοὺ ἐγὼ καὶ εἶπεν.

v. 4 : Cod. 25 εὐλογήσει.

v. 5 : Cod. 122 ἤκουε for ἤκουσε : 130 'Ισαὰκ λαλοῦντος.

v. 6 : Cod. 122 omits τοῦ before 'Ιακώβ : 130 reads ἰδοὺ for ἴδε.

v. 9 : Cod. 130 adds τε after ἁπαλούς.

v. 10 : Cod. 25 εὐλογήσει.

v. 14 : Cod. 130 adds αὐτοῦ after τῇ μητρὶ and reads καθὼς for
καθά.

v. 15 : Codd. 122, 130 omit αὐτὴν after ἐνέδυσεν.

v. 16 : Codd. 25, 130 read ἔθηκεν ἐπὶ τὰ γυμνά, omitting ἐπὶ τοὺς
βραχίονας αὐτοῦ καί.

v. 18 : Cod. 122 has ἔνεγκε for εἰσήνεγκε.

v. 19 : Cod. 25 καὶ πεποίηκα : 122 omits ἀπό.

This comparison gives eighteen corrections in the space of
twenty verses in one-twelfth of the MSS. collated.

To these corrections of MSS. which were actually collated may
be added, as an example of the additions which may be expected
from a further examination of the MSS., Lagarde's collation of the
same passage in the Zittau MS. which Holmes and Parsons mention in their list as No. 44, and which was partly collated for their
edition, but of which no various readings appear in Genesis.

The following is the collation of the Zittau MS. :—

v. 1 : τὸν υἱὸν αὐτοῦ Ἡσαῶ : om. μου after υἱέ.

v. 2 : om. εἶπε δὲ αὐτῷ Ἰσαάκ : ἰδοὺ ἐγὼ γεγήρηκα.

v. 4 : εὐλογήσει : πρὶν ἤ.

v. 6 : Ῥεβέκκα δὲ ἤκουσε λαλοῦντος ταῦτα καί : om. τοῦ before Ἰακώβ : νεώτερον for ἐλάσσω : ἐγὼ ἤκουσα : λαλοῦντος τοῦ πατρός σου : om. τὸν ἀδελφόν σου.

v. 7 : καὶ for ἵνα : με ἀποθανεῖν.

v. 8 : om. μου after υἱέ.

vv. 9–10 : om. ὡς φιλεῖ καὶ εἰσοίσεις τῷ πατρί σου.

v. 10 : om. εὐλογήσει : om. αὐτοῦ.

v. 11 : om. πρὸς Ῥεβέκκαν τὴν μητέρα αὐτοῦ and Ἡσαῦ.

v. 12 : om. ἐπ'.

v. 13 : ἄκουσον for ἐπάκουσον.

v. 14 : τῇ μητρὶ αὐτοῦ : καθὼς for καθά.

v. 15 : om. αὐτὴν after ἐνέδυσεν.

v. 16 : περὶ τοὺς βραχίονας.

v. 18 : καὶ εἶπε for εἶπε δέ.

v. 19 : τῷ πατρὶ αὐτοῦ : ἐποίησα : om. ἀπὸ τῆς θήρας μου.

ii. The Latin and Eastern versions of the Old Testament were made not from the Hebrew original but from the LXX. version. They have now to be used reversely, i.e. as indicating the LXX. text at the time at which they were written : and from the critical study of them more light is likely to be thrown upon the early recensions of the LXX. than from any other source. With the Eastern versions, i.e. the Egyptian (Sahidic, Memphitic, and Basmuric), Ethiopian, Armenian, Arabic, and Syriac, I am not competent to deal : the Latin versions are collected with singular care in the great work of Sabatier, nor, except in the cases of Cyprian and Lucifer of Cagliari, has modern criticism as yet improved to any considerable degree the texts which Sabatier used.

iii. The quotations from the LXX. in the Greek Fathers are an almost unworked field. With the Greek even more than with the Latin Fathers the texts require to be critically edited before the comparison of the quotations with

the MSS. of the LXX. can be satisfactorily made : but
the corroboration of the discovery of Lucian's recension,
which will be mentioned below, by the agreement of the
MSS. which are believed to contain it with the quotations
in Chrysostom and Theodoret, shows how much help may
be expected from this source.

The next step after collecting the materials is to group
the MSS. into classes or families. For this our chief
guide is the statement of Jerome that there were three
recensions of the LXX. in his time,—that of Hesychius
which was accepted in Egypt, that of Lucian which was
accepted from Constantinople to Antioch, that of Origen
which was accepted in Palestine[1]. The first step is to
recover, if possible, the texts of these several recensions.
And in the case of one of them, that of Lucian[2], we have
a remarkable clue. In a Paris MS. there is appended to
some marginal readings of several passages of the Fourth
Book of Kings a sign which is most probably interpreted
to be the Syriac letter *Lomad:* but this letter is said by
a tradition which comes through two channels, Greek and
Syriac, and contains no internal improbability, to have
been appended to the readings of Lucian's recension : it
is consequently inferred that these readings furnish a test
for the determination of the MSS. which contain Lucian's
recension. It is found that they coincide with the readings,
in the several passages, of Codd. 19 (Chisianus R vi. 38,
Lagarde's h), 82 (Parisinus Coislin 3, Lagarde's f), 93 (Arun-
delianus I D 2, Lagarde's m, in his later notation), 108
(Vaticanus 330, Lagarde's d, the basis, with 248, of the
Complutensian edition). These four MSS. are found to
hang together, and to have a peculiar text, throughout
the LXX. : their readings are also found to agree with

---

[1] S. Hieron. *Apol. adv. Ruffin.* Tom. ii. p. 522.

[2] It is unnecessary to repeat here the details respecting Lucian's edition
which are clearly and exhaustively given by Dr. Field, *Prolegomena in Hexapla
Origenis*, pp. lxxxvi *sqq.*

the quotations from historical books in Chrysostom and Theodoret, who may reasonably be supposed, assuming Jerome's statement to be accurate, to have used the text of Lucian. To the above-mentioned MSS. several others are found to be cognate, viz. 44 (the Zittau MS. mentioned above), 118 (Parisinus Graecus 6, Lagarde's p), 56 (Parisinus Graecus 5, Lagarde's k): and a MS. in the British Museum (Add. 20002, Lagarde's E). A comparison of these MSS. gives a single text which may reasonably be taken to represent Lucian's recension: and Lagarde has published it as such [1].

The next task of LXX. criticism will be to discover in a similar way the texts of the two other recensions. There are many indications of the path which research in that direction must follow: and the research would be full of interest. I do not propose to engage in it now because an even greater interest attaches to the question with which I propose specially to deal in this chapter, namely,

What can we learn about the text, or texts, of the LXX. before the three recensions of which Jerome speaks were made?

The answer to this question does not depend on the restoration of the text of those recensions. It is true that if we had the three recensions complete we should be able to infer that the readings in which they agreed probably formed part of a text which was prior to them: but we should still be unable to tell whether any given variant, i.e. any reading in which one of the three differed from the two others, or two of the three from the third, was part of an earlier text or a revision of it. We should also find that some of the existing MSS. and versions

---

[1] A specimen appeared in his *Ankündigung einer neuen ausgabe der griechischen übersezung des alten testaments*, Goettingen, 1882: and the first volume (Genesis--Esther) of a complete edition in 1883.

had readings which did not belong to any of the three recensions: and we should be in doubt whether these belonged to an earlier text or to a revision of it. It is consequently not necessary to possess the current texts of the third century in order to discover the text or texts of the preceding centuries. The discovery is not only interesting but important: and it is important in relation not only to textual criticism but also to exegesis. It is important in relation to textual criticism, because it may enable us to recognize in some existing MSS. the survivals of an earlier text than that of the three recensions: it is important in relation to exegesis: for as each recension reflects the state of knowledge of Hebrew, and the current opinion as to the interpretation of the Hebrew text, in the country in which it was made in the third century of the Christian era: so the texts which precede those recensions reflect the state of philology and of exegesis, in both Egypt and Palestine, during the first two centuries of the Christian era, and the two, or three, centuries which preceded it.

I have spoken of earlier texts, in the plural, rather than of the original text of the LXX., because there are many indications that the first and second centuries were no more free from variations of text than was the third. It was natural that it should be so. In the case of an original work like the *Aeneid,* or like the New Testament, there is a presumption that the scribe would endeavour to copy as accurately as he could the text before him, emending a passage only in the belief that it had been wrongly written by a previous scribe and in the hope of representing more accurately by his emendation what the author wrote. But in the case of a translation there is a constant tendency to make the text of the translation a more accurate representation of the text of the original. It may be assumed that a certain proportion, though perhaps only a small proportion, of the scribes of the LXX. were acquainted with Hebrew: it would be almost a religious obligation on such scribes, when they saw what they believed to be a mistranslation, to correct it. This was probably the case in an especial degree when certain texts came to have a dogmatic or controversial importance. Hence there is an *a priori* probability of the existence of varieties of text: and the probability will be found to be strongly confirmed by the detailed examination of some passages of the LXX. in the following pages.

What data have we for determining the question that has been proposed? How can we go behind the recensions of which Jerome speaks, and to one or other of which it may be presumed that the great majority of the existing MSS. belong?

The data consist partly in the quotations from the LXX. in early Greek writers, especially in Philo, in the New Testament, and in the Apostolic and sub-Apostolic Fathers, and partly in the quotations from the Latin versions which are found in early Latin writers. This statement assumes in regard to the Greek writers that they made use of the LXX. and not of another translation: but the assumption will be proved to be true when the quotations are examined. The points of similarity between them and the text of the LXX., the structure of the sentences, and the use of peculiar words and idioms, are altogether too numerous to admit of the hypothesis of the existence of another translation: the points of difference are, with hardly an exception, such as may be accounted for by the hypothesis of varieties of text and mistakes in transmission. The statement assumes also that the early Latin versions were made from the LXX.: this assumption also will be proved when the quotations are examined. The use of each of these classes of data, though more in the case of Greek than of Latin writers, is attended with the preliminary difficulty that the texts of the quotations have, in many instances, been altered by scribes in order to bring them into harmony with the Biblical texts of a later time. The difficulty is sometimes removed by the fact that the writer comments on a particular phrase and therefore establishes the fact of his having read it: and the probability of its existence in such a writer as Philo, in short passages which have no dogmatic importance, is very small: but at the same time there is no doubt that the data must be used with some degree of caution, and that the final results of the examination of them cannot be obtained until the texts of the several writers have themselves been critically studied.

These data may be dealt with in two ways. (1) The MSS. readings of a given passage may be compared with the quotations of it: the special use of this method is twofold: (*a*) it enables us to classify MSS., and to estimate their value, according as they do or do not agree with such early quotations; (*b*) it enables us also in certain cases to detect, and to account for, the recensions of the passage, and so obtain a clue to the history of its exegesis. (2) The quotations in a given writer may be gathered together: the special use of this method is also twofold: (*a*) it enables us to ascertain approximately the text which was in use in his time; (*b*) it enables us, upon a general estimate of the mode in which he quotes Scripture, to appreciate the value of the contributions which his quotations make to textual criticism.

The following pages contain examples of each of these methods.

(1) In the first portion a text of Genesis or Exodus is quoted from the Sixtine text: it is followed by (*a*) a short *apparatus criticus*, taken from Holmes and Parsons, and from Lagarde; (*b*) an account of passages in which it is

quoted in Philo, the New Testament, the Apostolic Fathers, and Justin Martyr; (c) an account, where useful, of the early Latin versions : to this is appended a short account of the conclusions to which the data point in regard to the criticism of the passages.

(2) In the second portion, the quotations of two books, the Psalms and Isaiah, in Philo, Clement of Rome, Barnabas, and Justin Martyr, are gathered together : and the bearing of each quotation upon the criticism or exegesis of the LXX. is estimated.

The following pages contain only examples of these methods, and not an exhaustive application of them : their object is to show in detail the help which the methods afford in the criticism of particular passages, and to stimulate students to pursue them further.

It may be convenient for those who are not familiar with the notation of MSS. of the LXX. to mention that in the following examples the MSS. are quoted according to their number in the list of Holmes and Parsons : Roman numerals (or capital letters) denote uncials, Arabic numerals denote cursives. The MSS. which have been more recently collated by Lagarde are quoted according to his notation : h=19, m=25 (in Lagarde's later notation, not in his *Genesis Graece*, m=93), x=29, z=44, y=122, t=130, r=135. The Codex Alexandrinus is usually here denoted by A instead of by the numeral III; and the Bodleian Codex of Genesis (Auct. T. inf. ii. 1) is denoted, as in Lagarde's *Genesis Graece*, by E (in his later notation E=the British Museum MS. Add. 20002). The Roman or Sixtine text is designated by R.

The quotations from the early Latin versions are for the most part due to the great collection of Sabatier, *Bibliorum Sacrorum Latinae Versiones antiquae*, Remis, 1743.

1. *Quotations from Genesis and Exodus.*

GENESIS i. 1, 2.

Ἐν ἀρχῇ ἐποίησεν ὁ θεὸς τὸν οὐρανὸν καὶ τὴν γῆν· ἡ δὲ γῆ ἦν ἀόρατος καὶ ἀκατασκεύαστος καὶ σκότος ἐπάνω τῆς ἀβύσσου· καὶ πνεῦμα θεοῦ ἐπεφέρετο ἐπάνω τοῦ ὕδατος.

Cod. 75 σκότος + ἦν, Codd. 68, 120, 121 σκότος + ἐπέκειτο.

Philo *Quis rer. divin. heres* 24 (i. 490) ἐν ἀρχῇ ἐποίησεν : id. *de Mundi Opif.* 7 (i. 5) ἐν ἀρχῇ . . . . τὴν γῆν = R. : id. *de Incorrupt. Mundi* 5 (ii. 491) ἐν ἀρχῇ . . . . ἀκατασκεύαστος = R.: id. *de Mundi Opif.* 9 (i. 7) σκότος ἦν ἐπάνω τῆς ἀβύσσου: id. *Leg. Alleg.* i. 13 (i. 50), *de Gigant.* 6 (i. 265) καὶ πνεῦμα . . . . ὕδατος = R.

Justin M. *Apol.* i. 59 = R. except τῶν ὑδάτων : id. *Apol.* i. 64 has the variant ἐπιφερομένου (probably a scribe's error for ἐπιφερόμενον) as well as τῶν ὑδάτων.

The insertion of ἦν after σκότος is supported by the early Latin versions, all of which have 'tenebrae *erant*:' its omission may be due to a Hebraizing revision of which there are further traces (*a*) in Justin's substitution of ἐπιφερόμενον (מְרַחֶפֶת *pres. part.*) for ἐπεφέρετο, (*b*) in his use of the plural τῶν ὑδάτων (הַמָּיִם) which is supported by *Excerpt. Theod.* 47, Clem. Alex. ed. Pott p. 980, and by the Latin 'super *aquas*' of Tertull. *de Baptismo* 3, 4 pp. 256, 257, *adv. Hermog.* 32 p. 282, *adv. Marc.* 4. 26 p. 546 : on the other hand, August. *de Gen. c. Manich.* i. 5 (i. 648), *de Gen. ad litt.* 1. 11, 13, 14 (iii. 120, 121), *Serm.* 226 (82) (v. 972), and Philastr. 109 p. 110 have 'super *aquam.*'

GENESIS i. 4, 5.

Καὶ εἶδεν ὁ θεὸς τὸ φῶς ὅτι καλόν· καὶ διεχώρισεν ὁ θεὸς ἀνὰ μέσον τοῦ φωτὸς καὶ ἀνὰ μέσον τοῦ σκότους· καὶ ἐκάλεσεν ὁ θεὸς τὸ φῶς ἡμέραν καὶ σκότος ἐκάλεσε νύκτα· καὶ ἐγένετο ἑσπέρα καὶ ἐγένετο πρωὶ ἡμέρα μία.

The variations of the MSS. are merely orthographical.

Philo *de Somniis* i. 13 (i. 632) διεχώρισεν . . . . σκότους = R. : id. *Quis rer. divin. heres* 33 (i. 496) καὶ διεχώρισεν . . . . νύκτα = R. except that ὁ θεὸς is omitted after ἐκάλεσεν, and ἐκάλεσε after σκότος: id. *de Mundi Opif.* 9 (i. 7) ἑσπέρα τε καὶ πρωία (*bis*) : *ibid.* τοῦ χρόνου μέτρον ἀπετελεῖτο εὐθὺς ὁ καὶ ἡμέραν ὁ ποιῶν ἐκάλεσε καὶ ἡμέραν οὐχὶ πρώτην ἀλλὰ μίαν ἢ λέλεκται οὕτως διὰ τὴν τοῦ νοητοῦ κόσμου μόνωσιν μοναδικὴν ἔχοντος φύσιν (cf. Joseph. *Antt.* 1. 1 καὶ αὕτη μὲν ἂν εἴη ἡ πρώτη ἡμέρα Μωϋσῆς δὲ αὐτὴν μίαν εἶπε).

GENESIS i. 9.

Καὶ εἶπεν ὁ θεὸς ϲγναχθήτω τὸ ὕδωρ τὸ ὑποκάτω τογ ογρανογ εἰϲ ϲγναγωγὴν μίαν καὶ ὀφθήτω ἡ ξηρά.

·Philo *de Mundi Opif.* 11 (i. 8) προστάττει ὁ θεὸς .... τὸ μὲν ὕδωρ .... ἐπισυναχθῆναι .... τὴν δὲ ξηρὰν ἀναφανῆναι.

Philo's quotation is indirect : but ἀναφανῆναι is supported by the Latin '*appareat*' in S. August. *de Gen. c. Manich.* i. 12 (i. 652), while the MSS. reading ὀφθήτω is supported by Tertull. *c. Hermog.* 29 p. 243, '*videatur* arida.'

GENESIS i. 10.

Καὶ τὰ ϲγϲτήματα τῶν ὑδάτων ἐκάλεϲε θαλάϲϲαϲ.

Philo *de Mundi Opif.* 11 (i. 8) τὴν μὲν ξηρὰν καλῶν γῆν τὸ δὲ ἀποκριθὲν ὕδωρ θάλασσαν.

Philo's use of the singular θάλασσαν is supported by S. August. *de Gen. c. Manich.* i. 12 (i. 652): but, as elsewhere, it is an open question whether the plural is due to a Hebraizing revision of an original θάλασσαν, or the singular to a Hellenizing version of an original θαλάσσας (מַיִּם).

GENESIS i. 24.

Ἐξαγαγέτω ἡ γῆ ψγχὴν ζῶϲαν κατὰ γένοϲ τετράποδα καὶ ἑρπετὰ καὶ θηρία τῆϲ γῆϲ κατὰ γένοϲ.

So Codd. A, X, 16, 68, 72, 73, 77, 120, 121, 128, 129. Cod. 76 ζῶσαν + καὶ τὰ κτήνη καὶ πάντα τὰ ἑρπετὰ τῆς γῆς : Cod. 75 *om.* κατὰ γένος .... τῆς γῆς : Cod. 55 *om.* κατὰ γένος *prior.* : Cod. 59 καὶ τετράποδα : Cod. 135 (r) *om.* καί ante θηρία : Cod. E *om.* καὶ θηρία : Cod. 108 *om.* τῆς γῆς : Codd. 15, 17, 19, 20, 25, 37, 55, 56, 61, 63, 106, 107, 108, 134, 135, z, τῆς γῆς + καὶ τὰ κτήνη καὶ πάντα τὰ ἑρπετὰ τῆς γῆς : Cod. 74 τῆς γῆς + καὶ πάντα τὰ ἑρπετά : post κατὰ γένος *poster.* Codd. 14, 31, 32, 78, 79, 131, t, *add.* καὶ τὰ κτήνη κατὰ γένος καὶ πάντα τὰ ἑρπετὰ τῆς γῆς κατὰ γένος : Cod. 25 *add.* καὶ πάντα τὰ ἑρπετὰ τῆς γῆς κατὰ γένος : Cod. 83 *add.* καὶ τὰ κτήνη κατὰ γένος : Cod. z *add.* καὶ τὰ κτήνη καὶ πάντα τὰ ἑρπετὰ τῆς γῆς κατὰ γένος.

Philo *de Mundi Opif.* 21 (i. 14) ἐξαγαγέτω ἡ γῆ κτήνη καὶ θηρία καὶ ἑρπετὰ καθ᾽ ἕκαστον γένος : id. *Leg. Alleg.* 2. 4 (i. 69) ἐξαγαγέτω . . . . θηρία=R.

Tertull. *c. Hermog.* 22, p. 241, 'producat terra animam viventem secundum genus quadrupedia et repentia et bestias terrae secundum genus ipsorum ': *ibid.* 29, p. 244 'vivam' is read for 'viventem,' and 'ipsorum' is omitted: S. Ambros. *Hexaem.* 6. 2 (i. 114) adds after "bestias terrae" et pecora secundum genus et omnia reptilia,' and S. August. *de Gen. ad litt. lib. imperf.* 53 (iii. 111) and *de Gen. ad litt.* 2. 16 (iii. 151) adds in the same place ' et pecora secundum genus.'

The variations in the text may probably be explained by the hypothesis that in very early times τετράποδα was substituted for the more usual κτήνη as the translation of בְּהֵמָה. That the two words were both found in very early times is shown by the fact that they both occur in Philo: and it seems less probable to suppose that the translators varied their usual translation of the Hebrew word than that τετράποδα came in as an early gloss or targum to emphasise the distinction between the 'winged fowls' of v. 21 and the land animals (τὰ χερσαῖα Philo i. 14) which were not created until the following day. This hypothesis that κτήνη rather than τετράποδα was the original word is confirmed by the quotation of the passage in S. Basil *in Hexaem. Hom.* ix. 2 (i. 81) ἐξαγαγέτω ἡ γῆ ψυχὴν ζῶσαν κτηνῶν καὶ θηρίων καὶ ἑρπετῶν, and in S. Cyril of Jerusalem *Catech.* 9. 13, p. 132 θηρία καὶ κτήνη καὶ ἑρπετὰ κατὰ γένος. This hypothesis also explains the other variants of the MSS.: for it clears the way for the further hypothesis that a scribe or reviser finding τετράποδα in some copies and κτήνη in others, and not noticing, or not knowing, that they were both admissible translations of the same Hebrew word, combined the phrases, adding after τῆς γῆς, or after κατὰ γένος, either the words καὶ τὰ κτήνη what would give the original of Augustine's quotation ' et pecora,' or the words καὶ τὰ κτήνη καὶ πάντα τὰ ἑρπετά, which are found in many cursives and are evidently the basis of the Latin ' et pecora secundum genus et omnia reptilia.'

GENESIS i. 26.

Ποιήϲωμεν ἄνθρωπον κατ᾽ εἰκόνα ἡμετέραν καὶ καθ᾽ ὁμοίωϲιν.

So all Codd.

Philo *de Mundi Opif.* 24 (i. 17) and *de confus. ling.* 35 (i. 432)

ποιήσωμεν ἄνθρωπον: id. *de Mundi Opif.* 24 (i. 16) ποιήσωμεν
ἄνθρωπον κατ᾽ εἰκόνα ἡμετέραν καὶ καθ᾽ ὁμοίωσιν: *ibid.* c. 23 . . . .
προσεπεσημήνατο εἰπὼν τῷ κατ᾽ εἰκόνα τὸ καθ᾽ ὁμοίωσιν εἰς ἔμφασιν
ἀκριβοῦς ἐκμαγείου τρανὸν τύπον ἔχοντος: id. *de mutat. nom.* 4 (i.
583) ποιήσωμεν ἄνθρωπον κατ᾽ εἰκόνα ἡμετέραν: id. *de confus. ling.*
33 (i. 430) ποιήσωμεν ἄνθρωπον κατ᾽ εἰκόνα ἡμετέραν καὶ καθ᾽
ὁμοίωσιν.

Clem. R. i. 33 ποιήσωμεν ἄνθρωπον κατ᾽ εἰκόνα καὶ καθ᾽ ὁμοίωσιν ἡμετέραν: Barnab. 5 ποιήσωμεν κατ᾽ εἰκόνα καὶ καθ᾽ ὁμοίωσιν ἡμετέραν:
id. 6 ποιήσωμεν κατ᾽ εἰκόνα καὶ καθ᾽ ὁμοίωσιν ἡμῶν τὸν ἄνθρωπον:
Justin M. Tryph. 62 = R.: Clem. Alex. *Paedag.* i. 12, p. 156
ποιήσωμεν ἄνθρωπον κατ᾽ εἰκόνα καὶ καθ᾽ ὁμοίωσιν ἡμῶν: id. *Strom.*
55, p. 662 . . . . κατ᾽ εἰκόνα καὶ ὁμοίωσιν ἡμετέραν.

The majority of early Latin quotations (Tertullian, Cyprian,
Hilary, Interpr. Irenaei, frequently Ambrose, Augustine) have
' Faciamus hominem ad imaginem et similitudinem nostram ' ;
the chief exceptions are S. Ambros. *Hexaem.* 6. 7 (i. 127)
' ad nostram imaginem et ad similitudinem nostram ': id. *de
Offic.* 1. 28 (ii. 35) ' ad imaginem nostram et secundum similitudinem.'

The passage is critically interesting on several grounds :

(1) The change in the position of the pronoun in Clement,
Barnabas, and the early Latin Fathers can hardly be ascribed to
accident or inexact quotation. The controversial importance of
the pronoun is shown by the Gnostic controversies, Epiphan.
Haeres. 23. 1, 5. The critical importance of the passage lies in
the indication which it furnishes of the existence of well-established
readings outside the existing MSS. of the LXX., and of the small
influence which early patristic citations exercised upon MSS. of the
LXX.

(2) The Hebrew has the pronoun with both words, and there
is a trace of a Hebraizing revision of the LXX. in the Paris and
Vatican MSS. of Origen *in Joann.* 13. 28 (iv. 238) κατ᾽ εἰκόνα ἡμετέραν
καὶ καθ᾽ ὁμοίωσιν ἡμετέραν: so also in the Coptic, Sahidic, and some
MSS. of the Arabic, and in the quotation in S. Ambros. *Hexaem.*
6. 7 given above. But this revision there is no trace in existing
MSS. of the LXX.

GENESIS i. 27.

Καὶ ἐποίησεν ὁ θεὸς τὸν ἄνθρωπον κατ᾽ εἰκόνα θεοῦ ἐποίησεν αὐτόν·
ἄρσεν καὶ θῆλυ ἐποίησεν αὐτούς.

Cod. 135 (r) τὸν ἄνθρωπον + ἐν εἰκόνι αὐτοῦ.

Philo *Leg. Alleg.* iii. 31 (i. 106) καὶ ἐποίησεν ὁ θεὸς τὸν ἄνθρωπον κατ᾽ εἰκόνα θεοῦ : id. *de Somniis* i. 13 (i. 632) ἐποίησεν .... αὐτόν= R. : id. *Quis rer. divin. heres* 33 (i. 496) ἐποίησε .... αὐτούς= R. : id. *ibid.* 49 (i. 506) ἐποίησε, γάρ, φησίν, ὁ θεὸς τὸν ἄνθρωπον, οὐκ εἰκόνα ἀλλὰ κατ᾽ εἰκόνα, where it is conceivable that there may be an implied criticism of Wisdom 2. 23 καὶ εἰκόνα τῆς ἰδίας ἰδιότητος ἐποίησεν αὐτόν.

It is possible that the quotation in Philo i. 106, which connects κατ᾽ εἰκόνα θεοῦ with the words that precede rather than with those that follow may go back to an earlier text, which followed the Hebrew in repeating the phrase κατ᾽ εἰκόνα θεοῦ [αὐτοῦ]: so Aquila and Theodotion ἔκτισεν ὁ θεὸς σὺν [Theod. *om.*] τὸν ἄνθρωπον ἐν εἰκόνι αὐτοῦ, ἐν εἰκόνι θεοῦ ἔκτισεν αὐτούς. Of such a text, or revision, there is a trace in Cod. 135, see above, and in Euseb. *Praepar. Evang.* ii. 27. 3, where Codd. C E F G I (Gaisf.) have the same version as that of Cod. 135.

GENESIS i. 31.

Καὶ εἶδεν ὁ θεὸς τὰ πάντα ὅσα ἐποίησε καὶ ἰδοὺ καλὰ λίαν.

Cod. 19 *om.* ὁ θεός : Codd. E. 15, 19, 20, 25 (m), 75, 127, 129, *om.* τά.

Philo *de migrat. Abraham.* 8 (i. 442) εἶδεν ὁ θεὸς τὰ πάντα ὅσα ἐποίησεν: id. *ibid.* 24 (i. 457) εἶδεν .... λίαν=R.: id. *Quis rer. divin. heres* 32 (i. 495) εἶδεν ὁ θεὸς τὰ πάντα ὅσα ἐποίησεν καὶ ἰδοὺ ἀγαθὰ σφόδρα (so Mangey: some MSS. πάντα).

Philo's reading σφόδρα is also the translation of Aquila and Symmachus, and hence may have been that of an earlier revision : and it is confirmed as a current reading by *Sirach* 39. 16 τὰ ἔργα κυρίου πάντα ὅτι καλὰ σφόδρα: of its variant πάντα there is also a trace in Gregory of Nyssa *Hexaem.* p. 84 (ed. Migne *Patrol. Gr.* XLIV) who has ἰδοὺ τὰ πάντα καλὰ λίαν: so Philastrius 79, p. 74 'ecce enim *omnia* valde erant bona.'

GENESIS ii. 1.

Καὶ συνετελέσθησαν ὁ οὐρανὸς καὶ ἡ γῆ καὶ πᾶς ὁ κόσμος αὐτῶν.

Codd. 19, 106, 107, z, συνετελέσθη.

Philo *Leg. Alleg.* i. 1 (i. 43) *Cod. Medic.* καὶ ἐτελέσθησαν οἱ οὐρανοὶ καὶ ἡ γῆ καὶ πᾶς ὁ κόσμος αὐτῶν, *Codd. rell.* .... ἡ γῆ καὶ πᾶσαι αἱ στρατιαὶ αὐτῶν.

The plural οἱ οὐρανοί is a closer translation of שָׁמַיִם than the singular ὁ οὐρανός: but the latter is the almost invariable form in the LXX.: στρατιά (στρατιαί) and κόσμος are both found as transla-- tions of צָבָא but the former is more usual: hence it is probable that an early form of the text had both οὐρανοί and στρατιαί: cf. Neh. 9. 6, where the two words are used in combination to translate the same Hebrew words as here, καὶ σοὶ προσκυνοῦσιν αἱ στρατιαὶ τῶν οὐρανῶν.

GENESIS ii. 2, 3.

Καὶ ϲγνετέλεϲεν ὁ θεὸϲ ἐν τῇ ἡμέρᾳ τῇ ἕκτῃ τὰ ἔργα αγτοŶ ἃ ἐποίηϲε· καὶ κατέπαγϲε τῇ ἡμέρᾳ τῇ ἐβΔόμῃ ἀπὸ πάντων τῶν ἔργων αγτοŶ ὧν ἐποίηϲε, καὶ εγλόγηϲεν ὁ θεὸϲ τὴν ἡμέραν τὴν ἐβΔόμην καὶ ἡγίαϲεν αγτὴν ὅτε ἐν αγτῇ κατέπαγϲεν ἀπὸ πάντων τῶν ἔργων αγτοŶ ὧν ἦρΞατο ὁ θεὸϲ ποιῆϲαι.

So Codd. A, X. 15, 25, 68, 72, 120, 128, 129, 130, 131. Codd. 59, 79 *om.* ἐν before τῇ ἡμέρᾳ: Codd. 37, 108, z κατέ- παυσεν + ὁ θεός: Codd. 16, 19, 38, 108 κατέπαυσεν ὁ θεὸς ἐν: Codd. 14, 20, 31, 32, 55, 57, 73, 76, 77, 78, 79, 83, 106, 134, 135 κατέπαυσεν + ἐν.

Philo *Leg. Alleg.* i. 2 (i. 43, 44) καὶ συνετέλεσεν ὁ θεὸς ἐν τῇ ἡμέρᾳ τῇ ἕκτῃ ἔργον αὐτοῦ ὃ ἐποίησεν, but immediately afterwards, ὅταν οὖν λέγη συνετέλεσεν ἕκτῃ ἡμέρᾳ τὰ ἔργα, νοητέον ὅτι οὐ πλῆθος ἡμερῶν παραλαμβάνει τέλειον δὲ ἀριθμὸν τὸν ἕξ: *ibid.* i. 6, 7 (i. 46) κατέπαυσεν οὖν τῇ ἑβδόμῃ ἡμέρᾳ ἀπὸ πάντων τῶν ἔργων αὐτοῦ ὧν ἐποίησε .... καὶ ηὐλόγησεν ὁ θεὸς τὴν ἡμέραν τὴν ἑβδόμην καὶ ἡγίασεν αὐτήν .... τὴν ἑβδόμην ηὐλόγησέ τε καὶ ἡγίασεν ὅτι ἐν αὐτῇ κατέ- παυσεν ἀπὸ πάντων τῶν ἔργων αὐτοῦ ὧν ἦρξατο ὁ θεὸς ποιῆσαι: id. *de posterit. Cain.* 18 (i. 237) καὶ κατέπαυσεν ὁ θεὸς ἐν τῇ ἡμέρᾳ ἑβδόμῃ ἀπὸ πάντων .... ποιῆσαι [ἑβδόμη . . . ποιῆσαι = R.].

Philo's agreement with the LXX. in reading ἐν τῇ ἡμέρᾳ τῇ ἕκτῃ is remarkable because (1) most MSS. of the Masoretic text have בַּיּוֹם הַשְּׁבִיעִי 'on the *seventh* day,' (2) Aquila, Symmachus, and Theodotion have τῇ ἑβδόμῃ, (3) Barnab. 15 has συνετέλεσεν τῇ [Cod. Sin.: Cod. Const. ἐν] ἡμέρα τῇ ἑβδόμῃ καὶ κατέπαυσεν ἐν αὐτῇ. The early Latin versions agree, as usual, with the LXX.: and the first indication of a variation is in Jerome *ad loc.* (*Hebr. quaest. in libro Genes.* p. 4, ed. Lagarde) 'pro die sexta in hebraeo diem septimam habet': the Syriac and Samaritan also agree with the LXX., and in two of Kennicott's MSS. הַשְּׁבִיעִי is absent.

The balance of external evidence must be held to be in favour of 'sixth' as opposed to 'seventh': but since both readings are of great antiquity, and also since, from the nature of the case, the external evidence for both readings is scanty, the question of the priority of the one reading over the other cannot be decided without regard to internal probability. It would be difficult to suggest a strong reason for changing 'sixth' to 'seventh': but the use which Jerome *l. c.* makes of the reading 'seventh' as an argument against Jewish sabbatarianism suggests the probability of 'seventh' having in very early times been changed to 'sixth' to avoid the apparent sanction which would be given to working on the Sabbath, if God were stated not to have ceased working until the seventh day had actually begun. In other words, the Masoretic text is probably correct, and the reading 'sixth' for 'seventh' is probably the earliest instance of a dogmatic gloss.

Philo's reading κατέπαυσεν ὁ θεὸς ἐν τῇ ἡμέρᾳ is supported not only by several excellent MSS. of the LXX., but also by the Latin version in Aug. *de Gen. ad litt.* 4. 1, 20, 37 (iii. 159, 166, 172) 'requievit *Deus in* die septimo': on the other hand, Irenaeus *Vet. Interpr.* 5. 28. 3 (i. 327) and Ambrose *Epist.* 44 (ii. 978) omit 'Deus': in Aug. *c. Adimant.* 1 (viii. 112) it is both inserted and omitted in the same chapter.

GENESIS ii. 4, 5.

Αὕτη ἡ βίβλος γενέσεως οὐρανοῦ καὶ γῆς ὅτε ἐγένετο ᾗ ἡμέρᾳ ἐποίησε κύριος ὁ θεὸς τὸν οὐρανὸν καὶ τὴν γῆν καὶ πᾶν χλωρὸν ἀγροῦ πρὸ τοῦ γενέσθαι ἐπὶ τῆς γῆς καὶ πάντα χόρτον ἀγροῦ πρὸ τοῦ ἀνατεῖλαι· οὐ γὰρ ἔβρεξεν ὁ θεὸς ἐπὶ τὴν γῆν καὶ ἄνθρωπος οὐκ ἦν ἐργάζεσθαι αὐτήν.

So Codd. 68, 120.

Cod. 75 ἡμέρα ᾗ ἐποίησε: Cod. 129 ἡ ἡμέρα ᾗ ἐποίησε: Codd. A 32, 38, 56, 57, 59, 72, 74, 107, 120, 128, 135 ἐποίησε κύριος ὁ θεός=R.: Codd. X. 14, 15, 16, 19, 20, 25 (m), 31, 37, 61, 73, 75, 76, 77, 78, 79, 82, 83, 106, 108, 127, 128, 129, 131, 134, tz, *om.* κύριος: Codd. X. (marg.), 19, 25 (m), 32, 57, 61, 73, 78, 79, 83, 108, 127 (marg.), 131, rt, ἔβρεξεν κύριος ὁ θεός: Codd. III. 14, 15, 16, 20, 37, 38, 55, 56, 59, 68, 72, 74, 75, 76, 77, 82, 106, 107, 120, 121, 128, 129 *om.* κύριος =R.: Codd. AE 14, 15, 16, 20, 25 (m), 32, 38, 55, 56, 57, 59, 72, 73, 74, 78, 79, 83, 127, 128, 129, 131, 134, rt, ἐργάζεσθαι τὴν γῆν.

All early Latin versions, e. g. S. Ambros. *in Luc.* 15 (i. 1464),

S. Aug. *de Gen. c. Manich.* 2. 1 (i. 663) read 'fecit Deus,' not 'Dominus Deus.' S. Aug. *ibid.* has 'cum factus esset dies 'quo fecit Deus,' which supports the readings of Codd. 75, 129 ἡμέρα or ἡ ἡμέρα.

Philo *Leg. Alleg.* i. 8 (i. 47) αὕτη ἡ βίβλος γενέσεως οὐρανοῦ καὶ γῆς ὅτε ἐγένετο [Cod. Vat. ἐγένοντο]: id. *de Mundi Opif.* 44 (i. 30) αὕτη ἡ βίβλος . . . . ἀνατεῖλαι=R. except that κύριος is omitted after ἐποίησε : id. *Leg. Alleg.* i. 9 (i. 47) ᾗ ἡμέρᾳ ἐποίησεν . . . . ἐργάζεσθαι τὴν γῆν=R. except that κύριος is also omitted, and τὴν γῆν is read instead of αὐτήν: these readings are repeated in the shorter citations which form the text of his commentary in the following page.

GENESIS ii. 6.

Πηγὴ δὲ ἀνέβαινεν ἐκ τῆς γῆς καὶ ἐπότιζε πᾶν τὸ πρόςωπον τῆς γῆς.

Cod. 16 ἀπὸ τῆς γῆς.

Philo i. 31=R. except ἀπὸ τῆς γῆς : i. 249, 573=R.

ἀπό is more commonly used than ἐκ as a translation of מִן, and the uniform translation *de terra* shows it to have been the reading of the text from which the early Latin versions were made.

GENESIS ii. 7.

Καὶ ἔπλαςεν ὁ θεὸς τὸν ἄνθρωπον χοῦν ἀπὸ τῆς γῆς· καὶ ἐνεφύςηςεν εἰς τὸ πρόςωπον αὐτοῦ πνοὴν ζωῆς καὶ ἐγένετο ὁ ἄνθρωπος εἰς ψυχὴν ζῶςαν.

Codd. 15, 16, 18, 19, 31, 37, 59, 61, 68, 72, 75, 79, 82, 106, 107, 108, 120, 121, z, χοῦν+λαβών.

Philo *de Mundi Opif.* 46 (i. 32) ἔπλασεν ὁ θεὸς ἄνθρωπον χοῦν λαβὼν ἀπὸ τῆς γῆς καὶ ἐνεφύσησεν εἰς τὸ πρόσωπον αὐτοῦ πνοὴν ζωῆς (but in the following commentary he interprets πνοήν by πνεῦμα, τὸ γὰρ ἐνεφύσησεν οὐδὲν ἦν ἕτερον ἢ πνεῦμα θεῖον ἀπὸ τῆς μακαρίας καὶ εὐδαίμονος ἐκείνης φύσεως ἀποικίαν τὴν ἐνθάδε στειλά- μενον . . .): id. *Leg. Alleg.* i. 12 (i. 50) καὶ ἔπλασεν . . . . ζῶσαν =R. except that λαβών is added after χοῦν: (in the following commentary he lays emphasis on the use of πνοήν instead of πνεῦμα, πνοὴν δὲ ἀλλ᾽ οὐ πνεῦμα εἴρηκεν ὡς διαφορᾶς οὔσης· τὸ μὲν γὰρ πνεῦμα νενόηται κατὰ τὴν ἰσχὺν καὶ εὐτονίαν καὶ δύναμιν ἡ δὲ πνοὴ ὡς ἂν αὔρα τίς ἐστι καὶ ἀναθυμίασις ἠρεμαία καὶ πραεία): id. *Leg. Alleg.* iii. 55 (i. 119) ἐνεφύσησε γὰρ εἰς τὸ πρόσωπον αὐτοῦ πνεῦμα ζωῆς ὁ θεὸς καὶ ἐγένετο ὁ ἄνθρωπος εἰς ψυχὴν ζωῆς: id. *Quod det. pot. insid.* 22 (i. 207) ἐνεφύσησεν εἰς τὸ πρόσωπον αὐτοῦ πνεῦμα ζωῆς καὶ ἐγένετο ὁ ἄνθρωπος εἰς ψυχὴν ζῶσαν, where there is a following commentary on the use of πνεῦμα): id. *Quis rer. divin. heres* 11 (i. 481) ἐνεφύσησε γάρ, φησίν, ὁ ποιητὴς τῶν ὅλων εἰς τὸ πρόσωπον αὐτοῦ πνοὴν ζωῆς καὶ ἐγένετο ὁ ἄνθρωπος εἰς ψυχὴν ζῶσαν (but the preceding remarks imply that either he read πνεῦμα or considered πνοήν to be its exact equivalent): id. *de plantat. Noe* 5 (i. 332), and (ps.-Philo) *de mundo* 3 (ii. 606) ἐνέπνευσε γάρ, φησίν, ὁ θεὸς εἰς τὸ πρόσωπον αὐτοῦ πνοὴν ζωῆς.

The variants which are found in Philo, ἐνέπνευσεν and ἐνεφύσησεν, πνοήν and πνεῦμα, have parallels in the Latin versions, which show that they existed side by side in very early times. Augustine not only mentions the fact of variation between *flavit* or *sufflavit*, and *spiravit* or *inspiravit*, and between *flatum vitae* and *spiritum vitae*, *de Gen. ad litt.* 7. 2 (iii. 211), *Epist.* 205 (146), *ad Consent.* c. 9 (ii. 770), but himself also varies, cf. *de Gen. ad litt.* 6. 1 (iii. 197), *ib.* 7. 5 (iii. 213), *de Gen. c. Manich.* 2. 10, 11 (i. 668, 669), *Epist.* 205 (146) *ut supra*, *de Civit. Dei* 13. 24 (vii. 346). He regards *flatum* as the more usual and correct word, and it is uniformly used by Tertullian, who also avoids *spiravit* and *inspiravit*, though he varies between *flavit*, *de Anima* 26, p. 284, *afflavit*, *Hermog.* 26, 31, pp. 242, 244, *inflavit*, *adv. Marc.* 2. 4, p. 383, and *insufflavit*, *de Resurr. carnis* 5, p. 328. *Spiritum* is found in Ambrose *in Ps. cxviii.* 10. 15 (i. 1091), *de bono mort.* c. 9 (i. 405), (but elsewhere *flatum*), and in Hilar. *in Ps. cxviii.* p. 299.

Symmachus and Theodotion have ἔπνευσεν, Aquila has ἐνεφύσησεν: and the hypothesis that the two readings coexisted in the earliest forms of the LXX. is supported by their combination in Wisdom 15. 11, where there is an evident reference to this passage, ὅτι ἠγνόησε τὸν πλάσαντα αὐτὸν καὶ τὸν ἐμπνεύσαντα αὐτῷ ψυχὴν ἐνεργοῦσαν καὶ ἐμφυσήσαντα πνεῦμα ζωτικόν. It may be further noted that ἐμπνεῖν is not elsewhere used to translate נפח, but that ἐμφυσᾶν is so used in Ezek. 22. 21: 37. 9: and that there is probably a reference to this passage in S. John 20. 20 καὶ τοῦτο εἰπὼν ἐνεφύσησεν καὶ λέγει αὐτοῖς λάβετε πνεῦμα ἅγιον: so also Justin M. *Dial.* 40 uses τοῦ ἐμφυσήματος in reference to Adam's creation.

The addition of λαβών to χοῦν, though probably no more than the epexegesis of a Hebraism, is probably very ancient, since it is found not only in Philo and many of the best MSS., but also in some early Latin versions, viz. Iren. *Vet. Interp.* 4. 20. 1 (i. 253) 'limum terrae *accipiens*': and in a more expanded form Iren. 5.

15. 1, i. 311 'et *sumpsit* Dominus limum de terra et finxit hominem': Philastr. 97, p. 93 'et *accepit* Dominus terram de limo et
plasmavit hominem': so Hilar. *in Ps. cxviii.* p. 299, Ambros. *in
Ps. cxviii.* 10. 15 (i. 1091). Another epexegetical variant in early
Latin was 'de limo terrae' Tert. *Hermog.* 26, p. 242 (but elsewhere, e.g. *adv. Marc.* 1. 24 p. 378 'limum de terra'): Augustine,
though he sometimes uses the words 'de limo terrae,' not only
speaks of them as an epexegesis of the Hebrew, but also states
expressly that in the Greek MSS. which he used (as in the Sixtine
text), λαβών was omitted, *de Civit. Dei* 24. 13 (vii. 345) 'et formavit
Deus hominem pulverem de terra . . . . quod quidam *planius inter-
pretandum putantes* dixerunt Et finxit Deus hominem de limo
terrae': after giving the reason for the interpretation he again
quotes 'et formavit Deus hominem pulverem de terra, *sicut Graeci
codices habent,* unde in Latinam linguam scriptura ista conversa est.'

Genesis ii. 8.

Καὶ ἐφύτεγςεν ὁ θεὸς παράδειςον ἐν Ἐδὲμ κατὰ ἀνατολάς.

Codd. AE 16, 19, 20, 25 (m), 32, 55, 57, 59, 73, 77, 78, 79,
106, 127, 128, 131, 135 [? not (r) Lag.], t, κύριος ὁ θεός.

Philo *Leg. Alleg.* i. 14 (i. 52), *de plant. Noe* 8 (i. 334), *de confus.
ling.* 14 (i. 414) καὶ ἐφύτευσεν . . . . ἀνατολάς = R.

The omission of κύριος is supported by the early Latin versions
(except S. Aug. *de doctr. Christ.* 3. 52 (iii. 62) 'Dominus Deus,'
elsewhere simply 'Deus'). But it would be difficult to frame any
theory to account for the omission or insertion of κύριος in this
part of Genesis. For example, יְהוָה occurs eleven times in this
chapter, viz. in vv. 4, 5, 7, 8, 9, 15, 16, 18, 21, 22; no existing
MS. of the LXX. translates it in every passage: and all MSS.
omit it in vv. 9, 19: one small group of MSS., viz. 25 (m), 73,
130 (t) agree in omitting it in vv. 4, 9, 19, 21 and inserting it
elsewhere: Codd. 82 (f) and z, omit it in vv. 4, 5, 7, 8, 9, 19, 21,
Cod. 106 agrees with them except as to v. 8, Cod. 108 (d) except
as to vv. 4, 5 and Cod. 19 (h) except as to vv. 5, 8. There is a
corresponding variety in the early Latin versions: but יְהוָה is
uniformly translated by Jerome wherever it occurs, except in v. 16,
where the subject of וַיְצַו is continued from the preceding verse.

GENESIS ii. 19.

Καὶ πᾶν ὃ ἐὰν ἐκάλεϲεν ἀγτὸ Ἀδὰμ ψγχὴν ζῶϲαν τοῆτο ὄνομα αγτῷ.

Codd. AE, 38, 127, 129 αὐτοῦ, Codd. 15, 18, 37, 61, 72, 75, 106, 107, ΓZ, αὐτοῖς.

Philo *Leg. Alleg.* ii. 4 (i. 68)=R.: id. *de mutat. nom.* 9 (i. 588) ὃ ἂν ἐκάλεσεν ὁ Ἀδάμ, τοῦτο ὄνομα τοῦ κληθέντος ἦν.

Philo's reading τοῦ κληθέντος is epexegetical : but it confirms the reading αὐτοῦ, which is further confirmed by the uniform '*ejus*' of the early Latin.

GENESIS ii. 24.

Ἕνεκεν τοΎτοΥ καταλείψει ἄνθρωπος τὸν πατέρα αΓτοῦ καὶ τὴν μητέρα καὶ προϲκολληθήϲεται πρὸϲ τὴν ΓΥναῖκα αΓτοῦ καὶ ἔϲονται οἱ ΔΎο εἰϲ ϲάρκα μίαν.

Codd. AE, 14, 15, 16, 31, 56, 57, 59, 61, 73, 75, 76, 77, 78, 82, 106, 127, 128, 129, 130 (t), 131, 134, ΓZ, μητέρα αὐτοῦ : Codd. AD (Grab.) E 25 (m), 31, 59, 68, 83, 120, 121, rtz, πρὸς τὴν γυναῖκα : Cod. A τῇ γυναικί.

Philo *Leg. Alleg.* ii. 14 (i. 75)=R., but omits αὐτοῦ after πατέρα : id. *de Gigant.* 15 (i. 272)=R. except ἐγένοντο γάρ for καὶ ἔσονται : id. *Fragm. ap. Joann. Damasc.* ii. 653, 654=R. except δύο for οἱ δύο.

The omission of αὐτοῦ after πατέρα is supported by Codd. א BDZ and other authorities in Matt. 19. 5, and by Cod. D in Mark 10. 7, and by the early Latin versions here, except only that Aug. *de Gen. ad litt.* 6 (iii. 198) has 'patrem *suum*.' The addition of αὐτοῦ to μητέρα is supported by Codd. א DM and other authorities in Mark 10. 7, but has against it all good MSS. in Matt. 19. 5, and all the early Latin versions here. The reading τῇ γυναικί for πρὸς τὴν γυναῖκα is supported by all uncial and most cursive MSS. in Matt. 19. 5, and by Codd. ACLN in Mark 10. 7 : also by the early Latin 'mulieri suae' or 'uxori suae:' it may be noted in reference to it that although the text of the quotation in the MSS. of Philo i. 75 is πρὸς τὴν γ., his commentary has the dative ... προσκολλᾶται καὶ ἑνοῦται τῇ αἰσθήσει (which is his exegesis of τῇ γυναικί) .... οὐκ ἡ γυνὴ κολλᾶται τῷ ἀνδρί.

GENESIS iii. 15.

Καὶ ἔχθραν θήϲω ἀνὰ μέϲον ϲογ καὶ ἀνὰ μέϲον τῆϲ γνναικὸϲ καὶ ἀνὰ μέϲον τογ ϲπέρματόϲ ϲογ καὶ ἀνὰ μέϲον τογ ϲπέρματοϲ αγτῆϲ· αγτόϲ ϲογ τηρήϲει κεφαλήν καὶ ϲγ τηρήϲειϲ αγτογ πτέρναν.

So Codd. AE, 14, 15, 16, 18, 19, 20, 25 (m), 31, 32, 37, 38, 55, 56, 57, 59, 61, 64, 68, 72, 73, 74, 76, 77, 78, 79, 82, 83, 107, 108, 120, 121, 128, 129, 130 (t), 131, 134, 135 (r): Cod. 75 καὶ ἔχθραν θήσω ἀνὰ μέσον σοῦ καὶ ἀνὰ μέσον τοῦ σπέρματος αὐτῆς· αὐτός σου τοιρήσει τὴν κεφαλὴν σοῦ δὲ αὐτοῦ τὴν πτέρναν : Codd. 106, z, τηρήσῃ and τηρήσῃς.

Philo Leg. Alleg. iii. 21 (i. 99)=R. except that he omits ἀνὰ μέσον before the second τοῦ σπέρματος: ibid. cc. 64–67 (i. 123, 124) he has the same omission, and the following comments: (1) τήρει δὲ ὅτι οὐκ εἶπεν 'ἔχθραν θήσω σοὶ καὶ τῇ γυναικὶ' ἀλλὰ ἀνὰ μέσον σοῦ καὶ τῆς γυναικός, the Hebraistic repetition of ἀνὰ μέσον being omitted : so also, a few lines below, τὸ δὲ 'ἀνὰ μέσον τοῦ σπέρματός σου καὶ τοῦ σπέρματος αὐτῆς' εἴρηται πάλιν φυσικῶς. (2) Τὸ δὲ 'αὐτός σου τηρήσει κεφαλὴν καὶ σὺ τηρήσεις αὐτοῦ πτέρναν' τῇ μὲν φωνῇ βαρβαρισμός ἐστι τῷ δὲ σημαινομένῳ κατόρθωμα : and, a few lines below, the commentary leaves no doubt that he read τηρήσει, since he explains it τὸ δὲ 'τηρήσει' δύο δηλοῖ· ἐν μὲν τὸ οἷον διαφυλάξει καὶ διασώσει, ἕτερον δὲ τὸ ἴσον τῷ ἐπιτηρήσει πρὸς ἀναίρεσιν.

Justin M. Tryph. 102 καὶ ἔχθραν θήσω ἀνὰ μέσον αὐτοῦ καὶ τῆς γυναικὸς καὶ τοῦ σπέρματος αὐτοῦ καὶ τοῦ σπέρματος αὐτῆς.

The early Latin versions, e.g. Lucif. Calar. de S. Athanas. i. 1, p. 67, ed. Hart., Ambros. de fug. saec. 7. 43 (i. 434) translate שׁוּף by 'observabit,' with the exceptions of Tert. de cult. fem. 1. 6, p. 152, Iren. Vet. Interp. 4. 40 who have 'calcabit.' In Cypr. Testim. 2. 9, p. 74, the MSS. vary between 'calcavit' (Codd. AB; so ed. Hartel) and 'observabit' 'observavit,' (Codd. LM; so ed. Fell). Notwithstanding this variant the text of the LXX. seems to be certain: the difficulty is in the interpretation : almost all Hebrew scholars maintain that the Hebrew word requires some such translation as that of Aquila προστρίψει or Symmachus θλίψει : and in the only two other passages in which שׁוּף occurs the LXX. render it by ἐκτρίβειν, Job 9. 17, and καταπατεῖν Ps. 138 (139). 10.

GENESIS iv. 3.

Καὶ ἐγένετο μεθ' ἡμέρας ἤνεγκε Κάιν ἀπὸ τῶν καρπῶν τῆς γῆς θυσίαν τῷ Κυρίῳ.

Cod. 72 κυρίῳ τῷ θεῷ, Codd. E, 129 τῷ θεῷ.

Philo *de sacrif. Abel. et Cain.* 13 (i. 171) καὶ ἐγένετο μεθ' ἡμέρας ἤνεγκε Κάιν ἀπὸ τοῦ καρποῦ τῆς γῆς δῶρον τῷ Κυρίῳ.

It is clear from the comments which immediately follow this quotation, and also from p. 176, that Philo read, as all MSS. of the LXX., ἀπὸ τῶν καρπῶν: the only other traces of the singular are in Tertull. *adv. Jud.* 5, p. 187, Lucif. Calar. *de S. Athan.* i. 1, p. 67, ed. Hart. The substitution of δῶρον for θυσίαν does not involve any change of meaning, the words being commonly interchanged in the LXX. as translations of פִּנְחָה, e. g. in the two following verses of this passage: and in p. 180 Philo himself uses θυσίαν in an indirect quotation of this passage τοῦ Κάιν μεθ' ἡμέρας φέροντος τὴν θυσίαν: the early Latin versions vary here, in sympathy with the Greek, between 'munus' ('munera') Tert. *adv. Jud.* 5, p. 138, Ambros. *de Cain et Abel* 1. 7 (i. 195), and 'sacrificium' Lucif. Calar. *pro S. Athan.* 1. 1, p. 67.

The reading of Codd. E, 129, τῷ θεῷ, though not that of the quotation in Philo, is supported by Heb. 11. 4 πλείονα θυσίαν Ἄβελ παρὰ Κάιν προσήνεγκεν τῷ θεῷ: but in 1 Clem. Rom. 4 there is the same difference as in the MSS. of the LXX. for Cod. A. reads τῷ θεῷ, Cod. C. τῷ κυρίῳ.

GENESIS viii. 21.

Ἔγκειται ἡ διάνοια τοῦ ἀνθρώπου ἐπιμελῶς ἐπὶ τὰ πονηρὰ ἐκ νεότητος αὐτοῦ.

Codd. 61, 78 τῶν ἀνθρώπων, Cod. 83 *om.* ἐπιμελῶς, Codd. AE, 15, 20, 37, 55, 61, 64, 68, 74, 83, 120, 121, 129, 130, 134, z, *om.* αὐτοῦ.

Philo *Quis rer. divin. heres* 59 (i. 516)=R. but *om.* αὐτοῦ: id. *Fragm. ap. Joann. Monach.* (ii. 663) ὅρα γὰρ αἷς ἐγκεχάρακται πάντων ἡ διάνοια ἐπιμελῶς.

The omission of αὐτοῦ is confirmed by the early Latin versions. The words ἐγκεχάρακται ἡ διάνοια in the fragment of Philo are remarkable as being an alternative translation of יֵצֶר לֵב which

others rendered by τὸ πλάσμα τῆς καρδίας (Euseb. Emis. *in Cat.*
Reg.=Procop. *in Gen.* p. 253, ap. Field's *Hexapla in loc.*). ἔγκειται ἐπιμελῶς are a gloss rather than a translation, and neither word
is elsewhere used to render יָצַר or its derivatives: and although
ἐγχαράσσειν, like ἔγκεισθαι, does not occur elsewhere in the LXX.,
yet the metaphor which it contains is in harmony with the other
translations of יָצַר, e. g. πλάσσειν (frequently), καταπλάσσειν (Jer.
1. 5), κατασκευάζειν (Is. 45. 7, 9), χωνεύειν (1 Kings 7. 3 (15)).

GENESIS ix. 25.

Ἐπικατάρατος Χαναὰν παῖς οἰκέτης ἔςται τοῖς ἀδελφοῖς αὐτοῦ.

> Cod. 59 *om.* παῖς, Cod. 72 *om.* οἰκέτης.

> Philo *de sobriet.* 7 (i. 397) ἐπικατάρατος Χαναὰν παῖς οἰκέτης δοῦλος
> δούλων ἔσται τοῖς ἀδελφοῖς αὐτοῦ, but *ibid.* 11 (i. 400)=R.

The text of Philo, i. 397 E, incorporates a gloss, δοῦλος δούλων,
which is Aquila's translation of the Hebrew text here: it helps to
show that παῖς οἰκέτης are to be taken together as in the Old Latin,
Ambros. *Ep.* 37 (ii. 931) 'servus domesticus erit fratribus suis.'

GENESIS ix. 27.

Πλατύναι ὁ θεὸς τῷ Ἰάφεθ καὶ κατοικησάτω ἐν τοῖς οἴκοις τοῦ Σήμ· καὶ
γενηθήτω Χαναὰν παῖς αὐτοῦ.

> Codd. plur. τοῖς σκηνώμασι τοῦ [Codd. 15, 64, 106 *om.*] Σήμ:
> Codd. D, 19, 58, 59, 108 ἔσται Χαναάν: Codd. AD, 31, 57,
> 58, 59, 71, 73, 75, 78, 83, 108, 128, 129, 130, r, αὐτῶν:
> Codd. 14, 16, 18, 25 (m), 32, 38, 76, 77, 79, 131, 134, t,
> αὐτῷ.

> Philo *de sobriet.* 12 (i. 401)=R. except the last clause γενέσθω
> Χαναὰν δοῦλος αὐτοῖς.

The texts from which the Old Latin versions were made
evidently varied between οἴκοις and σκηνώμασι, the former being
represented by 'domibus' in Ambros. *de Noe* 32 (i. 276), and the
latter by 'tabernaculis' in Philastr. 121, p. 128. That Philo read
οἴκοις is clear from his comment on the word p. 402.

Philo's reading αὐτοῖς, which finds no support elsewhere, may be
due to the transcriber and not to Philo himself, since in commenting upon it he substitutes the genitive, δοῦλον τὸν ἄφρονα τῶν τῆς
ἀρετῆς μεταποιουμένων, p. 403.

Genesis xii. 1–3.

Καὶ εἶπε κύριος τῷ Ἀβρὰμ Ἔξελθε ἐκ τῆς γῆς coy καὶ ἐκ τῆς cυγγενείας
coy καὶ ἐκ τοῦ οἴκου τοῦ πατρός coy καὶ Δεῦρο εἰς τὴν γῆν ἣν ἄν coι Δείξω·
καὶ ποιήcω cε εἰς ἔθνος μέγα καὶ εὐλογήcω cε καὶ μεγαλυνῶ τὸ ὄνομά coy
καὶ ἔcῃ εὐλογημένος· καὶ εὐλογήcω τοὺς εὐλογοῦντάς cε καὶ τοὺς καταρωμένους cε καταράcομαι· καὶ ἐνευλογηθήcονται ἐν coὶ πᾶcαι αἱ φυλαὶ τῆς γῆς.

Codd. A [D. Grabe], 15, 55, 74, 76, 129, 134 *om. καὶ δεῦρο* :
  Codd. A [D. Grabe] E 14, 15, 16, 18, 25 (m), 57, 72, 73,
  77, 78, 79, 82, 128, 129, 131, 135 (r), t, *ἔcῃ εὐλογητός*.

Philo *de migrat. Abraham.* 1 (i. 436) *καὶ εἶπε .... τῆς γῆς*=R.
 except (1) *ἄπελθε* for *ἔξελθε*, (2) *om. καὶ δεῦρο*, (3) *εὐλογητός* for
 εὐλογήμενος : *ibid.* 16 (i. 449) *μεγαλυνῶ τὸ ὄνομά σου* : *ibid.* 19,
 20, 21 (i. 453, 454) *ἔcῃ γάρ, φησίν, εὐλογητός .... εὐλογήσω,*
 φησί, τοὺς εὐλογοῦντάς σε καὶ τοὺς καταρωμένους σε καταράσομαι
 .... ἐνευλογηθήσονται ἔν σοι πᾶσαι αἱ φυλαὶ τῆς γῆς : id. *Quis*
 rer. divin. heres 56 (i. 513) *εἶπε κύριος .... ἔθνος μέγα*=R.
 except *πρός* for *δεῦρο εἰς*.

Acts 7. 3 *καὶ εἶπε πρὸς αὐτόν, Ἔξελθε ἐκ τῆς γῆς σου καὶ ἐκ τῆς συγ-*
 γενείας σου καὶ δεῦρο εἰς τὴν γῆν ἣν ἄν σοι δείξω [Cod. D *ἀπὸ τῆς*
 γῆς : Codd. BD *καὶ τῆς συγγενείας σου* : Cod. E *add.* post *συγγε-*
 νείας σου, καὶ ἐκ τοῦ οἴκου τοῦ πατρός σου].

1 Clem. R. 10. 2 *ἄπελθε ἐκ τῆς γῆς σου .... τῆς γῆς*=R. except
 (1) *ἄπελθε* for *ἔξελθε*, (2) *om. καὶ δεῦρο*, (3) *εὐλογηθήσονται* for
 ἐνευλογηθήσονται.

The reading *ἄπελθε*, which was certainly in Philo's text, inasmuch
as he comments upon it, p. 437, though not found in any MS. of
the LXX. is supported by Clement, and by the fact that *ἐξέρχεσθαι*
is very rarely, and not once in the Pentateuch, used to translate
יָלַךְ, while *ἀπέρχεσθαι* is frequently so used (18 times in Genesis):
but in the quotation of this passage in Acts 7. 3 all the MSS. have
ἔξελθε, which however is followed in Cod. D by *ἀπό*.

The omission of *καὶ δεῦρο* is also supported both by Clement *l. c.*
and by the fact that the words have no equivalent in the Hebrew :
but they also are found in all MSS. of Acts 7. 3. They are an
early and graphic gloss.

The reading *εὐλογητός* is emphasized by Philo i. 353 *ἔcῃ γάρ,*
φησίν, εὐλογητὸς οὐ μόνον εὐλογημένος, distinguishing the former as a
permanent and real quality, the latter as contingent on human
voices and opinions.

GENESIS xiv. 14 (xvii. 23).

Ἠριθμήϲε τοὺϲ ἰδίουϲ οἰκογενεῖϲ αὐτοῦ τριακοϲίουϲ δέκα καὶ ὀκτώ.

Cod. 129 *om. καί*: Codd. D (Gr.), 14 δέκα καὶ ὀκτὼ καὶ τριακοσίους: Codd. 15, 16, 18, 25 (m), 38, 55, 57, 59, 76, 77, 79,
82, 128, 131, 134, t, ὀκτὼ καὶ δέκα καὶ τριακοσίους: Cod. 78
ὀκτὼ καὶ δέκα τριακοσίους.

Barn. 9 καὶ περιέτεμεν Ἀβραὰμ ἐκ τοῦ οἴκου αὐτοῦ [Cod. C *om. ἐκ* . . . .
αὐτοῦ] ἄνδρας δέκα ὀκτὼ [ita Codd. אC, cett. δέκα καὶ ὀκτώ] καὶ
[Cod. p. *om.*] τριακοσίους.

The first part of the quotation in Barnabas is a summary of
Gen. 17. 23, the material point of the reference being not the
mention of circumcision but the number of persons circumcised,
upon which the writer founds an argument : τίς οὖν ἡ δοθεῖσα αὐτῷ
γνῶσις ; μάθετε ὅτι τοὺς δεκαοκτὼ πρώτους καὶ διάστημα ποιήσας λέγει
τριακοσίους. τὸ δεκαοκτὼ [Codd. bcn δέκα καὶ ὀκτώ]· I δέκα, H ὀκτώ·
ἔχεις Ἰησοῦν [Cod. א *om.* I . . . ὀκτώ: Cod. C *om.* ἔχεις Ἰη.]· ὅτι δὲ ὁ
σταυρὸς ἐν τῷ Τ ἤμελλεν ἔχειν τὴν χάριν, λέγει καὶ τριακοσίους. δηλοῖ οὖν
τὸν μὲν Ἰησοῦν ἐν τοῖς δυσὶν γράμμασιν καὶ ἐν τῷ ἑνὶ τὸν σταυρον, 'What,
then, was the knowledge given to him?' Observe that he mentions
the eighteen first, and then, with a pause, three hundred. In the
eighteen, i. e. I=ten, H=eight, you have (the initials of) Jesus
(ΙΗΣΟΥΣ). And because the Cross was to have its grace in (the
form) T, he mentions also three hundred : he thus indicates Jesus
in the two letters and the Cross in the third.

This shows that in the text which Barnabas used (1) the numbers
were probably expressed by the symbols ιητ ; (2) that, whether so
expressed or written in full, τ or τριακοσίους came last. There is a
similar variety in the MSS. in other enumerations of numbers, e. g.
Gen. 5. 6, 7, 8, etc., and it is difficult to determine whether the LXX.
originally followed the Hebrew in placing the larger number last
so that the text of the uncial MSS. and R here is due to Hellenizing
copyists, or followed the Greek usage in placing the larger number
first, so that the text of Barnabas, and of the MSS. which agree with
him, is due to a Hebraizing revision.

GENESIS xv. 5, 6.

Ἐξήγαγε δὲ αὐτὸν ἔξω καὶ εἶπεν αὐτῷ, ἀνάβλεψον δὴ εἰς τὸν οὐρανὸν καὶ
ἀρίθμηϲον τοὺϲ ἀϲτέραϲ εἰ δυνήϲῃ ἐξαριθμῆϲαι αὐτούϲ· καὶ εἶπεν, οὕτωϲ

ἔςται τὸ ϲπέρμα ϲογ· καὶ ἐπίϲτεγϲεν Ἀβρἀμ τῷ θεῷ καὶ ἐλογίϲθη αγτῷ εἰϲ
ΔΙΚΑΙΟϹΫΝΗΝ.

Codd. 15, 19, 37, 38, 61, 72, 77, 108, 129, 135 (r), z, om. δή:
Codd. 19, 108 ἐπίστευσε δέ for καὶ ἐπίστευσε.

Philo *Leg. Alleg.* iii. 13 (i. 95) ἐξήγαγεν αὐτὸν ἔξω καὶ εἶπεν, ἀνάβλεψον
εἰς τὸν οὐρανὸν καὶ ἀρίθμησον τοὺς ἀστέρας : id. *Quis rer. divin.
heres* 15–19 (i. 483–486) (15) ἐξήγαγεν αὐτὸν ἔξω καὶ εἶπεν
ἀνάβλεψον εἰς τὸν οὐρανόν . . . . (16) ἐξήγαγεν αὐτὸν ἔξω (*bis*) . . . .
(17) ἀνάβλεψον εἰς τὸν οὐρανὸν καὶ ἀρίθμησον τοὺς ἀστέρας ἐὰν
δυνηθῇς ἐξαριθμῆσαι αὐτούς· οὕτως ἔσται τὸ σπέρμα σοῦ . . . . (19)
(εὖ δὲ τὸ φάναι) λογισθῆναι τὴν πίστιν εἰς δικαιοσύνην αὐτῷ : id. *de
migrat. Abraham.* 9 (i. 443) ἐπίστευσεν Ἀβραὰμ τῷ θεῷ : id. *de
mutat. nomin.* 33 (i. 605) ἐπίστευσε δὲ Ἀβραὰμ τῷ θεῷ καὶ ἐλογίσθη
αὐτῷ εἰς δικαιοσύνην.

Rom. 4. 3 (τί γὰρ ἡ γραφὴ λέγει) ἐπίστευσεν δὲ Ἀβραὰμ τῷ θεῷ καὶ
ἐλογίσθη αὐτῷ εἰς δικαιοσύνην (so Codd. ℵ ABC *al.* : Codd. DFG
om. δέ).

Rom. 4. 18 (κατὰ τὸ εἰρημένον) οὕτως ἔσται τὸ σπέρμα σου.

Gal. 3. 6 καθὼς Ἀβραὰμ ἐπίστευσεν τῷ θεῷ καὶ ἐλογίσθη αὐτῷ εἰς
δικαιοσύνην.

James 2. 23 (καὶ ἐπληρώθη ἡ γραφὴ ἡ λέγουσα) ἐπίστευσεν δὲ Ἀβραὰμ
τῷ θεῷ καὶ ἐλογίσθη αὐτῷ εἰς δικαιοσύνην.

1 Clem. Rom. 10. 6 ἐξήγαγε δὲ [Cod. A *om.* δὲ] ὁ θεὸς τὸν Ἀβραὰμ
καὶ εἶπεν αὐτῷ· ἀνάβλεψον εἰς τὸν οὐρανὸν καὶ ἀρίθμησον τοὺς ἀστέρας
εἰ δυνήσῃ ἐξαριθμῆσαι αὐτούς· οὕτως ἔσται τὸ σπέρμα σου· ἐπίστευσεν
δὲ Ἀβραὰμ τῷ θεῷ καὶ ἐλογίσθη αὐτῷ εἰς δικαιοσύνην.

Justin M. *Dial.* 92 ἐπίστευσε δὲ τῷ θεῷ Ἀβραὰμ καὶ ἐλογίσθη αὐτῷ
εἰς δικαιοσύνην : *ibid.* 119 (ὃν γὰρ τρόπον ἐκεῖνος τῇ φωνῇ τοῦ θεοῦ)
ἐπίστευσε καὶ ἐλογίσθη αὐτῷ εἰς δικαιοσύνην.

Philo's omission of δή after ἀνάβλεψον is confirmed by 1 Clem.
Rom. 10. 6 : which also agrees with Rom. 4. 3, James 2. 23,
Justin. M. *Dial.* 92 in reading ἐπίστευσε δέ. Though the variation
is exegetically unimportant, the consensus of five early quotations
as against all existing MSS. except 19 (Cod. Chisianus) and 108
(= Cod. Vatican. 330, which forms the basis of the Complutensian
edition) is a remarkable testimony to the text which those MSS.
contain.

The common origin of all the quotations is indicated by the fact
that they agree in translating the active, יַחְשְׁבֶהָ, 'he counted,' by the
passive ἐλογίσθη.

Genesis xv. 13, 14.

Γινώσκων γνώϲῃ ὅτι πάροικον ἔϲται τὸ ϲπέρμα ϲου ἐν γῇ ογκ ἰδίᾳ καὶ δογλώϲογϲιν αγτογϲ καὶ κακώϲογϲιν αγτογϲ καὶ ταπεινώϲογϲιν αγτογϲ τετρακόϲια ἔτη· τὸ δὲ ἔθνοϲ ᾧ ἐὰν δογλεγϲωϲι κρινῶ ἐγώ· μετὰ δὲ ταγτα ἐξελεγϲονται ὧδε μετὰ ἀποϲκεγῆϲ πολλῆϲ.

Cod. 72 ἐν γῇ ἀλλοτρίᾳ: Cod. A, κακώσουσιν αὐτοὺς καὶ δουλώσουσιν αὐτούς: Codd. X, 37, 61, 107, 108, z, omit αὐτούς after κακώσουσιν: Codd. 19, 72, 81, omit καὶ ταπ. αὐτούς: Codd. X, 19, 37, 75, 77, 106, 108, 129, 130, z, ἔτη τετρακόσια: Codd. 14, 18, 19, 25 (m), 32, 57, 73, 75, 77, 78, 79, 131, t, καὶ τὸ ἔθνος.

Philo Quis rer. divin. heres 54 (i. 511) γινώσκων . . . . ἰδίᾳ, = R. : ibid. 55 (i. 512) τὸ δὲ ἔθνος . . . . πολλῆς, = R.

Acts 7. 6 ἔσται τὸ σπέρμα αὐτοῦ [Cod. ℵ σοῦ] πάροικον ἐν γῇ ἀλλοτρίᾳ καὶ δουλώσουσιν αὐτὸ [Cod. D αὐτοὺς] καὶ κακώσουσιν [Cod. C adds αὐτὸ] ἔτη τετρακόσια· καὶ τὸ ἔθνος, [Cod. C τὸ δὲ ἔθνος] ᾧ ἐὰν δουλεύσουσιν [Codd. ℵ BE al. δουλεύσωσιν] κρινῶ ἐγώ, ὁ θεὸς εἶπεν, καὶ μετὰ ταῦτα ἐξελεύσονται (καὶ λατρεύσουσίν μοι ἐν τῷ τόπῳ τούτῳ).

The critical interest of the passage lies chiefly in the evident tendency to harmonize the LXX. text and that of the Acts, which is shown (a) in the MSS. of the LXX. (1) in the substitution of ἀλλοτρίᾳ for οὐκ ἰδίᾳ, (2) in the omission of καὶ ταπεινώσουσιν αὐτούς, (3) in the variant καὶ τό for τὸ δέ: (b) in the MSS. of the Acts (1) in the substitution of σοῦ for αὐτοῦ, which is unquestionable, inasmuch as αὐτῷ both precedes and follows, (2) in the addition of αὐτούς and αὐτό to δουλώσουσιν and κακώσουσιν, (3) possibly in the variants τὸ δέ for καὶ τό and δουλεύσωσιν for δουλεύσουσιν.

The quotation of the passage in Clementin. 3. 43, p. 48 = R. except in omitting αὐτούς after κακώσουσιν: but in the continuation of the quotation it reads μετ' εἰρήνης with AX, 14, 15, 19, 25 (m), 32, 37, 38, 55, 57, 73, 74, 76, 77, 78, 106, 107, 108, 129, 134, rtz, and confirms the view that these words should be substituted for the ἐν εἰρήνῃ of R.

Genesis xviii. 1–3.

Ὤφθη δὲ αγτῷ ὁ θεὸϲ πρὸϲ τῇ δργῒ τῇ Μαμβρῇ καθημένογ αγτογ ἐπὶ τῆϲ θγραϲ τῆϲ ϲκηνῆϲ αγτογ μεϲημβρίαϲ· ἀναβλέψαϲ δὲ τοῖϲ ὀφθαλμοῖϲ αγτογ εἶδε καὶ ἰδογ τρεῖϲ ἄνδρεϲ εἱϲτήκειϲαν ἐπάνω αγτογ· καὶ ἰδὼν προϲέδραμεν εἰϲ ϲγνάντηϲιν αγτοῖϲ ἀπὸ τῆϲ θγραϲ τῆϲ ϲκηνῆϲ αγτογ καὶ προϲεκγνηϲεν ἐπὶ τὴν γῆν καὶ εἶπε Κύριε, εἰ ἄρα εὗρον χάριν ἐναντίον coy, μὴ παρέλθῃς τὸν παῖδά coy.

Cod. 25 (m) πρὸς τῇ θύρᾳ : Cod. 82 ἐπὶ τῇ θύρᾳ : Cod. 106. *om.* αὐτοῦ after σκηνῆς.

Justin M. *Dial.* 86 πρὸς τῇ δρυὶ τῇ Μαμβρῇ : *ibid.* 126 ὤφθη . . . . μεσημβρίας = R. exc. (1) καθημένῳ, (2) *om.* αὐτοῦ after ὀφθαλμοῖς, (3) συνέδραμεν for προσέδραμεν : *ibid.* 56 ὤφθη . . . . ἐπὶ τὴν γῆν καὶ εἶπε = R. except (1) ἐπὶ τῇ θύρᾳ, (2) *om.* αὐτοῦ after σκηνῆς and after ὀφθαλμοῖς, (3) συνέδραμεν for προσέδραμεν.

At the end of this quotation in c. 56 the text of Justin goes on καὶ τὰ λοιπὰ μέχρι τοῦ Ὥρθρισε δέ, i. e. the intervening words are omitted as far as c. 19. 28. But since, lower down in the same chapter, p. 278 b, Justin excuses himself from repeating some of the intervening words on the ground that they had been written down before, οὐ γὰρ γράφειν πάλιν τὰ αὐτὰ τῶν πάντων προγεγραμμένων δοκεῖ μοι, it is clear that the omission is due to the copyist.

GENESIS xviii. 10.

Ἐπαναcτρέφων ἥξω πρὸc cὲ κατὰ τὸν καιρὸν τοῦτον εἰc ὥραc καὶ ἕξει γίὸν Cάρρα ἡ γυνή coy.

Codd. 14, 16, 18, 25 (m), 38, 57, 73, 77, 78, 79, 128, 131, 135 (r) (HP) + t ἀναστρέφων.

Philo *de migrat. Abraham.* 22 (i. 456) = R. : *de Abrah.* 25, (ii. 20) ἐπανιὼν ἥξω πρὸς σὲ κατὰ τὸν καιρὸν τοῦτον εἰς νέωτα καὶ ἕξει υἱὸν Σάρρα ἡ γυνή σου.

Rom. 9. 9 (ἐπαγγελίας γὰρ ὁ λόγος οὗτος·) κατὰ τὸν καιρὸν τοῦτον ἐλεύσομαι καὶ ἔσται τῇ Σάρρᾳ υἱός.

The use of the classical εἰς νέωτα, 'next year,' is remarkable as a translation of כָּעֵת חַיָּה (which occurs infra c. 14, and 2 Kings 4. 16, 17, where it is rendered ὡς ἡ ὥρα ζῶσα). There is no trace of either the reading or the interpretation in the MSS. of the LXX. or in the early Latin versions: and it is a probable inference that the writer of the treatise *de Abrahamo*, whether Philo or another, had access to a revised, and otherwise unknown, edition of the LXX. : so in the same treatise, c. 32 (ii. 26), ἱερεῖον is substituted for πρόβατον in Gen. 22. 7, 8.

The quotation in Rom. 9. 9 is partly from v. 9, partly from v. 14, but not exactly from either.

GENESIS xviii. 20–23.

Εἶπε δὲ κύριος κραυγὴ Σοδόμων καὶ Γομόρρας πεπλήθυνται πρὸς μὲ καὶ
αἱ ἁμαρτίαι αὐτῶν μεγάλαι σφόδρα. καταβὰς οὖν ὄψομαι εἰ κατὰ τὴν κραυγὴν
αὐτῶν τὴν ἐρχομένην πρὸς μὲ συντελοῦνται· εἰ δὲ μὴ ἵνα γνῶ· καὶ ἀποστρέ-
ψαντες ἐκεῖθεν οἱ ἄνδρες ἦλθον εἰς Σόδομα· Ἀβραὰμ δὲ ἔτι ἦν ἑστηκὼς
ἐναντίον κυρίου καὶ ἐγγίσας Ἀβραὰμ εἶπε Μὴ συναπολέσῃς δίκαιον μετὰ
ἀσεβοῦς καὶ ἔσται ὁ δίκαιος ὡς ὁ ἀσεβής.

> Codd. AD, 15, 59, 68, 72, 82, 120, 121 *om.* πρὸς μέ after πεπλή-
> θυνται: Codd. 14, 16, 18, 19, 25 (m), 57, 73, 77, 78, 79,
> 108, 128, 131, t οἱ ἄνδρες ἐκεῖθεν: Codd. AD, 31, 37, 75, 76,
> 106, 107, 108, z *om.* ἔτι before ἦν: Cod. 132 ἑστὼς ἦν.

> Philo *de Cherub.* 6 (i. 142) ἔτι, γάρ, φησίν, ἦν ἑστηκὼς ἐναντίον κυρίου:
> id. *de Somniis* 2. 33 (i. 688) (Ἀβραάμ) ἐστιν ἑστὼς ἐναντίον κυρίου:
> id. *de poster. Cain.* 9 (i. 231) ἑστὼς ἦν ἐναντίον κυρίου καὶ ἐγγίσας
> εἶπε.

> Justin M. *Dial.* 56. p. 278 εἶπε δὲ κύριος .... ὁ ἀσεβής = R. except
> (1) *om.* πρὸς μέ after πεπλήθυνται, (2) οἱ ἄνδρες ἐκεῖθεν for ἐκεῖθεν
> οἱ ἄνδρες, (3) *om.* ἔτι before ἦν.

GENESIS xviii. 27.

Καὶ ἀποκριθεὶς Ἀβραὰμ εἶπε, Νῦν ἠρξάμην λαλῆσαι πρὸς τὸν κύριόν μου,
ἐγὼ δὲ εἰμι γῆ καὶ σποδός.

> Codd. 19, 59 *om.* τόν: Codd. 76, 129 τὸν θεόν: Codd. ADE,
> 14, 15, 16, 18, 19, 25 (m), 56, 57, 59, 61, 68, 73, 78, 79,
> 82, 108, 120, 121, 128, 131, 135 (r), t, *om.* μου.

> Philo *Quis rer. divin. heres* 7 (i. 477) ἐγγίσας, γάρ, φησίν, Ἀβραὰμ
> εἶπε Νῦν ἠρξάμην λαλεῖν πρὸς κύριον, ἐγὼ δέ εἰμι γῆ καὶ σποδός: id.
> *Quod Deus immut.* 34 (i. 296) (εὐθὺς ἔγνω) γῆν καὶ τέφραν
> (ὄντα).

1 Clem. Rom. 17 ἐγὼ δέ εἰμι γῆ καὶ σποδός.

The text of Philo i. 477 is sufficiently supported by the MSS. of
the LXX., and by its agreement with the Hebrew, to be probably
correct, with the exception of ἐγγίσας for ἀποκριθείς; but it may be
almost certainly inferred that ἐγγίσας existed in the text which Philo
used, and that it is not a mere accidental transfer of phrase from
v. 23, from the fact of his laying stress upon it in introducing the
second of the above two quotations i. 296 καὶ γὰρ Ἀβραὰμ ἔγγιστα
τῷ θεῷ ἑαυτὸν ποιήσας, εὐθὺς ἔγνω κ.τ.λ. The use of τέφρα for γῆ in

the second quotation is less probably correct, because the word does not occur in the LXX. except in the Apocryphal Books.

GENESIS xxi. 10.

Καὶ εἶπε τῷ Ἀβραάμ Ἔκβαλε τὴν παιδίςκην ταύτην καὶ τὸν υἱὸν αὐτῆς· οὐ γὰρ μὴ κληρονομήςει ὁ υἱὸς τῆς παιδίςκης ταύτης μετὰ τοῦ υἱοῦ μου Ἰςαάκ.

Codd. AD 15, 19, 20, 31, 32, 55, 56, 68, 74, 76, 77, 83, 108, 120, 121, 129 καὶ εἶπε=R.: Codd. X, 14, 16, 18, 25 (m), 38, 57, 59, 71, 73, 75, 76, 78, 79, 82, 106, 107, 128, 130 (t), 131, 134, 135 (r), z, om. καί.

Codd. AD, X, 15, 55, 56, 57, 68, 71, 74, 75, 76, 106, 107, 120, 121, 131, 134, 135+z τὴν παιδίσκην ταύτην: Codd. 14, 16, 18, 19, 20, 25 (m), 31, 32, 38, 59, 73, 77, 78, 82, 108, 128, 129, t, om. ταύτην.

Codd. D, X, 59, 72, 106+z, om. μή post γάρ: Codd. cett.=R.

Codd. 18, 20, 25 (m), 32, 55, 131, 134, 135 (r) κληρονομήσῃ: Codd. cett.=R.

Codd. III, 68, 108, 120, 121, om. ταύτης: Codd. cett.=R.

Philo de Cherubim 3 (i. 140) λέγει δὲ ἄντικρυς ἐκβαλεῖν τὴν παιδίσκην καὶ τὸν υἱόν.

Gal. 4. 30 ἔκβαλε τὴν παιδίσκην [Cod. A add. ταύτην] καὶ τὸν υἱὸν αὐτῆς· οὐ γὰρ μὴ [Codd. FG, 37, om. μή] κληρονομήσει [ita Codd. ℵ BDE al.: Codd. ACFGKL al. κληρονομήσῃ] ὁ υἱὸς τῆς παιδίσκης μετὰ τοῦ υἱοῦ τῆς ἐλευθέρας [Codd. DEFG al., add. μου Ἰσαάκ].

Justin M. Dial. 56. p. 276 καὶ εἶπε .... Ἰσαάκ=R. except om. καὶ before εἶπε, and μή after οὐ.

It is uncertain here, as elsewhere, whether the omission of καί before εἶπε is due to the Hellenizing tendencies of the copyists, or its insertion is due to a Hebraizing revision of the text. The latter is the more probable hypothesis, because there are other instances in Genesis in which the LXX. translators seem to ignore this use of ן, i. e. as introducing an apodosis or virtual apodosis : e. g. 3. 6 διανοιχθήσονται for καὶ διαν., 13. 9 ἐγὼ εἰς δεξιά for καὶ ἐγώ (Cod. 75 ἢ ἐγώ, Codd. E, 14, 16, 18, 31, 57, 73, 128 ἐγὼ δέ). The omission of ταύτην in some MSS. of the LXX. and its insertion by Cod. A in Gal. 4. 30 are probably harmonistic. The same hypothesis will account for its omission in the Latin versions quoted by Ambrose and Augustine (ap. Sabatier): and the harmonistic tendency is certainly shown in the addition μου Ἰσαάκ.

GENESIS xxii. 1, 2, 11, 12.

v. 1 καὶ ἐγένετο μετὰ τὰ ῥήματα ταῦτα ὁ θεὸς ἐπείραςε τὸν Ἀβραὰμ καὶ εἶπεν αὐτῷ Ἀβραὰμ Ἀβραάμ· καὶ εἶπεν Ἰδοὺ ἐγώ. v. 2 καὶ εἶπε Λάβε τὸν υἱόν ςου τὸν ἀγαπητὸν ὃν ἠγάπηςας τὸν Ἰςαάκ . . . . v. 11 καὶ ἐκάλεςεν αὐτὸν ἄγγελος κυρίου ἐκ τοῦ οὐρανοῦ καὶ εἶπεν Ἀβραὰμ Ἀβραάμ· ὁ δὲ εἶπεν ἰδοὺ ἐγώ. v. 12 καὶ εἶπε μὴ ἐπιβάλῃς τὴν χεῖρά ςου ἐπὶ τὸ παιδάριον μηδὲ ποιήςῃς αὐτῷ μηδέν.

v. 1 Codd. X, 71, 74, 83 ἐπείρασε=R.: Codd. cett. ἐπείραζεν.

Codd. 19, 20, 25, 31, 32, 56, 68, 71, 74, 75, 83, 107, 120, 121 εἶπεν αὐτῷ=R.: Codd. cett. εἶπε πρὸς αὐτόν.

Codd. 19, 31, 38, 61, 68, 71, 74, 76, 79, 83, 106, 107, 120, 121, 128, z καὶ εἶπεν Ἰδού=R.: Codd. cett. ὁ δὲ εἶπεν Ἰδού.

v. 11 Codd. 14, 16, 18, 25 (m), 38, 57, 77, 79, 128, t λέγων post οὐρανοῦ; Codd. cett. καὶ εἶπεν=R.

Philo de Somniis 1. 34 (i. 650)=R. except (1) ἐπείραζε for ἐπείρασε, (2) πρὸς αὐτόν for αὐτῷ, (3) ὁ δὲ εἶπεν for καὶ εἶπεν Ἰδού in v. 1, (4) λέγων for καὶ εἶπεν in v. 11.

It may be noted that the text of Philo agrees throughout with that of Codd. 14, 16, 18, 57, 77, 130 (t), and differs throughout from that of Codd. 71, 74, 83: that it agrees in three out of four cases (1) with Cod. 25 (m) ἐπείραζεν, ὁ δὲ εἶπεν, λέγων, (2) with Codd. 38, 79, 128 ἐπείραζεν πρὸς αὐτόν, λέγων, (3) with Codd. 129, 134, 135 ἐπείραζεν, πρὸς αὐτόν, ὁ δὲ εἶπεν.

GENESIS xxii. 3, 4.

Καὶ ἦλθεν ἐπὶ τὸν τόπον ὃν εἶπεν αὐτῷ ὁ θεὸς τῇ ἡμέρᾳ τῇ τρίτῃ καὶ ἀναβλέψας Ἀβραὰμ τοῖς ὀφθαλμοῖς αὐτοῦ εἶδε τὸν τόπον μακρόθεν.

Codd. 19, 37, 76, 82, 106, 134, z εἰς τὸν τόπον: Codd. cett. ἐπὶ τὸν τόπον=R.

Philo de poster. Cain. 6 (i. 229) Ἀβραὰμ ἐλθὼν εἰς τὸν τόπον ὃν εἶπεν αὐτῷ ὁ θεὸς τῇ τρίτῃ ἡμέρᾳ ἀναβλεψὰς ὁρᾷ τὸν τόπον μακρόθεν: (the following words ποῖον τόπον ; ἆρ᾽ εἰς ὃν ἦλθε ; show that he certainly read εἰς τὸν τόπον): de migrat. Abraham. 25 (i. 457) (ὅταν) ἐπὶ τὸν τόπον ὃν εἶπεν αὐτῷ ὁ θεὸς τῇ ἡμέρᾳ τῇ τρίτῃ παραγένηται : *ibid.* 30. i. p. 462 (ἀμφότεροι ἀνῆλθον) ἐπὶ τὸν τόπον ὃν εἶπεν ὁ θεός : *de Somniis* i. 11 (i. 630) ἦλθεν εἰς τὸν τόπον ὃν εἶπεν αὐτῷ ὁ θεός. καὶ ἀναβλέψας τοῖς ὀφθαλμοῖς αὐτοῦ εἶδε τὸν τόπον μακρόθεν.

Philo's testimony is evenly balanced between ἐπὶ τὸν τόπον and εἰς τὸν τόπον : and between the quotations in i. p. 229 and i. p. 457 there is the further difference that whereas the former connects τῇ τρίτῃ ἡμέρᾳ with ἀναβλέψας, as in the Hebrew, the latter connects it with the preceding clause. A presumption in favour of the former having been the current Alexandrian reading is afforded by the repetition of Philo's quotation in Clem. Alex. *Strom.* 5. 11 p. 690, ed. Pott. ὁ Ἀβραὰμ ἐλθὼν εἰς τὸν τόπον ὃν εἶπεν αὐτῷ ὁ θεὸς τῇ τρίτῃ ἡμέρᾳ ἀναβλέψας ὁρᾷ τὸν τόπον μακρόθεν. The early Latin verss., on the other hand, clearly connect τῇ τρίτῃ ἡμέρᾳ with the preceding clause : Ambros. *de Cain. et Ab.* 1. 8 (i. 197); *de Abrah.* 1. 8 (i. 305); so Jerome *Hebr. Quaest.* p. 33, ed. Lagarde.

GENESIS xxii. 16, 17.

Κατ᾽ ἐμαυτοῦ ὤμοϲα, λέγει κύριοϲ, οὗ εἵνεκεν ἐποίηϲαϲ τὸ ῥῆμα τοῦτο καὶ οὐκ ἐφείϲω τοῦ υἱοῦ ϲου τοῦ ἀγαπητοῦ δι᾽ ἐμέ, ἦ μὴν εὐλογῶν εὐλογήϲω ϲε καὶ πληθύνων πληθυνῶ τὸ ϲπέρμα ϲου ὡϲ τοὺϲ ἀϲτέραϲ τοῦ οὐρανοῦ καὶ ὡϲ τὴν ἄμμον τὴν παρὰ τὸ χεῖλοϲ τῆϲ θαλάϲϲηϲ.

Codd. AD X, 75, 135 εἰ μήν.

Philo *Leg. Alleg.* 3. 72 (i. 127)=R. (except the Attic ἕνεκα, for the Ionic εἵνεκεν, but *ibid.* p. 129 εἵνεκα).

Heb. 6. 13, 14 ὤμοσεν καθ᾽ ἑαυτοῦ λέγων εἰ μὴν εὐλογῶν εὐλογήσω σε καὶ πληθύνων πληθυνῶ σε [Codd. KL *al.* ἦ μήν].

GENESIS xxv. 21-23.

Ἐδέετο δὲ Ἰϲαὰκ κυρίου περὶ Ῥεβέκκαϲ τῆϲ γυναικὸϲ αὐτοῦ ὅτι ϲτεῖρα ἦν. ἐπήκουϲε δὲ αὐτοῦ ὁ θεὸϲ καὶ ϲυνέλαβεν ἐν γαϲτρὶ Ῥεβέκκα ἡ γυνὴ αὐτοῦ· ἐϲκίρτων δὲ τὰ παιδία ἐν αὐτῇ· εἶπε δέ, εἰ οὕτω μοι μέλλει γίνεϲθαι ἵνα τί μοι τοῦτο ; ἐπορεύθη δὲ πυθέϲθαι παρὰ κυρίου· καὶ εἶπε κύριοϲ αὐτῇ, δύο ἔθνη ἐν γαϲτρὶ ϲου εἰϲὶ καὶ δύο λαοὶ ἐκ τῆϲ κοιλίαϲ ϲου διαϲταλήϲονται· καὶ λαὸϲ λαοῦ ὑπερέξει καὶ ὁ μείζων δουλεύϲει τῷ ἐλάϲϲονι.

Codd. AE, 15, 30, 31, 59, 82, 106, 107, 129, 130, 134, z ἐδεῖτο : Cod. 75 κυρίῳ, Codd. 31, 135 κύριον, Codd. 19, 108 τοῦ κυρίου : Cod. 72, z, *om.* κυρίου : Codd. 106, z ὑπήκουσε

δέ: Codd. EX, 16, 18, 25 (m), 57, 59, 72, 73, 79, 128, 131, t
αὐτῷ ὁ θεός: Codd. ADE, 14, 15, 16, 18, 20, 25 (m), 30, 31,
38, 55, 57, 59, 68, 72, 73, 75, 77, 78, 79, 82, 83, 106, 107,
120, 121, 128, 129, 130 (t), 131, 134, 135, z ἔλαβεν: Codd.
19, 32, 56, 71, 74, 76, 108 συνέλαβεν = R.: Codd. ADE, 15,
16, 18, 25 (m), 30, 32, 56, 57, 59, 72, 75, 79, 82, 83, 106,
107, 128, 130 (t), 131, 134, 135, z ἐν τῇ γαστρί: Codd. 15,
72, 82, 106, 107 ἐστί.

Philo *Leg. Alleg.* iii. 29 (i. 105) δύο ἔθνη ἐν τῇ γαστρί σού ἐστι καὶ
δύο λαοὶ ἐκ τῆς κοιλίας σου διασταλήσονται καὶ λαὸς λαοῦ ὑπερέξει καὶ
ὁ μείζων δουλεύσει τῷ ἐλάσσονι: id. *de sacrif. Abel. et Cain.* 2
(i. 164) δύο ἔθνη ἐν τῇ γαστέρι σοῦ ἐστι .... καὶ δύο λαοὶ ἐκ τῆς
κοιλίας σου διασταλήσονται.

Rom. 9. 12 ὁ μείζων δουλεύσει τῷ ἐλάσσονι.

Barnab. 13 ἐδεῖτο δὲ Ἰσαὰκ περὶ Ῥεβέκκας τῆς γυναικὸς αὐτοῦ ὅτι στεῖρα
ἦν· καὶ συνέλαβεν [so Codd. ℵ and all others, except Cod. C,
which has οὐ συνέλαβεν]. εἶτα ἐξῆλθεν Ῥεβέκκα πυθέσθαι παρὰ
κυρίου· καὶ εἶπεν κύριος πρὸς αὐτήν, δύο ἔθνη ἐν τῇ γαστρί σου καὶ δύο
λαοὶ ἐν τῇ κοιλίᾳ σου καὶ ὑπερέξει λαὸς λαοῦ [so Cod. ℵ: Codd. C
and all others λαὸς λαοῦ ὑπερέξει] καὶ ὁ μείζων δουλεύσει τῷ
ἐλάσσονι.

The general correspondence of the quotation in Barnabas with
the text of the LXX. suggests that he was acquainted with it: but
the omission of several clauses, including those which have the
distinctive words ἐσκρίτων and διασταλήσονται, suggests also that
either (1) he purposely abbreviated the narrative, or (2) quoted
from a current manual of Scripture History.

GENESIS xxvii. 30.

Καὶ ἐγένετο ὡς ἂν ἐξῆλθεν Ἰακὼβ ἀπὸ προςώπου Ἰςαὰκ τοῦ πατρὸς αὐτοῦ
καὶ Ἡςαῦ ὁ ἀδελφὸς αὐτοῦ ἦλθεν ἀπὸ τῆς θήρας.

So Codd. X, 31, 32, 68, 83, 120, 121, 131, 134: Codd. 71,
106, 107 *om.* καὶ ἐγένετο: Codd. AD, 19, 20, 56, 59, 71, 72,
82, 107, 108, 129 *om.* ἄν: Codd. E, 14, 15, 16, 18, 25 (m)
[but with ὡς written above], 37, 55 [but with -σου erased
and -τε written above], 57, 58, 73, 75, 77, 78, 79, 130 (t),
135, yz ὅσον: Cod. 106 μετὰ τὸ ἐξελθεῖν: Cod. 128 ὅτε [but
ὡς ὅσον in margin]: Cod. 106 *om.* Ἰακὼβ and Ἰσαὰκ τοῦ
πατρός: Cod. E *om.* ἀπὸ τῆς θήρας: Cod. A *add.* αὐτοῦ.

Philo *de ebriet.* 2 (i. 358) ἐγένετο γάρ, φησίν, ὅσον ἐξῆλθεν Ἰακώβ, ἧκεν Ἡσαῦ ὁ ἀδελφὸς αὐτοῦ.

The text of Philo supports the reading ὅσον, of which ὡς ἄν was probably a corruption and ὡς a subsequent emendation : but its chief importance lies in its agreement with the shorter form of the Hebrew, which appears to underlie Jerome's translation 'et egresso Jacob foras venit Esau.' The hypothesis of the existence of a corresponding shorter Greek text would account for the MSS. omissions of καὶ ἐγένετο, Ἰσαὰκ τοῦ πατρός, and ἀπὸ τῆς θήρας.

GENESIS xxviii. 11–19.

v. 11 ·Καὶ ἀπήντησε τόπω καὶ ἐκοιμήθη ἐκεῖ· ἔδυ γὰρ ὁ ἥλιος· καὶ ἔλαβεν ἀπὸ τῶν λίθων τοῦ τόπου καὶ ἔθηκε πρὸς κεφαλῆς αὐτοῦ καὶ ἐκοιμήθη ἐν τῷ τόπω ἐκείνω.

Cod. z ὑπήντησε, Cod. 56 ἐν τόπω, Codd. 59, 76, 134 ἐν τῷ τόπω, Cod. 72 εἰς τόπον, Codd. 20, 82, 108, 130 πρὸς κεφαλήν.

Philo *de Somn.* 1 (i. 621)=R., except ἐν τόπω, ηὐλίσθη ἐκεῖ for ἐκοιμήθη ἐκεῖ, ὅτι εἰσῆλθεν ὁ ἥλιος for ἔδυ γὰρ ὁ ἥλιος, and πρὸς κεφαλήν for πρὸς κεφαλῆς : *ib.* 1. 11. i. p. 630 ὑπήντησεν ἐν τῷ τόπω, but p. 631 ὑπερφυέστατα δὲ ἔχει τὸ μὴ φάναι ἐλθεῖν εἰς τὸν τόπον ἀλλὰ ὑπαντῆσαι τόπω : *ib.* 1. 19. i. p. 638 ὑπήντησε τόπω· ἔδυ γὰρ ὁ ἥλιος.

Justin M. *Dial.* 58 = R.

v. 12 καὶ ἐνυπνιάσθη καὶ ἰδοῦ κλίμαξ ἐστηριγμένη ἐν τῇ γῇ ἧς ἡ κεφαλὴ ἀφικνεῖτο εἰς τὸν οὐρανὸν καὶ οἱ ἄγγελοι τοῦ θεοῦ ἀνέβαινον καὶ κατέβαινον ἐπ᾽ αὐτῇ.

Cod. 59 ἐπὶ τὴν γῆν : Codd. III, 20, 58, 59, 72, 75, 76², 82, 129, 134, 135, +E ἐπ᾽ αὐτῆς, Codd. 19, 37, 76¹, 79², 106, 107, +z ἐπ᾽ αὐτήν, Codd. I, 14, 15, 16, 18, 25 (m), 30, 31, 32, 55, 56, 57, 68, 71, 73, 77, 78, 79¹, 108, 120, 121, 128, 130 (t), 131 ἐπ᾽ αὐτῇ.

Philo *ibid.* i. p. 620=R. except ἐνυπνιάσθη Ἰακώβ, and ἐπ᾽ αὐτῆς : *ibid.* 1. 22. i. p. 641=R. except εἰς τὴν γῆν, and ἐπ᾽ αὐτῆς. Justin M. *ibid.*=R. except ἐπ᾽ αὐτῆς.

v. 13 ὁ δὲ κύριος ἐπεστήρικτο ἐπ᾽ αὐτῆς καὶ εἶπεν Ἐγώ εἰμι ὁ θεὸς Ἀβραὰμ τοῦ πατρὸς σου καὶ ὁ θεὸς Ἰσαάκ, μὴ φοβοῦ· ἡ γῆ ἐφ᾽ ἧς καθεύδεις ἐπ᾽ αὐτῆς σοι δώσω αὐτὴν καὶ τῷ σπέρματί σου.

Codd. 25 (m), 134 ἐστήρικτο : Codd. I, III, 15, 31, 37, 58,

72, 82, 83, 106, 108, 129, 130, +Eyz, *om.* εἰμί, Codd. cett.
=R. : Codd. III, 15, 56 (marg.), 58, 76, 82, 129, 130, 134
κύριος ὁ θεός, Codd. cett.=R.

Philo *ibid.* i. p. 620 καὶ ἰδοὺ κλῖμαξ ἐστηριγμένη ἐν τῇ γῇ καὶ ὁ κύριος
ἐστήλωται ἐπ᾽ αὐτῆς καὶ εἶπεν κ.τ.λ. = R. except τὴν γῆν ἐφ᾽ ἧς σὺ
καθεύδεις σοὶ δώσω: *ibid.* 1. 25. i. p. 644 (ἐμήνυε τὸ ὄναρ) ἐστηριγ-
μένον ἐπὶ τῆς κλίμακος τὸν ἀρχάγγελον κύριον *et paullo infra* μηδεὶς
δὲ ἀκούων ὅτι ἐπεστήρικτο . . . . : *ibid.* pp. 644, 646, 647 κύριος ὁ
θεὸς Ἀβραάμ . . . .
Justin M. *ibid.*=R. except (1) ἐπ᾽ αὐτήν, (2) κύριος ὁ θεός, (3) *om.*
ὁ θεός before Ἰσαάκ.

v. 14 καὶ ἔϲται τὸ ϲπέρμα ϲογ ὡϲ ἡ ἄμμος τῆϲ γῆϲ καὶ πλατγνθήϲεται ἐπὶ
θάλαϲϲαν καὶ λίβα καὶ Βορρᾶν καὶ ἐπὶ ἀνατολάϲ· καὶ ἐνεγλογηθήϲονται ἐν ϲοὶ
πᾶϲαι αἱ φγλαὶ τῆϲ γῆϲ καὶ ἐν τῷ ϲπέρματί ϲογ.

Codd. III, 20 τῆς θαλάσσης for τῆς γῆς : Codd. 16, 17 πληθυνθήσεται for πλατυνθήσεται : λίβα καὶ ἐπὶ βορρᾶν Codd. I, III, 14,
18, 25 (m), 38, 56, 57, 58, 59, 73, 78, 128, 129, 131 : ἐπὶ
λίβα καὶ ἐπὶ βορρᾶν Codd. 15, 19, 55, 72, 76, 77, 108, 134.

Philo *ibid.* i. p. 620=R. except ὁ χοῦς for ἡ ἄμμος, πληθυνθήσεται
for πλατυνθήσεται, and συγγένειαι for φυλαί : *ib.* 1. 28. i. p. 647
(continuing the commentary on v. 13) τὸ δὲ σοφίας γένος ἄμμῳ
γῆς ἐξομοιοῦται . . . . λέγεται γὰρ ὅτι πλατυνθήσεται ἐπὶ θάλασσαν
καὶ λίβα καὶ βορρᾶν καὶ ἀνατολάς . . . . ἐνευλογηθήσονται γὰρ ἐν σοί,
φησί, πᾶσαι αἱ φυλαί [both ἄμμος and φυλαί are repeated in
subsequent sentences, so as to leave no doubt that Philo had
them in his mind].
Justin M. *ibid.*=R. except νότον for λίβα, and *om.* ἐπί before
ἀνατολάς.

v. 15 καὶ ἰδοὺ ἐγώ εἰμι μετὰ ϲογ διαφγλάϲϲων ϲε ἐν τῇ ὁδῷ πάϲῃ ογ ἂν
πορεγθῆϲ καὶ ἀποϲτρέψω ϲε εἰϲ τὴν γῆν ταγτην· ὅτι ογ μή ϲε ἐγκαταλίπω ἕωϲ
τογ ποιῆϲαί με πάντα ὅϲα ἐλάληϲά ϲοι.

Codd. III, 14, 16, 18, 25 (m), 30, 32, 37, 38, 55, 57, 58, 59,
73, 78, 79, 106, 107, 108, 128, 129, 130 (t), 131, 134
+Ez, *om.* εἰμί : Codd. I, X, 15, 19, 20, 31, 56, 68, 71, 72,
74, 75, 76, 77, 82, 83, 120, 121, 135 ἐγώ εἰμι=R.

Philo *ibid.* i. p. 620 *om.* εἰμί, ᾗ ἄν for οὗ ἄν, ἐπιστρέψω for ἀποστρέψω,
ἅ for ὅσα : *ibid.* 1. 30. i. p. 637 ἰδοὺ γάρ, φησίν, ἐγὼ μετὰ σοῦ :
ibid. c. 31. i. p. 648 ἀποστρέψω σε εἰς τὴν γῆν ταύτην.
Justin M. *ibid. om.* εἰμί, *om.* τῇ before ὁδῷ, ᾗ ἄν for οὗ ἄν.

vv. 16, 17 καὶ ἐξηγέρθη Ἰακὼβ ͱ τογ ὕπνου αγτογ καὶ εἶπεν ὅτι ˮΕϲτι κγριοϲ ἐν τῷ τόπῳ τογτῳ ἐγὼ Δε ογκ ἤΔειν· καὶ ἐφοβήθη καὶ εἶπεν ῾Ωϲ φοβερὸϲ ὁ τόποϲ ογτοϲ· ογκ ἔϲτι τογτο ἀλλ᾽ ἢ οἶκοϲ θεογ καὶ αγτη ἡ πγλη τογ ογρανογ.

Codd. I, III, 20, 72, 75, 82 + z ἀπὸ τοῦ ὕπνου.

Philo *ibid.* 1. 31. i. p. 648 ἐξηγέρθη γάρ, φησίν, Ἰακὼβ καὶ εἶπεν ὅτι ἔστι κύριος ἐν τῷ τόπῳ τούτῳ, ἐγὼ δὲ οὐκ ᾔδειν .... c. 32 δικαίως οὖν ἐφοβήθη καὶ εἶπε θαυμαστικῶς ὡς φοβερὸς ὁ τόπος οὗτος: *de migrat. Abraham.* 1. i. p. 437 οὐκ ἔστι τοῦτο ἀλλ᾽ ἢ οἶκος θεοῦ. Justin M. *ibid.* = R.

vv. 18, 19 καὶ ἀνέϲτη Ἰακὼβ τὸ πρωί, καὶ ἔλαβε τὸν λίθον ὃν γπέθηκεν ἐκεῖ πρὸϲ κεφαλῆϲ αγτογ καὶ ἔϲτηϲεν αγτὸν ϲτηλην καὶ ἐπέχεεν ἔλαιον ἐπὶ τὸ ἄκρον αγτῆϲ. καὶ ἐκάλεϲε τὸ ὄνομα τογ τόπογ ἐκείνογ Οἶκος θεογ· καὶ Ογλαμλογϲ ἦν ὄνομα τῇ πόλει τὸ πρότερον.

Codd. 18, 32, 55, 75, 131, + t τῷ πρωί: Codd. 71, 76, 106, 107, 134, + z τὸ ἄκρον αὐτοῦ: Codd. I, III, 14, 15, 16, 18, 25 (m), 30, 55, 57, 58, 59, 72, 73, 75, 77, 78, 79, 82, 106, 107, 129, 130 (t), 131, 134, 135, + z ἐκάλεσεν Ἰακώβ: Codd. I, 31, 55, 56, 58, 59, 68, 72, 75, 76, 82, 83, 106, 107, 108, 120, 121, 130, 134 οὐλαμμαούς, Cod. 20 οὐλαμμαούζ, Cod. III οὐλαμμαύς, Cod. 74 οὐλαμαούς, Codd. 14, 16, 18, 25 (m), 38, 57, 73, 77, 78, 79, 128, 131, + t οὐλαμ. Justin M. *ibid.* τῷ πρωί, τὸ ἔλαιον, τὸ ἄκρον αὐτοῦ, *om.* ἐκείνου after τόπου, Οὐλαμμαούς.

In v. 11 Philo's ηὐλίσθη for ἐκοιμήθη points to a coordinate translation or revision of the LXX., for although לין is always elsewhere translated by κοιμᾶσθαι in the Pentateuch, in the other historical books it is uniformly translated by αὐλίζεσθαι. εἰσῆλθεν for ἔδυ also points to a coordinate translation or revision, for whereas בֹא is only rendered three times in the Pentateuch by δύειν, it is frequently (about 150 times) rendered by εἰσέρχεσθαι: the corresponding phrase for sunrise is ὁ ἥλιος ἐξῆλθεν Gen. 19. 23.

In v. 12 εἰς τὴν γῆν receives no support from the MSS. of the LXX., except the partial support of Cod. 59 ἐπὶ τὴν γῆν, which is itself favoured by the Old Latin 'super terram,' Aug. *de Civit. Dei* 16. 38 (vii. 449); on the other hand ἐν τῇ γῇ is confirmed by 'in terra,' Tertull. *adv. Marc.* 3. 24. p. 412. The concurrence of

Philo and Justin in the reading ἐπ' αὐτῆς gives to it a strong probability.

v. 13, Philo's reading ἐστήλωται for ἐπεστήρικτο also points to a coordinate translation or revision, inasmuch as στηλοῦν is elsewhere found as the translation of יצב, e.g. Codd. A Judges 18. 16, 17; 1 Sam. 17. 16; 2 Kings 17. 10, but not ἐπιστηρίζειν and only once στηρίζειν. The revision to which ἐστήλωται may be presumed to have belonged was apparently Hebraistic, for στηλοῦν is in several places used by Aquila where the LXX. have a more colourless word, e.g. Ps. 73 (74). 17, LXX. σὺ ἐποίησας πάντα τὰ ὅρια τῆς γῆς, Aquila ἐστήλωσας.

In v. 14 Philo's reading χοῦς for ἄμμος points in the same direction: the former word is the ordinary translation of עָפָר, whereas the latter is only found as such in Gen. 13. 16, where it is probably transferred from 22. 17, in which passage the Hebrew word is not עָפָר but חוֹל.

The reading πληθυνθήσεται also points in the same direction: this is the only passage in which פָּרַץ is translated by πλατύνειν, but it is translated by πληθύνειν in 1 Chron. 4. 38, Ps. 105 (106). 29. There is a trace of a revision of the same word in Ps. 24 (25). 17 (where it is used to translate not פָּרַץ but רָחַב): the MSS. reading in that passage, ἐπληθύνθησαν, could hardly have been the reading when the extant extracts from the Hexapla were made, inasmuch as a distinction is drawn between Theodotion and Interpres Sextus, who have that reading, and Aquila and Interpres Quintus, who are said to read the same as the LXX.: hence ἐπλατύνθησαν must there be considered to be the original reading, and ἐπληθύνθησαν to be a revision of it.

The reading συγγένειαι for φυλαί is another instance of the same kind. Both words are found as translations of מִשְׁפָּחָה, but while the latter is more frequently so used in the Pentateuch, the former is more frequent in the other historical books.

In v. 15 the concurrence of Philo and Justin in the omission of εἰμί makes that omission probable: and the probability is supported by its omission in Clem. Alex. *Paed.* i. 7. p. 131. But there is a great want of uniformity of practice in the several groups of MSS. as to its insertion or omission here and in v. 13. Some MSS. agree with Philo and Justin in inserting it in v. 13 and omitting it here, viz. Codd. 14, 16, 18, 25, 38, 55, 57, 59, 73, 78, 79, 107, 128 : some MSS. insert it in both places, viz. Codd. 19, 20, 32, 56, 68, 74, 75, 76, 77, 120, 121, 135 : some omit it in both places, viz. Codd. III, 37, 58, 106, 108, 129, 130, Ez.

It may be added that the variants of Philo in this passage help to support the hypothesis, to which many other facts lead, that the treatise *De Somniis* belongs to a generation subsequent to that of Philo himself.

Genesis xlix. 10.

Οὐκ ἐκλείψει ἄρχων ἐξ Ἰούδα καὶ ἡγούμενος ἐκ τῶν μηρῶν αὐτοῦ ἕως ἐὰν ἔλθῃ τὰ ἀποκείμενα αὐτῷ· καὶ αὐτὸς προςδοκία ἐθνῶν.

Codd. 20, 37, 58, 72 οὐδὲ ἡγούμενος.

Codd. I, III, VII, 15, 18, 19, 20, 55, 56, 58, 71, 74, 75, 76, 82, 108, 120, 121, 129 τὰ ἀποκείμενα αὐτῷ : Codd. 30, 31, 37, 38, 57, 59, 73, 75, 78, 79, 83, 107, 127, 128, 134 ᾧ ἀπόκειται, so also, but in the margin, Codd. X, 29, 64 : Codd. 32, 84, 135 ὃ ἀπόκειται αὐτῷ: Codd. 14, 16, 25 (m), 77, 85, 106, 131, + tz ὃ ἀπόκειται : Cod. 72 τὸ ἀποκείμενον αὐτῷ ὃ ἀπόκειται.

Justin M. *Apol.* i. c. 32. p. 73 (Cod. A) (1)=R., except ὃ ἀπόκειται, (2) .... ἕως ἂν ἔλθῃ ᾧ ἀπόκειται τὸ βασίλειον : *ibid.* c. 54. p. 89,=R., except ὃ ἀπόκειται : *Dial.* c. 52. p. 271 ἕως ἂν ἔλθῃ τὰ ἀποκείμενα αὐτῷ : Cod. A. *marg.* ὃ ἀπόκειται : *ibid.* c. 120. p. 348, (1) ἕως ἂν ἔλθῃ τὰ ἀποκείμενα αὐτῷ=R., (2) (μέχρι γὰρ τῆς παρουσίας τοῦ Χριστοῦ ἡ προφητεία προεκήρυσσεν) ἕως ἂν ἔλθῃ ᾧ ἀπόκειται, (3) δυνατὸν δὲ ἦν μοι, ἔφην, ὦ ἄνδρες, μάχεσθαι πρὸς ὑμᾶς περὶ τῆς λέξεως ἣν ὑμεῖς ἐξηγεῖσθε λέγοντες εἰρῆσθαι· Ἕως ἂν ἔλθῃ τὰ ἀποκείμενα αὐτῷ· ἐπειδὴ οὐχ οὕτως ἐξηγήσαντο οἱ ἑβδομήκοντα ἀλλ'· Ἕως ἂν ἔλθῃ ᾧ ἀπόκειται.

It is clear from the third of the three quotations in *Dial.* c. 120, (1) that there was a difference of opinion in Justin's time between Jews and Christians as to the interpretation of the passage, (2) that notwithstanding the reading τὰ ἀποκείμενα in the chief existing MS. of his writings, Justin himself not only read ᾧ ἀπόκειται, but held that to be the true reading of the LXX. This fact is of much importance in relation to the question of the trustworthiness of the quotations in Justin's MSS. : it shows that no sound argument can be based upon them except in cases where Justin's own commentary makes it certain that they contain the text which he used.

The varieties of reading may perhaps be explained on the hypothesis that the original version followed a common Hellenistic idiom in reading ᾧ τὸ ἀποκείμενον (τὰ ἀποκείμενα) αὐτῷ, and that ὃ ἀπόκειται was a gloss or alternative translation for τὸ ἀποκείμενον which found its way into the text: hence the readings ὃ ἀπόκειται αὐτῷ and ὃ ἀπόκειται come from an earlier reading ᾧ ὃ ἀπόκειται αὐτῷ. This hypothesis is supported by the combination of the original reading and the gloss in the remarkable Venice Cod. 72 τὸ ἀποκείμενον αὐτῷ ὃ ἀπόκειται. There is a different survival of the original reading in Epiphanius i. 332 ᾧ τὰ ἀποκείμενα : and there is a noteworthy rendering in the Clementines, 3. 49. p. 50, ed. Lag. ἕως ἂν ἔλθῃ οὗ ἐστίν.

The early Latin versions, with the exception of Cyprian *Testim.* 1. 21. p. 55, who has 'deposita illi,' are in favour of ᾧ ἀπόκειται : viz. Novatian *de Trinit.* 9 (p. 711 in Tertull. ed. Rig.) 'cui repromissum est,' Ambros. *de bened. Patr.* 4 (i. 518), 'cui repositum est,' Iren. *Vet. Interp.* 4. 10. p. 239, Hilar. *in Ps. lix.* p. 158, Hieron. *Hebr. Quaest.* p. 69, ed. Lag., and in several other passages, e. g. *in Esai.* lib. 4. c. 11 (iv. 162, Vall.); Rufinus *de bened. Patr.* 1. 3. p. 9 has 'veniant ea quae reposita sunt,' but adds 'et velut in aliis exemplaribus habetur Veniat is cui repositum est.' Augustine *de Civit. Dei* 16. 41 (vii. 452), *ibid.* 18. 6 (vii. 492) has 'quae reposita sunt ei.'

EXODUS ii. 13, 14.

Καὶ λέγει τῷ ἀδικοῦντι Διατί σὺ τύπτεις τὸν πλησίον; ὁ δὲ εἶπε Τίς σε κατέστησεν ἄρχοντα καὶ δικαστὴν ἐφ' ἡμῶν; μὴ ἀνελεῖν με σὺ θέλεις ὃν τρόπον ἀνεῖλες χθὲς τὸν Αἰγύπτιον;

Cod. VII ἢ δικαστήν.

Codd. 14, 16, 25, 30, 32, 37, 52, 53, 54, 56, 72, 73, 74, 75, 77, 78, 82, 108, 118, 130 ἐφ' ἡμᾶς : Codd. II, III, VII, X, 18, 19, 29, 53, 57, 58, 59, 71, 76, 84, 106, 107, 128, 129, 131, 134, 135 ἐφ' ἡμῶν = R.

Codd. III, VII, X, 16, 18, 25, 29, 32, 52, 54, 55, 56, 57, 73, 76, 78, 85, 129, 130, 131, 135 ἢ ἀνελεῖν : Codd. II, 14, 19, 30, 37, 53, 58, 59, 71, 72, 74, 75, 77, 82, 84, 106, 107, 108, 118, 128, 134 μὴ ἀνελεῖν = R.

Acts vii. 26–28 (the narrative portion of the text differs from that of Exodus, but the dialogue nearly agrees and is probably a quotation) : (ἄνδρες ἀδελφοί ἐστε') ἱνατί ἀδικεῖτε ἀλλήλους ; (ὁ

δὲ ἀδικῶν τὸν πλησίον ἀπώσατο αὐτὸν εἰπών)· Τίς σε κατέστησεν
ἄρχοντα καὶ [Cod. Laud. ἢ] δικαστὴν ἐφ' ἡμῶν [Codd. DE al. ἐφ'
ἡμᾶς] ; μὴ ἀνελεῖν με σὺ θέλεις ὃν τρόπον ἀνεῖλες ἐχθὲς τὸν
Αἰγύπτιον ;

1 Clem. Rom. 4 τίς σε κατέστησεν κριτὴν ἢ [ita Cod. Alex., καὶ
Cod. Constant.] δικαστὴν ἐφ' ἡμῶν ; μὴ ἀνελεῖν με σὺ θέλεις
ὃ τρόπον ἀνεῖλες ἐχθὲς τὸν Αἰγύπτιον ;

There is a probable reference to the passage in Luke xii. 14,
where the MSS. vary as follows :—

Cod. ℵ	τίς με κατέστησεν κριτὴν ἢ μεριστὴν ἐφ' ὑμῶν ;			
Codd. BL al.	,,	,,	,,	,,	ἐφ' ὑμᾶς ;
Codd. A al.	,,	,,	δικαστὴν	,,	ἐφ' ὑμᾶς ;
Codd. D al.	,,	,,	κριτὴν	om.	ἐφ' ὑμᾶς ;
Cod. 157	,,	,,	ἄρχοντα καὶ δικαστὴν ἐφ' ὑμᾶς ;		

If the reading of Cod. 157 be dismissed, as being obviously
harmonistic, the chief importance of this reference in Luke, when
taken together with the quotation in Clement, lies (1) in its substitution of κριτὴν for ἄρχοντα, and of μεριστὴν for δικαστήν ; (2) in its
use of ἤ for καί. In regard to (1), there is no instance in the LXX.
of the use of κριτής to render שׂר, but the combination κριτὴν καὶ
δικαστήν is found in 1 Sam. 24. 16, 1 Esdr. 8. 23 : the word μεριστήν,
which is not found elsewhere in Biblical Greek, is omitted here not
only by Cod. D, but also by the Curetonian Syriac and by Tertullian
adv. Marc. 4. 28. p. 445, who, in quoting the Gospel, has 'quis me,
inquit, judicem constituit super vos?' but in quoting Exodus in the
same place has 'quis te constituit magistrum aut judicem super
nos?' In regard to (2), the agreement of the Gospel and Clement
in reading ἤ is supported by the quotation in Tertullian l. c.

That both the Acts and Clement are quoting the LXX. is shown
by their use of ἐχθές, which word is not in the Hebrew.

Exodus iii. 2.

Ὄφθη δὲ αὐτῷ ἄγγελος κυρίου ἐν πυρὶ φλογὸς ἐκ τοῦ βάτου· καὶ ὁρᾷ ὅτι ὁ
βάτος καίεται πυρί, ὁ δὲ βάτος οὐ κατεκαίετο.

Codd. III, VII, 14, 16, 25, 29, 30, 32, 52, 54, 57, 58, 64, 72,
73, 74, 75, 76, 77, 78, 83, 84, 106, 107, 130, 132, 134 ἐν
φλογὶ πυρός : Codd. II, X, 11, 19, 53, 55, 56, 59, 71, 82,
128, 129, 131, 135 ἐν πυρὶ φλογός, = R.

Codd. 53, 72 οὐ κατακαίεται.

Philo *de profugis* 29 (i. 170) (φάσκων ὅτι) ὁ βάτος καίεται καὶ οὐ κατακαίεται.

Acts 7. 30 ὤφθη αὐτῷ ἐν τῇ ἐρήμῳ τοῦ ὄρους Σινᾶ ἄγγελος [ita Codd. א ABC: Codd. DEHP *al.* add. κυρίου] ἐν φλογὶ πυρὸς [ita Codd. א BDHP *al.* : Codd. ACE *al.* ἐν πυρὶ φλογὸς] βάτου. Justin M. *Dial.* 60. p. 283=R., except ἐκ βάτου.

The reading ἐν φλογὶ πυρός in Exodus has in its favour (1) the fact that it is supported by MSS. of different groups : (2) the fact that, although the passage is not quoted directly by Philo, the phrases (ὁ βάτος) περισχεθεὶς πολλῇ φλογί, and τὸ φλέγον πῦρ, *Vit. Mos.* i. 12, ii. p. 92, point to ἐν φλογὶ πυρός. On the other hand the reading ἐν πυρὶ φλογός is supported by Justin not only in the quotation given above, but also by the more important paraphrase *Apol.* i. 63. p. 96 : (3) the early Latin versions, which have ' in (de) flamma ignis,' e.g. Cypr. *Testim.* 2. 19. p. 86 : Ambros. *de Spirit. Sanct.* i. 14 (vii. 629) : August. *de Trin.* i. 23 (viii. 785).

EXODUS vi. 2–4.

'Ελάλησε δὲ ὁ θεὸς πρὸς Μωυσῆν καὶ εἶπε πρὸς αὐτὸν 'Εγὼ κύριος καὶ ὤφθην πρὸς 'Αβραὰμ καὶ 'Ισαὰκ καὶ 'Ιακώβ, θεὸς ὢν αὐτῶν, καὶ τὸ ὄνομά μου κύριος οὐκ ἐδήλωσα αὐτοῖς.

Codd. 19, 108, 118 ἐγὼ κύριος ὁ θεός, Cod. 55 ἐγὼ ὁ θεός, Cod. 53 *om.* καί before ὤφθην.

Cod. 118 τὸ ὄνομά μου κύριος ὤν, Codd. 25, 32, *om.* κύριος.

Philo *de mutat. nom.* 2 (i. 580) τὸ ὄνομά μου οὐκ ἐδήλωσα αὐτοῖς. Justin M. *Dial.* 126. p. 355 ἐλάλησε δὲ κύριος πρὸς Μωσῆν καὶ εἶπε πρὸς αὐτὸν 'Εγὼ εἰμι κύριος καὶ ὤφθην πρὸς τὸν 'Αβραὰμ καὶ 'Ισαὰκ καὶ 'Ιακώβ θεὸς αὐτῶν, καὶ τὸ ὄνομά μου οὐκ ἐδήλωσα αὐτοῖς.

Justin's omission of ὤν after θεός may belong to an earlier text than that of any existing MS. of the LXX., inasmuch as it follows the Hebrew in making θεός an essential part of the predicate (i.e. 'I appeared to Abraham .... *as* their God, yet my name I did not disclose to them'), and not an additional clause.

His omission of κύριος after τὸ ὄνομά μου is apparently, but not really, supported by Philo, for Philo's commentary, *l. c.*, makes it clear that κύριος (or κύριον) was in his text. For he plays upon the grammatical sense of κύριον ὄνομα, i.e. a 'proper name,' and quotes this passage to prove that God had never revealed His

'proper name,' and he immediately goes on to say, τοῦ γὰρ ὑπερ-
βατοῦ μετατεθέντος ἑξῆς ἂν τοιοῦτος εἴη λόγος· Ὄνομά μου τὸ κύριον οὐκ
ἐδήλωσα αὐτοῖς ἀλλὰ τὸ ἐν καταχρήσει διὰ τὰς εἰρημένας αἰτίας : ' Remov-
ing the transposition, there will result such a sentence as the
following : My proper name I did not declare to them, but my
wrongly applied name, for the reasons stated.'   The transposition
can only be that of τὸ ὄνομά μου κύριον in the original sentence to
ὄνομά μου τὸ κύριον in the new sentence which Philo forms: and
this makes it clear that κύριον was in his text.

The reading of Cod. 118 κύριος ὤν may be a survival of an
original ὤν, without κύριος, transferred from 3. 24 as the translation
of the Tetragrammaton.

2. *Quotations from the Psalms and Isaiah in Philo, Clement, Barnabas, and Justin Martyr.*

1. Philo.

I. *Quotations from the Psalms.*

The quotations from the Psalms in the Philonean literature so nearly correspond with the LXX. version in its
current form, as to make it certain that the writer or writers
used that version.

In some passages there are no variants worthy of note:—

Ps. 36 (37). 4 is quoted without variant in *De Plantatione Noe* 7
(i. 335) and *De Somniis* ii. 37 (i. 690).

Ps. 74 (75). 9 is similarly quoted in *Quod Deus immut.* 17
(i. 284).

Ps. 79 (80). 5 is similarly quoted in *De Migrat. Abraham.* 28
(i. 460).

In some passages the variants are only of grammatical
forms :—

Ps. 22 (23). 1 is quoted (twice) in *De Agricultura* 12 (i. 308),
and in *De Mutatione Nominum* 20 (i. 596), in each case with
ὑστερήσει for the current ὑστερήσῃ. [So Codd. S 165, 277, 278.]

Ps. 30 (31). 18 is quoted in *De Confus. Ling.* 11 (i. 410), and Ps. 41 (42). 4 in *De Migrat. Abraham.* 28 (i. 460) with the variants respectively of γενέσθω, ἐγένετο for the later forms γενηθήτω [γενηθήτωσαν], ἐγενήθη of the existing MSS. of the LXX.

Ps. 100 (101). 1 is quoted in *Quod Deus immut.* 16 (i. 284) with the Hellenistic ἔλεον [as in S² and 95 cursive MSS.] for the current Attic ἔλεος.

Even when the variations are greater they are not important :—

In Ps. 45 (46). 5 all existing MSS. of the LXX., but one, agree with the Hebrew in having the plural τοῦ ποτάμου τὰ ὁρμήματα εὐφραίνουσι τὴν πόλιν τοῦ θεου. But in *De Somniis* ii. 38 (i. 691) Philo has the singular τὸ ὅρμημα τοῦ ποτάμου εὐφραίνει : as in Cod. 184. There is an indication that he here follows an earlier text of the LXX. than any that has come down to us in the fact that the Cod. Sangermanensis of the Old Latin, and also Hilary and Ambrose have 'Fluminis impetus laetifi*cat*': and it is to be noted that the Latin of the Verona Psalter has the singular, though the Greek has the plural.

Ps. 93 (94). 9 is quoted in *De Plantat. Noe* 7 (i. 334) with three variants, viz. (1) the present participles ὁ φυτεύων, ὁ πλάσσων are substituted for the aorists ὁ φυτεύσας, ὁ πλάσας which are found in all MSS. of the LXX.: (2) the plural ὀφθαλμούς is used instead of the singular ὀφθαλμόν [so Codd. BS¹ of the LXX.] : (3) ἐπιβλέπειν is used for the LXX. κατανοεῖν, and in the future instead of the present : in this last point Philo follows the Hebrew more closely, and agrees with Jerome's *Psalter* as against the Old Latin. The same passage is also quoted in the treatise *De Mundo* (ii. 608) without the two former of the variants just mentioned, but with ἐπιβλέπει for κατανοεῖ.

In Ps. 26 (27). 1, where all MSS. of the LXX. have Κύριος φωτισμός μου, *De Somniis* i. 13 (i. 632) has φῶς : and in this he agrees with Aquila and Symmachus.

Ps. 113. 25 (115. 17) is quoted indirectly, but in harmony with the current text, in *De Profugis* 11 (i. 555) νεκροὶ δὲ .... οὐκ αἰνέσουσι κύριον : and Ps. 83 (84). 11 is clothed in a philosophical

paraphrase in *Quis rer. divin. heres* 58 (i. 515) μίαν γὰρ ἡμέραν . . . .
βούλεσθαι βιῶναι μετὰ ἀρετῆς ἢ μυρία ἔτη ἐν σκιᾷ τοῦ θανάτου.

It may be noted that Philo in quoting the Psalms never
uses the word ψαλμός or its compounds, but always ὕμνος or
one of its compounds : e.g. i. 596, quoting Ps. 22 (23). 1,
ᾄδεται δὲ καὶ ἐν ὕμνοις ᾆσμα τοιοῦτον: i. 335, quoting Ps. 36 (37).
4, ὁ τοῦ Μωϋσέως θιασώτης . . . ἐν ὑμνῳδίαις ἀνεφθέγξατο : i. 460,
quoting Ps. 41 (42). 4, ἐν ὕμνοις εἴρηται : i. 284, quoting Ps.
100 (101). 1, ὁ ὑμνῳδὸς εἶπέ που : i. 555 (quoting Ps. 113. 25
(115. 17) as given above), ὡς καὶ ἐν ὕμνοις λέγεται. And that
ὕμνοις was the older designation is shown by the subscription
to the Second Book of Psalms, which is found in most MSS.,
ἐξέλιπον οἱ ὕμνοι Δαυὶδ τοῦ υἱοῦ Ἰεσσαί.

II. *Quotations from Isaiah.*

Philo appears to quote Isaiah only twice :—

In *De Somniis* ii. 25 (i. 681) he quotes the figure of the vine
from Is. 5. 7, ἀμπελὼν κυρίου παντοκράτορος οἶκος τοῦ Ἰσραήλ, the only
variant being that, as is the case in many passages of the LXX.,
especially in the Minor Prophets, צְבָאוֹת is translated instead of
being transliterated. The passage is quoted as having been said
by τις τῶν πάλαι προφητῶν, and by him ἐπιθειάσας, 'under in-
spiration.'

In *De Mutat. Nom.* 31 (i. 604) he quotes Is. 57. 21 χαίρειν οὐκ ἔστι
τοῖς ἀσεβέσιν εἶπε θεός : that the quotation is from the LXX. is shown
by the rendering of שָׁלוֹם by χαίρειν : it is ordinarily translated by
εἰρήνη, Aquila and Symmachus so translate it in this passage, nor is
it rendered by χαίρειν in any other passage of the LXX., except the
parallel passage Is. 48. 22.

In *De Exsecrat.* 7 (ii. 435) ἡ γὰρ ἔρημος, ᾗ φησὶν ὁ προφήτης,
εὔτεκνός τε καὶ πολύπαις may be an echo of Is. 54. 1.

But the resemblance of words is slight : and it may be inferred
from 1 Sam. 2. 5, Ps. 113. 9, that the phrase was a conventional
and even proverbial one.

2. Clement of Rome.

I. *Quotations from the Psalms.*

In the majority of passages in which the Psalms appear to be quoted in Clement of Rome there is a precise agreement with either the current text of the LXX., or the text of existing MSS.: i.e. the variations are only such as exist between different MSS. of the LXX., and the quotations of Clement must be reckoned to be an additional item of great value for the determination of the text of the LXX.

For example :—

Ps. 50 (51). 3–19 is quoted in c. 18 with only the following variants from the Sixtine text: στήρισον is read in v. 12 for στήριξον, as in Codd. BS, 27, 55: τὰ χείλη and τὸ στόμα are transposed in v. 15.

Ps. 61 (62). 5 is quoted in c. 15 with the Hellenistic εὐλογοῦσαν, as in Codd. BS¹ 27, 55, Verona Psalter, for the current classical εὐλογοῦν.

Ps. 31 (32). 1, 2 is quoted in c. 50 with οὗ οὐ μὴ λογίσηται, as in Codd. ABS¹ and 12 cursives, for ὃ οὐ .... of Cod. S², the majority of cursives, and the Sixtine text.

Ps. 36 (37). 35–37 is quoted in c. 14 with (1) the variants ἀσεβῆ [Cod. Alex.], τὸν ἀσεβῆ [Cod. Const.] as in the LXX. where Codd. BS¹ omit and Cod. A inserts the article: (2) ἐξεζήτησα as in Codd. 99, 183 for the current ἐζήτησα.

Ps. 49 (50). 16–23 is quoted in c. 35 with a few unimportant, and two important, variants: (1) in v. 21 the current text of the LXX. (i.e. Cod. B and all cursives except 188: the long lacuna in Cod. A begins two verses earlier) has the phrase ὑπέλαβες ἀνομίαν, the word ἀνομίαν having no equivalent in the Hebrew and spoiling the sense. Clement agrees with Cod. S¹ in reading ἄνομε which, though without a Hebrew equivalent, is in entire harmony with the spirit of the passage and adds to its force. The Latin of the Verona Psalter has 'inique,' which is retained in the Vulgate: but this word appears to have been taken not as a vocative but as an adverb: hence the translation in the Prayer-Book version 'Thou thoughtest *wickedly* that . . . .': it may be noted that the only variant in the MSS. of the LXX., Cod. 188, also substitutes an adverb, ἀδίκως: (2) in v. 22 Clement adds after ἁρπάσῃ the words ὡς λέων in which he is supported by both the Greek and the Latin of the Verona Psalter: but the words are probably only a reminiscence of Ps. 7. 2.

The general fidelity of Clement to the text of the LXX. is sometimes shown by his reproduction of its mistranslation: for example in Ps. 50 (51). 8 the Hebrew clearly means (as it is translated in the English Revised Version):

> 'Behold thou desirest truth in the inward parts;
> And in the hidden part thou shalt make me to know wisdom.'

But the LXX., which is followed by Clement, c. 18. 6, translates בַּטֻּחוֹת by τὰ ἄδηλα, and appears to destroy the parallelism of the verse by joining it to the second member, viz. :

> ἰδοὺ γὰρ ἀλήθειαν ἠγάπησας·
> τὰ ἄδηλα καὶ τὰ κρύφια τῆς σοφίας σου ἐδήλωσάς μοι.

(At the same time it is conceivable that the original LXX. version may have been εἰς τὰ ἄδηλα, and that it was misunderstood and altered by a scribe.)

But in at least one case there are variations from the LXX. text which suggest the same hypothesis which is suggested by some of the quotations in Barnabas, viz. that of the existence of 'revised' or 'adapted' editions of the Psalms.

> Ps. 3. 6 ἐγὼ ἐκοιμήθην καὶ ὕπνωσα,
> ἐξηγέρθην ὅτι κύριος ἀντιλήψεται μου
> [Codd. S¹ 210 ἀντελάβετο μου]

is quoted in c. 26 in the form ἐκοιμήθην καὶ ὕπνωσα, ἐξηγέρθην ὅτι σὺ μετ' ἐμοῦ εἶ, where the last phrase is probably incorporated from Ps. 22 (23). 4 (οὐ φοβηθήσομαι κακὰ) ὅτι σὺ μετ' ἐμοῦ εἶ.

II. *Quotations from Isaiah.*

Several of Clement's quotations from Isaiah are composite, and will be considered separately in the next chapter. The other quotations are for the most part faithful reproductions of the LXX. text, and in several cases afford interesting contributions to the criticism of it.

Is. 1. 16–20 is quoted in c. 8 : (1) Cod. Const. follows the great majority of MSS. of the LXX., and the Old Latin, in reading λούσασθε, καθαροὶ γένεσθε : Cod. A agrees with two cursives 93, 144, in reading καί before καθαροί : (2) Cod. A reads ἀφέλεσθε for ἀφέλετε, in agreement with Justin M. *Tryph.* 18, but against all MSS. of the LXX. and Justin M. *Apol.* 44, 61 : (3) Cod. A reads χήρᾳ for χήραν, in agreement with Codd. B¹, 144, 147¹ of the LXX. but against all other MSS. : (4) Cod. Const. follows Cod. B and the majority of cursives of the LXX., and the Old Latin, in reading δεῦτε διελεγχθῶμεν (διαλεχθῶμεν), Cod. A of Clement agrees with Codd. AS and 16 cursives of the LXX. in inserting καί after δεῦτε.

Is. 29. 13 as quoted in c. 15 affords many points of interest.

In the LXX., Cod. B and the majority of cursive MSS. (with many minor variants in the cursives) read ἐγγίζει μοι ὁ λαὸς οὗτος ἐν τῷ στόματι αὐτοῦ καὶ ἐν τοῖς χείλεσιν αὐτῶν τιμῶσί με ἡ δὲ καρδία αὐτῶν πόρρω ἀπέχει ἀπ᾽ ἐμοῦ. Codd. AS, 26, 49, 87, 91, 97, 198, 306, 309 read ἐγγίζει μοι ὁ λαὸς οὗτος τοῖς χείλεσιν αὐτῶν τιμῶσί με ἡ δὲ καρδία αὐτῶν πόρρω ἀπέχει ἀπ᾽ ἐμοῦ.

In Clement, Cod. A has οὗτος ὁ λαὸς τοῖς χείλεσί με τιμᾷ ἡ δὲ καρδία αὐτῶν πόρρω ἄπεστιν ἀπ᾽ ἐμοῦ : Cod. C has ὁ λαὸς οὗτος τῷ στόματί με τιμᾷ ἡ δὲ καρδία αὐτῶν πόρρω ἀπέχει ἀπ᾽ ἐμοῦ.

In the N. T., the following is, except where otherwise noted, the reading of the chief MSS. of Mark 7. 6 : οὗτος ὁ λαὸς [Codd. BD ὁ λαὸς οὗτος] τοῖς χείλεσίν με τιμᾷ [Cod. D, a, b, c, ἀγαπᾷ] ἡ δὲ καρδία αὐτῶν πόρρω ἀπέχει [Cod. D ἀφέστηκεν, Cod. L ἄπεστιν] ἀπ᾽ ἐμοῦ. In Matt. 15. 8 some MSS. viz. CEF, and the Peschitta, have the longer form which is found in Cod. B of the LXX.; and Cod. D, which is supported by most early Latin quotations, has ἐστὶν ἀπ᾽ ἐμοῦ for ἀπέχει ἀπ᾽ ἐμοῦ.

It is a legitimate inference that, before the time of

Clement, the quotation had become detached from its context, and that οὗτος ὁ λαός, having lost its proper predicate ἐγγίζει, and having assimilated the following predicate τιμῶσι (which thereby became τιμᾷ), the antithesis was accentuated by the loss of one or other of the phrases ἐν τῷ στόματι or ἐν τοῖς χείλεσι. The quotation is one which naturally became common in a time of religious revival, and it not less naturally tended to become so in its shortest form. Hence it was so written by many of the scribes of the LXX., and became the current text of one of its recognized recensions.

Hence the shorter form is found

(1) In all MSS. of St. Mark: while some good MSS. of St. Matthew give the longer form.

(2) In Clement, though the shorter form is found in both MSS., Cod. A has τοῖς χείλεσι, Cod. C τῷ στόματι.

(3) Justin M. shows by his repeated indirect quotations of it that the shorter form was in frequent use in the Judaeo-Christian controversies, *Tryph.* 27, 39, 80: and at the same time he alone of early writers goes behind the quotation to its original meaning, and in *Tryph.* 78 quotes the whole passage in accordance with the Hebrew, omitting only τῷ στόματι αὐτῶν (or equivalent words) ἐγγίζει μοι ὁ λαὸς οὗτος· τοῖς χείλεσιν αὐτῶν τιμῶσί με, ἡ δὲ καρδία αὐτῶν πόρρω ἀπέχει ἀπ' ἐμοῦ.

(4) Almost all the early Latin quotations of the passage give it in the shorter form, indicating that the current version was based upon the corresponding recension of the LXX.: e. g. Iren. *Vet. Interp.* 4. 12, Cypr. *Ep.* 67. 2, p. 736, Ambros. *in Psalm.* 36, vol. i. 810 d. But at the same time it is clear from Jerome *in Isai.* 29, tom. iv. 393, that a version of the longer form was also in existence.

Is. 53 is quoted entire in c. 16.

The following are the more noteworthy variants: (1) In v. 2, Clement agrees with Codd. AS, 22, 26, 36, 48, (62), 86, 90, 93, 106, 144, 147, 198, 233, 306, 308, in placing ἐναντίον αὐτοῦ immediately after ἀνηγγείλαμεν: so Tertull. *c. Marc.* 3, pp. 671, 676, Annuntiavimus de illo [coram ipso] velut [sicut] parvulus, Cyprian *Testim.* 2. 13. p. 77, Lactant. *Instit.* 4. 16, and the majority of early

Latin writers. (2) In v. 3 Clement reads ἐκλεῖπον παρὰ τὸ εἶδος τῶν ἀνθρώπων : the LXX. has many variants, chiefly, ἐκλεῖπον, or ἐκλεῖπον τὸ εἶδος [so Codd. 22, 48, 51, 62, 90, 93, 106, 144, 233, 308] παρὰ τοὺς υἱοὺς τῶν ἀνθρώπων or παρὰ πάντας ἀνθρώπους [so Codd. A, 26, 198, 239, 306]. None of these translations, in either Clement or the LXX., correspond to the Hebrew of this verse : but the difference between Clement and the LXX. affords a remarkable proof that the translation has been transferred to this place from c. 52. 14, for each of the translations is a possible translation of the latter half of that verse. Consequently they must have been made independently, and this fact suggests the hypothesis that the Greek of this verse, whichever of the two translations be adopted, represents an alternative, but now lost, Hebrew text. (3) In v. 6 Clement reads ὑπὲρ τῶν ἁμαρτιῶν ἡμῶν : all existing MSS. of the LXX. read ταῖς ἁμαρτίαις ἡμῶν, but the early Latin quotations, e. g. Cyprian *Testim.* 2. 13. p. 77, Lactant. *Instit.* 4. 16 support Clement by reading *propter peccata nostra :* so Jerome *in Isai.* 53, tom. iv. 615 *propter iniquitates nostras.*

Is. 60. 17 is quoted in c. 42 with the variants (*a*) ἐπισκόπους for the ἄρχοντας of all MSS. of the LXX., and (*b*) διακόνους for ἐπισκόπους. In regard to (*a*) it may be noted (1) that Clement and the LXX. agree in rendering the abstract פְּקֻדָּה by the concrete words ἄρχοντας, ἐπισκόπους, whereas Aquila has ἐπίσκεψιν, Symmachus ἐπισκοπήν: (2) that the same word is translated by ἐπισκόπους in 2 Kings 11. 18, and by ἐπισκέψεως in 1 Chron. 26. 30 : (3) that the concrete פָּקִיד is rendered in LXX., Gen. 41. 34 by the local Egyptian word τοπάρχας, in Symmachus by ἐπισκόπους, in LXX., Judges 9. 28 by ἐπίσκοπος, in LXX., 2 Chron. 24. 11 by προστάτης, in LXX., Esth. 2. 3 by κωμάρχας. It follows that Clement may very possibly have had before him a revised text of the LXX. in which ἐπισκόπους was used in the present passage. In regard to (*b*) it may be noted that the Hebrew נֹגֵשׂ which Clement here renders by διακόνους, the LXX. by ἐπισκόπους, Aquila and Theodotion by πράκτορας, Symmachus by ἐπιστάτας, is rendered in Job 3. 18: 39. 7 by φορολόγος.

3. Barnabas.

I. *Quotations from the Psalms.*

In three cases the quotation agrees with the Sixtine text of the LXX., and there is no important variant from that text in the MSS. of the LXX. itself: viz. Ps. 21 (22). 19, 117 (118). 12 and 22 are all quoted in Barn. 6.

In four unimportant cases the text of Barnabas differs from the Sixtine text, but is supported by good MSS. of the LXX.

In Ps. 1. 1, quoted in c. 10, Cod. S of Barnabas agrees with Codd. BS and 42 cursives in reading ἐπὶ καθέδραν for ἐπὶ καθέδρᾳ.

In Ps. 1. 5, quoted in c. 11, Barnabas agrees with Codd. A, 268 of the LXX. in omitting the article before ἀσεβεῖς.

In Ps. 17 (18). 45, quoted in c. 9, Barnabas agrees with Codd. S¹, 179, 286 of the LXX. in reading ὑπήκουσαν for ὑπήκουσεν, and with S², 205, 206 in reading μου for μοι.

In Ps. 21 (22). 17, quoted in c. 6, Barnabas is supported by two cursives, 81, 206, in reading περίεσχε for περίεσχον.

Some cases suggest the hypothesis that a Greek text of the psalms was in existence, which was based upon the LXX. but altered by a Greek hand in the same way as, for example, in modern times hymns are sometimes altered by the compiler of a hymn-book.

Ps. 21 (22). 23 διηγήσομαι τὸ ὄνομά σου τοῖς ἀδελφοῖς μου, ἐν μέσῳ ἐκκλησίας ὑμνήσω σε is quoted in c. 6 in the form ἐξομολογήσομαί σοι ἐν ἐκκλησίᾳ ἐν μέσῳ ἀδελφῶν μου καὶ ψαλῶ σοι ἀνὰ μέσον ἐκκλησίας ἁγίων. The fact that elsewhere in the same chapter Barnabas quotes exactly the LXX. text of the same psalm seems to show that he is not using another translation of the Hebrew: but it must be noted (1) that ἐξομολογεῖσθαι does not occur in the LXX. as a translation of סָפַר, (2) that ψάλλειν does not occur in the LXX. as a translation of הִלֵּל.

Other cases suggest the hypothesis that psalms were in

existence which breathed the spirit, and adopted the Greek phraseology, of the existing psalms, but which were never incorporated into the psalter and only exist in these fragments :

Ps. 33 (34). 13 τίς ἐστιν ἄνθρωπος ὁ θέλων ζωήν, ἀγαπῶν ἡμέρας ἰδεῖν ἀγαθάς; is recalled by c. 9 τίς ἐστιν ὁ θέλων ζῆσαι εἰς αἰῶνα ;

Ps. 41 (42). 3 πότε ἥξω καὶ ὀφθήσομαι τῷ προσώπῳ τοῦ θεοῦ; is recalled by c. 6 ἔν τινι ὀφθήσομαι τῷ κυρίῳ θεῷ καὶ δοξασθήσομαι ;

Ps. 50 (51). 19 θυσία τῷ θεῷ πνεῦμα συντετριμμένον, καρδίαν συντετριμμένην καὶ τεταπεινωμένην ὁ θεὸς οὐκ οὐδενώσει is recalled by c. 2 θυσία τῷ θεῷ πνεῦμα συντετριμμένον, ὀσμὴ εὐωδίας τῷ κυρίῳ καρδία δοξάζουσα τὸν πεπλακότα αὐτήν.

Ps. 89 (90). 4 χίλια ἔτη ἐν ὀφθαλμοῖς σου ὡς ἡ ἡμέρα ἡ ἐχθὲς ἥτις διῆλθε is recalled by c. 15 ἰδοὺ σήμερον ἡμέρα ἔσται ὡς χίλια ἔτη.

In at least one case, in c. 5, there is a cento from several psalms, which will be discussed separately in the next chapter.

It must be noted that there is no difference in the mode of quotation between passages which are undoubtedly from the LXX. and other passages which are best explained by the hypothesis of the existence of altered versions or centos : undoubted quotations are introduced by e.g. Δαυὶδ ... λέγει ὁμοίως c. 10, λέγει κύριος ἐν τῷ προφήτῃ c. 9, λέγει πάλιν ὁ προφήτης c. 6, other quotations by e.g. λέγει πάλιν Κύριος c. 6, πάλιν τὸ πνεῦμα τοῦ Κυρίου λέγει c. 9, λέγει ὁ προφητεύων ἐπ' αὐτῷ c. 5, αὐτὸς δέ [*sc.* ὁ Κύριος] μοι μαρτυρεῖ λέγων c. 15. The point is of importance as an indication of the current opinion in regard to the limits of the Canon of Scripture. It seems likely that as any writer or speaker of exceptional spiritual force was regarded as a προφήτης, so what he wrote or said was regarded as the utterance of the Spirit of God through him.

II. *Quotations from Isaiah.*

In most cases the quotations follow the current text of the LXX., with only such variations as are found in existing MSS. of the LXX.; but in some cases the original meaning is clearly disregarded and the quotation adapted to the immediate point in hand.

Is. 1. 2 is quoted in c. 9 with the addition ταῦτα εἰς μαρτυρίαν after κύριος ἐλάλησεν.

Is. 1. 10 is quoted in c. 9 with the substitution of τοῦ λαοῦ τούτου for Σοδόμων.

Is. 1. 11–14 is quoted in c. 2 with (*a*) the omission, in Cod. Sin., of κριῶν after ὁλοκαυτωμάτων, (*b*) the omission of καὶ ἡμέραν μεγάλην after τὰ σάββατα. v. 13 is also quoted in c. 15 with the same omission of καὶ ἡμ. μεγ.

Is. 3. 9 is quoted in c. 6 with the variant ὅτι for διότι.

Is. 5. 21 is quoted in c. 4: Cod. Sin., as also Cod. 91 of the LXX., omits, Cod. Const. retains ἐν in the phrase οἱ συνετοὶ ἐν ἑαυτοῖς.

Is. 33. 13 ἀκούσονται οἱ πόρρωθεν ἃ ἐποίησα, γνώσονται οἱ ἐγγίζοντες τὴν ἰσχύν μου is quoted in c. 9 with a Hebraistic addition to ἀκούσονται and with the omission of the second subject, viz. ἀκοῇ ἀκούσονται οἱ πόρρωθεν ἃ ἐποίησα γνώσονται, which shows that the words are quoted without reference to their original meaning and application.

Is. 33. 16, 17 . . . τὸ ὕδωρ αὐτοῦ πιστόν· βασιλέα μετὰ δόξης ὄψεσθε, οἱ ὀφθαλμοὶ ὑμῶν ὄψονται γῆν πόρρωθεν, ἡ ψυχὴ ὑμῶν μελετήσει φόβον is quoted in c. 11 in the form τὸ ὕδωρ αὐτοῦ πιστόν· βασιλέα μετὰ δόξης ὄψεσθε καὶ ἡ ψυχὴ ὑμῶν μελετήσει φόβον κυρίου: here also the severance of τὸ ὑδ. αὐ. πιστόν from the preceding sentence to which they belong, and the addition of κυρίου to the last words, show that the words are quoted as words pertinent to the point in hand, without reference to their original meaning and application.

Is. 40. 3 φωνὴ βοῶντος ἐν τῇ ἐρήμῳ is quoted in c. 9 with the prefix ἀκούσατε τέκνα, and it is clear that, as in Matt. 3. 3, Mk. 1. 3, Luke 3. 4, ἐν τῇ ἐρήμῳ is taken with βοῶντος rather than with the following ἐτοιμάσατε: Cod. Sin. of Barnabas reads φωνή as in the LXX., but Cod. Const. reads φωνῆς, making the word depend on ἀκούσατε.

Is. 42. 6, 7 is quoted exactly in c. 14, with the exceptions (*a*) ὁ θεός σου for ὁ θεός: (β) Cod. Sin. has ἰσχύσω for ἐνισχύσω: so Justin M. in his three quotations of the passage, *Tryph.* 26, 65, and 122: (γ) καί is read before ἐξαγαγεῖν: so Cod. XII and most cursives of the LXX.: (δ) πεπεδημένους is read for δεδεμένους: so Justin M. in the three quotations just mentioned: this change points to a revised text since πεπεδημένος is a more frequent translation of אָסִיר: (ε) καί is omitted, with most MSS. of the LXX., with Justin M. *Tryph.* 26, 65, and in agreement with the Hebrew, before καθημένους.

Is. 45. 1 λέγει κύριος ὁ θεὸς τῷ χριστῷ μου Κύρῳ is quoted in c. 12, probably (i. e. in Codd. Sin.[1] Const. as against Codd. Barb. Med. Sin[3].) with the change of Κύρῳ into κυρίῳ, obviously on apologetic grounds.

Is. 45. 2 is quoted in c. 11 with the variants (*a*) in Codd. Sin. Const. πύλας for θύρας, a change in the translation of דֶּלֶת which is sometimes found in the LXX., (*b*) ἀοράτους is omitted, as in Cod. A[1], (*c*) γνῶσιν for γνῷς, a middle term between the two readings existing in the γνωσῃ of Cod. A.

Is. 49. 6 (Cod. A) ἰδοὺ τέθεικά σε [Codd. BS, *al.* add εἰς διαθήκην γένους] εἰς φῶς ἐθνῶν τοῦ εἶναί σε εἰς σωτηρίαν ἕως ἐσχάτου τῆς γῆς· οὕτως λέγει κύριος ὁ ῥυσάμενός σε ὁ θεὸς Ἰσραήλ is quoted in c. 14 as in the Alexandrine text with (*a*) the substitution of λυτρωσάμενος for ῥυσάμενος; (*b*) the omission of the article, as in Codd. BS[3], and six cursives, before θεός; (*c*) all MSS. of Barnabas, except Cod. Sin., also omit Ἰσραήλ after θεός. It may be also noted that here, as elsewhere, the clause οὕτως λέγει . . . is detached from its proper context and adapted to the immediate purpose of the writer.

Is. 50. 6, 7 is quoted in c. 5 with the omission of 6 *b*, 7 *a*: i. e. the final clause of the antithesis, being sufficient for the purpose, is given instead of the whole: the only variant is τέθεικα for ἔδωκα, as in the preceding quotation.

Is. 50. 8, 9 (Cod. B) τίς ὁ κρινόμενός μοι; ἀντιστήτω μοι ἅμα· καὶ τίς ὁ κρινόμενός μοι· ἰδοὺ κύριος κύριος βοηθήσει μοι· τίς κακώσει με; ἰδοὺ πάντες ὑμεῖς ὡς ἱμάτιον παλαιωθήσεσθε καὶ σὴς καταφάγεται ὑμᾶς is quoted in c. 6 with omissions and with an apologetic adaptation to Christ:

the variants are (*a*) ἅμα is omitted, (*c*) ἢ τίς is used for καὶ τίς, (*c*) the second κρινόμενος is changed to δικαιούμενος in Codd. Sin. Const.: so also Cod. 26 of the LXX., δικαζόμενος Codd. cett., (*d*) the clauses ἰδοὺ κύριος . . . . , τίς κακώσει με are omitted, as not being pertinent to the purpose of the quotation, (*e*) οὐαὶ ὑμῖν ὅτι is substituted for ἰδού: but it is possible that these words are meant not to be part of the quotation but only to call the attention to what follows: *Woe to you, for* (*as the prophet says*) '*Ye shall all wax old* . . . .'

Is. 58. 4–10 is quoted in c. 3 with the following variants:—

In v. 4 Barnabas inserts the words λέγει κύριως after νηστεύετε: the insertion of the words in MSS. of the LXX. is somewhat arbitrary, e. g. they are inserted in the next verse by Codd. 239, 306.

In v. 5 Barnabas agrees with 13 cursives and the Old Latin, as against the other MSS., in inserting ἐγώ before ἐξελεξάμην: he reads οὐκ ἄνθρωπον ταπεινοῦντα τὴν ψυχὴν αὐτοῦ for καὶ ἡμέραν ταπεινοῦν ἄνθρωπον τὴν ψυχὴν αὐτοῦ, in which he is supported, against all the MSS. of the LXX., by Cypr. *Testim.* 3. 1, p. 108 *diem humiliare hominem animam suam*, Hieron. *in Zach.* 7, tom. vi. 833 *neque ut humiliet homo animam suam:* he reads the plurals κάμψητε, ὑποστρώσητε [Cod. Const. omits] for the singulars κάμψης, ὑποστρώσῃ, and he gives the special predicate ἐνδύσησθε τὸ σάκκον.

In v. 6 the words οὐχὶ τοιαύτην νηστείαν ἐγὼ [most cursives omit ἐγώ] ἐξελεξάμην are expanded into the more emphatic form ἰδοὺ αὕτη ἡ [Cod. Sin. omits ἡ] νηστεία ἣν ἐγὼ ἐξελεξάμην, in which he is supported, against all existing MSS. of the LXX., by Clem. Alex. *Paed.* 3. 12, p. 305.

In v. 7 (1) the order of the clauses πτωχοὺς ἀστέγους εἴσαγε εἰς τὸν οἶκόν σου, and γυμνὸν ἐὰν ἴδῃς περίβαλε is inverted: so also in the Old Latin in Hieron. *in Zach.* tom. vi. 833 *si videris nudum operi eum et pauperem et absque tecto induc in tabernaculum tuum:* but all the other quotations of the passage in early Latin writers follow the current order of the clauses, with the exception of Auct. Quaest. V. T. *ap.* S. Aug. tom. iii. *append.* p. 145*e*, which omits the translation of the clause πτωχοὺς . . . . οἶκόν σου. (2) πτωχοὺς is omitted, as in Tertull. *c. Marc.* 4, p. 651*c*, 730 *b* (but elsewhere *mendicos* is inserted): possibly because of the practical difficulty of a literal observance of the injunction, which may also account for the substitution of *peregrinum* in Iren. *Vet. Interp.* 4. 17. (3) A new clause is added, ἐὰν ἴδῃς ταπεινόν, and the predicate of the following clause, viz. οὐκ ὑπερόψῃ is placed as its apodosis : the use of ταπεινόν here, and the omission of πτωχούς in the preceding clause, may be explained on the supposition that in some editions of the LXX. the former word rather than the latter was used, as in five other passages of Isaiah, to translate עָנִי.

The text of the passage in Barnabas is evidently ' conflate ': the quotations in the early Latin writers mentioned above indicate that in one text, as in Barnabas and perhaps through the influence of the cognate passages, Ezek. 18. 7, 16, the clause about clothing the naked was placed next to that about feeding the hungry, probably without any further change : and that another text followed the Hebrew order. When Barnabas, or a reviser whom he followed, put these two texts together, in order to avoid the repetition of γυμνόν, he used ταπεινόν, which some texts contained in the preceding clause, as the object of the repeated ἐὰν ἴδῃς and made the predicate οὐχ ὑπερόψῃ αὐτόν common to the two last clauses.

In v. 8 it is almost certain, although the reading is corrected, perhaps by the original scribe, in Cod. Sin., that Barnabas read ἱμάτια for ἰάματα : it is obviously a scribe's error, but it is found in Codd. S² and ³, 91¹, 106¹, 147 of the LXX., and, in the translation *vestimenta*, in Tert. *de Resurr. Carnis*, pp. 576 c, 577 a, Cyprian *Testim.* 3. 1, p. 108, *de Orat. Domin.* 33, p. 291, *de Op. et eleem.* 4, p. 376. Jerome notes it as the current Latin reading, *In Isai.* 58, tom. iv. 693.

In v. 9 the MSS. of Barnabas vary between βοήσεις and βοήσῃ, and between ἐπακούσεται and εἰσακούσεται : in each case the latter of the two readings mentioned is the reading of all the MSS. of the LXX. except one.

In v. 10 Barnabas agrees with Codd. A, 26, 49, 106 in adding σου to τὸν ἄρτον : so also all the early Latin quotations.

Is. 61. 1 is quoted in c. 14 almost exactly as in the current text of the LXX., from which there are no important variants : but both in the LXX. and Barnabas there is an interesting instance of the interchange of πτωχοῖς and ταπεινοῖς as translations of עָנִי (see above, p. 73): in the LXX. Codd. AB and most cursives have πτωχοῖς, Cod. S¹ has ταπεινοῖς, in Barnabas the fragmentary MSS. have ταπεινοῖς and add χάριν, Cod. S. has πτωχοῖς.

Is. 65. 2 Cod. B ἐξεπέτασα τὰς χεῖράς μου ὅλην τὴν ἡμέραν πρὸς λαὸν ἀπειθοῦντα καὶ ἀντιλέγοντα, τοῖς πορευομένοις ὁδῷ οὐ καλῇ is quoted in c. 12 in the form ὅλην τὴν ἡμέραν ἐξεπέτασα τὰς χεῖράς μου πρὸς λαὸν ἀπειθῆ [so Cod. Sin., Codd. Const. cett. ἀπειθοῦντα] καὶ ἀντιλέγοντα ὁδῷ δικαίᾳ μου. The insertion of the words ὁδῷ δικαίᾳ μου, which are obviously suggested by the following clause of the LXX., is probably a rhetorical softening of the harshness of the absolute use of ἀντιλέγειν.

In at least two passages the resemblance to the text of Isaiah is hardly strong enough to warrant the supposition that they are directly quoted from it : viz.

c. 16 ἰδοὺ οἱ καθελόντες τὸν ναὸν τοῦτον αὐτοὶ αὐτὸν οἰκοδομήσουσιν recalls Is. 49. 17 καὶ τάχυ οἰκοδομηθήσῃ ὑφ' ὧν κατῃρέθης : c. 6 καὶ ἔθηκέν με ὡς στερεὰν πέτραν recalls Is. 50. 7 τὸ δὲ πρόσωπόν μου ἔθηκα ὡς στερεὰν πέτραν (which is quoted exactly in c. 5 ; see above, p. 186).

It is a hypothesis for which there is no direct evidence, and which at the same time is not contrary to analogy, to suppose that besides the canonical books themselves, there were manuals of prophecy as well as anthologies, which had a certain authority and were accordingly quoted as of authority, in the same way as e.g. Clement of Alexandria (*Strom.* 3. 20) quotes the 'Two Ways' as ἡ γραφή. This hypothesis will serve also to explain the quotations in c. 6. 13 ἰδοὺ ποιῶ τὰ ἔσχατα ὡς τὰ πρῶτα, c. 11. 10 καὶ ὃς ἂν φάγῃ ἐξ αὐτῶν ζήσεται εἰς τὸν αἰῶνα (which appears to be a summary of Ezek. 47. 12).

4. Justin Martyr.

It is desirable, before considering any of Justin's quotations, to point out that the text of his genuine works practically rests upon a single MS. of the fourteenth century,

Cod. Paris 450, dated 1364. The value of that MS. can
be tested in two ways: (1) the same MS. contains other
works of which other and earlier MSS. remain: three of
these works, ps-Justin *Epistola ad Zenam* and *Cohortatio
ad Gentiles*, and Athenagoras *de Resurrectione*, it has in
common with another Paris MS., No. 451, which was written
in 914, i.e. 450 years earlier. Omitting unimportant orthographical variations, it differs from these three treatises in
169 passages, in only a small proportion of which (according
to Otto 17, according to Harnack 5 or 6) is it probable that
the later MS. has the better reading. In other words, in
that part of the MS. which admits of comparison with these
three works there are not less than 150 passages which
require emendation. If the mistakes in the two Apologies
and Trypho be in the same ratio, as they may fairly be
presumed to be, the number of such mistakes will be very
large. (2) In a few passages we can compare the MS. with
quotations from Justin in other works which have well-
attested texts: e.g. Justin, *Apol.* ii. 2 with Euseb. *H. E.* 4.
17: this comparison gives the same results as the preceding: the number of mistakes is considerable. In other
words the Paris Codex 450 contains a careless and inac-
curate text which a critic need not scruple to alter[1].

The only other complete MS. of Justin's genuine writings
is one which was once in the Jesuits' Library at Paris, and
hence is known as the *Codex Claromontanus*, but which is
now in the Middlehill collection at Cheltenham. It was
written in 1541, and is merely a copy of the Paris Cod.
450[2].

There are two late MSS. which contain fragments of

---

[1] This account of the MSS. of Justin is entirely based upon Professor
Harnack's elaborate account of them in the *Texte und Untersuchungen zur
Geschichte der altchristliche Literatur*, Bd. i. Leipzig, 1882, entitled *Die
Ueberlieferung der griechischen Apologeten des II Jahrhunderts in der alten
Kirche und im Mittelalter*.

[2] See, for details, the *Theologische Literaturzeitung* for 1876, No. 13.

Justin's genuine works: (1) in the Vatican Library, Cod. Ottobonianus Gr. 274, written in the fifteenth century, contains chapters 65–67 of the Apology: (2) in the National Library at Paris, Cod. Supplem. Gr. 190, is only a worthless transcript, made in the seventeenth century, of some extracts from one or other of the earlier printed editions.

It thus appears that our only authority for almost all Justin's text is the Paris MS. 450, of 1364: and considering the character of that MS. it will not be necessary for a student to treat the text of Justin, as it exists in that MS., with the same reverential respect, and the same reluctance to assume the existence of an error, which he would feel in the case e.g. of the Alexandrine MS. of Clement.

This account of the existing MS. evidence for Justin's text forms a necessary preface to an examination of his quotations, because some untenable arguments have been based upon the correspondence or non-correspondence of those quotations with the existing MSS. of both the Old and the New Testaments. The most important of such arguments are those of Credner's *Beiträge zur Einleitung in die biblischen Schriften*: the agreements and differences between Justin's text and the biblical texts are stated in that work with great minuteness: but the arguments which are based upon them are practically without value because they assume that the text of the Paris MS. represents Justin's own quotations from the biblical texts of his time. It may be shown, in disproof of that assumption, that the scribe of that MS., or of its original, neglected Justin's own quotations and copied them for himself from some other MS.: sometimes, indeed, as in the quotation from Psalm 71 (72) in *Tryph.* 64, he was not at the trouble to copy out more than the beginning and ending of the passage, but after transcribing a few verses wrote '... and so forth until the words ....' (καὶ τὰ λοιπὰ ἄχρι τοῦ ...)

The following three instances will be sufficient to establish this point:—

(1) In Ps. 18 (19). 6 it is clear from two short quotations in *Tryph.* 69, *Apol.* i. 54 that Justin read ἰσχυρὸς (ὡς γίγας δραμεῖν ὁδόν), because in each case he comments upon the word : the same inference may be drawn from *Tryph.* 76. But in the MS. of *Tryph.* 64, in which the first six verses of the psalm are quoted at length, the word ἰσχυρός is omitted. It is thus evident that in transcribing *Tryph.* 46 the scribe did not follow Justin's text. The insertion of the word in the text which Justin used is to be noted because there is no trace of it in any existing MS. of the LXX.: it was probably used in some recension as a gloss of γίγας or as a substitute for it, γίγας being a rare word, which Hesychius *s.v.* explains by ἰσχυρός. It is possible that the true text of Justin himself may be not that of the MS. as given above, but ὡς ἰσχυρὸς δραμεῖν ὁδόν, and that γίγας may be an interpolation : but however this may be, the fact remains that ἰσχυρός was in his text of the Psalms and that it is not in the text of the Psalms which is transcribed in the MS.

(2) In Ps. 95 (96). 10 it is clear from Justin's words in *Tryph.* 73 that he read ὁ κύριος ἐβασίλευσεν ἀπὸ τοῦ ξύλου, because he comments upon the fact that the Jews omitted those words on account of their evident reference to the crucified Jesus. But in the quotation of the psalm which immediately follows the words are omitted, as they are in all existing MSS. of the Psalter, except the Verona Psalter and Cod. 156 (a Basle MS. of uncertain date). It is obvious that the scribe did not follow Justin's own text, but transcribed the Psalm from a MS. which contained the current text. The absence of the words from all MSS. of the LXX., except the two mentioned above, is a fact of great importance in regard to the textual tradition of the LXX., especially in face of the facts (1) of the use which was made of them in the Judaeo-Christian controversies, for they are used against the Jews not only by Justin but also by Tertullian, *adv. Jud.*, pp. 144, 146 : (2) of the words *a ligno* being found in almost all early Latin quotations of the passage (Hilary is probably the only exception). The existence of the words in the two Greek MSS. which contain them may be accounted for by the fact that both those MSS. are accompanied by a Latin version : and the form in which they occur in the Basle MS., viz. απο τω ξυλω,

suggests the hypothesis that they are there only an attempt at retranslation by a mediaeval scribe.

(3) *Ps.* 71 (72). 17 is quoted twice in *Tryph.* 121 in the form ὑπὲρ τὸν ἥλιον ἀνατελεῖ (*sc.* τὸ ὄνομα αὐτοῦ). There can be no doubt that this was Justin's reading, for he supports his quotation of the passage by a quotation from Zach. 6. 12 ἀνατολὴ ὄνομα αὐτοῦ, and his commentary is πυρωδέστερος γὰρ αὐτοῦ ὁ τῆς ἀληθείας καὶ σοφίας λόγος καὶ φωτεινότερος μᾶλλον τοῦ ἡλίου δυνάμεών ἐστι. But in the quotation of the whole psalm in *Tryph.* 34, and in the similar quotation (which the scribe has shortened) in *Tryph.* 64, the scribe follows the current reading of the LXX., πρὸ τοῦ ἡλίου διαμενεῖ τὸ ὄνομα αὐτοῦ.

It is clear from these instances that the longer quotations in the Paris MS. of Justin cannot be trusted as representatives of Justin's own text, and that arguments based upon them alone fall to the ground. But it is also clear that the untrustworthiness of the longer quotations does not affect the shorter quotations which form an integral part of Justin's own text, and which are in many cases confirmed by his comments.

The following is an examination of some of these shorter quotations, with one longer quotation which invites special treatment, in order to ascertain what light they throw upon the text of the LXX.

I. *Quotations from the Psalms.*

Ps. 3. 6 is quoted in *Tryph.* 97, and in *Apol.* i. 38 : in both quotations ἀντελάβετο is read, with Codd. S¹, 210, as against the common reading ἀντιλήψεται. There is a similar variation of tenses in the early Latin quotations : but the preponderance of testimony is in favour of the past as against the future : the former is found in Lactant. *Instit.* 4. 19, and in the Codex Sangermanensis : the latter is found first in Hilar. *in Psalm.* 131, tom. i. 505 : in Cypr. *Testim.* 2. 24, p. 91 the MSS. vary : both are found in Ambrose and Augustine.

Ps. 21 (22). 3 is quoted not only as part of the long quotation in *Tryph.* 98, but twice separately in *Tryph.* 99. In each case the reading is that of the current text of the LXX. καὶ οὐκ εἰς ἄνοιαν ἐμοί: but Justin seems to have read not ἄνοιαν but ἄγνοιαν, for his words are (*Tryph.* 99) ἀλλ᾽ ἵνα μή τις λέγῃ Ἠγνόει οὖν ὅτι μέλλει πάσχειν, ἐπάγει ἐν τῷ ψαλμῷ εὐθύς. Καὶ οὐκ εἰς ἄνοιαν ἐμοί. ὅνπερ τρόπον οὐδὲ τῷ θεῷ εἰς ἄνοιαν ἦν τὸ ἐρωτᾶν τὸν Ἀδὰμ ποῦ ἐστὶν οὐδὲ τὸν Καῖν ποῦ Ἅβελ ἀλλ᾽ εἰς τὸ ἕκαστον ἐλέγξαι ὁποῖός ἐστι καὶ εἰς ἡμᾶς τὴν γνῶσιν πάντων διὰ τοῦ ἀναφανῆναι ἐλθεῖν . . . . The whole point turns not upon folly but upon knowledge or ignorance: and ἠγνόει would be unintelligible unless ἄγνοιαν followed.

The passage raises a wider question than that of Justin's reading : neither εἰς ἄνοιαν nor εἰς ἄγνοιαν gives any intelligible meaning, or is an approximate translation of the Hebrew. The meaning of the Hebrew וְלַיְלָה וְלֹא־דוּמִיָּה לִי is clearly that there was no cessation of his crying in the night. The alteration of a single letter would give this meaning to the Greek, and I do not hesitate to suggest that the LXX. wrote not εἰς ἄνοιαν but εἰς ἀνείαν (i. e. remission or cessation, from ἀνίημι). But the word was a rare one: the only recorded instance of it is in a Paris MS. (Colbert, No. 4249) of ps-Athanas. *Praecepta ad Antiochum* (*Opp.* ed. Bened. ii. 253, and, separately, ed. G. Dindorf, Lipsiae, 1857), c. 5, in a passage based upon Hermas, *Mand.* 5. 1, where it is probably a scribe's error for ἀγνείαν. It was consequently unknown to the early scribes of the LXX., who substituted for it, with a complete disregard of the meaning of the passage, one or other of two words, ἄνοιαν and ἄγνοιαν, which they knew better. A single MS., Cod. 167 (British Museum, No. 5553), has the reading εις αυιαν, which may be a survival of εἰς ἀνείαν.

Ps. 23 (24). 7 is quoted in *Tryph.* 85, *Apol.* i. 51 in the form ἐπάρθητε πύλαι αἰώνιοι ἵνα εἰσέλθῃ ὁ βασιλεὺς τῆς δόξης. The reading of all existing MSS. of the LXX. is καὶ εἰσελεύσεται : and this current reading is found both in the quotation of the whole psalm in *Tryph.* 36, and in the shorter quotation in *Tryph.* 127. But ἵνα εἰσέλθῃ is a closer rendering of the Hebrew : and Jerome's Psalter has *et ingrediatur*, for which *ut ingrediatur* may reasonably be conjectured, as opposed to the *et introibit* of the Verona Psalter and the Codex Sangermanensis. In other words ἵνα εἰσέλθῃ may be supposed to be the reading which existed in the recension of the LXX., which was followed not only by Justin but also by the Old Latin versions.

Ps. 81 (82). 7 is quoted in *Tryph.* 124 with a comment on the difference between the Jewish and the LXX. interpretation. As the text stands it is not clear wherein the difference lies: the longer quotation has probably undergone the fate of most of the longer quotations in Justin, and is no longer in the form in which he wrote it. But the reading of the shorter quotation ἰδοὺ δὴ ὡς ἄνθρωποι ἀποθνήσκετε, upon which emphasis is laid as being the reading of the LXX., though not found in any existing MS., is probably supported by the reading of Cod. S¹ δε δη ως ανθρωποι, which may be conjectured to be an imperfect transcription of ἴδε δὴ ὡς ἄνθρωποι .... If this be so, it must be supposed that the LXX. followed the Hebrew in connecting ὑμεῖς with the preceding clause: and this view is supported by Jerome's Psalter *dii estis et filii excelsi omnes vos*.

It will be seen from these instances that the shorter quotations present in almost every case some point of interest in regard to the critical study of the LXX.: this fact makes the untrustworthiness of the longer quotations more to be regretted, and leads the student to anticipate with hope the possible discovery of a MS. of Justin which shall preserve his quotations from the LXX. in their original form.

There is at least one instance, that of Psalm 95 (96). 1–10, in which it seems likely that this original form has been preserved: and it invites examination because the psalm is not only quoted twice by Justin, viz. in *Apol.* i. 41 and in *Tryph.* 73, but also exists in two forms in the LXX., in the Psalter and in 1 Chronicles 16. 23–31. In regard to the quotation in the Trypho it was pointed out above that it cannot be a transcription of the text which Justin used: but since the two phrases, εἴδωλα δαιμονίων and ἀπὸ τοῦ ξύλου, which were certainly in Justin's text, though they are absent from the longer quotation in the Trypho are found in the quotation in the Apology, it may be assumed (1) that the two texts were originally the same, (2) that the Apology represents the text which Justin used. It may further be noted that the text in the Trypho corresponds, almost exactly, to the Vatican text of the LXX. Psalter, and represents the same tradition as that text: whereas the text in the Apology corresponds more nearly to that of 1 Chronicles. (In addition to the longer quotations, vv. 1–3 are quoted in *Tryph.* 74, v. 5 in *Tryph.* 55, 73, 79, 83, v. 10 in *Tryph.* 73.)

The following is a detailed examination of the quotations:

vv. 1, 2. The form of these verses in the Psalter (=Trypho) is ᾄσατε τῷ κυρίῳ ᾆσμα καινόν, ᾄσατε τῷ κυρίῳ πᾶσα ἡ γῆ· ᾄσατε τῷ κυρίῳ, εὐλογήσατε τὸ ὄνομα αὐτοῦ, εὐαγγελίζεσθε ἡμέραν ἐξ ἡμέρας τὸ σωτήριον αὐτοῦ. There is no noteworthy variant.

The form in 1 Chronicles and the Apology is shorter: ᾄσατε τῷ κυρίῳ πᾶσα ἡ γῆ· ἀναγγείλατε ἐξ ἡμέρας εἰς ἡμέραν τὸ σωτήριον [so Codd. AS and most cursives: Cod. B and some cursives σωτηρίαν] αὐτοῦ.

v. 3. The form in most MSS. of the Psalter (=Trypho), is ἀναγγείλατε [ἀπαγγείλατε] ἐν τοῖς ἔθνεσι τὴν δόξαν αὐτοῦ, ἐν πᾶσι τοῖς λαοῖς τὰ θαυμάσια αὐτοῦ: Cod. A¹, the Verona Psalter, and *Tryph.* 74, omit the first half of the verse, making ἐν πᾶσι .... θαυμάσια αὐτοῦ coordinate with τὸ σωτήριον as an object of εὐαγγελίζεσθε in v. 2.

The whole verse is omitted in the Apology, and in Codd. ABS, and several cursives, in 1 Chronicles: the MSS. which contain it read as in the Psalms with the substitution of ἐξηγεῖσθε for ἀναγγείλατε.

v. 4 is the same in all four passages: except that 1 Chronicles and Justin agree with about 80 cursive MSS. of the Psalter in reading ὑπὲρ πάντας instead of ἐπὶ πάντας.

v. 5. The form in almost all MSS. of the Psalter (=Trypho) is ὅτι πάντες οἱ θεοὶ τῶν ἐθνῶν δαιμόνια, ὁ δὲ κύριος τοὺς οὐρανοὺς ἐποίησεν.

The form in 1 Chronicles is ὅτι πάντες οἱ θεοὶ τῶν ἐθνῶν εἴδωλα καὶ ὁ θεὸς ἡμῶν οὐρανοὺς [ABS οὐρανὸν] ἐποίησεν: the Apology (so also *Tryph.* 55, 73, but not 79, 83) substitutes εἴδωλα δαιμονίων for εἴδωλα, and follows with ὁ δὲ θεὸς τοὺς οὐρανοὺς ἐποίησεν. The phrase εἴδωλα δαιμονίων is supported by Iren. *Vet. Interp.* 3. 5 alone among early Latin authorities, and by Clem. Alex. *Protrept.* c. 4 alone among early Greek authorities: εἴδωλα is used elsewhere, but δαιμόνια is not, as a translation of אֱלִילִים. The phrase in Justin, if notwithstanding its absence in *Tryph.* 79, 83 it be really his, is perhaps an intentional combination of the two readings.

v. 6. The form in the Psalter (=Trypho) is ἐξομολόγησις καὶ ὡραιότης ἐνώπιον αὐτοῦ, ἁγιωσύνη καὶ μεγαλοπρέπεια ἐν τῷ ἁγιάσματι αὐτοῦ.

The form in most MSS. of 1 Chronicles and in the Apology is δόξα καὶ ἔπαινος κατὰ πρόσωπον αὐτοῦ, ἰσχὺς καὶ καύχημα ἐν τόπῳ αὐτοῦ [*Apol.* ἐν τόπῳ ἁγιάσματος αὐτοῦ, Codd. 19, 93, 108 ἐν τῷ ἁγιάσματι αὐτοῦ, Codd. 106, 120, 134, 144, 236, 243 ἐν τόπῳ ἁγίῳ αὐτοῦ]. The form of the last clause in Justin seems to be a combination of the readings of the Psalter and of Chronicles: as in the preceding verse.

v. 7 is the same in the Psalter and 1 Chronicles, except that the former reads ἐνέγκατε and τίμην where the latter has δότε and ἰσχύν. But in the Apology, which otherwise agrees with 1 Chronicles, Justin has the remarkable reading δότε τῷ κυρίῳ τῷ πατρὶ τῶν αἰώνων for δότε τῷ κυρίῳ αἱ πατριαὶ τῶν ἐθνῶν. The origin of this reading may probably be traced in Codd. BS of the passage in 1 Chronicles, which read πατρί for αἱ πατριαί. Justin may have found a similar reading in the copy which he used: and πατρὶ τῶν ἐθνῶν being an unusual expression was changed to τῷ πατρὶ τῶν αἰώνων, a phrase which may be compared with the current philosophical phrase τῷ πατρὶ τῶν ὅλων.

In vv. 8, 9, 10 the form in the Psalter (=Trypho) is—

8   ἐνέγκατε τῷ κυρίῳ δόξαν ὀνόματι αὐτοῦ,
    ἄρατε θυσίας καὶ εἰσπορεύεσθε εἰς τὰς αὐλὰς αὐτοῦ·

9   προσκυνήσατε τῷ κυρίῳ ἐν αὐλῇ ἁγίᾳ αὐτοῦ,
    σαλευθήτω ἀπὸ προσώπου αὐτοῦ πᾶσα ἡ γῆ.

10   εἴπατε ἐν τοῖς ἔθνεσιν Ὁ κύριος ἐβασίλευσε,
    καὶ γὰρ κατώρθωσε τὴν οἰκουμένην, ἥτις οὐ σαλευθήσεται,
    κρινεῖ λαοὺς ἐν εὐθύτητι.

The only noteworthy variant is in v. 10, where AS² and most cursives read ὅτι κύριος : BS¹ are supported in reading ὁ κύριος by the short quotation in *Tryph.* 73, and by the Old Latin.

The form in most MSS. of 1 Chronicles is—

8 Cod. A: [Codd. BS omit] δότε τῷ κυρίῳ δόξαν ὀνόματι αὐτοῦ,
  λάβετε δῶρα καὶ ἐνέγκατε κατὰ πρόσωπον αὐτοῦ.
  καὶ προσκυνήσατε κυρίῳ [Cod. A τῷ κ.] ἐν αὐλαῖς ἁγίαις
  αὐτοῦ.

9 φοβηθήτω ἀπὸ προσώπου αὐτοῦ πᾶσα ἡ γῆ,
  κατορθωτήτω [S¹ καὶ κατ.] ἡ γῆ καὶ μὴ σαλευθήτω.

10 εὐφρανθήτω ὁ οὐρανὸς καὶ ἀγαλλιάσθω ἡ γῆ
  καὶ εἰπάτωσαν ἐν τοῖς ἔθνεσιν Κύριος βασιλεύων [Cod. A
  ἐβασίλευσεν].

The form in the Apology is—

8 λάβετε χάριν καὶ εἰσέλθετε κατὰ πρόσωπον αὐτοῦ,
  καὶ προσκυνήσατε ἐν ταῖς αὐλαῖς ἁγίαις αὐτοῦ·

9 φοβηθήτω ἀπὸ προσώπου αὐτοῦ πᾶσα ἡ γῆ,
  καὶ κατορθωτήτω καὶ μὴ σαλευθήτω.

10 εὐφρανθήτωσαν ἐν τοῖς ἔθνεσιν·
  ὁ κύριος ἐβασίλευσεν ἀπὸ τοῦ ξύλου.

The noteworthy points in this text of the Apology are (1) the agreement with Codd. BS in the omission of the first clause of v. 8, (2) the use of χάρις for δῶρον or θυσία as a translation of מִנְחָה : this would be even more important if it were certain that Justin knew Hebrew : (3) the omission of εἴπατε in v. 10, which it is certain that Justin read, inasmuch as he twice quotes εἴπατε ἐν τοῖς ἔθνεσιν in *Tryph.* 73 : if this be restored, it may be assumed that the subjects of εὐφρανθήτωσαν in his text were ὁ οὐρανὸς καὶ ἡ γῆ, as in 1 Chronicles : (4) the reading ἀπὸ τοῦ ξύλου, for which see above, p. 189.

It will be noted that, in the form of the psalm in the Psalter, (1) the two members of vv. 8, 9 respectively give an intelligible antithesis, (2) the words καὶ γὰρ . . . σαλευθήσεται in v. 10 not only destroy the poetical structure of the passage, but also introduce an idea which is not germane to the rest of the verse. It will also be noted that the clause of v. 8 which is found in Cod. A in 1 Chronicles similarly destroys the parallelism of that verse, and that its omission, as in Codd. BS and the Apology, gives to vv. 8, 9 a perfect poetical structure and an intelligible sequence of ideas. It seems very probable that the words came into this place in the Psalter from the similar passage in Ps. 28 (29). 2 : that when they had become an ordinary part of the text, the second clause of v. 9 was omitted to restore the lost parallelism : and that subsequently the second clause of v. 9 was reinserted, in a wrong place, between the two clauses of v. 10. The antithesis which is found in 1 Chronicles, and probably also in Justin, between the two clauses of v. 10 is confirmed by Ps. 96 (97). 1.

II. *Quotations from Isaiah.*

The quotations are very numerous, as may be expected in a writer who deals so largely with the Messianic controversy. They are almost always worth study, and in some cases will be found to make material contributions to the textual criticism of the LXX. Some of the more important quotations occur more than once : but it is rarely the case that such double or triple quotations agree throughout : in some instances the scribe has apparently copied out a current text, in others he has preserved Justin's own text. It may be noted that the very fact of such variations in the case of double quotations confirms the view which has been advanced above as to the inexpediency of drawing inferences from the existing MS. of Justin's text in the case of single quotations, except where Justin's commentary makes his readings certain.

The following are examples of the contributions which Justin's quotations make to the textual criticism of Isaiah :

Is. 3. 10. The LXX. reading is δήσωμεν τὸν δίκαιον ὅτι δύσχρηστος ἡμῖν ἐστί : there is no variant. *Tryph.* 17, 133, both of which are long quotations, have δήσωμεν, but *Tryph.* 136, 137, both of which are short quotations, have ἄρωμεν, and in 137 Justin remarks upon the reading, saying that ἄρωμεν is the true reading of the LXX. and δήσωμεν the Jewish reading: he adds a remark, which is important for the consideration of other passages besides this, that earlier in his treatise, i.e. in c. 17, he had himself quoted the Jewish reading by way of concession to those with whom he was arguing. It may be noted that Barnabas c. 6 has δήσωμεν; Hegesipp. ap. Euseb. *H. E.* 2. 23, 15, and Clem. Al. *Strom.* 5. 14, p. 714, have ἄρωμεν: Tertull. *c. Marc.* 3. 22 has *auferamus*, but Jerome *in Isai.* 3, tom. iv. p. 57, has *alligemus*. Neither reading is a translation of the Hebrew text as we have it: but the fact that the Jews had and insisted upon a translation which implies another text, is an indication that the Hebrew text of the passage as we have it is not identical with the Hebrew text of the second century.

The fact that there are no variants in the MSS. of the LXX. is important in its bearing upon the tradition of the LXX. text: it confirms the view that we owe that text to Jewish rather than to Christian scribes.

Is. 7. 10–17 is quoted at length in *Tryph.* 43, 66 : v. 14 also in *Apol.* 33, and v. 14 *a* in *Tryph.* 67, 71, 84.

In v. 10 there is no variant: in v. 11 Justin's MS. supports the reading τοῦ θεοῦ of Cod. S and 10 cursives as against θεοῦ : in v. 12 there is no variant: in v. 13 the addition of Ἡσαίας to εἶπεν is supported, and ἀκούετε is read for ἀκούσατε.

In v. 14 *Tryph.* 43 reads καλέσεται (perhaps by a not uncommon scribe's error for καλέσετε, which is found in Cod. XII and several cursives, and in the Old Latin), and *Tryph.* 66 reads καλέσουσι (which is found in several cursives and is the common reading in the Greek Fathers, no doubt on account of its being the reading of Matt. 1. 23) : the same two quotations in the Trypho, and also the short quotations in 67, 71, 84 have ἐν γαστρὶ λήψεται, which is read in Codd. AS, XII, 26, 41, 90, 106, 144, 239, 306. But *Apol.* 33 has the singular reading ἰδοὺ ἡ παρθένος ἐν γαστρὶ ἕξει καὶ τέξεται υἱὸν καὶ ἐροῦσιν ἐπὶ τῷ ὀνόματι αὐτοῦ Μεθ' ἡμῶν ὁ θεός. The reading ἐν γαστρὶ ἕξει is repeated in the same chapter in a way which shows that Justin must have read it, for he uses συλλαβεῖν to explain it: and the passage is the more remarkable because Justin lays stress on giving it αὐτολεξεί, 'word for word.' The ἐροῦσι is perhaps the source of the καλέσουσι in Matthew: but otherwise there is no trace of this translation of the second clause of the verse, which is perhaps a unique survival of a lost Targum.

In v. 15 *Tryph.* 43 agrees with the current text of the LXX. in reading καὶ ἐκλέξασθαι, but *Tryph.* 66 agrees with AS² and 17 cursives in reading ἐκλέξεται.

In v. 16 both quotations agree with AS² and 14 cursives in reading τοῦ before ἐκλέξασθαι : in the same verse *Tryph.* 43 reads ἀπειθεῖ πονηρά for the current LXX. reading ἀπειθεῖ πονηρίᾳ : only two cursives have a variant, viz. Codd. 93, 305 which read πονηρίαν, and the early Latin quotations read *non credit* (*credet, credidit*) *malitiae*, or (Iren. *Vet. Interp.* 3. 21) *non consentiet nequitiae*. But the translation in August. *lib.* 8 *de Gen. ad lit.*, tom. 3. 237 *contemnet malitiam*, taken in connexion with the use of the accusative case in Justin and two MSS. of the LXX. and with the fact that ἀπωθεῖν is frequently used as the translation of מאס, ' to despise,' gives a plausibility to Wolf's conjecture that ἀπειθεῖ is a scribe's mistake for ἀπωθεῖ.

But in v. 16 both quotations agree in inserting c. 8. 4, and it is evident from Tertull. *c. Jud.* 9, p. 141, *c. Marc.* 3. 12, p. 673, that the insertion existed in the text which Tertullian used. It may be that the insertion is due only to a scribe's reminiscence of the inserted passage, which has part of the same protasis, πρὶν ἢ γνῶναι τὸ παιδίον . . . ., as a clause of v. 16 : but this does not altogether explain the fact of its being so far recognized as to be used with emphasis in the Judaeo-Christian controversy.

Is. 29. 14 is quoted thrice, *Tryph.* 32, 78, 123 : in each case with a slight variation which may be compared with both the LXX. and with the quotation of the passage in 1 Corinthians 1. 19.

LXX. ἀπολῶ τὴν σοφίαν τῶν σοφῶν [several cursives add αὐτοῦ, or αὐτῶν] καὶ τὴν σύνεσιν τῶν συνετῶν [the same cursives add αὐτοῦ or αὐτῶν] κρύψω [Cod. 301 ἀθετήσω].

1 *Cor.* 1. 19 ἀπολῶ τὴν σοφίαν τῶν σοφῶν καὶ τὴν σύνεσιν τῶν συνετῶν ἀθετήσω.

Tryph. 32 ἀφελῶ τὴν σοφίαν τῶν σοφῶν καὶ τὴν σύνεσιν τῶν συνετῶν αὐτῶν κρύψω.

id. 78 ἀφελῶ τὴν σοφίαν τῶν σοφῶν αὐτῶν τὴν δὲ σύνεσιν τῶν συνετῶν ἀθετήσω.

id. 123 ἀπολῶ τὴν σοφίαν τῶν σοφῶν καὶ τὴν σύνεσιν τῶν συνετῶν κρύψω.

The reading ἀφελῶ is supported by Tert. *c. Marc.* 3. 6, p. 670

auferam sapientiam sapientium illorum, ibid. 5. 11, p. 793 : but the same writer also shows the existence of various readings, for *ibid.* 4. 25, p. 719 he has *perdam sapientiam sapientium* : at the same time it must be noted that ἀπολλύω is the ordinary translation of אָבַד, and that ἀφαιρέω is never elsewhere used as the translation of it. The addition of αὐτῶν to σοφῶν, in c. 78, and to συνετῶν in c. 32, is in harmony with the Hebrew, and is supported by good cursives of the LXX.: the omission of the words both in 1 Corinthians and in the uncials of the LXX. is probably due to an adaptation to the immediate purpose of the writer.

Is. 42. 1–4 is quoted in *Tryph.* 123, 135, and the quotations which differ in many respects from each other, so that they cannot both be due to the scribe's transcription from a current text, have some points of interest in relation to the similar quotation in St. Matt. 12. 18–21.

The following is a detailed comparison of the four texts :

LXX.	*St. Matt.* 12. 18–21.	*Tryph.* 123.	*Tryph.* 135.
Ἰακὼβ [Codd. 106, 302, 305 ἰδοὺ Ἰακὼβ] ὁ παῖς μου ἀντιλή-ψομαι αὐτοῦ·	ἰδοὺ ὁ παῖς μου ὃν ἡρέτισα·	ὁ παῖς μου ἀντι-λήψομαι αὐτοῦ,	ὁ παῖς μου ἀντι-λήψομαι αὐτοῦ·
		Ἰακὼβ	Ιακὼβ
Ἰσραὴλ ὁ ἐκλεκ-τός μου προσεδέ-ξατο αὐτὸν ἡ ψυχή μου·	ὁ ἀγαπητός μου [εἰς] ὃν ηὐδόκησεν ἡ ψυχή μου·	Ἰσραὴλ ἐκλεκτοῦ μου·	καὶ Ἰσραὴλ ὁ ἐκ-λεκτός μου προσ-δέξεται αὐτὸν ἡ ψυχή μου·
ἔδωκα τὸ πνεῦμά μου ἐπ' αὐτόν, κρίσιν τοῖς ἔθνε-σιν ἐξοίσει.	θήσω τὸ πνεῦμά μου ἐπ' αὐτόν καὶ κρίσιν τοῖς ἔθνεσιν ἀπαγγελεῖ	θήσω τὸ πνεῦμά μου ἐπ' αὐτόν καὶ κρίσιν τοῖς ἔθνεσιν ἐξοίσει	δέδωκα τὸ πνεῦ-μά μου ἐπ' αὐτόν· καὶ κρίσιν τοῖς ἔθνεσιν ἐξοίσει.

It will be noted (1) that both quotations in Justin agree with the LXX. in asserting, what St. Matthew agrees with the Hebrew in omitting, the names Jacob and Israel. That the insertion of the words in Justin is not accidental is proved by his quoting them separately, c. 123, and giving them a Messianic interpretation : (2) that *Tryph.* 123 agrees with St. Matthew in reading θήσω, but that the passage has not been altered to harmonize with St. Matthew is made probable by the retention in both Justin's quotations of the LXX. ἐξοίσει as against ἀπαγγελεῖ.

It may also be noted that while the translation of בְּחִיר by ἀγαπητός is peculiar to St. Matthew, the rest of St. Matthew's phrase is identical with Theodotion's translation of רָצְתָה נַפְשִׁי.

LXX.	St. Matt. 12. 18–21.	Tryph. 123.	Tryph. 135.
οὐ κεκράξεται οὐδὲ ἀνήσει [βοήσει Cod. 308],	οὐκ ἐρίσει οὐδὲ κραυγάσει,	οὐκ ἐρίσει οὔτε κράξει,	οὐ κεκράξεται
οὐδὲ ἀκουσθήσεται ἔξω ἡ φωνὴ αὐτοῦ·	οὐδὲ ἀκούσει τις ἐν ταῖς πλατείαις τὴν φωνὴν αὐτοῦ·	οὔτε ἀκούσεταί τις ἐν ταῖς πλατείαις τὴν φωνὴν αὐτοῦ·	οὐδὲ ἀκουσθήσεται ἔξω ἡ φωνὴ αὐτοῦ·

It will be observed that the LXX. ἀνήσει does not exist in any of the other quotations : that it was the original LXX. translation is made probable by the fact (1) that נָשָׁא is rendered by ἀνίημι in three other passages of Isaiah (more commonly, both in Isaiah and elsewhere, by αἴρω), (2) that it underlies the Old Latin versions *dimittet* and *relinquet*, Hieron. *Ep.* 121 *ad Algas.* qu. 2, tom. i. 848, *in Isai.* 42, tom. iv. 506, and *cessabit* August. *de Civit. Dei* 20. 30. That it was felt to be a difficult expression may perhaps be inferred from its omission not only in *Tryph.* 135, above, but also in Tertull. *c. Marc.* 4. 23, p. 717, Cypr. *Testim.* 2. 13, p. 78. And that the βοήσει of Cod. 308 was an early variant is shown by Tertull. *c. Jud.* 9, p. 143 *neque contendit neque clamavit*, where the quotation must be from Isaiah and not from St. Matthew, because *foris* and not *in plateis* follows.

κάλαμον τεθλασμένον [Codd. A 23, 41, 87, 91, 97, 106, 228, 308, 309, συντεθλασμένον] οὐ συντρίψει, καὶ λίνον καπνιζόμενον οὐ σβέσει ἀλλ' εἰς ἀλήθειαν ἐξοίσει κρίσιν.	κάλαμον συντετριμμένον οὐ κατεάξει καὶ λίνον τυφόμενον οὐ [D οὐ μὴ] σβέσει ἕως ἂν ἐκβάλῃ εἰς νῖκος τὴν κρίσιν.	κάλαμον συντετριμμένον οὐ κατεάξει καὶ λίνον τυφόμενον οὐ μὴ σβέσει ἀλλὰ εἰς ἀλήθειαν ἐξοίσει κρίσιν.	κάλαμον τεθραυσμένον οὐ συντρίψει καὶ λίνον τυφομένον οὐ σβέσει ἕως οὗ νῖκος ἐξοίσει κρίσιν.

The variations between (*a*) τεθλασμένον, συντεθλασμένον, συντετριμμένον, and τεθραυσμένον, (*b*) συντρίψει and κατεάξει, correspond to variations in the early Latin versions between (*a*) *fractam, confractam, contusam*, and *quassatam*, (*b*) *conteret, comminuet, fregit, confringet*: they must therefore be taken to mark an early difficulty, and a consequent early variety, in the rendering of the contrast between נָצַ֫ץ and שָׁבַ֫ר.

The variations in the rendering of the last clause may perhaps be best explained by noting that εἰς νῖκος is interchanged with εἰς τέλος as a translation of נֶצַח or לָנֶ֫צַח, 'for ever,' i.e. utterly or completely: it is consequently conceivable that it may have come to be used as an equivalent for εἰς ἀλήθειαν or ἐν ἀληθείᾳ, 'truly' or 'really.'

ἀναλάμψει καὶ οὐ θραυσθήσεται [S σβεσθήσεται] ἕως ἂν θῇ ἐπὶ τῆς γῆς κρίσιν·	ἀναλήψει καὶ οὐ μὴ θραυσθήσεται ἕως ἂν θῇ ἐπὶ τῆς γῆς κρίσιν·	ἀναλήψει καὶ οὐ θραυσθήσεται ἕως ἂν θῇ ἐπὶ τῆς γῆς κρίσιν·
καὶ ἐπὶ τῷ ὀνόματι αὐτοῦ ἔθνη ἐλπιοῦσι·	καὶ τῷ ὀνόματι αὐτοῦ ἔθνη ἐλπιοῦσι	καὶ ἐπὶ τῷ ὀνόματι αὐτοῦ ἐλπιοῦσιν ἔθνη	καὶ ἐπὶ τῷ ὀνόματι αὐτοῦ ἐλπιοῦσιν ἔθνη

The reading of Justin's MS., ἀναλήψει, would no doubt be in an earlier MS. ἀναλήμψει, which was originally only a scribe's error for ἀναλάμψει.

The omission of the clause ἀναλάμψει . . . . κρίσιν in St. Matthew is perhaps best explained by the hypothesis of a homoioteleuton κρίσιν . . . . κρίσιν in an early MS.

The absence of any trace either in the MSS., or in the quotations, or in the early Latin versions, of any variation in the last clause, in other words the fact that all early recensions of the LXX. agreed in translating וּלְתוֹרָתוֹ אִיִּים יְיַחֵ֫לוּ by (ἐπὶ) τῷ ὀνόματι αὐτοῦ ἔθνη ἐλπιοῦσι, whereas the later revisers, Aquila, Symmachus, and Theodotion, agreed with modern scholars in translating the passage by τῷ νόμῳ αὐτοῦ νῆσοι ἐλπιοῦσι, seems to point to a lost variant in the Hebrew text.

Is. 53 is largely quoted, and some of the quotations are useful contributions to the criticism of the LXX. The following are the more noteworthy.

v. 2 is quoted in *Apol.* i. 50, *Tryph.* 13, 42, in each case placing the words ὡς παιδίον immediately before ὡς ῥίζα. This is the reading of Codd. AS, XII, 22, 26, 36, 48, 86, 90, 93, 106, 144, 147, 198, 233, 306, 308, and of Clem. Rom. i. 16. 2.

v. 8 *b* is quoted in *Apol.* i. 51, *Tryph.* 13, with the variant ἥκει for ἤχθη, and in *Tryph.* 43 ἤχθην. ἥκει is found also in Codd. 62, 90, 144, 147, 233, and in Clem. Rom. i. 16. 9 : but the Latin versions all have *ductus est* or *adductus est.*

v. 9 is quoted in *Apol.* i. 51, *Tryph.* 13, with the reading οὐδὲ (οὐχ) εὑρέθη δόλος ἐν τῷ στόματι αὐτοῦ, in agreement with Codd. AS², XII, 26, 36, 41, 49, 51, 86, 90, 91, (93), 104, 106, 144, 147, 198, 228, 233, 239, 306, 308, 309, [Codd. 87, 97 have οὐδὲ δόλος, Cod. B has οὐδὲ δόλον, without εὑρέθη]. It seems probable that the original reading was οὐδὲ δόλος, which is a literal rendering of the Hebrew, and that (*a*) δόλον arose from assimilation to the preceding ἀνομίαν, (*b*) εὑρέθη was supplied by way of exegesis. The antiquity of the accusative δόλον is shown by its translations *insidias* in Cypr. *Testim.* 2. 15, p. 80, and *dolum* in August. *de Civit. Dei* 18. 29, tom. 7. 510, and elsewhere : Faustin. *de Trinit.* 3. 4, further proves its existence by the reading *neque dolum in ore locutus est.* But Tertull. *c. Jud.* 10, p. 144, has *nec dolus in ore ejus inventus est.*

v. 12 is quoted in *Apol.* i. 51, *Tryph.* 13, with only a slight variation from the current text of the LXX.: but at the beginning of Apol. i. 50 it is prefixed to the quotation of c. 52. 13—53. 8, and instead of the current text αὐτὸς ἁμαρτίας πολλῶν ἀνήνεγκε καὶ διὰ τὰς ἀνομίας αὐτῶν παρεδόθη is the important variant αὐτὸς ἁμαρτίας πολλῶν εἴληφε καὶ τοῖς ἀνόμοις ἐξιλάσεται. This last clause brings the Greek into harmony with the Hebrew וְלַפֹּשְׁעִים יַפְגִּיעַ, 'he made intercession for the transgressors,' but there is no trace of the reading elsewhere : it must be taken to be part of a lost revision of the LXX. of which Justin made use but which is otherwise unknown.

V. ON COMPOSITE QUOTATIONS FROM THE SEPTUAGINT.

IT would be improbable, even if there were no positive evidence on the point, that the Greek-speaking Jews, who were themselves cultured, and who lived in great centres of culture, should not have had a literature of their own. It is no less improbable that such a literature should have consisted only of the Apocalyptic books, and the scanty fragments of other books, which have come down to us. It may naturally be supposed that a race which laid stress on moral progress, whose religious services had variable elements of both prayer and praise, and which was carrying on an active propaganda, would have, among other books, manuals of morals, of devotion, and of controversy. It may also be supposed, if we take into consideration the contemporary habit of making collections of *excerpta*, and the special authority which the Jews attached to their sacred books, that some of these manuals would consist of extracts from the Old Testament.

The existence of composite quotations in the New Testament, and in some of the early Fathers suggests the hypothesis that we have in them relics of such manuals. The passages which are examined in the following chapter are more consistent with such a hypothesis than with any other. The view that they are mere misquotations in which the several writers have, through defect of memory, blended several passages into one is rendered improbable by the whole character of the quotations which they make from the Old Testament : it will be clear from the preceding chapter that such quotations were ordinarily made with great accuracy, and that the existence of a discrepancy between them and the existing MSS. points not to an inaccuracy on the part of the writer but to a variation in the current text. The view, which might otherwise be tenable, that such passages are combinations, such as might be made by any writer who was familiar with the text of the Old Testament, is set aside by the fact that in some cases the same, or nearly the same, combinations occur in different writers. Two instances of this will be found below, viz. (1) the composite quotation, Jer. 2. 12, 13, Is. 16. 1, 2, which is found in both Barnabas 11, and in Justin M. *Tryph.* 114: (2) the composite quotation from the Psalms and Isaiah, which is found in the New Testament, Romans 3. 10–18 and in Justin M. *Tryph.* 27.

1. Clement of Rome.

(1) c. XV.

In c. 15 there is a passage which is composed of Ps. 77 (78). 36, 37 : 30 (31). 18 : 11 (12). 4 *b*–5 :

Ps. 77 (78) ἠγάπησαν αὐτὸν ἐν τῷ στόματι αὐτῶν
καὶ τῇ γλώσσῃ αὐτῶν ἐψεύσαντο αὐτῷ [so Cod. Alex.
and Clem. Alex. : Cod. Const. ἔψεξαν αὐτόν]·
ἡ δὲ καρδία αὐτῶν οὐκ εὐθεῖα μετ᾽ αὐτοῦ
οὐδὲ ἐπιστώθησαν ἐν τῇ διαθήκῃ αὐτοῦ.
Ps. 30 (31) (διὰ τοῦτο) ἄλαλα γενηθήτω τὰ χείλη τὰ δόλια,
Ps. 11 (12) γλῶσσα μεγαλορήμων [so Cod. Const. : Cod. Alex.
γλῶσσαν μεγαλορήμονα],
τοὺς εἰπόντας τὴν γλῶσσαν ἡμῶν μεγαλυνοῦμεν
τὰ χείλη ἡμῶν παρ᾽ ἡμῖν ἐστίν· τίς ἡμῶν κύριός ἐστιν ;
ἀπὸ τῆς ταλαιπωρίας τῶν πτωχῶν καὶ ἀπὸ τοῦ στεναγμοῦ
τῶν πενήτων,
νῦν ἀναστήσομαι, λέγει Κύριος,
θήσομαι ἐν σωτηρίῳ· παρρησιάσομαι ἐν αὐτῷ.

The text of Clement is not certain: recent editors, Lightfoot, and Gebhardt and Harnack, insert the first clause of Ps. 11 (12). 4 *a* ἐξολοθρεύσαι κύριος πάντα τὰ χείλη τὰ δόλια after τὰ χείλη τὰ δόλια, and follow Cod. Alex. in reading the accusative γλῶσσαν μεγαλορήμονα: this gives a good grammatical construction for τοὺς εἰπόντας but destroys the parallelism. The harshness of the construction without a governing verb was evidently seen by the scribe of Cod. Const. for he prefaces τοὺς εἰπόντας by the words καὶ πάλιν, as though it were a separate quotation. But this confirms his reading.

Whether the words be inserted or not, the sense of the cento is consecutive.

The same cento is also found in Clement of Alexandria, *Strom.* 4. 6, p. 577: that it comes from the same source is shown by the use of the words διὰ τοῦτο, which are not found in the LXX., in introducing the half verse from Ps. 30 (31): and it is to be noted that whereas in Clement of Rome the quotations from Is. 29. 13, Ps. 61 (62). 5, which precede it, are separated from it and from each other by the introduction of the words πάλιν λέγει . . . . καὶ πάλιν λέγει, in Clement of Alexandria there is no such distinction between the quotations, and the whole series of passages forms a single cento.

(2) c. XXII.

In c. 22, after quoting Ps. 33 (34). 12–18 with great fidelity to the existing text of the LXX., instead of the following verses of the Psalm, Clement adds Ps. 31 (32). 10,

> πολλαὶ αἱ μάστιγες τοῦ ἁμαρτωλοῦ,
> τοὺς δὲ ἐλπίζοντας ἐπὶ κύριον ἔλεος κυκλώσει,

which preserves the sequence and antithesis of the passage so well that the whole quotation may be taken to be a separate current poem, formed of the second part of Ps. 33 (34)—the psalm is divided by the διάψαλμα after v. 11— with an abridged ending, which has been transferred from Ps. 31 (32).

(3) c. XXXIV.

In c. 34 there is a passage in which Daniel 7. 10 and Isaiah 6. 3 are blended together.

The passage in Daniel is—

'Thousand thousands ministered unto him, and ten thousand times ten thousand stood before him.'

The passage in Isaiah is (after the description of the seraphim with six wings)—

'And one cried unto another and said Holy, holy, holy is the Lord of hosts; the whole earth is full of his glory.'

The passage in Clement is—

μύριαι μυριάδες παρειστήκεισαν αὐτῷ καὶ χίλιαι χιλιάδες ἐλειτούργουν αὐτῷ καὶ ἐκέκραγον· Ἅγιος, ἅγιος, ἅγιος κύριος σαβαώθ, πλήρης πᾶσα ἡ κτίσις τῆς δόξης αὐτοῦ.

(4) c. L.

In c. 50 there is a passage in which Is. 26. 20 and probably either Ezek. 37. 12, 13 or 4 Esdr. 2. 16 are blended together.

The passage in Isaiah is—

'Enter thou into thy chambers and shut thy doors about thee: hide thyself for a little moment, until the indignation be overpast.'

The passage in Ezekiel is—

'Behold, I will open your graves and cause you to come up out of your graves, O my people.'

The passage in 4 Esdras is—

'Those that be dead will I raise up again from their places, and bring them out of the graves: for I have known my name in Israel.'

The passage in Clement is—

εἰσέλθετε εἰς τὰ ταμεῖα μικρὸν ὅσον ὅσον ἕως οὗ παρέλθῃ ἡ ὀργὴ καὶ ὁ θυμός μου· καὶ μνησθήσομαι ἡμέρας ἀγαθῆς καὶ ἀναστήσω ὑμᾶς ἐκ τῶν θηκῶν ὑμῶν.

(5) c. LVI.

In c. 56 there is a passage which is composed of Ps. 117 (118). 18, Prov. 3. 12, and Ps. 140 (141). 5:

Ps. 117 (118) παιδεύων ἐπαίδευσέν με ὁ κύριος,
καὶ τῷ θανάτῳ οὐ παρέδωκέν με·

Prov. 3 ὃν γὰρ ἀγαπᾷ κύριος παιδεύει [so Codd. AS in LXX., Cod. B ἐλέγχει]
μαστιγοῖ δὲ πάντα υἱὸν ὃν παραδέχεται.

Ps. 140 (141) παιδεύσει με γάρ (φησι) δίκαιος ἐν ἐλέει καὶ ἐλέγξει με,
ἔλαιον δὲ ἁμαρτωλῶν μὴ λιπανάτω τὴν κεφαλήν μου.

But the want of cohesion between the third quotation and the two first makes it probable that this is rather a series of quotations on a cognate subject than a single quotation from a composite poem.

2. Barnabas.

(1) c. V.

In c. 5 there is a passage which is composed of Ps. 118 (119). 120: 21 (22). 17 :

Ps. 118 (119) καθήλωσόν μου τὰς σάρκας,
Ps. 21 (22) ὅτι πονηρευομένων συναγωγαὶ ἐπανέστησάν μοι.

It is immediately preceded by the quotation of Ps. 21 (22). 21, but the καί which (in Codd. Sin. Const.) immediately precedes seems to mark it as a separate quotation.

Neither of the quotations corresponds exactly to the text of the LXX.: (1) in Ps. 118 (119) the LXX. text is καθήλωσον ἐκ τοῦ φόβου σου τὰς σάρκας μου : (2) in Ps. 21 (22) it is συναγωγὴ πονηρευομένων περιέσχον με. In other words the quotation is not from the LXX. but from a psalm based upon the LXX.: but it possibly has a critical value in that it may help to solve the difficulty which the words καθήλωσόν μου τὰς σάρκας present in Ps. 118 (119). These words are not in any sense a translation of the Hebrew, which means

'My flesh trembleth for fear of thee:' and they have no
appreciable bearing upon the context. They must have
been in early MSS. of the LXX. because they are translated in the Old Latin versions ' Confige (infige) timore tuo
carnes meas :' and Hilary, Ambrose, and Augustine comment upon the unusual expression. A clue to the original
reading is afforded by Aquila's translation ἡλώθη . . . . ἡ σάρξ
μου: and it may be conjectured that the present reading is
due to a scribe's recollection of the composite psalm which
Barnabas here quotes, or possibly adapts.

(2) c. XI.

In c. 11 is a passage composed of Jerem. 2. 12, 13 and
Is. 16. 1, 2 :

λέγει γὰρ ὁ προφήτης (Jer. 2. 12)· ἔκστηθι οὐρανέ, καὶ ἐπὶ τούτῳ πλεῖον
φριξάτω ἡ γῆ ὅτι δύο καὶ πονηρὰ ἐποίησεν ὁ λαὸς οὗτος· ἐμὲ ἐγκατέλιπον πηγὴν ζωῆς καὶ ἑαυτοῖς ὤρυξαν βόθρον θανάτου· (Is. 16. 1) μὴ πέτρα ἔρημός
ἐστιν τὸ ὄρος τὸ ἅγιόν μου Σινᾶ ; ἔσεσθε γὰρ ὡς πετεινοῦ νοσσοὶ ἀνιπτάμενοι
νοσσιᾶς ἀφῃρημένης.

The critical interest of the quotation is considerable: the
text of the quotation from Jeremiah is in some points
nearer to the Hebrew than the LXX. is, but the substitution
of βόθρον θανάτου, 'an empty pit into which they will fall and
be killed,' is a complete change of the metaphor: the text
of that from Isaiah is nearer to the LXX., and preserves the
points in which the LXX. differs from the Hebrew: it may
therefore be presumed to be quoted from the LXX. If so,
it affords an important correction of the LXX. text: for
whereas all the MSS. of the LXX. have Σιών, the context
and the Hebrew require Σινᾶ, which is read in all MSS. of
Barnabas.

The quotation has the further interest of being also
found, with some changes, in Justin M. *Tryph.* 114, where
the whole of it is attributed to Jeremiah. Justin's quotation consists of Jer. 2. 13, Is. 16. 1, Jer. 3. 8 :

οὐ.ὶ ὑμῖν, (Jer. 2. 13) ὅτι ἐγκατελίπετε πηγὴν ζῶσαν καὶ ὠρύξατε ἑαυτοῖς λάκκους συντετριμμένους οἳ οὐ δυνήσονται συνέχειν ὕδωρ· (Is. 16. 1) μὴ ἔρημον ᾖ οὗ ἐστὶ τὸ ὄρος Σιὼν ὅτι Ἱερουσαλὴμ βιβλίον ἀποστασίου ἔδωκα ἔμπροσθεν ὑμῶν;

It may be noted, without discussing in full the critical points of the quotation, (1) that Justin's text follows the LXX. in having λάκκους συντετριμμένους for the βόθρον θανάτου of Barnabas: (2) that it preserves the Σιὼν of the LXX. text as against the Σινᾶ of Barnabas.

(3) c. XVI.

In c. 16 is a passage composed of Is. 40. 12 : 66. 1.

(Is. 40. 12) τίς ἐμέτρησεν τὸν οὐρανὸν σπιθαμῇ ἢ τίς τὴν γῆν δρακί; οὐκ ἐγώ; λέγει κύριος (Is. 66. 1) ὁ οὐρανός μοι θρόνος ἡ δὲ γῆ ὑποπόδιον τῶν ποδῶν μου· ποῖον οἶκον οἰκοδομήσετέ μοι; ἢ τίς τόπος τῆς καταπαύσεώς μου;

The text of the quotation from c. 40 nearly corresponds to the LXX., τῇ χειρὶ τὸ ὕδωρ being omitted, as it is also in the quotation in Clem. Alex. *Protrept*. 8, which shows that a recension in which the words were omitted was current: that of the quotation from c. 66 agrees throughout with Codd. AS, except only τίς τόπος for ποῖος τόπος, and with Cod. 26 except only in omitting λέγει κύριος after οἰκοδομήσετέ μοι.

3. Justin Martyr.

(1) *Tryph.* c. XXVII.

The most interesting of the composite quotations in Justin is that of *Tryph.* 27. It forms part of the same cento which is quoted by St. Paul, *Romans* 3. 10–18, and is made up of passages from Ps. 13 (14). 1, 2, 3 (or 52 (53). 2, 3): 5. 9: 139 (140). 4: 9. 28 (10. 7). Is. 59. 7, 8.

P

Ps. 13 (14). 1 b.	Rom. 3.	Tryph. 27.
	v. 10.	
οὐκ ἔστι ποιῶν χρηστό-τητα[οὐκ ἔστιν ἕως ἑνός].	οὐκ ἔστιν δίκαιος οὐδὲ εἷς.	

Ps. 52 (53). 2 b.
οὐκ ἔστι ποιῶν ἀγαθόν

Ps. 13 (14). 2, 3 a: 52 (53). 3, 4.	vv. 11, 12.	
..... τοῦ ἰδεῖν εἰ ἔστι συνιῶν ἢ ἐκζητῶν τὸν θεόν.	οὐκ ἔστιν ὁ συνιῶν, οὐκ ἔστιν ὁ ἐκζητῶν τὸν θεόν·	
πάντες ἐξέκλιναν, ἅμα ἠχρειώθησαν,	πάντες ἐξέκλιναν, ἅμα ἠχρειώθησαν,	πάντες (γὰρ) ἐξέκλιναν, ἅμα [MS. ἄρα] ἠχρειώθησαν·
οὐκ ἔστι ποιῶν χρηστό-τητα [Ps. 52 ἀγαθὸν] οὐκ ἔστιν ἕως ἑνός·	οὐκ ἔστιν ὁ ποιῶν χρη-στότητα, οὐκ ἔστιν ἕως ἑνός·	οὐκ ἔστιν ὁ συνιῶν, οὐκ ἔστιν ἕως ἑνός·

Ps. [13 (14) 3:] 5. 10 b.	v. 13.	
τάφος ἀνεῳγμένος ὁ λάρυγξ αὐτῶν,	τάφος ἀνεῳγμένος ὁ λάρυγξ αὐτῶν,	ταῖς γλώσσαις αὐτῶν ἐδολιοῦσαν,
ταῖς γλώσσαις αὐτῶν ἐδολιοῦσαν·	ταῖς γλώσσαις αὐτῶν ἐδολιοῦσαν·	τάφος ἀνεῳγμένος ὁ λάρυγξ αὐτῶν·

Ps. [13 (14). 3 :] 139 (140). 4.		
ἰὸς ἀσπίδων ὑπὸ τὰ χείλη αὐτῶν·	ἰὸς ἀσπίδων ὑπὸ τὰ χείλη αὐτῶν·	ἰὸς ἀσπίδων ὑπὸ τὰ χείλη αὐτῶν·

Ps. [13 (14) 3:] 9. 28 (10. 7).	v. 14.	
οὗ ἀρᾶς τὸ στόμα αὐτοῦ γέμει καὶ πικρίας·	ὧν τὸ στόμα ἀρᾶς καὶ πικρίας γέμει·	

[Ps. 13 (14). 3] Is. 59. 7, 8.	vv. 15, 16, 17.	
οἱ δὲ πόδες αὐτῶν τα-χινοὶ ἐκχέαι αἷμα [Ps. 13 (14). ὀξεῖς οἱ πόδες αὐτῶν ἐκχέαι αἷμα].	ὀξεῖς οἱ πόδες αὐτῶν ἐκχέαι αἷμα·	

..... σύντριμμα καὶ   σύντριμμα καὶ ταλαι-   σύντριμμα καὶ ταλαι-
-αλαιπωρία ἐν ταῖς ὁδοῖς   πωρία ἐν ταῖς ὁδοῖς   πωρία ἐν ταῖς ὁδοῖς
αὐτῶν,   αὐτῶν,   αὐτῶν,
καὶ ὁδὸν εἰρήνης οὐκ   καὶ ὁδὸν εἰρήνης οὐκ   καὶ ὁδὸν εἰρήνης οὐκ
οἴδασι·   ἔγνωσαν·   ἔγνωσαν·

Ps. 35 (36). 1 *b.*   v. 18.
οὐκ ἔστι φόβος θεοῦ   οὐκ ἔστι φόβος θεοῦ
ἀπέναντι τῶν ὀφθαλμῶν   ἀπέναντι τῶν ὀφθαλμῶν
αὐτοῦ.   αὐτῶν.

There can be no reasonable doubt that the text of Ps. 13 (14) has been tampered with to make it agree with the quotation by St. Paul. The verses and words inserted above in square brackets are not found either in the Hebrew or in the majority of MSS. of the LXX.: they are found in BS[1], but omitted by AS[2] and 94 cursives. Jerome, *Praef. in Isai.* 57, tom. iv. 667, writes on the subject of their insertion, and says that all Greek commentators obelized them, and so admitted that they were not in the original text of the LXX. but in the Κοινή.

(2) *Tryph.* c. XXIV.

In *Tryph.* 24 are two quotations which might be considered to be one, except that the introduction of the phrase βοᾷ διὰ Ἡσαίου appears to make a distinction between them.

The second quotation is from Is. 65. 1, 2, 3 *a.*

The first quotation is composite and is drawn partly from Is. 2. 5, 6, 9 and partly from unknown sources :

δεῦτε σὺν ἐμοὶ πάντες οἱ φοβούμενοι τὸν θεόν,
οἱ θέλοντες τὰ ἀγαθὰ Ἱερουσαλὴμ ἰδεῖν·

δεῦτε πορευθῶμεν τῷ φωτὶ κυρίου·
ἀνῆκε γὰρ τὸν λαὸν αὐτοῦ τὸν οἶκον Ἰακώβ·

δεῦτε πάντα τὰ ἔθνη συναχθῶμεν εἰς Ἱερουσαλὴμ
τὴν μηκέτι πολεμουμένην διὰ τὰς ἀνομίας τῶν λαῶν.

The source of the first strophe is unknown. The second strophe is from Is. 2. 5 *b*, 6 *a*, with Ἰακώβ, as in many cursives, instead of Ἰσραὴλ which is read by Codd. ABS. It is also evident that ἀνῆκε is used by Justin in the sense of 'pardoned,' as in Is. I. 14 οὐκέτι ἀνήσω τὰς ἁμαρτίας ὑμῶν : but that is clearly not the sense in which it is used by the LXX. here, or in which Justin himself uses it in a more exact quotation of the passage in *Tryph.* 135 : the Hebrew נָטַשׁ, and the context require it to mean 'forsook.' The source of the third strophe is also unknown.

The three strophes evidently form part of a fine poem, a relic probably of the Judaeo-Christian poetry, of which the Sibylline Books are almost the only other remaining monument.

(3) *Apol. I.* c. LII.

In the First Apology c. 52 is a passage which, though assigned to Zechariah, differs so widely from the text of Zechariah as to be in reality a composite quotation, into which some passages of Zechariah enter.

1   ἐντελοῦμαι τοῖς τέσσαρσιν ἀνέμοις
    συνάξαι τὰ ἐσκορπισμένα τέκνα,
    ἐντελοῦμαι τῷ βορρᾷ φέρειν
    καὶ τῷ νότῳ μὴ προσκόπτειν·
5   καὶ τότε ἐν Ἰερουσαλὴμ κοπετὸς μέγας,
    οὐ κοπετὸς στομάτων ἢ χειλέων,
    ἀλλὰ κοπετὸς καρδίας·
    καὶ οὐ μὴ σχίσωσιν αὐτῶν τὰ ἱμάτια,
    ἀλλὰ τὰς διανοίας·
10 κόψονται φυλὴ πρὸς φυλήν·
    καὶ τότε ὄψονται εἰς ὃν ἐξεκέντησαν
    καὶ ἐροῦσι· τί κύριε ἐπλάνησας ἡμᾶς ἀπὸ τῆς ὁδοῦ σου ;
    ἡ δόξα ἣν εὐλόγησαν οἱ πατέρες ἡμῶν
    ἐγενήθη ἡμῖν εἰς ὄνειδος.

ll. 1, 2 are a reminiscence, but not a quotation, of LXX. Zech.
2. 6 ἐκ τῶν τεσσάρων ἀνέμων τοῦ οὐρανοῦ συνάξω ὑμᾶς, λέγει κύριος.

ll. 3, 4 are a similar reminiscence of LXX. Is. 43. 6 ἐρῶ τῷ βορρᾷ
Ἄγε, καὶ τῷ Λιβὶ Μὴ κώλυε.

l. 5 resembles Zech. 12. 11 μεγαλυνθήσεται ὁ κοπετὸς ἐν Ἰερουσαλήμ.

ll. 6, 7 cannot be traced.

ll. 8, 9 resemble Joel 2. 13 διαρρήξατε τὰς καρδίας ὑμῶν καὶ μὴ τὰ
ἱμάτια ὑμῶν.

l. 10 expresses the same idea as Zech. 12. 12 καὶ κόψεται ἡ γῆ κατὰ
φυλὰς φυλάς.

l. 11 is a translation of Zech. 12. 10: whether it is that of the
LXX. is uncertain: the majority of the MSS. in that passage have
the singular reading ἐπιβλέψονται πρὸς μὲ ἀνθ' ὧν κατωρχήσαντο, which
Jerome notes as having arisen from a mistake of the Seventy, who
confounded דקרו from דָּקַר, 'to pierce,' with רקדו from רָקַד, 'to
dance': but (1) Codd. 22, 23, 26, 36, 57, 62, 68, 86, 87, 95, 97,
114, 157, 185, 228, 238, 240, some of which, e.g. 26, 86, are of
authority, read ἐξεκέντησαν; (2) ἐξεκέντησαν was read by the Greek
Fathers, e.g. Clem. Alex. p. 984, and hence also in ps.-Ignat. ad
Trall. 10; (3) it was read in the recension which underlies the Latin
version used by Tertullian, who uses pupugerunt or compugerunt in
contexts which show clearly that he is quoting Zecharias, e.g.
c. Judaeos c. 14, p. 148, c. Marc. 3, p. 671, by Cyprian Testim. 2,
p. 294, and by Lactantius Instit. 4. 18. It may reasonably be
supposed that St. John's quotation, c. 18. 37, is from the same
recension: it may also not unreasonably be supposed, from the use
which was made of the quotation in the Judaeo-Christian controversy, that the alteration in the text of the LXX. was from ἐξεκέντησαν
to κατωρχήσαντο, and not the reverse, and that it was made by Jews
and not by Christians. This hypothesis will be still more probable
if it be true that the LXX. text has been handed down by a Jewish
rather than by a Christian tradition.

l. 12 is a quotation of LXX. Is. 63. 17.

ll. 13, 14 are a quotation of LXX. Is. 64. 11 with the exception
of the substitution of εἰς ὄνειδος for πυρίκαυστος: the LXX. text of the
passage is quoted exactly in Apol. i. 47, which is one of many
indications that this cento was a separate poem.

It may be noted as a common feature of all these quotations, whether from Clement, Barnabas, or Justin, that they
are introduced by the same formulae which are used for
quotations of single passages of the canonical books. The

formulae are, in Clement, (1) λέγει [*sc.* τὸ ἅγιον πνεῦμα], (2) διὰ τοῦ πνεύματος τοῦ ἁγίου οὕτως παρακαλεῖται ἡμᾶς, (3) λέγει γὰρ ἡ γραφή, (4) γέγραπται γάρ, (5) οὕτως φησὶν ὁ ἅγιος λόγος. In Barnabas, (1) λέγει ὁ προφητεύων ἐπ᾽ αὐτῷ, (2) λέγει ὁ προφήτης, (3) πῶς λέγει κύριος καταργῶν αὐτόν ; In Justin M., (1) βοᾷ [*sc.* τὸ ἅγιον πνεῦμα], (2) διὰ Ζαχαρίου τοῦ προφήτου προφητευθέντα ἐλέχθη οὕτως.

VI. ON ORIGEN'S REVISION OF THE LXX. TEXT OF JOB[1].

THERE is ample evidence that the original LXX. text of the book of Job was much shorter than that which has come down to us in existing MSS.; that the original text was revised by Origen in order to bring it into conformity with the Hebrew; that the passages which were absent from the LXX. text, but present in the Hebrew, were supplied by him from the version of Theodotion; and that the text of all existing Greek MSS. is the revised and composite text which Origen thus formed.

The divergences between the earlier and the later texts are indicated by Origen himself (*Epist. ad African.*, Op. ed. Delarue, vol. i. p. 15) as consisting in the omission in the Greek of 'frequently three or four, sometimes fourteen or nineteen verses': the total amount of such omissions is said by Jerome to have been 700 or 800 verses (*Praef. in Hiob*, tom. ix. 1097).

The passages which were absent from the original LXX. text, and which were supplied by Origen from Theodotion, were marked by him in his text of the Hexapla with an

---

[1] The author thinks it due both to himself and to Professor G. Bickell to say that although he had read his dissertation *De indole ac ratione Versionis Alexandrinae in interpretando libro Jobi* (Marburg, 1862) before delivering the lecture on which the present essay is based, and derived from it, as he has since derived from his papers in the *Zeitschrift für katholische Theologie*, some valuable hints, the views which he here sets forth were suggested to him independently, in the course of his examination of early quotations from the LXX., by the fact that Clement of Alexandria (*Strom.* 4. 26, p. 641) quotes, or appears to quote, c. xxxvi. 10-12 in the form which it had before Origen's revision: that is to say vv. 10 *b*, 11 are omitted.

asterisk: and these asterisks have been preserved in three distinct groups of authorities :

(1) They are found in two Greek MSS. of the LXX., the Colbert MS. 1952 in the *Bibliothèque Nationale* at Paris, and the Vatican MS. 346 (which was collated for Holmes and Parsons, and is numbered 248 in their list).

(2) They are also found in at least two Latin MSS., viz. the Bodleian MS. (Cod. Lat. 2426, which contains the Old Latin version, and Jerome's version separately); and a MS. which was formerly in the monastery of Marmoutiers (Cod. Majoris Monasterii), and which was published by Martianay in his edition of Jerome, vol. i, and reprinted by Sabatier in his *Bibliorum Sacrorum Latinae Versiones Antiquae.*

(3) They are also found in the Syro-Hexaplar version, i. e. the Syriac version which the monophysite bishop, Paulus Telensis, made in A. D. 617, from one of Eusebius's copies of Origen's Hexapla. The book of Job in this version exists only in one MS., now in the Ambrosian Library at Milan, which has been published (1) by Middledorp in the *Codex Syriaco-hexaplaris* (Berlin, 1835), (2) more recently in facsimile by Ceriani (Milan, 1876).

To these three texts and versions which preserve Origen's asterisks has recently been made the important addition of a version of the text itself as it existed before Origen's time. It is the Sahidic (= Thebaic) version, which is (with the exception of the last leaves, which are at Naples) contained in a MS. in the Museum Borgianum at Rome: its only lacuna, c. xxxix. 9–xl. 7, can be supplied from a Sahidic MS. at Paris [1].

It is of importance to note that these several sources of

---

[1] The only information which I possess of this version is contained in a letter of Bishop Agapios Bsciai to the *Moniteur de Rome* of October 26, 1883, quoted at length by Lagarde *Mittheilungen*, No. 21, p. 203. The letter is sufficient for the present purpose inasmuch as it contains a list of the passages which the Sahidic version omits.

evidence in the main agree: they differ, as must be expected when critical marks are transferred from one MS. to another at wide intervals of time, in the length of the obelized passages: but they agree in all important instances, and there is an especial agreement between the Syro-Hexaplar and the Sahidic versions.

The question to the consideration of which the present essay is designed to be a contribution is, How are we to account for these wide divergences between the original and the later texts of the LXX.?

i. It seems probable that some of them are due to a careless or unintelligent correction of the text by Origen or his scribe: of this the following four passages are examples:

In c. ix. 3 there is a double version of לֹא יַעֲנֶנּוּ, (1) οὐ μὴ ὑπακούσῃ αὐτῷ, (2) ἵνα μὴ ἀντείπῃ. The former of these is due to Symmachus and Theodotion: the latter is probably a modification of an original LXX. reading οὐ μὴ ἀντείπῃ, which has survived in the readings οὐδὲ μὴ ἀντείπῃ in Cod. 254, and οὐδ' οὐ μὴ ἀντείπῃ in the margin of Cod. 250.

In c. xxiii. 14, 15 the translation of the Hebrew of v. 14 is omitted, and v. 15 is translated twice,

(1) v. 14 διὰ τοῦτο ἐπ' αὐτῷ ἐσπούδακα·
    νουθετούμενος δὲ ἐφρόντισα αὐτοῦ.

(2) v. 15 ἐπὶ τούτῳ ἀπὸ προσώπου αὐτοῦ κατασπουδασθῶ·
    κατανοήσω καὶ πτοηθήσομαι ἐξ αὐτοῦ.

Of these two versions the first is that of the LXX., the second that of Theodotion. That is to say, Origen substituted the more accurate version of Theodotion for that of the LXX., but either he or his scribe erased v. 14 by mistake for v. 15.

In c. xxviii. 26, 27 there is apparently a double rendering of אָז רָאָה וַיְסַפְּרָהּ, viz. (1) οὕτως ἰδὼν ἠρίθμησε, (2) τότε εἶδεν αὐτὴν καὶ ἐξηγήσατο αὐτήν. The first of these renderings is probably the translation of the LXX., since ἀριθμεῖν is used to translate סָפַר in xiv. 16, xxxviii. 37, xxxix. 2: the second is that of Theodotion. But the translation of לְמָטָר חֹק is omitted: and the first of the above translations takes its place, so that the passage gives no intelligible sense. The explanation is probably to be found in the fact that according to Codd. Marm. Bodl. and the Syr.-Hex. and Sahid. the words καὶ ὁδὸν ... ἐξηγήσατο αὐτὴν were inserted from Theodotion: when this was done the words οὕτως ἰδὼν ἠρίθμησε of the original translation should have been erased: when they were left in by the negligence or ignorance of a scribe, the object of ὅτε ἐποίησεν, i.e. ὑετῷ πρόσταγμα (or equivalent words), was omitted as destroying the symmetry of the στίχοι.

The original form of the LXX. translation of vv. 24–28 may be supposed to have been as follows:

23   ὁ θεὸς εὖ συνέστησεν αὐτῆς τὴν ὁδόν,
      αὐτὸς δὲ οἶδε τὸν τόπον αὐτῆς·

24   αὐτὸς γὰρ τὴν ὑπ' οὐρανὸν πᾶσαν ἐφορᾷ,
      εἰδὼς τὰ ἐν τῇ γῇ πάντα·

25   [ὅτε] ἐποίησεν ἀνέμων σταθμόν,
      ὕδατός τε μέτρα [ἡτοίμασε]

26   ὅτε ἐποίησεν [ὑετῷ πρόσταγμα]
      [ὁδόν τε κυδοιμῶν]·

27   [τότε] ἰδὼν ἠρίθμησε,
      ἑτοιμάσας ἐξιχνίασεν·

28   εἶπε δὲ ἀνθρώπῳ, Ἰδοὺ ἡ θεοσέβειά ἐστι σοφία, •
      τὸ δὲ ἀπέχεσθαι ἀπὸ κακῶν ἐστὶν ἐπιστήμη.

The words in brackets are conjectural: the reason for each of them is as follows: in vv. 24, 25 Cod. B reads πάντα ἐποίησεν, Codd. AC¹ 254 πάντα ἃ ἐποίησεν ἐποίησεν δέ, Codd. 23, 55, 68, 157, 160, 161, 250, 252, 255, 256, 257, 260, 261 πάντα ἃ ἐποίησεν, Codd. 106, 110, 137, 139, 147, 248, 249, 255, 258, 259 πάντα τε ἃ ἐποίησεν, Codd. 138, 251, 254 πάντα ὅσα ἐποίησεν: since ὅτε follows in the next verse, and since the Hebrew אָז requires τότε (which Theodotion has) in v. 27, it may be conjectured, in face of the great variety of readings, and not out of harmony with it, that ὅτε was read here. In v. 25 the missing translation of תִּכֵּן may be supplied by ἡτοίμασε, since the same Hebrew verb is translated by ἑτοιμάζειν in the song of Hannah, 1 Sam. 2. 3. In v. 26 the missing translation of לַמָּטָר is clearly, as elsewhere, ὑετῷ and that of חֹק may be πρόσταγμα, as in c. xxvi. 10: the translation of וְדֶרֶךְ לַחֲזִיז קֹלוֹת was probably ὁδόν τε κυδοιμῶν as in c. xxxviii. 25.

In c. xxix. 10, 11 the words כִּי אֹזֶן שָׁמְעָה וַתְּאַשְּׁרֵנִי are translated, (1) οἱ δὲ ἀκούσαντες ἐμακάρισάν με, (2) more literally, ὅτι οὖς ἤκουσε καὶ ἐμακάρισέ με: the first of these translations takes the place of the translation of קוֹל־נְגִידִים נֶחְבָּאוּ, 'the voice of the nobles was hid': and it, rather than the second, is likely to have been the LXX. translation because the noun אֹזֶן (in the dual) is translated by the verb ἀκούειν elsewhere, viz. c. xiii. 17, Ezek. ix. 5: x. 13. Cod. 248 obelizes v. 11, the Syr. Hex. and Sahid. obelize vv. 10 *b*, 11 *a*. These facts taken together seem to point to the existence of an earlier text, and the simplest hypothesis as to its form is that v. 11 in the Hebrew is a duplication of v. 10, and that vv. 10 *b*, 11 *a* in the Greek are a duplication of vv. 9 *b*, 10 *a*.

ii. It is conceivable that some of the divergences are due to the circumstances under which the translation was originally made. It was made after Judaism had come into contact with Greek philosophy. It may be presumed to have been intended not only for Greek speaking Jews but also for aliens. The tendency, which found its highest literary expression in Philo, to show that Judaism was in harmony with Greek culture, may have influenced the mind of the translator, and led him to soften down some of the vivid Semitic anthropomorphisms, and throw a veil over some of the terrors of the law. Even in the Pentateuch which from its greater sacredness, and from its liturgical use, was translated with especial fidelity, a paraphrase or circumlocution sometimes takes the place of the literal expression of an idea which a philosopher would have found difficult to assimilate: and it is natural to expect that a poetical book, to which no idea of special sanctity was attached, and which had no liturgical use, should be translated with some freedom.

But the hypothesis of the intentional omission of passages which were out of harmony with the Hellenized theology of Alexandria, though it may in some cases be true, is inadequate, because, in the first place, it would account for only a small proportion of the passages which were absent from the original version: and because, in the second place, many passages which remain have the same theological character as those which are omitted.

The same remarks would apply to the hypothesis that the omissions are due to the difficulty of the language in certain passages: it would account for only a few of the obelized passages: it would not explain the fact that many passages are omitted of which the translation is easy, and that many remain of which the translation is difficult.

Two other hypotheses remain : the one is that the book was more or less arbitrarily curtailed by the translator: the other is that at a time subsequent to its first translation the original Hebrew text was amplified, and that the original LXX. text represents, in the main, this original Hebrew.

The first of these hypotheses is improbable, nor does it admit of either proof or disproof. The second is not without its difficulties, but it at least bears examination. I propose in the following pages to test its truth, and its sufficiency as an explanation of the facts, by enquiring how far the passages which Origen inserted can be omitted without detriment to the argument of the poem.

The passages to which the hypothesis is chiefly applicable occur in the third (c. xxii–xxxi) and fourth (c. xxxii–xxxvii) groups of speeches: but there are also some passages in the second group (c. xiv–xxi) and in the fifth (c. xxxviii–xlii. 6). I propose to give some examples from the second and third groups, but to deal mainly with the fourth, the speeches of Elihu : there is the more reason for doing this because the speeches of Elihu are, from the point of view of a critic, the most interesting portion of the book, and because it is hoped that the hypothesis which is here adduced may help to solve some of the more difficult problems which the criticism of those speeches involves.

i. *The second group of Speeches :* c. xiv–xxi.

c. xvii. 3–5.

vv. 3–5 *a* are obelized in Cod. Colb. and in the Sahid. :
vv. 3–5 in Cod. Marm. : vv. 3 *b*, 4 *b*, 5 *a* in Syr.-Hex.

The obelized words are difficult of explanation in both
the Hebrew and the Greek : their omission gives a consecutive sense which is even clearer in the Greek than in
the Hebrew. It may be noted that the Greek and Hebrew
of v. 2 are quite different : but since the Greek is in harmony
with the sense of the non-obelized verses 1, 6, 7, 8 it may
be supposed that it represents a lost Hebrew verse, which
was displaced when vv. 3–5 were inserted : in other words
v. 2 in the Hebrew belongs to the added portion, but in
the Greek belongs to the original.

1	ὀλέκομαι[1] πνεύματι φερόμενος,	*I am consumed, being agitated in spirit (?) :*
	δέομαι δὲ ταφῆς καὶ οὐ τυγχάνω·	*I pray for the grave, and obtain it not.*
2	λίσσομαι κάμνων,	*I am weary with entreating.*
	καὶ τί ποίησας ;	*And what hast thou done ?*
3	ἔκλεψαν δέ μου τὰ ὑπάρχοντα ἀλλότριοι·	And strangers have stolen my goods,
	τίς ἐστιν οὗτος ; τῇ χειρί μου συνδεθήτω·	Who is this one? let him strike hands with me :
4	ὅτι καρδίαν αὐτῶν ἔκρυψας ἀπὸ φρονήσεως,	For thou hast hid their heart from understanding :
	διὰ τοῦτο οὐ μὴ ὑψώσῃς αὐτούς·	Therefore shalt thou not exalt them.

[1] In this, as in the other quotations in this chapter which are arranged in
parallel columns, inasmuch as neither a critical discussion of the meaning of
the variants of the Greek text nor a philological discussion of the meaning of
the Hebrew would be pertinent to its main point, (1) the LXX. is quoted,
except where otherwise specified, from the Sixtine text, (2) the Revised English
Version has been followed wherever the meaning of the Hebrew approximates
to that of the Greek. Where the Hebrew text varies to any great extent
from the Greek, an independent translation of the latter has been given.
The Roman type indicates the Revised Version, the Italic type indicates an
independent translation of the Greek : the larger type indicates what the author
believes to have been the original text of the book, the smaller type the passages
which he believes to have been added.

5 τῇ μερίδι ἀναγγελεῖ κακίας,
   ὀφθαλμοὶ δὲ ἐφ' υἱοῖς ἐτάκησαν·

?
Even the eyes of his children *failed* :

6 ἔθου δέ με θρύλλημα ἐν ἔθνεσι,

Thou didst make me also a by-word among the people :

   γέλως δὲ αὐτοῖς ἀπέβην·

And I *became a laughing-stock to them.*

7 πεπώρωνται γὰρ ἀπ' ὀργῆς οἱ ὀφθαλμοί μου,
   πεπολιόρκημαι μεγάλως ὑπὸ πάντων.

Mine eye also is dim by reason of *wrath,*
I am besieged greatly by all men.

c. xxi. 28–33.

These verses are obelized in all the authorities : and Cod. 248 adds to them v. 27 *b.*

The sense will be found to run on, and even more clearly in the Greek than in the Hebrew, from v. 27 to v. 34. The obelized section may be regarded as a poetical expansion of either v. 27 or v. 34 *a.*

27 ὥστε οἶδα ὑμᾶς,
   ὅτι τόλμῃ ἐπικεῖσθέ μοι.

So that I know you,
That with boldness ye set upon me :

28 ὥστε ἐρεῖτε, Ποῦ ἐστιν οἶκος ἄρχοντος ;
   ·καὶ ποῦ ἐστιν ἡ σκέπη τῶν σκηνωμάτων τῶν ἀσεβῶν ;

So that ye will say, Where is the house of the prince?
And where is the shelter of the tents of the wicked?

29 ἐρωτήσατε παραπορευομένους ὁδόν,
   καὶ τὰ σημεῖα αὐτῶν οὐκ ἀπαλλοτριώσετε.

Ye asked them that go by the way,
And their tokens *ye shall not estrange.*

30 ὅτι εἰς ἡμέραν ἀπωλείας κουφίζεται ὁ πονηρός
   εἰς ἡμέραν ὀργῆς αὐτοῦ ἀπαχθήσονται.

That the evil man is reserved to the day of calamity,
That they *shall be* led forth to the day of wrath.

31 τίς ἀπαγγελεῖ ἐπὶ προσώπου αὐτοῦ τὴν ὁδὸν αὐτοῦ ;
   καὶ αὐτὸς ἐποίησε, τίς ἀνταποδώσει αὐτῷ ;

Who shall declare his way to his face?
And who shall repay him what he hath done?

32 καὶ αὐτὸς εἰς τάφους ἀπηνέγχθη,
   καὶ αὐτὸς ἐπὶ σωρῶν ἠγρύπνησεν.

Yet *hath he been* borne to the grave,
And *hath kept* watch over the tomb :

33	ἐγλυκάνθησαν αὐτῷ χάλικες χειμάρρου		The *cups of the brook have been* sweet unto him,
	καὶ ὀπίσω αὐτοῦ πᾶς ἄνθρωπος ἀπελεύσεται,		And all men shall draw after him,
	καὶ ἔμπροσθεν αὐτοῦ ἀναρίθμη- τοί·		As there were innumerable before him :
34	πῶς δὲ παρακαλεῖτέ με κενά ;		How then comfort ye me in vain ?
	τὸ δὲ ἐμὲ καταπαύσασθαι ἀφ' ὑμῶν οὐδέν.		And rest for me from you is there none.

ii. *The third group of Speeches:* c. xxii–xxxi.

c. xxiv. 14 c–18 a.

These verses are obelized in Codd. Colb. Marm., and in the Syr.-Hex. and Sahidic : so also in Cod. Vat. except v. 14 c, and in Cod. Bodl. except vv. 14 c, 15 a, b.

The omission of the obelized verses gives an intelligible sequence of ideas. In LXX. v. 13 Job enquires why God does not visit the wicked who oppress the poor and know not the way of righteousness. The answer is at once given in LXX. v. 14 a, b, that when He takes cognizance of their deeds He delivers them over to darkness : and this idea of punishment is continued in v. 18 b, 'may their portion be cursed upon earth, and their fruits be withered.'

The insertion of the obelized section, on the contrary, interrupts the sequence, and appears almost like a digression leading off from the double sense of σκότος. In v. 14 b it is used in the sense of 'Sheol,' but in v. 14 c it is apparently taken in the sense of 'night,' and this leads to the thought of the thief and the adulterer.

The entire absence of correspondence between the Greek and the Hebrew in vv. 13 a, 14 a, b, 18 c, 19, 20 a, b makes it possible to suppose that the introduction of the obelized section led to changes in the verses immediately preceding and following it.

13 αὐτὸς δὲ διὰ τί τούτων ἐπισκοπὴν οὐ πεποίηται ;	*Why has he not made a visitation for these things ?*
ἐπὶ γῆς ὄντων αὐτῶν καὶ οὐκ ἐπέγνωσαν,	*Upon earth they were, and they acknowledged him not,*
14 ὁδὸν δὲ δικαιοσύνης οὐκ ᾔδεισαν	*But the way of righteousness they knew not,*
οὐδὲ ἀτραποὺς αὐτῆς ἐπορεύθησαν.	*Neither walked they* in the paths thereof.
γνοὺς δὲ αὐτῶν τὰ ἔργα,	*But when he took knowledge of their works*
παρέδωκεν αὐτοὺς εἰς σκότος,	*He delivered them over to darkness.*
καὶ νυκτὸς ἔσται ὡς κλέπτης·	*And at night he shall be as a thief :*
15 καὶ ὀφθαλμὸς μοιχοῦ ἐφύλαξε σκότος,	*The eye also of the adulterer waiteth for the* darkness,
λέγων, Οὐ προνοήσει με ὀφθαλμός,	*Saying, No eye shall see me,*
καὶ ἀποκρυβὴν προσώπου ἔθετο·	*And he putteth a covering on his face :*
16 διώρυξεν ἐν σκότει οἰκίας,	*In the dark they dig through houses,*
ἡμέρας ἐσφράγισαν ἑαυτούς,	*They shut themselves up in the day-time,*
οὐκ ἐπέγνωσαν φῶς.	*They know not the light.*
17 ὅτι ὁμοθυμαδὸν αὐτοῖς τὸ πρωῒ σκιὰ θανάτου,	*For the morning is to all of them as the shadow of death,*
ὅτι ἐπιγνώσεται ταράχας σκιᾶς θανάτου.	*For he shall* know the terrors of the shadow of death.
18 ἐλαφρός ἐστιν ἐπὶ πρόσωπον ὕδατος·	*He is swift upon the face of the waters :*
καταραθείη ἡ μέρις αὐτῶν ἐπὶ γῆς,	*May their* portion *be* cursed *upon earth,*
19 ἀναφανείη δὲ τὰ φυτὰ αὐτῶν ἐπὶ γῆς ξηρά·	*May their trees appear barren upon earth.*
ἀγκαλίδα γὰρ ὀρφανῶν ἥρπασαν·	*For they plundered the armful (gleanings ?) of orphans.*
20 εἶτ' ἀνεμνήσθη αὐτοῦ ἡ ἁμαρτία·	*Then his sin was remembered,*
ὥσπερ δὲ ὁμίχλη δρόσου ἀφανὴς ἐγένετο·	*And as the mist of dew he vanished ;*

σ‚ντριβείη δὲ πᾶς ἄδικος ἴσα   *And may every unrighteous man*
ξύλῳ ἀνιάτῳ.   *be broken like a tree that cannot*
   be healed.

c. xxvi. 5–11.

The following verses are obelized :

vv. 5–10 in Codd. Colb. Marm., vv. 5–11 in the Syr.-Hex. and Sahid., vv. 6–10 in the Cod. Vat. In Cod. Bodl. c. xxvi forms a continuation of the speech of Bildad in c. 25 : there are five asterisks, but it is not clear where they are meant to begin and end.

The omission would make the description of the power of God shorter, but not less emphatic : the obelized verses give a poetical expansion of the main idea, but do not materially add to it.

It may be noted that v. 14 *a*, *b*, also is obelized in the Syr.-Hex. As that verse stands (1) its first two clauses ἰδοὺ . . . . ἐν αὐτῷ would be less intelligible if it had been preceded by only the short enumeration of God's ways which the omission of vv. 5–11 would leave, (2) its last clause is in intelligible sequence with vv. 12, 13, and it may possibly have been immediately preceded by a clause which was omitted when vv. 5–11, 14 *a*, *b*, were inserted.

c. xxviii. 13-22.

The following verses are obelized :

vv. 13–19 in Cod. Vat.

vv. 14–19 in Codd. Colb. Marm., and in the Syr.-Hex. and Sahid.

v. 21 in Codd. Colb. Vat. Marm. : v. 21 *b* in Codd. Bodl. and in the Syr.-Hex. and Sahid.

v. 22 *a* in the Syr.-Hex. and Sahid.

The sequence of ideas is not in any way disturbed by the omission of the section vv. 14–19, which amplify the main thought of the passage with singular poetical beauty, but do not add to its substance.

Q

It will be noted that v. 20 is a repetition in both form and substance of v. 12, and v. 21 *a*, in substance though not in form, of v. 13 : and also that v. 22 is in substance analogous to vv. 14 sqq. Consequently v. 23 begins an answer which is common to both the sections vv. 11–19 and 20–22.

There is another fact which enters into the consideration of the original form of the passage, viz. that Clement of Alexandria (*Strom.* 6. 6, p. 763) possibly, or probably, quotes vv. 20, 21 in a form which does not survive in any existing MS. of the LXX. : λέγει ὁ ᾅδης τῇ ἀπωλείᾳ· εἶδος μὲν αὐτοῦ οὐκ εἴδομεν, φωνὴν δὲ αὐτοῦ ἠκούσαμεν. If these words be a quotation from this passage, they may be taken to be a relic either of the original form of the passage, which was modified when vv. 14–19 were inserted, or of the poem which was incorporated with it.

12 ἡ δὲ σοφία πόθεν εὑρέθη ; ποῖος δὲ τόπος ἐστὶ τῆς ἐπιστή- μης ;	Where shall wisdom be found? And where is the place of understanding ?
13 οὐκ οἶδε βροτὸς ὁδὸν αὐτῆς, οὐδὲ μὴν εὑρέθη ἐν ἀνθρώποις.	Man knoweth not the *way* thereof : Neither is it found *among men :*
14 ἄβυσσος εἶπεν Οὐκ ἔνεστιν ἐν ἐμοί· καὶ ἡ θάλασσα εἶπεν Οὐκ ἔνεστιν μετ' ἐμοῦ.	The deep saith, It is not in me : And the sea saith, It is not with me.
15 οὐ δώσει συγκλεισμὸν ἀντ' αὐτῆς, καὶ οὐ σταθήσεται ἀργύριον ἀντάλλαγμα αὐτῆς.	*He shall not give . . . for it :* Neither shall silver be weighed for the price thereof.

vv. 16, 17, 18, 19   * * *
  * * *
	* * *
	  * * *

20 [ἡ δὲ σοφία πόθεν εὑρέθη ; · ποῖος δὲ τόπος ἐστὶ τῆς συνέσεως;	[Whence then cometh wisdom ? And where is the place of understanding ?
21 λέληθε πάντα ἄνθρωπον,]	Seeing it is hid from the eyes of all living,]
καὶ ἀπὸ πετεινῶν τοῦ οὐρανοῦ ἐκρύβη.	And kept close from the fowls of the air.

22 ἡ ἀπώλεια καὶ ὁ θάνατος εἶπαν   Destruction and death say
ἀκηκόαμεν δὲ αὐτῆς τὸ κλέος   We have heard a rumour thereof
    with our ears :

23 ὁ θεὸς εὖ συνέστησεν αὐτῆς τὴν   God understandeth the way
ὁδόν,   thereof,
αὐτὸς δὲ οἶδε τὸν τόπον αὐτῆς.   And he knoweth the place
    thereof.

c. xxxi. 1–4.

These verses are obelized in Cod. 248, and in the Syr.-
Hex. and Sahid. : parts of vv. 1–3 are obelized in Codd.
Marm. Bodl.

The verses are in no way necessary to the general argument ; the section which begins with c. xxxi. 6 is in a
more natural sequence with c. xxx. than c. xxxi. 1.

iii. The Speeches of Elihu.

1. The first speech, c. xxxii. 6–xxxiii.

In the first speech of Elihu there are two groups of
obelized passages, (1) xxxii. 11–17, (2) xxxiii. 28–33.

(1) xxxii. 11–17.

The following verses are obelized :

v. 11 in Cod. Marm. : 11 *b* in Codd. Colb. Vat., and in Syr.-Hex.
v. 12 in Codd. Colb. Vat. Marm., in Syr.-Hex., and Sahid.
v. 13 in Codd. Colb. Marm. : 13 *a* in Sahid.
v. 14 in Cod. Marm.
v. 15 in Codd. Colb. Marm., in Syr.-Hex. and Sahid.
v. 16 in Codd. Colb. Vat. Marm., in Syr.-Hex. and Sahid.
v. 17 in Cod. Marm.

It is probable that vv. 11–17 were all absent from the
original text. It will be noted that the Hebrew has the
same clause at the end of v. 10 and at the end of v. 16,
אֲחַוֶּה דֵעִי אַף־אָנִי : the intervening words form a separable
section : and the connexion of ideas between v. 10 and the

beginning of v. 17 is close and natural, 'I said, Hearken to me; I also will shew mine opinion, *For* I am full of words.'

6 νεώτερος μέν εἰμι τῷ χρόνῳ ὑμεῖς
  δέ ἐστε πρεσβύτεροι
  I am young, and ye are very old :

  διὸ ἡσύχασα φοβηθεὶς τοῦ ὑμῖν
  ἀναγγεῖλαι τὴν ἐμαυτοῦ ἐπιστήμην.
  Wherefore I held back, and durst not shew you mine opinion.

7 εἶπα δὲ Ὅτι οὐχ ὁ χρόνος [Cod.
  A εἶπον δὲ ὅτι χρόνος] ἐστὶν
  ὁ λαλῶν,
  I said, Days should speak,

  ἐν πολλοῖς δὲ ἔτεσιν οἴδασι
  σοφίαν.
  And multitude of years should teach wisdom.

9 οὐχ οἱ πολυχρόνιοί εἰσι σοφοί,
  οὐδ' οἱ γέροντες οἴδασι κρίμα.
  It is not the ancients that are wise, Nor the aged that understand judgment

10 διὸ εἶπα, ἀκούσατέ μου, καὶ ἀναγ-
   γελῶ ὑμῖν ἃ οἶδα.
   Therefore I said, Hearken to me, I also will shew mine opinion.

11 ἐνωτίζεσθέ μου τὰ ῥήματα, ἐρῶ
   γὰρ ὑμῶν ἀκουόντων,
   ἄχρις οὗ ἐτάσητε λόγους.
   Give ear unto my words,
   For I will speak while ye listen,
   Until ye have searched out what to say.

12 καὶ μέχρι ὑμῶν συνήσω,
   καὶ ἰδοὺ οὐκ ἦν ἐν Ἰὼβ ἐλέγχων,
   Yea I attended unto you,
   And behold there was none that convinced Job,

   ἀναποκρινόμενος ῥήματα αὐτοῦ
   ἐξ ὑμῶν·
   Or that answered his words among you,

13 ἵνα μὴ εἴπητε Εὕρομεν σοφίαν
   κυρίῳ προσθέμενοι·
   Beware lest ye say, We have found wisdom, *being joined to the Lord.*

14 ἀνθρώπῳ δὲ ἐπετρέψατε λαλῆσαι
   τοιαῦτα ῥήματα.
   But it was a man that ye permitted to speak such words :

15 ἐπτοήθησαν, οὐκ ἀπεκρίθησαν
   ἔτι,
   ἐπαλαίωσαν ἐξ αὐτῶν λόγους·
   They are amazed, they answer no more :
   They have not a word to say.

16 ὑπέμεινα οὐ γὰρ ἐλάλησα,
   ὅτι ἔστησαν οὐκ ἀπεκρίθησαν.
   I waited, for I spake not,
   Because they stood still, and answered no more.

17 (ὑπολαβὼν δὲ Ἐλιοὺς λέγει,
   πάλιν λαλήσω)
   πλήρης γάρ εἰμι ῥημάτων
   ὠλέκει γάρ με τὸ πνεῦμα τῆς
   γαστρὸς.
   For I am full of words
   The spirit *of my belly* con-straineth me.

18 ἡ δὲ γαστήρ μου ὥσπερ ἀσκὸς
    γλεύκους ζέων δεδεμένος,
  ἢ ὥσπερ φυσητὴρ χαλκέως ἐρρη-
    γώς.
19 λαλήσω ἵνα ἀναπαύσωμαι,

  ἀνοίξας τὰ χείλη·

Behold my belly is as wine that
   hath no vent ;
Or like a smith's bellows burst-
   ing :
I will speak that I may be re-
   freshed,
I will open my lips and answer.

There are two other points, besides the fact of their
being obelized, which give an exceptional character to
vv. 11–17.

(1) With the exception of v. 18 b (where the LXX. probably read חָרָשׁ, 'a smith,' instead of חָדָשׁ, ' new') the translation of the rest of the speech follows the Hebrew closely,
whereas that of vv. 11–17 in several instances varies widely
from it.

(2) The obelized verses are characterized by great
varieties of reading, especially in vv. 11, 16, which, on the
hypothesis which has been offered, form the points of
junction between the original and the added portions.
The more noteworthy of these variants are the following :

In v. 11 Codd. BS¹ and the Syr.-Hex. omit ἐρῶ γάρ, which makes
the sentence unintelligible ; Cod. A, and other Codd. which are
mentioned by Olympiodorus (ap. Field's Hexapla *in loc.*) add after
ἀκουόντων the duplicate, and more accurate, translation ἰδοὺ ἤκουσα
τοὺς λόγους ὑμῶν· ἐνωτισάμην μέχρι συνέσεως ὑμῶν : so Cod. 23, with
the addition of γὰρ after ἰδού, and with a further duplication of καὶ
ἕως ὑμῶν συνήσω after συνέσεως ὑμῶν. It must be supposed that there
were several concurrent versions of the passage, and that the reading
of the Sixtine text, which is that of the majority of MSS., is a scribe's
compound.

In v. 16 Cod. A has ἐλάλησαν : Cod. 254 has ἐσίγησαν for ἔστησαν :
Codd. 106, 110, 137, 138, 139, 147, 161, 249, 251, 255, 256, 258,
260, 261, Colb., and the Syr.-Hex. add ὅτι ἀποκριθῶ κἀγὼ μέρος after
ἀπεκρίθησαν, so, without ὅτι, 259 : of these words Cod. Colb. mentions that μέρος (τὸ μέρος μου) is due to Symmachus. It may be noted

that although the words represent the Hebrew אֶעֱנֶה אַף־אֲנִי חֶלְקִי they leave the following half of the verse, 16 *b*, which is a repetition of v. 10 *b*, untranslated. This is entirely in harmony with the hypothesis that 16 *b* was only needed to serve as a point of junction between the added section and the following words of the original text .... ' For I am full of words.' It may be further noted, as a mark pointing in the same direction, that the want of such words in the current text of the LXX. probably accounts for the interpolation, which has no equivalent in the Hebrew, πάλιν λαλήσω.

(2) xxxiii. 27–33.

Three sets of facts must be considered in relation to this section.

(i) The following verses are obelized :

vv. 28–29 in Codd. Colb. Vat. Marm. Bodl., in the Syr.-Hex. and Sahid.

vv. 31–33 in Codd. Colb. Bodl., in the Syr.-Hex. and Sahid.

vv. 32–33 in Codd. Vat. Marm.

In other words vv. 27, 30 are the only verses of the section which remain in the Colbert text of the Greek, in the Bodleian text of the Latin, or in the Syriac and Sahidic versions.

(ii) After v. 30 Codd. A, 23, and the margin of the Syr.-Hex., insert the following words :

ὑπολαβὼν δὲ Ἐλιοὺς λέγει,
ἀκούσατέ μου σόφοι, ἐπιστάμενοι ἐνωτίζεσθαι τὸ καλόν·
ὅτι εἴρηκεν Ἰώβ [23 omits Ἰώβ] Ἰδοὺ ταῦτα πάντα ἐργᾶται ὁ ἰσχυρός
ὁδοὺς τρεῖς μετὰ ἀνδρός,
τοῦ ἐπιστρέψαι ψυχὴν αὐτοῦ ἐκ διαφθορᾶς,
τοῦ φωτίσαι αὐτῷ ἐν φωτὶ ζώντων.

Of these words, lines 1, 2 are the beginning of c. xxxiv, as it stands in most MSS. : the Sixtine text omits τὸ καλόν. It will be noted below that vv. 3, 4 of c. xxxiv are obelized, so that not only lines 1, 2, but also the words ὅτι εἴρηκεν

Ἰώβ, belong to that chapter. This fact is a strong corroboration of the hypothesis that at any rate vv. 31–33 did
not form part of the original text. The words that follow,
ἰδοὺ ταῦτα ... ζώντων, are a duplicate, and more exact, translation of vv. 29, 30. They are altogether out of place in
the mouth of Job, and do not contain the opinions which
Elihu proceeds to answer.

(iii) Neither the text nor the meaning of the Greek of
v. 27 is certain: but no meaning can be attached to any
form of the text which will bring it into harmony with the
Hebrew: and neither the Greek nor the Hebrew is in
intelligible sequence with the context.

The general result is that, in the original text of the
speech, vv. 28, 31, 32, 33 were certainly omitted, and that
the speech ended with v. 30, which is not obelized in any
of the MSS. or versions, and the true form of which is
preserved in the duplicate translation in Codd. A, 23. To
these omissions that of v. 27 should probably be added:
but although v. 29 is obelized by all the authorities,
the fact that it is preserved with v. 30 in the duplicate
translation, and that it coheres well with the general
sense of the passage, raises a presumption in favour of
its retention.

The following is suggested as having been probably the
original form of the passage, the inserted portions being
printed in smaller type:

26 εὐξάμενος δὲ πρὸς κύριον καὶ   He prayeth unto God and he is
   δεκτὰ αὐτῷ ἔσται,   favourable unto him,
   εἰσελεύσεται προσώπῳ ἱλαρῷ σὺν   So that he seeth his face with
   ἐξηγορίᾳ·   joy,
   ἀποδώσει δὲ ἀνθρώποις δικαιο-   And he restoreth unto man his
   σύνην   righteousness:

27   εἶτα τότε ἀπομέμψεται ἄνθρωπος
     ἑαυτῷ
     λέγων Οἷα συνετέλουν;

Καὶ οὐκ ἄξια ἤτασέ με ὧν ἥμαρτον·	And it was not requited unto me:
28 σῶσον ψυχήν μου τοῦ μὴ ἐλθεῖν εἰς διαφθοράν, καὶ ἡ ζωή μου φῶς ὄψεται.	He hath redeemed my soul from going into the pit, And my life shall behold the light.
29 ἰδοὺ ταῦτα πάντα ἐργᾶται ὁ ἰσχυρὸς ὁδοὺς τρεῖς μετὰ ἀνδρός· 30 [Codd. A, 23.] τοῦ ἐπιστρέψαι ψυχὴν αὐτοῦ ἐκ διαφθορᾶς, τοῦ φωτίσαι αὐτῷ ἐν φωτὶ ζών- των [Codd. BCS cett.]	Lo, all these things doth God work, Twice, yea thrice, with a man, To bring back his soul from the pit That he may be enlightened with the light of the living.
ἀλλ' ἐρρύσατο τὴν ψυχήν μου ἐκ θανάτου, ἵνα ἡ ζωή μου ἐν φωτὶ αἰνῇ αὐτόν.	But he rescued my soul from death, That my life might praise him in the light.
31 ἐνωτίζου Ἰὼβ καὶ ἄκουέ μου, κώφευσον καὶ ἐγώ εἰμι λαλήσω.	Mark well, O Job, hearken unto me: Hold thy peace and I will speak.
32 εἰ εἰσί σοι λόγοι, ἀποκρίθητί μοι· λάλησον, θέλω γὰρ δικαιωθῆναί σε.	If thou hast anything to say answer me: Speak for I desire to justify thee.
33 εἰ μή, σὺ ἄκουσον μου· κώφευσον καὶ διδάξω σε.	If not, hearken thou unto me: Hold thy peace, and I will teach thee wisdom.

2. The second speech of Elihu, c. xxxiv.

In the second speech of Elihu there are two groups of obelized passages, (1) vv. 3–7, (2) vv. 23–33.

(1) vv. 3–7.

The following verses are obelized:

vv. 3, 4 in Codd. Colb. Vat. Marm. Bodl., and in the Syr.-Hex. and Sahid.

vv. 6 b, 7 in Codd. Colb. Marm. Bodl., and in the Syr.-Hex. and Sahid.

v. 8 a in Cod. Bodl. and in the Syr.-Hex.

The variants are not important except in v. 8, where the most noteworthy are the following:

Codd. 139, 147, 256 omit οὐχ ἁμαρτὼν οὐδὲ ἀσεβήσας: Codd. A, 23 read οὐδέ, Codd. CS², 106, 110, 137, 138, 139, 147, 157, 160, 161, 248, 250, 251, 252, 253, 254, 255, 256, 257, 258, 259, 261, read οὐδ᾽ ὅλως, Cod. 249 reads ἢ ὁδοῦ, Cod. 260 reads ἢ οὐδ᾽ ὅλως, for ἢ οὐδ᾽ οὐ of Cod. B and the Sixtine text: Cod. A adds ὁδοῦ after κοινωνήσας.

The omission of vv. 3, 4 is supported, as mentioned above, by the readings of Codd. A, 23 in v. 30 of the preceding chapter: and it helps rather than hurts the sense of the passage. The main difficulty is that of v. 8 a which has no equivalent in the Hebrew, and which, as the passage stands, affords no intelligible sense: this may account for its being obelized in Cod. Bodl. and the Syr.-Hex. The difficulty may perhaps be solved by noting that if v. 6 b be rightly obelized, v. 6 is left without a second member, and by conjecturing that 8 a is that second member. On this hypothesis the whole passage originally read as follows: the added portions are printed, as before, in smaller type.

2	ἀκούσατέ μου σοφοί, ἐπιστάμενοι ἐνωτίζεσθε.	Hear my words, ye wise men; And give ear unto me ye that have knowledge.
3	ὅτι οὖς λόγους δοκιμάζει καὶ λάρυγξ γεύεται βρῶσιν.	For the ear trieth words As the palate tasteth meat.
4	κρίσιν ἑλώμεθα ἑαυτοῖς, γνῶμεν ἀνὰ μέσον ἑαυτῶν ὅ τι καλόν.	Let us choose for us that which is right: Let us know among ourselves what is good.
5	ὅτι εἴρηκεν Ἰώβ, Δίκαιός εἰμι, ὁ Κύριος ἀπήλλαξέ μου τὸ κρίμα	For Job hath said, I am righteous, And God hath taken away my right:
6	ἐψεύσατο δὲ τῷ κρίματί μου· βίαιον τὸ βέλος μου ἄνευ ἀδικίας.	*And hath been false in my judgment,* My wound is incurable, though I am without transgression.

7   τίς ἀνὴρ ὥσπερ Ἰώβ   What man is like Job

πίνων μυκτήρισμον ὥσπερ ὕδωρ   Who drinketh up scorning like water

8   οὐχ ἁμαρτὼν οὐδὲ ἀσεβήσας,   *Though I have not sinned nor dealt wickedly*

οὐδὲ [Codd. A, 23, or οὐδ' ὅλως as in CS² and most cursives] κοινωνήσας μετὰ ποιούντων τὰ ἄνομα   *Nor gone* in company with the workers of iniquity,

τοῦ πορευθῆναι μετὰ ἀσεβῶν   *So as to* walk with wicked men.

(2) vv. 23–33.

The following verses are obelized :

v. 22 *b* in Codd. Colb. 255.

v. 23 in Codd. Colb. Bodl. Marm., and in the Syr.-Hex. and Sahid. : it is omitted in the early Latin.

v. 25 *b* in the Syr.-Hex. and Sahid.

vv. 25–34 in Codd. Colb. Marm. Bodl.

vv. 28–33 in Cod. Vat. and in the Syr.-Hex. and Sahid.

The omission of the section vv. 23 (or 22)–33 would in no way affect the argument of the speech; the answer of Elihu in vindication of God against Job is fitly concluded with either v. 21 or v. 22, and in v. 34 he turns again to the 'men of understanding,' in the full assurance that they will say that Job has spoken without knowledge.

3. *The third speech of Elihu*, c. xxxv.

In the third speech of Elihu there are two obelized passages, (1) vv. 7 *b*–10 *a*, (2) vv. 15–16.

(1) vv. 7 *b*–10 *a*.

These verses are obelized in Codd. Colb. Marm., in the Syr.-Hex. and Sahid. : vv. 8–10 *a* in Cod. Bodl.

The argument is made clearer and more pointed by the omission of the passage, which has no necessary connexion with the rest of the speech.

(2) vv. 15–16.

These verses are obelized in Codd. Colb. Marm. Bodl., and in the Syr.-Hex. and Sahid.

The passage, like the preceding, is in no way necessary to the argument: and the hypothesis that it is an addition to the original text is supported by the fact that the LXX. has a different ending to the speech, viz. the clause of v. 14 κρίθητι . . . ὡς ἔστι, which is no less difficult than the Hebrew, but which is both more appropriate and more emphatic than vv. 15, 16.

The connexion of ideas in the speech, from v. 5, will be seen from the following reprint of it :

5 ἀνάβλεψον εἰς τὸν οὐρανὸν καὶ ἴδε,
κατάμαθε δὲ νέφη ὡς ὑψηλὰ ἀπὸ
σοῦ.

Look unto the heavens and see,
And behold the skies which are higher than thou.

6 εἰ ἥμαρτες, τί πράξεις ;

If thou hast sinned, what doest thou against him ?

εἰ δὲ καὶ πολλὰ ἠνόμησας, τί δύνασαι ποιῆσαι ;

And if thy transgressions be multiplied, what doest thou unto him ?

7 καὶ εἰ [Codd. A, 23, 249 ;
Codd. B cett. ἐπεὶ δὲ οὖν]
δίκαιος εἶ, τί δώσεις αὐτῷ

If thou be righteous, what givest thou him ?

ἢ τί ἐκ χειρός σου λήψεται ;

8 ἀνδρὶ τῷ ὁμοίῳ σοι ἡ ἀσέβειά σου,
καὶ υἱῷ ἀνθρώπου ἡ δικαιοσύνη σου·

Or what receiveth he of thine hand ?
Thy wickedness may hurt a man as thou art ;
And thy righteousness may profit a son of man.

9 ἀπὸ πλήθους συκφαντούμενοι κεκράξονται,
βοήσονται ἀπὸ βραχίονος πολλῶν

By reason of the multitude of oppressions they cry out,
They cry for help by reason of the arm of the mighty.

10 καὶ οὐκ εἶπε Ποῦ ἔστιν ὁ θεὸς ὁ ποιήσας με,

But none saith, Where is God my maker,

ὁ κατατάσσων φυλακὰς νυκτερινάς,

Who ordereth the watches of the night

11 ὁ διορίζων με ἀπὸ τετραπόδων γῆς

Who separateth me from the beasts of the earth,

ἀπὸ δὲ πετεινῶν οὐρανοῦ [Codd. 23, 253 add σοφίζει ἡμᾶς].

And from the fowls of heaven?

12 ἐκεῖ κεκράξονται καὶ οὐ μὴ εἰσακούσῃ

There they cry, but none giveth answer,

καὶ [Codd. A, 23, 161 omit] ἀπὸ ὕβρεως πονηρῶν

Because of the pride of evil men.

13 ἄτοπα γὰρ οὐ βούλεται ἰδεῖν ὁ Κύριος·

Surely God will not hear vanity,

αὐτὸς γὰρ ὁ παντοκράτωρ ὁρατής ἐστι

For the Almighty himself is an observer

14 τῶν συντελούντων τὰ ἄνομα

Of those who commit unrighteousness,

καὶ σώσει με.

And he will save me.

κρίθητι δὲ ἐναντίον αὐτοῦ

Plead thou in his sight

εἰ δύνασαι αὐτὸν αἰνέσαι ὡς ἔστι

If thou canst praise him as he is.

15 καὶ νῦν ὅτι οὐκ ἔστιν ἐπισκεπτόμενος ὀργὴν αὐτοῦ, καὶ οὐκ ἔγνω παράπτωμά τι σφόδρα.

But now, because he hath not visited in his anger, Neither doth he greatly regard arrogance.

16 καὶ Ἰὼβ ματαίως ἀνοίγει τὸ στόμα αὐτοῦ, ἐν ἀγνωσίᾳ ῥήματα βαρύνει.

Therefore doth Job open his mouth in vanity, He multiplieth words without knowledge.

---

4. The fourth speech of Elihu, c. xxxvi–xxxvii.

So large a part of this speech is obelized, that it will be most conveniently considered as a whole. The antiquity of the shorter form is shown by the fact, which has been mentioned above, that Clement of Alexandria (Strom. 4. 26, p. 641) quotes it: i.e. in quoting c. xxxvi. 10–12 he omits the obelized portions.

The following are the obelized passages:

c. xxxvi.

v. 5 in Cod. Colb.: 5 b in Codd. Vat. Marm., and in the Syr.-Hex. and Sahid.

vv. 6, 7 in Codd. Colb. Vat. Marm., and in the Syr.-Hex. and Sahid.: v. 7 in Cod. Bodl.

vv. 8, 9 in Codd. Vat. Marm. Bodl., and in the Syr.-Hex. and Sahid.

vv. 10, 11 in Codd. Vat. Marm. Bodl. : vv. 10 *b*, 11 in Cod. Colb. and in the Syr.-Hex. and Sahid.

v. 13 in Codd. Vat. Marm. Bodl., and in the Syr.-Hex. an~ Sahid.

v. 16 in Codd. Colb. Vat. Marm. Bodl., and in the Syr.-Hex. and Sahid.

v. 19 *b* in Cod. Marm.

v. 20 in Codd. Colb. Vat. Marm., and in the Syr.-Hex. and Sahid : v. 20 *b* in Cod. Bodl.

v. 21 in Codd. Vat. Marm. Bodl.: v. 21 *b* in Cod. Colb. and in the Syr.-Hex. and Sahid.

v. 22 to c. xxxvii. 6 in Cod. Vat.

vv. 22 *a*, 23 *a* in the Sahid.

v. 24 *b*, 25 *a* in Codd. Colb. Marm. Bodl., and in the Syr.-Hex. and Sahid.

v. 26 in Codd. Colb. Vat. Marm. Bodl., and in the Syr.-Hex. and Sahid.

v. 27 in the Codd. Vat. Marm. Bodl.: v. 27 *b* in the Syr.-Hex. and Sahid.

v. 28 *a* in Codd. Vat. Marm. Bodl., and in the Syr.-Hex. and Sahid.

v. 29 in Codd. Colb. Vat. Marm. Bodl., and in the Syr.-Hex. and Sahid.

v. 30 in Codd. Vat. Marm. Bodl. and in the Syr.-Hex.: v. 30 *a* in Cod. Colb.

c. xxxvii.

v. 1 in Codd. Colb. Vat. Marm. Bodl.: v. 1 *a* in the Syr.-Hex.

vv. 2–5 *a* in Codd. Colb. Vat. Marm. Bodl. and 2 *b*–5 *a* in the Syr.-Hex.

v. 5 *b* in the Sahid.

vv. 6 *b*, 7 *a* in Codd. Colb. Bodl., and in the Syr.-Hex. and Sahid.

v. 9 *b* in Codd. Colb. Marm.

v. 10 Cod. Vat. : v. 10 *a* Codd. Colb. Marm. Bodl. and in the Sahid.

v. 11 in the Syr.-Hex. and Sahid.

v. 12 in Cod. Colb. and in the Syr.-Hex. and Sahid. : v. 12 *a* in Cod. Marm.

v. 13 in Cod. Vat.: v. 13 *b*, *c* in Cod. Bodl. and in the Syr.-Hex. and Sahid.

v. 18 in Codd. Marm. Bodl. and in the Sahid.: v. 18 *b* in the Syr.-Hex.

(1) c. xxxvi. 5–21.

5 γίνωσκε ὅτι ὁ κύριος οὐ μὴ ἀπο-ποιήσηται τὸν ἄκακον,	*Know that God will not cast away the guiltless man,*
δυνατὸς ἰσχύϊ καρδίας·	He is mighty in strength of understanding.
6 ἀσεβῆ οὐ μὴ ζωοποιήσῃ	He preserveth not the life of the wicked,
καὶ κρίμα πτωχῶν δώσει.	But giveth to the afflicted their right.
7 οὐκ ἀφελεῖ ἀπὸ δικαίου ὀφθαλ-μοὺς αὐτοῦ καὶ μετὰ βασιλέων εἰς θρόνον καὶ καθίει αὐτοὺς εἰς νῖκος καὶ ὑψωθήσονται.	He withdraweth not his eyes from the righteous, But with kings upon the throne He setteth them for ever and they are exalted.
8 καὶ οἱ πεπεδημένοι ἐν χειροπέδαις συσχεθήσονται ἐν σχοινίοις πε-νίας·	And those that are bound in fetters, Shall be taken in the cords of affliction ;
9 καὶ ἀναγγελεῖ αὐτοὺς τὰ ἔργα αὐτῶν καὶ παραπτώματα αὐτῶν ὅτι ἰσχύσουσι·	*And he shall shew* them their works, And their transgressions, that they have behaved themselves proudly.
10 ἀλλὰ τοῦ δικαίου εἰσακούσεται·	*But he will give ear unto the righteous :*
καὶ εἶπεν ὅτι ἐπιστραφήσονται ἐξ ἀδικίας·	And commandeth that they return from iniquity.
11 ἐὰν ἀκούσωσι καὶ δουλεύσωσι, συντελέσουσι τὰς ἡμέρας αὐτῶν ἐν ἀγαθοῖς, καὶ τὰ ἔτη αὐτῶν ἐν εὐπρεπείαις·	If they hearken and serve him, They shall spend their days in prosperity And their years in pleasures.
12 ἀσεβεῖς δὲ οὐ διασώζει,	*But the ungodly will he not pre-serve,*
παρὰ τὸ μὴ βούλεσθαι αὐτοὺς εἰδέναι τὸν κύριον καὶ διότι νουθετούμενοι ἀνήκοοι ἦσαν·	*For that they were not willing to know the Lord. And because when admonished they hearkened not.*
13 καὶ ὑποκριταὶ καρδίᾳ τάξουσι θυμόν·	But they that are godless in heart lay up anger,

οὐ βοήσονται ὅτι ἔδησεν αὐτούς·

They cry not for help when he bindeth them.

14 ἀποθάνοι τοίνυν ἐν νεότητι ἡ ψυχὴ αὐτῶν,

ἡ δὲ ζωὴ αὐτῶν τιτρωσκομένη ὑπὸ ἀγγέλων

Their soul dieth in youth,

And their life *wounded by angels,*

15 ἀνθ᾽ ὧν ἔθλιψαν ἀσθενῆ καὶ ἀδύνατον·

κρίμα δὲ πραέων ἐκθήσει.

Because they afflicted the weak and helpless,

And he will execute judgment for the meek.

16 καὶ προσεπιηπάτησέν σε ἐκ στόματος ἐχθροῦ,

ἄβυσσος κατάχυσις ὑποκάτω αὐτῆς,

καὶ κατέβη τράπεζά σου πλήρης πιότητος

17 οὐκ ὑστερήσει δὲ ἀπὸ δικαίων κρίμα,

Judgment shall not fail from the righteous,

18 θυμὸς δὲ ἐπ᾽ ἀσεβεῖς ἔσται,

But wrath shall be upon the wicked,

δι᾽ ἀσέβειαν δώρων ὧν ἐδέχοντο ἐπ᾽ ἀδικίαις·

For the wickedness of the gifts which they received for unrighteousnesses.

19 μή σε ἐκκλινάτω ἑκὼν ὁ νοῦς δεήσεως

ἐν ἀνάγκῃ ὄντων ἀδυνάτων·

Let not thy mind willingly turn thee aside from entreaty,

When the helpless are in distress.

20 καὶ πάντας τοὺς κραταιοῦντας ἰσχύν·

μὴ ἐξελκύσῃς τὴν νύκτα,

τοῦ ἀναβῆναι λαοὺς ἀντ᾽ αὐτῶν·

21 ἀλλὰ φύλαξαι μὴ πράξῃς ἄτοπα·

But take heed that thou do not iniquity.

ἐπὶ τούτων γὰρ ἐξείλου ἀπὸ πτωχείας·

If the non-obelized verses 5 *a,* 10 *a,* 12, 14, 15, 17, 18 *a,* be read consecutively it will be found that they give a consecutive and appropriate sense. They are a contrast, in clearly defined antithesis, of God's dealings with the righteous and the wicked.

In the same way if vv. 5 *b*, 6, 7, 8, 9, 10 *b*, 11, 13, be read consecutively they also give a consecutive and intelligible sense. They form two connected sections: in vv. 6, 7 there is a contrast between God's dealings with the righteous and the wicked: in the other verses there is a contrast between the effects of God's discipline upon the righteous whom he has afflicted for their transgressions, and the godless who 'cry not for help when he bindeth them.' The only verse from which some words seem to have fallen away is 10 *b*, which requires an additional member to connect it, without harshness, with v. 9, and to explain its initial καί.

So far as these verses of the LXX. are concerned they form two interwoven but separable poems.

The main difficulties of the passage lie (1) in the non-obelized verse 19, and (2) in the obelized verses 16, 20, 21 *b*.

In regard to (1) there is almost certainly a corruption of the text. The note of the wickedness of bribed judgments having been struck in v. 18 *b* it is natural to expect by way of antithesis an exhortation against receiving bribes in v. 19: the words as they stand are barely intelligible, and it may be inferred from the fact that μὴ ἐκκλινάτω σε is a good translation of אַל־יַטֶּךָ, that the other words represent a lost translation of וְרָב־כֹּפֶר, 'the greatness of the ransom.' If this be so, the next non-obelized words, v. 21 'But take heed that thou do not iniquity' will follow in natural sequence.

In regard to (2) vv. 16, 20 are altogether unintelligible as they stand: the varieties of reading in v. 16 point to a corruption of the text: and both verses, as also 21 *b*, appear to be fragments of other translations of the Hebrew, since single phrases in each of them correspond to single phrases of the Hebrew, which were worked into an early text of the LXX. by an unintelligent scribe.

(2) xxxvi. 22–xxxvii. 13.

22 ἰδοὺ ὁ ἰσχυρὸς κραταιώσει ἐν
    ἰσχύϊ αὐτοῦ·
    τίς γάρ ἐστι κατ' αὐτὸν δυνάστης;

23 τίς δέ ἐστιν ὁ ἐτάζων αὐτοῦ τὰ
    ἔργα;
    ἢ τίς ὁ εἰπών, Ἔπραξεν ἄδικα.

24 μνήσθητι ὅτι μεγάλα ἐστὶν αὐτοῦ
    τὰ ἔργα

    ὧν ἦρξαν ἄνδρες,
25 πᾶς ἄνθρωπος εἶδεν ἐν ἑαυτῷ,

    ὅσοι τιτρωσκόμενοί εἰσι βροτοί.

26 ἰδοὺ ὁ ἰσχυρὸς πολύς, καὶ οὐ
    γνωσόμεθα·
    ἀριθμὸς ἐτῶν αὐτοῦ καὶ ἀπέραν-
    τος.

27 ἀριθμηταὶ δὲ αὐτῷ σταγόνες
    ὑετοῦ,
    καὶ ἐπιχυθήσονται ὑετῷ εἰς νε-
    φέλην·

28 ῥυήσονται παλαιώματα
    ἐσκίασε δὲ νέφη ἐπὶ ἀμυθήτων
    βροτῶν.

ὥραν ἔθετο κτήνεσιν,
οἴδασι δὲ κοίτης τάξιν·

ἐπὶ τούτοις πᾶσιν οὐκ ἐξίσταταί
    σου ἡ διάνοια,
οὐδὲ διαλλάσσεταί σου ἡ καρδία
    ἀπὸ σώματος.

29 καὶ ἐὰν συνῇ ἀπέκτασιν [Cod.
    Β ἀπέκτασις] νεφέλης,
    ἰσότητα σκηνῆς αὐτοῦ·
30 ἰδοὺ ἐκτενεῖ ἐπ' αὐτὸν ἠδώ[1],

Behold, God doeth loftily in his
    power,
Who is a *mighty one* like unto
    him?

Who enquireth into his works ?

Or who can say, Thou hast
    wrought unrighteousness?
Remember that thou magnify his
    work,

Every man hath seen in himself,

?

Behold, God is great, and we
    know him not :
The number of his years is un-
    searchable.
Numbered by him are the drops
    of rain,
And they shall be poured forth in
    rain into cloud :

?

And he hath made the clouds over-
    shadow the countless race of
    men.

He hath set a season to the beasts
And they know the order of their
    lying down.
At all these things thy mind is not
    astonished,
Nor is thy heart parted from thy
    body.

And if thou dost understand the
    spreading of the clouds,
The . . . . of his pavilion :
Behold, he will stretch his bow
    thereon,

---

[1] For this, which is the reading of almost all MSS., Codd. A, 23 read τὸ τόξον,
which is the correct translation of the Hebrew אורו : here, as in some other
passages, ר and ד were confused, so that ἠδώ is a transliteration of אידו.

καὶ ῥιζώματα θαλάσσης ἐκάλυψεν.	And he covereth the bottom of the sea :
31 ἐν γὰρ αὐτοῖς κρινεῖ λαούς,	For by these he judgeth the peoples,
δώσει τροφὴν τῷ ἰσχύοντι [Cod. B ἀκούοντι].	He giveth meat *to him that is strong.*
32 ἐπὶ χειρῶν ἐκάλυψε φῶς	He covereth his hands with the lightning.
καὶ ἐνετείλατο περὶ αὐτῆς ἐν ἀπαντῶντι·	And giveth it a charge that it strike the mark :
33 ἀναγγελεῖ περὶ αὐτοῦ φίλον αὐτοῦ κύριος, κτῆσις καὶ περὶ ἀδικίας.	
c. xxxvii. 1 καὶ ἀπὸ ταύτης ἐταράχθη ἡ καρδία μου	At this also my heart was troubled,
καὶ ἀπερρύη ἐκ τοῦ τόπου.	And is moved out of its place.
2 ἄκουε [Codd. A, 23, 254, add Ἰὼβ] ἀκοὴν ἐν ὀργῇ θυμοῦ κυρίου,	
καὶ μελέτη ἐκ στόματος αὐτοῦ ἐξελεύσεται.	*And meditation shall go forth from his mouth.*
3 ὑποκάτω παντὸς τοῦ οὐρανοῦ ἡ ἀρχὴ αὐτοῦ,	*Beneath the whole heaven is his government,*
καὶ τὸ φῶς αὐτοῦ ἐπὶ πτερύγων τῆς γῆς.	And his light unto the ends of the earth.
4 ὀπίσω αὐτοῦ βοήσεται φωνῇ,	*Behind him shall he shout with a voice,*
βροντήσει ἐν φωνῇ ὕβρεως αὐτοῦ·	He *shall thunder* with the voice of his majesty.
καὶ οὐκ ἀνταλλάξει αὐτούς, ὅτι ἀκούσει φωνὴν αὐτοῦ.	? *For thou shalt hear his voice.*
5 βροντήσει ὁ ἰσχυρὸς ἐν φωνῇ αὐτοῦ θαυμάσια·	God *shall thunder* marvellously with his voice,
ἐποίησε γὰρ μεγάλα ἃ οὐκ ᾔδειμεν,	Great things doeth he, which we cannot comprehend.
6 συντάσσων χιόνι Γίνου ἐπὶ γῆς,	For he saith to the snow, Fall thou on the earth ;
καὶ χειμὼν ὑετὸς	Likewise to the shower of rain
καὶ χειμὼν ὑετῶν δυναστείας αὐτοῦ.	And to the showers of his mighty rain.
7 ἐν χειρὶ παντὸς ἀνθρώπου κατασφραγίζει	He sealeth up the hand of every man,
ἵνα γνῷ πᾶς ἄνθρωπος τὴν ἑαυτοῦ ἀσθένειαν·	That all men may know *their weakness* :
8 εἰσῆλθε δὲ θηρία ὑπὸ τὴν σκέπην	Then the beasts go into their coverts,

ἡσύχασαν δὲ ἐπὶ κοίτης.

9 ἐκ ταμιείων ἐπέρχονται ὀδύναι,

    ἀπὸ δὲ ἀκρωτηρίων ψῦχος

10 καὶ ἀπὸ πνοῆς ἰσχυροῦ δώσει
    πάγος·
    οἰακίζει δὲ τὸ ὕδωρ ὡς ἐὰν βού-
    ληται

11 καὶ ἐκλεκτὸν καταπλάσσει νε-
    φέλη·
    διασκορπιεῖ νέφος φῶς αὐτοῦ,

12 καὶ αὐτὸς κυκλώματα διαστρέ-
    ψει,
    ἐν θεεβουλαθώθ, εἰς ἔργα αὐ-
    τῶν·
    πάντα ὅσα ἂν ἐντείληται αὐ-
    τοῖς,

13 ταῦτα συντέτακται παρ' αὐτοῦ
    ἐπὶ τῆς γῆς,
    ἐάν τε εἰς παιδείαν ἐὰν εἰς τὴν
    γῆν αὐτοῦ
    ἐὰν εἰς ἔλεος εὑρήσει αὐτόν.

And remain in their dens.

Out of the chambers *come forth*
    .... (?)

And from the extremities cold,
By the breath of God ice is
    given
And he steereth the water as he
    wills

?

He spreadeth abroad the cloud of
    his light,
And he himself will turn about
    its circuits:

?

All things whatsoever he com-
    mandeth them:
These things are ordered by him
    upon the earth,
Whether it be for correction or
    for his earth
Or for mercy, *he shall find him.*

It will probably be found, after a more minute comparison of the Greek text with both the Hebrew and the other versions, that, in this section, four poems, two of them original and two added, have been fused together. Each of the poems has the same theme, the greatness of God as seen in nature, and its effect on the mind of man.

The first of the non-obelized, and therefore presumably original, poems seems to consist of c. xxxvi. 22, 23, 24 *a*, and the section ὥραν ἔθετο κτήνεσιν which is in some MSS. placed at the end of c. xxxvi. 28 and in others in the middle of c. xxxvii. 5. It may reasonably be supposed that this section forms the end of an enumeration of some of the works of God, which has been replaced by the added verses 26, 27, 28.

The second of the non-obelized poems seems to consist of the fragments c. xxxvii. 5 *b*, 6 *a*, 7 *b* (?), 8, 9 *a*. It begins with the second half of a verse of which the first half

probably resembled the beginning of two other poems, viz.
xxxvi. 22 a, 26 a. The poem, like the preceding, enumerates some of the works of God; (compare the mention
of the beasts in xxxvi. 28 and xxxvii. 8).

The third poem seems to consist of the obelized passages
c. xxxvi. 26, 27, 28 a, b, 29, 30, 31, 32, 33, 34 (=xxxvii. 1).
It begins, like the first poem, with a declaration of the
greatness of God, and proceeds to an enumeration of his
works; and it concludes with a description of the effect of
the consideration of those works upon the mind of Elihu
(καὶ ἀπὸ ταύτης ἐταράχθη ἡ καρδία μου, καὶ ἀπερρύη ἐκ τοῦ
τόπου αὐτῆς) which is in apparent contrast with the effect on
the mind of Job (c. xxxvi. 28 [xxxvii. 5] ἐπὶ τούτοις πᾶσιν
οὐκ ἐξίσταταί σου ἡ διάνοια, οὐδὲ διαλλάσσεταί σου ἡ καρδία
ἀπὸ σώματος).

The fourth poem seems to consist of the obelized
passages c. xxxvii. 2–5 a, 6 b, 7 a (and b?), 9 b, 10–13. This
poem is more fragmentary than the others, and contains at
least two verses, 11, 12, which in their existing form are
not intelligible.

It is probable that the remainder of the chapter, vv.
14–24, forms another poem: it contains many philological
difficulties, but only one obelized verse, v. 18, and therefore
it comes less than the preceding parts of the speech within
the scope of this chapter.

The result of the enquiry is that the hypothesis which
was advanced at the outset explains satisfactorily the
majority of the passages which Origen supplied from Theodotion. In other words it seems probable that the book of
Job originally existed in a shorter form than at present; and
that in the interval between the time of the original translation and that of Theodotion large additions were made to
the text by a poet whose imaginative power was at least not
inferior to that of the original writer. The additions are in

general harmony with the existing text, though they do not always exactly fit in to their place : nor is it likely that the difficulties will be solved until the ten factors which are necessary to their solution have each engaged the attention of skilled specialists, namely, the philology and the textual criticism not only of the Hebrew, but also of the Greek, the Syro-Hexaplar, the Sahidic, and the Latin versions. Of these ten factors, only the first two, namely the philology and the textual criticism of the Hebrew, have as yet been dealt with by competent scholars.

VII. ON THE TEXT OF
ECCLESIASTICUS.

THE text of Ecclesiasticus has come down to us in a form
which, as it is frequently unintelligible, must be presumed
to be corrupt: but since it is a translation of which the
original is lost, and since, consequently, its textual difficulties cannot be explained by reference to that original,
we cannot, in all cases, know for certain whether they are
due to imperfections in the translation itself or to an imperfect tradition of it. It has the further element of uncertainty that, like all paroemiastic literature, it was altered
from time to time. The wisdom of the fathers gave place
to the wisdom of the children: one generation had little
scruple in correcting, amplifying, and supplementing the
proverbial sayings of its predecessors. And since there
are some parts of the book in which the Latin and Syriac
texts differ not only from the Greek text but also from
one another, it must be presumed that the original text
was not only altered but altered in different ways, in different countries, or at different times.

The probability of recovering the original text of the
whole book is consequently small. But for the greater
part of it we have the same means of determining the text
that we have in the case of the New Testament; that is
to say, we have not only the Greek MSS. but also early
versions which point to a text that is probably earlier than
that of the earliest existing MSS. It is remarkable, considering the great intrinsic interest of the book, its importance in the history of ethics, and the place which it has

occupied in Christian theology, that so few attempts have been made to apply these means to the determination of the text where it is doubtful, and to the recovery of it where it is at present corrupt and unintelligible. The present essay is a study in that direction: its object is to show both how much remains to be done and how far the existing materials help us to do it. It will begin by a short survey of those materials, and proceed to apply them to the criticism of some passages.

1. GREEK MSS.

The Greek MSS. which contain Ecclesiasticus, and of which collations have been published, are the following:—

Uncial MSS.: Codices Alexandrinus A, Vaticanus B, Sinaiticus S, Ephraemi rescriptus C (in Tischendorf *Monumenta Sacra*, vol. i), Codex Venetus, a MS. of the 8th or 9th century, No. 1 in the Ducal Library (Holmes and Parsons, No. 23).

Cursive MSS.: No. 55[1], a Vatican MS. (No. 1 of Queen Christina's MSS.) probably of the twelfth century: No. 68, a Venice MS. (No. 5 in the Ducal Library) probably compiled from earlier MSS. by order of Cardinal Bessarion, very partially collated for Holmes and Parsons: No. 70, a MS. of the 15th century in the Library of St. Anne at Augsburg, probably the same as that which was collated by D. Hoeschel (see below); only c. 1 was collated for Holmes and Parsons: No. 106, a Ferrara MS. described as being apparently written 'in charta papyracea Aegyptiaca,' and dated A.D. 734? (*The First Annual Account of the Collation of the MSS.* Oxford, 1789, p. 64): No. 155, a MS. of the 11th century, formerly in the Meerman Collection at the Hague, and now in the Bodleian Library (Auct. T. II. 4): No. 157, a Basle MS.: No. 248, a Vatican MS. (346) of about the fourteenth century: No. 253, a Vatican MS.

---

[1] The numbers are those of Holmes and Parsons: the references in the following pages to the cursive MSS., with the exception of No. 155, which has been collated independently, are made from the MS. collations, now in the Bodleian Library, and not from the printed edition. The numbers which are placed in brackets, e.g. (157), are those in which the collator has made no note of variation from the printed text which he used, and in which, consequently, the reading of the MS. is inferred, more or less uncertainly, *e silentio*.

(336) also of about the fourteenth century : No. 254, a Vatican MS. (337) of about the thirteenth century : No. 296, a Vatican MS. (Codex Palatinus, No. 337) probably of the eleventh century : No. 307, an incomplete Munich MS. (129, formerly 276) of the fourteenth century : No. 308, a Vatican MS., described by Holmes and Parsons (Praef. ad libr. Ecclesiastici) as Codex Palatinus *Vindobonensis* : but the MS. collation was made at Rome, and describes it simply as ' MS. Palatinus,' without further identification : (there is no trace of it in Stevenson's catalogue of the Codices Graeci Palatini). In 1604 D. Hoeschel published an edition of Ecclesiasticus with variants from a MS. in the Library of St. Anne at Augsburg, which he does not further identify, but which is probably of the fifteenth century (Holmes, *Ninth Annual Account*, Oxford, 1797, p. 25).

In addition to these there are many MSS. of which no published collations exist : of these probably the most important are the palimpsests of the 6th or 7th century at St. Petersburg, which Tischendorf promised to publish in his *Monumenta Sacra*, vol. viii.   Two Vienna MSS., Cod. Theol. Gr. xi (quoted below as Vienna 1) and Cod. Theol. Gr. cxlvii (=Vienna 2), both of which were brought by Busbecq from Constantinople, have been partially collated for this work.

It is desirable in the first instance to form a working conception of the character and relations of the chief MSS., in order to ascertain what kind of presumption for or against a reading is afforded by the fact of its occurring in a particular MS. or group of MSS.   Such a conception may to some extent be derived from an examination of other books of the Bible in the same MSS.   But there are two considerations which limit that extent : the first, which is the less important one, is that the MSS. of the whole Bible were written by different hands, and that no two scribes can be assumed to have copied with precisely the same degree of accuracy : the second, which is the more important consideration, is that different books or groups of books may be supposed to have been copied from different originals. The main ground for this supposition in the case of the two books of Wisdom is that though they are always placed together, their place, like that of other books which were probably circulated separately, is different in different MSS., for example,

In the Sinaitic MS. the order (omitting the earlier books) is . . . Major Prophets, Minor Prophets, Psalms, Proverbs, Ecclesiastes, Canticles, Wisdom, Ecclesiasticus, Job.

In the Alexandrian MS. the order is . . . Minor Prophets, Major Prophets, Esther, Tobit, Judith, Esdras, Maccabees, Psalms, Job, Proverbs, Ecclesiastes, Canticles, Wisdom, Ecclesiasticus.

In the Vatican MS. the order is . . . Psalms, Proverbs, Ecclesiastes, Canticles, Job, Wisdom, Ecclesiasticus, Esther, Judith, Tobit, Minor Prophets, Major Prophets.

In the Ferrara MS. (Holmes and Parsons, No. 106) the order is . . . Job, Proverbs, Wisdom, Ecclesiasticus, Major Prophets, Minor Prophets, 1 and 2 Maccabees, Psalms.

These differences of position seem to be best explained by the hypothesis that, although at the time when the MSS. were written there had come to be a general agreement as to the books which should be included, the books, or small groups of them, existed in separate MSS.

It is consequently possible that the original MS. from which the scribe of e.g. the Vatican MS. copied Ecclesiasticus may have been different from that from which he, or his earlier colleague, copied the Pentateuch. So that no inference lies from the accuracy or inaccuracy of the one text to the accuracy or inaccuracy of the other. Hence the MSS. of each book must be separately considered in relation to the book: and a general estimate, or working conception, of their value, and of their relation to each other, must be formed before the text of the book can be considered.

The following is an endeavour to show the way in which such an examination may be made upon the comparatively

neutral ground of grammatical forms and usages, i.e. upon
ground on which the scribe was not led to vary the reading by
a desire to harmonize, or to interpret, or to paraphrase it.

1. *Forms of Words.*

In 1. 3 : 18. 6 all MSS., without a variant, have a form of the
Hellenistic ἐξιχνιάζω : in 42. 18 they have, also without a variant, a
form of the Classical ἐξιχνεύω : in 6. 27 all MSS. except Codd. 253,
307 have a form of ἐξιχνεύω, but in 18. 4 Codd. 253, 307 agree with
Codd. ACS, 155, against Cod. B and the rest, in having a form of
ἐξιχνιάζω.

1. 6 : Codd. ACS, 23 have the classical form πανουργήματα, Codd.
B, cett. the Hellenistic πανουργεύματα : so also in 42. 18 Codd. AS¹,
307 πανουργήμασιν, Codd. B, cett. πανουργεύμασιν.

1. 27 : Codd. ACS, 55, 70, 106, 157, 254, 296, 307 πραΰτης :
Codd. B, (23), (155), (248), (253) πραότης. But in 3. 17 : 4. 8 :
10. 28 : 36. 28 all important MSS. read πραΰτης : and in 45. 4 Cod.
A reads πραότης, against the πραΰτης of all other MSS.

27. 13 : Codd. AS προσώχθισμα : Codd. BC προσόχθισμα.

40. 5 : Codd. AS, 106, 157, 253, 307 μήνιμα : Codd. 55, 155,
254 μῆνις : Cod. 308 μήνισμα : Cod. 248 μίμημα : Codd. BC μηνίαμα,
a word which is not elsewhere found.

2. *Inflexions.*

4. 3 : Codd. AS παρωργισμένην : Codd. BC παρoργισμένην.

8. 6 : Codd. AS, 23, 106, 157, 248 ἐν γήρᾳ : Codd. BC, cett. ἐν
γήρει.

14. 14 : Codd. AS, 55, 106, 155, 157, 248, 253, 254, 296 παρελ-
θέτω : Codd. BC, (23) παρελθάτω.

14. 18 : Codd. AS δένδρου δασέως : Codd. BC δένδρου δασέος.

15. 2 : Codd. AS, 55, 106, 155, 157, 248, ὑπαντήσει : Codd. BC,
(254), (296) ὑπαντήσεται : Codd. 23, 253 ἀπαντήσεται. The future
of ὑπαντάω in late Greek seems to have been ὑπαντήσομαι : Sext.
Emp. *adv. Phys.* 10. 60, p. 644, probably after the analogy of
ἀπαντάω. (But the future active of ἀπαντάω is found, without variant,
in Mark 14. 13).

15. 3 : Codd. ACS, 155, 157, 254, 296, 307 ποτίσει : Codd. B, (55),
(106), (248), (253) ποτιεῖ. So c. 24. 31.

15. 4 : Codd. ACS, 23 στηρισθήσεται: Codd. B, cett. στηριχθήσεται: but elsewhere in the book, viz. 24. 10: 29. 32: 42. 17, the form with χ is found without any important variant.

17. 27 : Codd. ACS, cett. ἐν ᾅδου: Cod. B ἐν ᾅδους: Cod. S¹ ἐν ᾅδη.

28. 26 : Codd. AS¹ ὀλισθῇς : Codd. BCS² ὀλισθήσῃς [S² -σις]. All the other aorist forms of the word in the book are, as usual in Hellenistic Greek, first aorist forms, viz. 3. 24: 9. 9: 14. 1: 25. 8, without important variant except Cod. C in 9. 9 ὀλισθῇς for ὀλισθήσῃς.

3. *Use of the paroemiastic future.*

3. 3 : Codd. ACS¹, 106, (157), 253, 254, 296, 397 ἐξιλάσκεται : Codd. B, 23. (55), (155), (248). (308) ἐξιλάσεται.

4. 13 : Codd. ACS, 23, 55, 106, 157, 248, 253, 254, 307 εὐλογεῖ : Cod. B εὐλογήσει.

4. 17 : Codd. ACS², 55, 157, 248, 254, 296 πορεύσεται : Codd. BS¹, (23), 70, 106, (155), (253), (308) πορεύεται.

11. 1 : Codd. ACS, 23, 55, 106, 155, (157), 248, 254, 307 ἀνυψώσει [307, ὑψώσει] : Codd. B, 296, 308 ἀνύψωσε.

12. 3 : Codd. AS, 23, 155, (157), 248, 253, 254 οὐκ ἔσται : Codd. BC, 55, (106), 296, (308) οὐκ ἔστι.

16. 25 : Codd. AS, 23, 55, 106, 157, 248, 253, 254 ἐκφανῶ : Codd. BC ἐκφαίνω.

19. 30 : Codd. ACS, 55, 106, 155, 157, 248, 253, 254 ἀναγγελεῖ : Cod. B ἀναγγέλλει.

4. *Omission or insertion of the Article.*

(a) *Instances of insertion in Cod. A and other MSS., and of omission in Cod. B :*

6. 23 : Codd. AS, 155, 157, 307 τὴν γνώμην μου : Codd. B cett. γνώμην μου.

7. 19 : Codd. AS, 23, 55, 106, 155, 157, 248, 296, 307 ἡ γὰρ χάρις αὐτῆς : Codd. B, 253, (254), (308) καὶ γὰρ χάρις.

7. 20 : Codd. AS, 55, 106, (157), 248, 253, 296, 307 διδόντα τὴν ψυχὴν αὐτοῦ : Codd. B, (23), (155), (308) διδόντα ψυχὴν αὐτοῦ.

10. 4 : Codd. AS, 23, 55, 106, 155, 157 ἡ ἐξουσία τῆς γῆς : Codd. BC, 248. (253), (254) ἐξουσία τῆς γῆς.

12. 2 : Codd. AS, 23, 55, 106, 155, 157, 248, 253, 254, 307 παρὰ τοῦ ὑψίστου : Codd. BC, (296) παρὰ ὑψίστου.

15. 5 : Codd. ACS, 55, 106, 157, 307, 308 τὸ στόμα : Codd. B (23), (155), (248), (253), (254) στόμα.

21. 20 : Codd. ACS, 55, 155, 157, 254, 308 τὴν φωνήν : Codd. B, (23), (106), (248) φωνήν.

46. 9 : Codd. ACS, 55, 106, 155, 248, 254 ἐπὶ τὸ ὕψος τῆς γῆς : Codd. B, (23), (157), (253) ἐπὶ ὕψος τῆς γῆς.

(β) *Instances of omission in Cod. A and others, and insertion in Cod. B :*

4. 28 : Codd. ACS, 55, 106, 155, 157, 248, 253, 254, 296, 307 ἕως θανάτου : Codd. B, 23, (308) ἕως τοῦ θανάτου.

7. 8 : Codd. AS, 23, 55, 106, 155, 157, 248, 253, 254, 307 ἐν γὰρ μιᾷ : Codd. BC ἐν γὰρ τῇ μιᾷ.

12. 5 : Codd. AS, 55, 106, 155, 157, 248, 253, 254, 296, 307 ταπεινῷ : Codd. BC, (23) τῷ ταπεινῷ.

12. 7 : Codd. AS, 248, 253, 307 ἁμαρτωλοῦ : Codd. BC, (23), (55), (106), (155), (157), (296) τοῦ ἁμαρτωλοῦ.

5. *Syntactical usages.*

4. 17 : Codd. B, (55), 157, (254), 296, (308) have δὲ *in apodosi*, φόβον δὲ καὶ δειλίαν ἐπάξει : Codd. ACS, 23, 106, 155, 248, 253, 307 omit δέ. This use of δὲ is so rare in Biblical Greek that it is more likely to have been added by Cod. B than omitted by the other MSS. : and it is noteworthy that in one of the two instances, both of which are disputed, of the same usage in the N. T., viz. 1 Pet. 4. 18, it is Cod. B which, against almost all other MSS., both uncial and cursive, inserts δὲ in the quotation from Prov. 11. 31.

9. 12 : Cod. A μὴ εὐδοκήσῃς εὐδοκίᾳ ἀσεβῶν : Codd. CS, 157, 248 ... εὐδοκίαις : Codd. B, (55), (155) ... ἐν εὐδοκίᾳ : Codd. 23, 106, 254, 296, 307. There is a similar variation elsewhere in the construction of εὐδοκεῖν : it is found with ἐν in 2 Kings 22. 20 ; 1 Chron. 29. 3 ; Ps. 43 (44). 3 ; 48 (49). 13 ; 67 (68). 16 ; 146 (147). 10 ; Hab. 2. 4 ; Mal. 2. 17 ; 1 Macc. 10. 47 : without ἐν in 1 Esdr. 4. 39 ; Sir. 18. 31 ; 1 Macc. 1. 43.

11. 7 : Codd. AS, 23, 55, 248, 254, 307 have πρὶν ἤ c. subj. followed in v. 8 by πρὶν c. infin., in both cases with a negative main sentence : in 18. 19 : 19. 17 : 23. 20 they have πρὶν ἤ c. infin. with

an affirmative main sentence. In 11. 7 Cod. B has πρὶν c. subj. followed in v. 8 by πρὶν ἢ c. infin. There are similar variations in the construction of πρὶν ἢ in the N. T.: (1) when used with the infinitive, there was a tendency to drop ἤ, which is found without variant only in Matt. 1. 18, Acts 7. 2, whereas it is omitted in Matt. 26. 34 by all good MSS. except L, in Matt. 26. 75 by all except A, in Mark 14. 30 by אD, and in Acts 2. 20 by אACD: (2) its use with the subjunctive tended to disappear, for in Luke 2. 26 Codd. א³L and others add ἂν to ἤ, Cod. B omits ἤ and inserts ἄν, and in Luke 22. 34 Codd. אBL substitute ἕως for πρὶν ἤ, which is read by A only of the greater uncials.

41. 2 : Codd. AS, 55, 155, (157), 307, 308 ἐλασσουμένῳ ἐν ἰσχύϊ: Codd. BC, (23), (106), (248), (253), (254) ἐλασσουμένῳ ἰσχύϊ.

44. 5 : Codd. AS, 55, 106, 155, (157), 248, 254, 296 κεχορηγη-μένοι ἐν ἰσχύϊ: Codd. B, 23, 253, 308 κεχορηγημένοι ἰσχύϊ.

45. 2 : Codd. AS ὡμοίωσεν αὐτὸν ἐν δόξῃ ἁγίων: Codd. BC cett. . . . δόξῃ ἁγίων.

45. 15 : Codd. A, 25, 106, 155, 157, 248, 254 ἐγενήθη αὐτῷ εἰς διαθήκην αἰώνιον καὶ τῷ σπέρματι αὐτοῦ ἐν ἡμέραις οὐρανοῦ : Codd. BC, cett. . . . καὶ ἐν τῷ σπέρματι αὐτοῦ . . .

46. 5 : Codd. AS, 155 ἐπήκουσεν αὐτῶν μέγας κύριος λίθοις χαλάζης: Codd. BC, cett. . . . ἐν λίθοις χαλάζης.

It will be noted that although, as is usually the case, no MS. is uniform in either its forms or its syntax, the Hellenistic forms and constructions preponderate in the Vatican Codex. It will also be noted that in almost all cases the majority of MSS. are against that Codex in these respects. The more difficult question remains undecided, whether the Hellenisms or the Classicalisms belong to the original text : in other words whether a Hellenistic text was purged of some of its Hellenisms by purist scribes with the view of rendering the work more acceptable to educated persons, or whether a Classical text was altered by Hellenistic scribes who substituted a more familiar for a less familiar form or phrase.

2. LATIN AND SYRIAC VERSIONS.

1. *The Latin Versions.* The old Latin version, which was left untouched by Jerome, has come down to us in the following MSS.

(1) The Toledo MS., the collation of which was first published by Bianchini in his *Vindiciae Biblicae*, Verona, 1748, from which work it was reprinted by Vallars in the Benedictine edition of St. Jerome, vol. x : (2) the Codex Amiatinus, the text of which is printed at length by Lagarde, *Mittheilungen*, p. 283 : (3) the MSS. collated by Sabatier, viz. two Corbey MSS., one St. Germain MS., and one MS. of St. Theodoric of Reims.

But it is probable that the large quotations from the book in St. Augustine's *Speculum* (last edited by Weihrich in the Vienna *Corpus Scriptorum Ecclesiasticorum*, vol. xiii) represent a more current form of the text than any of the above MSS.

2. *The Syriac Versions.* There are two Syriac versions, the Peschitta and the Syro-Hexaplar.

(*a*) The Peschitta, or current Syriac version, was first printed, with a Latin translation, in Walton's Polyglott, vol. iv : it has more recently been edited, with the help of six MSS. in the British Museum, by Lagarde (*Libri Veteris Testamenti Apocryphi Syriace*, 1861): the photographic reproduction of the oldest MS., that of the Ambrosian Library, has not yet been completed. (*b*) The Syro-Hexaplar version has been published for the first time, from an Ambrosian MS., in photographic facsimile by Ceriani in his *Monumenta sacra et profana*, vol. vii, Milan, 1874.

There are some parts of the book in which the Latin and Syriac differ so widely from both the Greek and one another as to force upon us the hypothesis that the original text underwent in very early times different recensions. But for the greater part of the book the Latin and the two forms of the Syriac clearly point, with whatever differences in detail, to the same original as the Greek. The relation of the Latin and the Syro-Hexaplar to the Greek is clearly one of derivation. The relation of the Peschitta to the Greek must be considered to be still *sub judice:* nor

can it be determined with any approach to scientific com-
pleteness until after the exact study of the Greek text itself,
to which the present essay is designed to be a contribution.

The question of this relation of the Peschitta to the Greek is
extremely complex. There are some passages in which the Syriac
appears either to be based on an earlier Greek text than that which
has come down to us, or to have been revised by reference to the
Hebrew. There are, on the other hand, passages in which both
the Greek and the Syriac have an unintelligible phrase which points
to a mistranslation of the same Hebrew original. For example, in
25. 15 the Greek οὐκ ἔστι κεφαλὴ ὑπὲρ κεφαλὴν ὄφεως, and the Syriac
equivalent 'No head is more bitter than the head of a serpent,'
point to a mistranslation of ראש, viz. 'head' for 'venom': but
there is nothing to determine whether the mistranslation is common
to the two versions, or was derived by one from the other. The
question of derivation will be positively determined by the examination of the passages, some of which are mentioned below, in which
an error which has grown up inside the Greek text, is copied by the
Syriac : for example, if it be true that in 5. 6 the Greek originally
read παρ' αὐτοῦ, with a verb such as ἐλεύσεται in place of ἔλεος, the
Syriac, which is a translation of παρ' αὐτῷ without an expressed
verb, must be presumed to be derived from a Greek text in which
παρ' αὐτῷ was read, and from which the verb had already disappeared.
So also, if it be true that in 25. 17 the reading ἄρκος is a mistake for
ἄρκυς, and that σάκκον (σάκκος) was a gloss upon ἄρκυς, even if it be
not an equivalent early reading, with the same signification, the Syriac
'sackcloth' can only be a misinterpretation of the Greek σάκκον.

But a more important question than that of the relation
of the Peschitta to the Greek is that of the contributions
which both the Latin and the Syriac make to the determination of the original text. It will be found that all
three versions are more or less corrupt, that they also have
a common tendency to paraphrase, and that in a large
proportion of passages each of them supplements the other.
The justification of this remark can of course only be found
in the examination of a considerable number of passages :
the two following are taken, almost at random, as examples :

(1) xx. 27, 28.

Cod. Amiat.	*Peschitta.*

ὁ σοφὸς ἐν λόγοις προάξει
ἑαυτὸν
καὶ ἄνθρωπος φρόνιμος
ἀρέσει μεγιστᾶσιν·
ὁ ἐργαζόμενος γῆν ἀνυ-
ψώσει θημωνίαν αὐτοῦ
καὶ ὁ ἀρέσκων μεγιστᾶσιν
ἐξιλάσεται ἁμαρτίαν

sapiens in verbis pro-
ducet seipsum
et homo prudens place-
bit magnatis:
qui operatur terram suam
exaltabit   acervum
fructuum
et qui operatur iustitiam
ipse exaltabitur:
qui vero placet magnatis
effugiet iniquitatem

He who is full of the
sayings of wisdom,
how shall he show
himself small?
And a wise servant shall
be lord over princes.

The first four lines of the Latin give two well-balanced couplets:

> A man who is clever in speech will advance himself,
> And a man of understanding will be pleasing to princes:

> He who works his land will raise a high heap of corn,
> And he who works justice will himself be raised.

The fifth line of the Latin,

> He who is pleasing to princes will escape injustice,

is out of harmony with the context, and is easily understood as a gloss upon the second line. But it is a translation of the fourth line of the Greek, where it is equally out of place. It seems probable that the fourth line of the Greek was originally a gloss upon the second line, that the original fourth line should be restored from the Latin fourth line, and that the Latin fifth line was added when the present fourth line of the Greek had superseded the original fourth line.

The Syriac seems to paraphrase the first couplet and to omit the second: its diminished paroemiastic force makes it difficult to take it as the original form.

(2) xxviii. 3-7.

S. Aug. *Spec.* p. 142.	*Peschitta.*
ἄνθρωπος ἀνθρώπῳ συντηρεῖ ὀργήν, καὶ παρὰ κυρίου ζητεῖ ἴασιν;	homo homini servat iram, et a Deo quaerit medellam?	A man who cherishes wrath against a man, How should he ask for healing from God?

ἐπ' ἄνθρωπον ὅμοιον αὐτῷ
οὐκ ἔχει ἔλεος,

in hominem similem sibi non habet misericordiam,

He who is himself a man is not willing to forgive,

καὶ περὶ τῶν ἁμαρτιῶν αὐτοῦ δεῖται;

et de peccatis suis deprecatur?

shall any one forgive that man's sins?

αὐτὸς σὰρξ ὢν διατηρεῖ μῆνιν
τίς ἐξιλάσεται τὰς ἁμαρτίας αὐτοῦ;

ipse dum caro sit servat iram,
et propitiationem petit a Deo?
quis exorabit pro delictis illius?

μνήσθητι τὰ ἔσχατα καὶ παῦσαι ἐχθραίνων,
καταφθορὰν καὶ θάνατον καὶ ἔμμενε ἐντολαῖς·

memento novissimorum et desine inimicari,
tabitudo enim et mors imminent in mandatis:

Remember death, and lay aside enmities,
the grave and destruction, and abstain from sinning:

μνήσθητι ἐντολῶν καὶ μὴ μηνίσῃς τῷ πλησίον

memorare timorem Dei et non irascaris proximo

Remember the commandment and hate not thy neighbour before God:

καὶ διαθήκην ὑψίστου καὶ πάριδε ἄγνοιαν.

memorare testamenti altissimi et despice ignorantiam proximi.

nay, give him that of which he is in want.

Each of the first three couplets of the passage in the Greek and Latin appears to express the same idea in a slightly altered form. But while the duplication of an idea is common, the triplication of it is so unusual as to suggest the hypothesis that one of the forms is a gloss. The hypothesis is supported by the fact that the sixth line of the Latin is clearly another form of the second, and that it is introduced out of place between the two lines of the third couplet, so that the six lines of the Greek are represented by seven lines in Latin. It is even more strongly supported by the fact that the third couplet is altogether omitted from the Peschitta.

In the fourth couplet of the Latin 'tabitudo enim et mors imminent' clearly show a corruption of 'imminent' for 'immane' = ἔμμενε, and a consequent corruption of the nominatives 'tabitudo' and 'mors' for the genitives 'tabitudinis' and 'mortis.'

The last line of the Syriac is also clearly corrupt. The exhortation of the Greek and Latin 'overlook the ignorance (transgression) of thy neighbour' is in entire harmony with the drift of the passage: the exhortation to almsgiving is a commonplace which gives no suitable antithesis to the preceding half of the couplet.

The whole passage consists, in other words, of two quatrains which are best represented by the first two and the last two couplets of the Greek text: but the third couplet of the Greek text is an intrusive gloss.

3. EXAMINATION OF SOME IMPORTANT INSTANCES OF VARIATION.

I now proceed from the short survey of the materials to the examination of some passages in which the variants are important, and in which the text can only be determined by the help of whatever critical aids we possess.

i. 13.

Codd. ACS, 23, 70, 155, 157, 248, 253, 296, 307, Vienna 1 ἐν ἡμέρᾳ τελευτῆς αὐτοῦ εὐλογηθήσεται: Codd. B, (55), (106), (308), (254), Vienna 2 . . . εὐρήσει χάριν.

Latin: 'in die defunctionis suae benedicetur.'

Syriac: *Pesch.* 'in the end of his days he shall be blessed.'

It seems clear that εὐλογηθήσεται is the correct reading: the diplomatic evidence against εὐρήσει χάριν is supported by the fact that that phrase does not appear to be used absolutely in the LXX., but always with the addition ἐν ὀφθαλμοῖς (ἔναντι, ἐνώπιον) αὐτοῦ (κυρίου), e.g. *infra*, iii. 18.

i. 23.

Codd. ACS¹, 23, 157, 253, Vienna 1 ὕστερον αὐτῷ ἀναδώσει εὐφροσύνην: Codd. B, (55), 106, 155, (248), (254), 296, (308), Vienna 2
.... εὐφροσύνη: Cod. 70 ἀναδώσει εἰς εὐφροσύνην.

Latin: 'et postea redditio jucunditatis.'

Neither εὐφροσύνη nor εὐφροσύνην seems to be grammatically
possible: the former because it involves a neuter sense for ἀναδώσει,
the latter because ἀναδώσει has no subject. The Latin suggests
the conjecture that the original reading was ἀνάδοσις εὐφροσύνης:
the substitution of ἀνάδωσις for ἀνάδοσις by an early scribe would be
a not uncommon change, and would sufficiently account for the
variants.

iii. 10.

Codd. ABCS, 106, 157, 254, 296, 308, Vienna 1 οὐ γάρ ἐστί σοι
δόξα πρὸς ἀτιμίαν: Cod. 253 .... δόξα ὡς ἀτιμία: Cod. 155
.... δόξα ἀτιμίαν: Vienna 2 πρς ἀτιμία.

Codd. (23), (55), (248) .... δόξα πατρὸς ἀτιμία.

Latin: 'non enim est tibi [Cod. Am. omits] gloria sed confusio.'
Syriac: Pesch. 'for it will not be a glory to thee: Syr.-Hex. 'for
it will not be an honour as a disgrace to thee': (the subject 'the
shame of thy father,' is continued from the preceding clause).

The difficulties in the way of accepting πατρὸς ἀτιμία as the original reading are mainly (1) the difficulty of accounting for the
corruption of so simple and obvious a phrase into πρὸς ἀτιμίαν in
the majority of MSS., (2) the absence of an equivalent phrase in
both the Latin and the Syriac. If πρὸς ἀτιμίαν were the reading of
only a small group of MSS., it might have been supposed that
some one scribe had written πατρὸς in the contracted form πρς, and
that the copyists of this MS., mistaking the contraction, had adapted
ἀτιμία to the supposed preposition. But this hypothesis hardly accounts for the facts (1) that πρὸς ἀτιμίαν is read by MSS. of such
different character as those enumerated above, (2) that the Syro-
Hexaplar supports the reading ὡς ἀτιμία of Cod. 253.

iii. 26.

Codd. ACS, 23, 55, 106, 155, 157, 248, 253, 254, 296, 307,
Vienna 1 ὁ ἀγαπῶν κίνδυνον ἐν αὐτῷ ἀπολεῖται: Codd. B, (308)
.... ἐν αὐτῷ ἐμπεσεῖται.

Latin: 'qui amat periculum in illo [Cod. Tolet. 'ipso'] peribit.'

It may be noted that although B probably stands alone, the quotation in S. Aug. *de civit. Dei* i. 27 'qui amat periculum *incidit* in illud' shows that it preserves an ancient variant.

iv. 11.

Codd. ACS, 23, 55, 157, 248, 253, 296, 307 ἡ σοφία υἱοὺς αὐτῆς [55, 157, 248, 296 ἑαυτῆς] ἀνύψωσε: Codd. B, 155, (254), (308) . . . . υἱοὺς ἑαυτῇ ἀνύψωσεν: Cod. 106 αὐτῇ υἱοὺς ὕψωσε.

Latin: the MSS. agree in reading 'sapientia filiis suis vitam :' they differ in regard to the verb, Cod. Tolet. 'inspirabit,' Cod. Amiat. 'spirat,' Cod. S. Germ. 'inspiravit,' Codd. cett. 'inspirat.'

The Latin seems to show that the Greek verb was originally ἐψύχωσε or ἐνεψύχωσε: and this hypothesis is confirmed by what appears to be a reference to this passage in Clem.-Alex. *Strom.* 7. 16, p. 896 ἡ σοφία, φησὶν ὁ Σολομών, ἐνεφυσίωσε [ἐνεφύσησε? cp. supra, p. 148] τὰ ἑαυτῆς τέκνα.

iv. 15.

Codd. ACS, 23, 55, 106, 155, 157, 248, 253, 296, 307, Vienna 2 ὁ προσέχων αὐτῇ κατασκηνώσει πεποιθώς: Codd. B, (254), (308) ὁ προσελθών. . . . .

Latin: 'qui intuetur illam permanebit [Cod. Amiat. 'permanet'] confidens.'

There is a similar variation of readings in 1 Tim. 6. 3, where Cod. S¹ reads καὶ μὴ προσέχεται ὑγιαίνουσιν λόγοις, which is supported by the uniform translation of the Latin 'acquiescit, (-cet)' whereas all the other Greek MSS. read προσέρχεται.

v. 6.

Codd. ACS, 55, 106, 155, 253, 254, 296, 307, Vienna 2 ἔλεος γὰρ καὶ ὀργὴ παρ' αὐτῷ: Codd. B, 23, (308) . . . . παρ' αὐτοῦ: Codd. 157, 248 . . . . παρ' αὐτῷ ταχυνεῖ.

Latin: 'misericordia enim et ira ab illo cito proximat' [so Codd. Tolet. Amiat.: Codd. cett. 'proximant.']

Syriac: *Pesch.* 'for mercy and wrath are with him.'

The Latin confirms the reading of Codd. 157, 248 in respect of ταχυνεῖ, but suggests that παρ' αὐτοῦ was read rather than παρ' αὐτῷ. The Syriac on the other hand is in harmony with the majority of Greek MSS. The absence of a verb would be out of harmony with the verses which precede and follow : whereas the introduction of ταχυνεῖ makes the verse closely parallel to v. 7 ὅ ἐξάπινα γὰρ ἐξε-λεύσεται ὀργὴ κυρίου.

The exegetical difficulty of the verse lies in ἔλεος : for the whole of v. 6 δ seems to be an answer to the sinner's plea 'His compassion is great, he will make propitiation for the multitude of my sins :' and it is conceivable that the corruption of the text is greater than either the MSS. or the versions show. The exegesis seems to point to an original reading [ἐξ]ελεύσεται γὰρ ὀργὴ παρ' αὐτοῦ 'for wrath shall come forth from him, and his anger shall abide upon sinners.' The next verse, assuming that the sinner will accept this assurance, and repent, urges him to do so speedily : on the ground that not only will wrath come forth but that it will do so speedily : hence ἐξάπινα ἐξελεύσεται would be not a repetition but a natural expansion of the supposed ἐξελεύσεται in v. 6 δ.

The clause ἔλεος γὰρ καὶ ὀργὴ παρ' αὐτοῦ is found also in 16. 12 where the mention of mercy as well as wrath is quite appropriate, and is amplified in the following clause δυνάστης ἐξιλασμῶν καὶ ἐκχέων ὀργήν.

vii. 18.

Codd. AS, 23, 155, 157, Vienna 1 μὴ ἀλλάξῃς φίλον ἀδιαφόρου : Codd. BC, (55), (253), (254), 296, 308, Vienna 2 μὴ ἀλλάξῃς φίλον ἕνεκεν (εἵνεκεν) ἀδιαφόρου : Cod. 106 μὴ ἀλλάξῃς φίλον ἀδιαφόρου κατὰ μηδέν : Cod. 248 μὴ ἀλλάξῃς φίλον ἀδιαφόρου μηδὲ ἕν : Cod. 307 μὴ ἐλέγξῃς φίλον ἕνεκεν ἀδιαφόρου.

Latin : Codd. Am., S. Theod. 'Noli praevaricari [Cod. Am. -re] in amicum pecunia differenti :' ('praevaricari in . . . .'=παρα-βαίνειν, e.g. Is. 66. 24 'qui praevaricati sunt in me :' cf. Rom. 4. 15 'ubi enim non est lex nec praevaricatio.')

Syriac : Pesch. 'Barter not a friend for money.'

It must be gathered both from the Latin and the Syriac that the word in the genitive, whether ἀδιαφόρου or another word, was taken to mean 'money' : but (1) διάφορον, not ἀδιάφορον, is the Hellenistic word which has this sense : e.g. Corpus Inscr. Graec. 2347 c, 56 τὸ ἀποτεταγμένον εἰς τὸν στέφανον ἐκ τοῦ νόμου διάφορον 'the money assigned for the crown in accordance with the law :' 2 Macc. 1. 35 πολλὰ διάφορα ἐλάμβανε καὶ μετεδίδου 'he took and distributed many sums of money :' (2) the Latin 'differenti' points to a reading διαφόρου in the text which the Latin translator used : the addition

'pecunia' may be regarded as having been added either by the
translator to define the uncertain meaning of ' differenti,' or as a
gloss at a subsequent time.

The original text of the LXX. was thus, in all probability, μὴ
ἀλλάξῃς φίλον διαφόρου : the other readings are attempts to explain
ἀδιαφόρου, as is most clearly seen in Cod. 307, which changes the
meaning to ' Do not rebuke a friend for a trifling cause.'

x. 17.

Codd. ACS, 23, 106, 155, (157), 248, 254, 296, 307 ἐξῆρεν
αὐτοὺς [C, αὐτάς, S¹, 23, 296, ἐξ αὐτῶν] καὶ ἀπώλεσεν αὐτούς
[C, αὐτάς] : Codd. B, (308) ἐξήρανεν ἐξ αὐτῶν : Cod. 55 ἐξήρανεν αὐτούς.

Latin : ' arefecit ex ipsis et disperdidit illos [eos].'

Syriac : *Pesch.* ' he destroyed them, and overthrew them.'

The reading ἐξήρανεν is supported by the Latin : but it has (1)
the exegetical difficulty that it would be a mild word inserted
among strong ones, (2) the critical difficulty that it does not account for the reading ἐξ αὐτῶν, with which it is incompatible. On
the other hand ἐξῆρεν, which is always elsewhere in the Apocryphal
books constructed with an accusative followed by ἐξ, e.g. 1 Macc.
12. 53 : 14. 7, 36, not only gives a congruous meaning, but also
accounts for both αὐτοὺς and ἐξ αὐτῶν. It may be conjectured that
the latter phrase was in the original text ἐξ ἀνθρώπων [i.e. ΕΞΑΥΤΩΝ
=ΕΞΑΝΩΝ] : the words ' he put them away from among men and
destroyed them ' would thus find a natural balance in the following
clause, ' he caused their memorial to cease from off the earth.'

x. 27.

Codd. A, 106, 157, 296, Vienna 1 κρείσσων ἐργαζόμενος καὶ περισσεύων [157, -εὗον] ἐν πᾶσιν ἢ περιπατῶν δοξαζόμενος καὶ ὑστερῶν
[106, 296, Vienna 1 ἀπορῶν] ἄρτων [106, Vienna 1 ἄρτου].

Cod. B κρείσσων ἐργαζόμενος ἐν πᾶσιν ἢ περιπατῶν ἢ δοξαζόμενος καὶ
ἀπορῶν ἄρτων.

Cod. 155 κρείσσων ἐργαζόμενος ἐν πᾶσιν ἢ περιπατῶν δοξαζόμενος καὶ
ἀπορῶν ἄρτου.

Cod. S κρείσσων ἐργαζόμενος ἢ [S² omits ἢ and adds ἐν πᾶσιν] καὶ
περισσεύων ἐν πᾶσιν [S² omits ἐν π.] ἢ περιπατῶν δοξαζόμενος καὶ
ἀπορῶν ἄρτων.

Codd. ·3, 248 κρείσσων γὰρ ὁ ἐργαζόμενος καὶ περισσεύων ἐν πᾶσιν ἢ
ὁ δοξαζόμενος καὶ ἀπορῶν ἄρτου.

Codd. 55, 254, Vienna 2 κρείσσων ἐργαζόμενος ἐν πόνοις ἢ περιπατῶν
δοξαζόμενος καὶ ἀπορῶν ἄρτων.

Cod. 307 κρείσσον ἐργαζόμενος ἐν πᾶσιν ἢ περιπατῶν ἐργαζόμενος καὶ
ἀπορῶν ἄρτων.

Latin : ' melior est qui operatur et abundat in omnibus quam qui
gloriatur et eget pane.'

Syriac : *Pesch.* : ' better is one who works and abounds in riches,
than one who boasts and wants food.'

The Latin and Syriac show that Codd. 23, 248 have preserved
the original text. The variants from that text may probably be
accounted for thus :—the earliest variant may have been that wh.ch
is found in Cod. A, and which added περιπατῶν as a gloss to δοξοζό-
μενος : a later scribe finding ἢ περιπατῶν in some copies took it to
be a correction for καὶ περισσεύων, and omitted the latter [hence
Cod. B], and since ἐν πᾶσιν was difficult to explain after ἐργαζόμενος
it was altered to ἐν πόνοις [so Cod. 55] : a later scribe restored καὶ
περισσεύων but retained the ἢ [so Cod. S¹] which was further corrected by omitting the ἢ, and placing the restored καὶ περισσεύων
after instead of before ἐν πᾶσιν [so Cod. S²].

xi. 9.

Codd. ACS, 23, 248, 296, 307, Vienna 1 περὶ πράγματος οὗ οὐκ
ἔστι σοι μὴ ἔριζε : Codd. B, (55), (106), 155, (157), (254), (308),
Vienna 2 . . . . οὗ οὐκ ἔστι σοι χρεία. . . . .

Latin : ' de ea re quae te non molestat ne certeris :' [but the
original scribe of Cod. Tolet. omitted ' re.']

Syriac : *Pesch.* ' if it be in thy power do not contend :' *Syr.-Hex.*
' about a matter which is not a trouble to thee do not contend.'

It seems probable that the MSS. from which χρεία is absent preserve the original reading, and that οὗ is to be explained as an ordinary instance of inverse attraction. If ἐρίζειν be used here in its
sense of a legal contest, the meaning will be ' contend not (at law)
about a matter which is not thine.'

xii. 12.

The following is the text of Cod. A :—μὴ στήσῃς αὐτὸν παρὰ σεαυτῷ
μὴ ἀναστρέψας σε στῇ ἐπὶ τὸν τόπον σου· μὴ καθίσῃς αὐτὸν ἐκ δεξιῶν
σου μήποτε ζητήσῃ τὴν καθέδραν σου.

The variants on this text are Codd. B, 23, 106, 155, 308 παρὰ
σεαυτόν : Cod. 106 omits μὴ ἀναστρέψας . . . . τόπον σου : Codd.
BC, 55, 253, (254), 296, (307) ἀνατρέψας : Cod. 23, 248
καταστρέψας (248 μή ποτε κ.) : Cod. 155 εστη=σε στῇ : Cod.
253 ἵνα μὴ ἀνατρέψας εἰς τὸν τόπον σου στῇ : Codd. 296, 308 ἐπὶ
τοῦ τόπου σου : Codd. 106, 248 add λαβεῖν after καθέδραν σου.

Latin : (see below).

Syriac : *Pesch.* ' set him not near thee,
            lest, turning round, he stand in thy place :
            set him not at thy right hand,
            lest he desire to take thy seat.'

It is obvious that the two pairs of phrases are in effect duplicates
of each other : but it is not clear whether or not the duplication
be intended by the writer. The Greek of all MSS. except Cod.
106, and also the Syriac, would be quite intelligible on the hypothesis of an intentional duplication : and some analogies could be
found for it elsewhere in the book.

But the Latin suggests the hypothesis that one of the two pairs
of phrases is a gloss of the other, since it arranges them in the
order in which they would occur if a gloss had been incorporated
into the text.

The earliest text is probably that of S. August. *Speculum*, p. 130,
which agrees with Codd. Amiat., S. Germ., S. Theod. : (the supposed glosses are here printed in italics) :

' non statuat illum penes te
nec sedeat ad dexteram tuam
ne conversus stet in loco tuo
ne forte conversus in locum tuum inquirat cathedram tuam.'

The Toledo MS. has—

' non statuas illum penes te *in loco tuo*
nec sedeat ad dexteram tuam
ne forte conversus in locum tuum inquirat cathedram tuam.'

The later MSS. and the Vulgate are based upon this, and
have—

' non statuas illum penes te in loco tuo
nec sedeat ad dexteram tuam
ne forte conversus in locum tuum inquirat cathedram tuam.'

If the words printed in italics be omitted from the oldest of these texts, the remainder will suggest that the original Greek text was—

μὴ στήσῃς αὐτὸν παρὰ σεαυτῷ
μὴ ἀνατρέψας σε στῇ ἐπὶ τὸν τόπον σου.

The only important variants in the Greek are ἀναστρέψας and ἀνατρέψας: the uniform translation 'conversus' in all the Latin MSS. indicates that the former is the older reading. It may be supposed that the common use of the verb in the LXX. as a neuter was unknown to some of the Greek scribes, and that (1) they added σε to it, (2) substituted ἀνατρέψας for it : the interchange of ἀναστρέφω ἀνατρέπω is not infrequent : there is an instance of it below, v. 16, where Codd. S, 22, read ἀναστρέψαι, Codd. AB, ἀνατρέψαι.

xiv. 20.

Codd. S², 106, 248, 253 μακάριος ἀνὴρ ὃς ἐν σοφίᾳ μελετήσει καλά [S² omits καλά] : Codd. AB, (23), (55), 155, 157, (254), (296), 308, Vienna 1 τελευτήσει : Cod. 307 τελευτᾷ.

Latin : S. August. *Speculum*, p. 468 'Felix sapiens qui in sapientia sua veritatem et justitiam meditatur :' *Cod. Amiat.* ' beatus vir qui in sapientia sua morietur et qui in justitia sua meditatur :' Codd. cett. and Vulg. ' beatus vir qui in sapientia morabitur et qui in justitia sua meditabitur.'

Syriac : *Pesch.* 'Blessed is the man who thinks upon wisdom, and meditates upon understanding :' *Syr.-Hex.* 'Blessedness is for the man who in wisdom meditates well.'

The original reading was clearly μελετήσει = ' meditabitur :' the Latin duplicates ' morietur' ' meditabitur' show the combination of two Greek texts, and the antiquity of both of them : the later ' morabitur' is possibly an emendation of ' morietur.'

xv. 6.

Codd. AS¹, 106, 248—

εὐφροσύνην καὶ στέφανον ἀγαλλιάματος εὑρήσει,
καὶ ὄνομα αἰῶνος [106, Vienna 1, αἰώνιον] κατακληρονομήσει [106, Vienna 1, κληρονομήσει, 248 adds αὐτόν]

Codd. BC, (23), (55), 155, 157, 253, (254), 296, 307, 308—

εὐφροσύνην καὶ στέφανον ἀγαλλιάματος [155, 307 ἀγαλλιάσεως] καὶ ὄνομα αἰώνιον [23, 155, 157, 253 αἰῶνος] κατακληρονομήσει.

Latin : 'jucunditatem et exultationem thesaurizabit super illum, et nomine aeterno hereditabit illum.'

Syriac: *Pesch.* 'With joy and gladness will he fill him, and he will cause him to possess an everlasting name.'

The difficulty as to εὑρήσει is that the preceding verses seem to require the subject κύριος to be continued: hence most Greek MSS. omitted εὑρήσει.

The key to the original text is supplied by the Latin 'thesaurizabit:' the original text may be supposed to have been (reading ἀγαλλιάσεως with Codd. 155, 307)—

ΑΓΑΛΛΙΑϹΕωϹΘΗϹΑΥΡΙϹΕΙ, i.e. ἀγαλλιάσεως θησαυρίσει: but a careless scribe passed from one Ϲ to another and wrote ΑΓΑΛΛΙΑϹΕωϹΑΥΡΙϹΕΙ, i.e. αγαλλιασεως αυρισει: and since αυ was a not uncommon error for ευ, and ι for η, the word αυρισει which followed αγαλλιασεως was interpreted as εὑρήσει.

xvi. 3.

Codd. AS, 23, 155, (157), 248, 253, 254, 296 μὴ ἔπεχε ἐπὶ τὸ πλῆθος αὐτῶν: Codd. BC, 308 .... ἐπὶ τὸν τόπον αὐτῶν: Codd. 106, 307 omit the clause.

The Latin 'ne respexeris in labores eorum' points to a reading κόπον or πόνον: but the context makes τὸ πλῆθος almost certain, since the following clause is κρείσσων γὰρ εἷς ἢ χίλιοι.

xvi. 17.

Codd. AS, 23, 106, 155, 157, 248, 253, 307 μὴ εἴπῃς ὅτι [248 omits], ἀπὸ κυρίου ἀποκρυβήσομαι, καὶ ἐξ ὕψους [S¹ ὑψίστου] τίς μου μνησθήσεται; Codd. BC, 55, (254), 296, (308) μὴ ἐξ ὕψους ....
Latin: 'non dicas a deo [*Cod. Tolet.* 'ab eo'] abscondar, et ex summo quis mei memorabitur?'
Syriac: *Pesch.* 'Say not, I shall be hidden from the sight of the Lord, and in the height of heaven who will remember me?'
The Latin and Syriac confirm the reading of Codd. AS.

xvi. 18.

Codd. AS, 23, 155, 157, 253, 254, 296, 307, Vienna 1
ἰδοὺ ὁ [155 omits ὁ] οὐρανὸς καὶ ὁ οὐρανὸς τοῦ οὐρανοῦ
ἄβυσσος καὶ γῆ [S, 296 ἡ γῆ] ἐν τῇ ἐπισκοπῇ αὐτοῦ σαλευθήσονται
[23, 253 σαλεύονται, 155 σαλευθήσεται]
Codd. B, (55), (308)—
ἰδοὺ ὁ οὐρανὸς καὶ ὁ οὐρανὸς τοῦ οὐρανοῦ τοῦ θεοῦ,
ἄβυσσος καὶ γῆ σαλευθήσονται ἐν τῇ ἐπισκοπῇ αὐτοῦ.

Cod. 106—

ἰδοὺ ὁ οὐρανὸς τοῦ οὐρανοῦ
ἄβυσσος καὶ γῆ καὶ τὰ ἐν αὐτοῖς ἐν τῇ ἐπισκοπῇ αὐτοῦ σαλευθήσονται.

So Cod. 248, except that καὶ ὁ οὐρανὸς is retained.

Latin : 'Ecce caelum et caeli caelorum, abyssus et universa terra, et quae in eis sunt in conspectu illius commovebuntur' [in Cod. Tolet. 'commovebuntur' is added by a later hand].

Syriac : Pesch. 'Behold the heaven and the heaven of heavens, the deep, and the earth, stand by his manifestation upon them :' Syr.-Hex. '.... are trembling at his visitation of them.'

It is probable that τοῦ θεοῦ has come into the Greek text as an alternative translation of an original Hebrew אל, as in Is. 14. 13. But the insertion seems to make τοῦ θεοῦ a predicate, 'the heaven and the heaven of heaven is God's:' which destroys the parallelism with the following verse.

xvii. 27.

Codd. ACS, 106, 155, 157, 248, 296, 307 ἀντὶ ζώντων καὶ διδόντων ἀνθομολόγησιν : Codd. B, (23), (55), (253), (254), (308) ἀντὶ ζώντων καὶ ζώντων καὶ διδόντων ἀνθομολόγησιν. Latin : 'cum - vivis et dantibus confessionem Deo.'

It is only an inference from the silence of the collators to suppose that any MS. supports B in the addition καὶ ζώντων : the addition is most like only the error of a scribe who wrote the words for καὶ διδόντων, and afterwise corrected them. But the fact of the words occurring, if they do occur, in other MSS. would be an important contribution to the genealogy of those MSS.

xviii. 32.

Codd. ACS, 155, 157, 248, 254—

μὴ εὐφραίνου ἐπὶ πολλῇ τρυφῇ [248 adds σου]
μὴ [Codd. C, (157), 248, 254, Vienna I, μηδέ, Cod. 155 καὶ μηδέ] προσδεηθῇς συμβολῇ [248 συμβουλῆς, Vienna I συμβουλῇ] αὐτῆς.

Cod. B, (55), (253), 307 μηδὲ [307 μὴ] προσδεθῇς.
Cod. 106 μηδὲ συνδεθῇς . . . .
Cod. 23 καὶ εὐφραίνου . . . . καὶ προσδεθῇς.
Latin : Codd. Am. Corb.
            'ne oblecteris in turbis nec inmodicis,
            ad duas est enim commissio illorum :'

Cod. Tol.

'ne oblecteris in turbis nec inmodicis delecteris,
ad duas est enim commissio illorum:'

S. August. *Specul.* 134–5

'ne oblecteris in turbis
nec inmodicis delecteris:'

Codd. cett., and Vulg.

'ne oblecteris in turbis nec inmodicis:
assidua enim est commissio eorum.'

Syriac: *Pesch.* 'Delight not in a multitude of delights, lest at
length thou become poor:' *Syr.-Hex.* 'Delight not in a multitude of delights, and do not tie thyself to a portion of them.'

The Latin 'commissio' (probably = 'comissatio,' for which
'comissa' is found, cf. Ducange *s. v.*) points to συμβολή having been
in the nominative case in the text which it translated. *Assidua* also
points to the possibility of the difficult variants προσδεθῆς, προσδεηθῆς
being the representatives of a lost adjective. But there is no apparent
clue to the original reading.

xix. 22.

Codd. ACS[1], 106, 155, (157), 254, 308 καὶ οὐκ ἔστι βουλὴ ἀμαρ-
τωλῶν φρόνησις: Codd. B, (23), (55), (248), (253), (296) καὶ
οὐκ ἔστιν ὅπου βουλὴ ἁμαρτωλῶν φρόνησις.

Latin: 'et non est cogitatus peccatorum prudentia.'

The use of the classical οὐκ ἔστιν ὅπου (= οὐδαμοῦ) in Cod. B,
which is possibly not supported by any other MS., is improbable.

xxi. 17.

Codd. ACS, 23, 155, 157, 253, 254 στόμα φρονίμου ζητηθήσεται ἐν
ἐκκλησίᾳ, καὶ τοὺς λόγους αὐτοῦ διανοηθήσονται ἐν καρδίᾳ: Cod. B,
(106), (248), (296) . . . διανοηθήσεται. Latin: 'verba ejus
cogitabunt in cordibus suis.'

The singular διανοηθήσεται is unintelligible on account of the
accusative τοὺς λόγους: the subject of the plural διανοηθήσονται is
clearly implied in the preceding clause.

xxii. 27.

Codd. AS, 155, 296, 308 ἐπὶ τῶν χειλέων μου σφραγῖδα πανούργων:
Codd. BC, (23), (55), (106), 157, (248), (253), (254) . . . .
πανοῦργον.

Latin: 'super labia mea signaculum certum.'

It is probable .that πανοῦργον is correct: it is found in a good sense elsewhere in the book, = 'clever,' e. g. 6. 32 : but a doubt arises from the fact that it is always used in the LXX. of persons and not of things: hence possibly here σφρ. πανούργων = 'a seal of clever men,' i. e. cunningly devised: cf. βουλὰς πανούργων Job 5. 12.

xxiii. 10.

Codd. AS, 55, 157, 254 ὁ ὀμνύων καὶ [Codd. AS καὶ ὁ] ὀνομάζων διὰ παντὸς τὸ ὄνομα κυρίου ἀπὸ ἁμαρτίας οὐ μὴ καθαρισθῇ : Codd. BC, 23, (106), 155, (248), (253) omit τὸ ὄνομα κυρίου.

Latin : ' omnis jurans et nominans in toto a peccato non purgabitur.'

Syriac: *Pesch.* ' Whoever swears on any (slight) occasion, it is an abominable thing, nor will he be guiltless:' *Syr.-Hex.* 'He who swears, and names Him, on any (slight) occasion will not be guiltless.'

The antithetical clause οἰκέτης ἐξεταζόμενος seems to require a single participle here : and the variants are best explained by the hypothesis that ὁ ὀνομάζων τὸ ὄνομα κυρίου was added in early times as a gloss of ὁ ὀμνύων : the phrase apparently comes from Lev. 24. 16, and the separation of it into two parts by the insertion of διὰ παντὸς probably accounts for the loss of the words τὸ ὄνομα κυρίου in most MSS., including those from which the Latin translation was made.

xxiv. 17.

Codd. AS, 23, 55, 106, 155, (157), 248, 253, 254, 296 ἐγὼ ὡς ἄμπελος ἐβλάστησα χάριν (248 εὐωδίαν): Codd. BC, (308) βλαστήσασα.

Latin: 'ego quasi vitis fructificavi suavitatem [*Cod. Amiat.* 'in suavitate '] odoris.'

Syriac: *Pesch., Syr.-Hex.* 'I am like unto a vine of fairest beauty.'

The Latin is remarkable as supporting not only Codd. AS, cett. against BC, but also the reading εὐωδίαν of Cod. 248 against all the other MSS.

xxv. 15.

Codd. A, Vienna 2 συνοικῆσαι [Cod. A συνοίκησε] λέοντι καὶ δράκοντι εὐδόκησε, ἢ συνοικῆσαι μετὰ γυναικὸς πονηρᾶς : Codd. BCS¹, 253 συνοικῆσαι λέοντι καὶ δράκοντι [253 δράκοντι καὶ λέοντι] εὐδοκήσω ἢ ἐνοικῆσαι μετὰ γυναικὸς πονηρᾶς : Codd. S², 23, 55, 155, 296,

Vienna 1 . . . *εὐδοκῆσαι ἢ συνοικῆσαι* . . .: Codd. 106, 254 . . .
εὐδοκῆσαι ἢ οἰκῆσαι . . .: Cod. 248 . . . *εὐδοκῶ ἢ συνοικῆσαι*: Vienna
2 . . . *εὐδόκησε ἢ συνοικῆσαι* . . .

Latin: 'commorari leoni et draconi placebit quam habitare cum
muliere nequam.'

Syriac: *Syr.-Hex.* 'I prefer to live with a serpent and with a lion,
than to dwell in the house with a wicked woman.'

The Syriac supports the personal *εὐδοκήσω* or *εὐδοκῶ* against the
impersonal *εὐδόκησε*, and the Latin supports the future *εὐδοκήσω*
against the present *εὐδοκῶ*. It seems probable that the reading
εὐδοκῆσαι has arisen from the influence of the following *ἐνοικῆσαι*, and
that the impersonal *εὐδόκησε* of Cod. A is only a scribe's error for
εὐδοκῆσαι. It is probable that *ἐνοικῆσαι* is correct rather than *συνοικῆσαι*
in the second clause, because the meaning of the former 'to live in
the house' is more suitable to the passage than the meaning of the
latter, which in relation to a woman is almost always 'to cohabit.'

XXV. 17.

Codd. AS, 23, 55, 106, 155, 157, 248, 253, 254, 296, Vienna 1, 2
(*πονηρία γυναικὸς*) *σκοτοῖ τὸ πρόσωπον* [254, 308 *τὴν ὅρασιν*] *αὐτῆς
ὡς ἄρκος*: Codd. BC, (308) . . . . *ὡς σάκκον*.

Latin: 'obcaecat [obcaecavit, obcaecabit] vultum suum tanquam
ursus, et quasi saccum ostendit.'

Syriac: *Pesch., Syr.-Hex.* 'it makes her face dark as the colour
of sackcloth.'

The Latin shows the antiquity of both the Greek readings,
ἄρκος and *σάκκον*.

ἄρκος (=*ἄρκτος*) is unintelligible: it can hardly be doubted that
the original reading was *ἄρκυς* in the sense of a net for the hair: so
Hesychius *ἄρκυς· γυναικεῖον κεκρύφαλον*. For headdresses of this
kind, see Baumeister, *Denkmäler des klassischen Altertums*, fig. 81
(a Pompeian wall-picture, from *Mus. Borbon.* vi. 18) and fig. 392
(a Herculanean picture from *Antic. di Ercol.* i. 79).

σάκκον has probably the same sense as *ἄρκυς*: it was a cloth
like that of the terra-cotta which is pictured in Baumeister, fig. 850
(from Stackelberg's *Gräber der Hellenen*). The neuter form of the
word does not occur elsewhere.

It may be conjectured that each of the two words *ἄρκυς* and *σάκκον*
(*σάκκος*) had a local or restricted use, and the one was substituted

for the other by the scribe of a different locality. The Latin translator, finding the corrupt reading ἄρκος translated it 'ursus,' and not understanding σάκκον, but taking it for an accusative, constructed the new clause 'et quasi saccum ostendit.'

The meaning of the passage, whether ἄρκυς or σάκκον be read, is 'the wickedness of a woman changes her appearance, and darkens her countenance as when a wimple is drawn over it.'

XXV. 21.

Codd. AS, 106, 155, (157), 308 γυναῖκα ἐν κάλλει μὴ ἐπιποθήσῃς:
Codd. 55, 254, 296 γυναῖκα ἐν κάλλει μὴ ἐπιθυμήσῃς: Codd. BC,
(23), (253) γυναῖκα μὴ ἐπιποθήσῃς: Cod. 248 γυναῖκα μὴ ἐπιποθήσῃς
εἰς τρυφήν.

Latin: 'non concupiscas mulierem in specie.'

The first clause of the verse, μὴ προσπέσῃς ἐπὶ κάλλος γυναικός, is inadequately balanced by the reading of Codd. BC, and although the reading of the majority of MSS. ἐν κάλλει is supported by the Latin, 'in specie,' yet it is too nearly a repetition of ἐπὶ κάλλος to be quite satisfactory. Hence there is a probability that the true reading is preserved in Cod. 248 εἰς τρυφήν, in the sense of the Latin 'luxuria.'

XXV. 25.

Codd. AS, 23, 106, 155, (157), 253, 254 (μὴ δῷς) . . . μηδὲ
γυναικὶ πονηρᾷ παρρησίαν: Codd. BC, (55), 296, 308 . . . μηδὲ
γυναικὶ πονηρᾷ ἐξουσίαν: Cod. 248 . . . παρρησίαν ἐξόδου.

Latin: 'nec mulieri nequam veniam prodeundi.'
Syriac: Syr.-Hex. 'nor to a wicked woman liberty.'

The antithetical clause μὴ δῷς ὕδατι διέξοδον seems to favour the reading παρρησίαν in the sense of 'freedom of speech,' in which sense it is used in Job 27. 10, Prov. 1. 20. But the Latin shows that ἐξουσίαν, in the sense of 'liberty to go out of doors,' was an early variant, to which ἐξόδου was probably added as a gloss.

xxvi. 5.

Codd. AS², 55, 106, 155, 157, 248, 253, 296 ἐπὶ τῷ τετάρτῳ
προσώπῳ ἐφοβήθην: Codd. BC, (23), (254) . . . ἐδεήθην. Latin:
'et in quarto facies mea metuit.'

The variation of reading is probably due to the unusual construction of φοβεῖσθαι with ἐπί: but ἐδεήθην gives no intelligible sense. The Latin connects προσώπῳ ἐφοβήθην, 'I was afraid in countenance.'

xxvii. 27.

Codd. AS², 55, 106, 155, 157, 253, 254, 296, 307, 308 ὁ ποιῶν πονηρὰ εἰς αὐτὰ κυλισθήσεται [106, 254 ἐγκυλισθήσεται]: Codd. B, (23) . . . εἰς αὐτὸν κυλισθήσεται: Cod. 248 ποιοῦντι πονηρὰ ἐπ' αὐτὸν κυλισθήσεται.

Latin: S. Aug. *Speculum*, p. 142, Cod. S. Theod. 'facienti nequissimum consilium super illum devolvetur:' Codd. Tolet. Amiat. 'facienti nequissimum super ipsum devolvetur.'

Syriac: *Pesch.*, *Syr.-Hex.* 'he who devises evil will fall into it.'

The most noteworthy point is the agreement of the Latin with Cod. 248 in the possible but harsh construction 'to him that doeth mischief, it will roll upon him:' the reading of Cod. B is grammatically impossible, but critically interesting because it preserves in αὐτὸν the middle link between the reading of Cod. 248 and that of the majority of MSS., i. e. it may be supposed that when the dative ποιοῦντι was changed into the nominative, αὐτὸν was in some cases retained by an unintelligent scribe from an earlier MS.

xxviii. 1.

Codd. ABCS, 68, 157, 253, 296, 307, Vienna 1 τὰς ἁμαρτίας αὐτοῦ (157, 253 αὐτῶν) διαστηριῶν διαστηριεῖ: Codd. 23, (106), (248), 254, Vienna 2 τὰς ἁμαρτίας αὐτοῦ (254 αὐτῶν) διατηρῶν διατηρήσει: Cod. 55 τὰς ἁμαρτίας αὐτῶν διατηρήσει: Cod. 155 διατηριῶν διατηρήσει: Cod. 308 (apparently) διαστηριῶν διατηρήσει.

Latin: 'et peccata illius servans servabit.'

Syriac: *Pesch.*, *Syr.-Hex.* 'for all his sins will be carefully preserved for him,' i. e. for God.

The reading διατηρῶν διατηρήσει is confirmed not only by the versions but also by the context. The purport of the context is evidently that a man should not avenge himself upon one who has wronged him, but wait for the vengeance of God. The Pauline 'I will recompense, saith the Lord' is here expressed as 'their sins he will surely keep (in remembrance).' In the reading διαστηριῶν διαστηριεῖ there is (1) the grammatical difficulty that the use of the participle in the future would probably be without a parallel, (2) that the meaning 'their sins he will surely confirm' is not relevant to the context.

xxix. 4.

Codd. AS, 23, 106, 155, 157, 248, 253, 296, 307 πάρεσχον κόπον [307 κόλπον] τοῖς βοηθήσασιν αὐτοῖς : Codd. BC, (55), (254), (308) . . . πόνον. Latin: 'praestiterunt molestiam his qui se adiuvaverunt (adiuverunt).'

κόπος and πόνος are similarly interchanged elsewhere, e. g. Job 3. 10; Ps. 9. 35 (10. 14): 54 (55). 10, 11; Wisd. 10. 10.

xxix. 7.

(1) Codd. AS¹, 55, 155, 157, 248, 254, 296, Vienna 1 πολλοὶ οὖν χάριν πονηρίας ἀπέστρεψαν (Codd. 55, 106, 157, 254 add χεῖρα, 248 adds τὸν ἄνθρωπον) : Codd. S², 23, 253, 307 πολλοὶ οὐ χάριν πονηρίας ἀπέστρεψαν : Cod. B, (308) πολλοὶ χάριν πονηρίας ἀπέστρεψαν : Cod. 106 πολλοὶ χάριν πονηρίας ἀπέστρεψαν χεῖρα.

(2) Codd. ABS, 106, 155, 157, 254, 296, (307), 308 ἀποστερηθῆναι δωρεὰν εὐλαβήθησαν : Codd. 23, 55, 248, 253, Vienna 2 ἀποστερηθῆναι δὲ . . . : Cod. 248 omits δωρεάν.

Latin: 'multi non causa nequitiae non fenerati sunt sed fraudari gratis timuerunt.'

Syriac: *Pesch.* 'many turn away from lending, by no means on account of wickedness, but because they are afraid of an empty quarrel:' *Syr.-Hex.* (the last clause) '. . . but they shall be deprived because they feared without cause.'

In the first clause it is possible that both οὖν and οὐ may be correct. The latter word is required by the whole structure of the passage, and is supported both by good Greek MSS. and by the versions. The former is possible, because the verse is of the nature of an inference from v. 6.

The verb ἀπέστρεψαν requires an object, and the analogy of v. 9 leads us to expect a personal object : hence the τὸν ἄνθρωπον of Cod. 248 seems preferable to the χεῖρα of other MSS.

In the second clause δὲ is clearly necessary, and the retention of it in Cod. 248 shows that that MS. is based upon one which read οὐ in the first clause.

xxix. 13.

Codd. AS, 23, 55, 106, 155, 157, 254, 296, 307, 308 ὑπὲρ ἀσπίδα κράτους (157 κράνους) καὶ ὑπὲρ [55 omits] δόρυ ὁλκῆς : Codd. BC, (248), (253) . . . ὑπὲρ δόρυ ἀλκῆς.

T

Latin : 'super scutum potentis et super lanceam.'

Syriac : *Pesch.* 'a strong shield, and a spear, and a wall will it be for war.'

The reading ὀλκῆς is not only better attested, but is also a more common word in later prose and Hellenistic Greek than the poetical ἀλκῆς : 'it (sc. almsgiving) will fight for him in the face of the enemy better than a strong shield or a heavy spear.'

XXX. 11, 12, 13.

Cod. 248

1 μὴ δῷς αὐτῷ ἐξουσίαν ἐν νεότητι

  καὶ μὴ παρίδῃς τὰς ἀγνοίας αὐτοῦ

  κάμψον τὸν τράχηλον αὐτοῦ ἐν νεότητι

  καὶ θλάσον τὰς πλευρὰς αὐτοῦ ὡς ἔστι νήπιος

5 μὴ ποτε σκληρυνθεὶς ἀπειθήσῃ σοι·

  καὶ ἔσται σοι ὀδύνη ψυχῆς.

  παίδευσον τὸν υἱόν σου καὶ ἔργασαι ἐν αὐτῷ

  ἵνα μὴ ἐν τῇ ἀσχημοσύνῃ αὐτοῦ προσκόψῃς.

Codd. ABCS, 23, 55, 68, 155, 157, 253, 296, 308 omit vv. 2, 3, 6 : Cod. 106 omits vv. 2, 3 : Cod. (254) places vv. 2, 3 after v. 8.

The variants are : v. 1, Cod. 307 δός : v. 4, Codd. A, 106, 155 ἕως ἐστί : v. 5, Codd. ACS, 157, 307, 308 ἀπειθήσει, Cod. 155 ἐπιθήσει : v. 6, Cod. 106 adds ἐξ αὐτοῦ after σοι : v. 7, Cod. C has ὡς ἔστι νήπιος for ἔργασαι ἐν αὐτῷ : v. 8, Cod. 296 . . . ἐν τῇ αἰσχύνῃ αὐτοῦ προσκόψῃς, Cod. 55 . . . ἐν τῇ αἰσχημοσύνῃ σου προσκόψῃς, Cod. 308 . . . ἐν τῇ αἰσχημοσύνῃ σου προσκόψῃ.

Latin :   'non des illi potestatem in juventute

                et ne despicias cogitatus illius :

                curva cervicem ejus in juventute

                et tunde latera illius dum infans est,

                ne forte induret et non credat tibi

                et erit tibi dolor animi :

                doce filium tuum et operare in illum

                ne in turpitudinem illius offendas.'

Syriac : *Syr.-Hex.*

'Give him not power in his youth,

  Nor forgive him all his transgressions :

  Keep low his heart while he is young,

  And break his back while he is little :

Lest when he is grown strong he rebel against thee.
Teach thy son grief of mind,
And show thyself rough towards him :
Lest he cause thee to stumble by his foolishness.'

Both the Latin and the Syriac confirm the general reading of
Cod. 248 against all the other MSS. But the original of the Syriac
translation of vv. 6, 7 was evidently different from any Greek text
which has survived.

xxx. 39 (xxxiii. 31).

Codd. ACS, 23, 55, 157, 253, 254, 296, 307, Vienna 2

εἰ ἔστι σοι οἰκέτης ἔστω ὡς σύ
ὅτι ἐν αἵματι ἐκτήσω αὐτόν·
εἰ [S¹ om.] ἔστι σοι οἰκέτης ἄγε αὐτὸν ὡς ἀδελφόν,
ὅτι ὡς ἡ ψυχή σου ἐπιδεήσεις αὐτῷ.

Codd. B, (308)

εἰ ἔστι σοι οἰκέτης ἔστω ὡς σύ
ὅτι ἐν αἵματι ἐκτήσω αὐτόν·
εἰ ἔστι σοι οἰκέτης ἄγε αὐτὸν ὡς σεαυτόν,
ὅτι ὡς ἡ ψυχή σου ἐπιδεήσεις αὐτῷ.

Cod. 106

εἰ ἔστι σοι οἰκέτης [marg. add. πιστὸς] ἔστω ὡς σύ
ὅτι ἐν αἵματι ἐκτήσω αὐτόν·
ἄγε αὐτὸν ὡς ἀδελφόν,
ὅτι ὡς ἡ ψυχή σου ἐπιδεήσεις αὐτῷ.

Cod. 155

εἰ ἔστιν σοι οἰκέτης ἄγαγε αὐτὸν ὡς ἀδελφόν,
ὅτι ὡς ἡ ψυχή σου ἐπιδέησις αὐτῷ.

Cod. 248

εἰ ἔστι σοι οἰκέτης, ἔττω σοι ὡς ἡ ψυχή σου
ὅτι ἐν αἵματι ἐκτήσω αὐτόν·
εἰ ἔστι σοι οἰκέτης ἄγε αὐτὸν ὡς ἀδελφὸν
ὅτι ὡς ἡ ψυχή σου ἐπιδεήσεις αὐτῷ.

Latin :

' Si est tibi servus fidelis, sit tibi quasi anima tua :
quasi [Cod. Tol. ' et sicut '] fratrem sic eum tracta,
quoniam in sanguine animae comparasti eum.'
[Cod. Tol. ' . . . animae tuae': ' parasti ' in the margin.]

Syriac: *Pesch.*

' If thou hast one bond-servant, let him be to thee as thyself,
Because like thyself will be the loss :

If thou hast one bond-servant, treat him as thy brother;
Fight not against the blood of thy soul.'

The passage is one of the most difficult in the book: it seems evident, both from the Greek MSS. and from the Latin, that part of it has been duplicated. The key to the diversities of the Greek MSS. seems to be afforded by the Latin, which makes it probable (1) that εἰ ἔστι σοι οἰκέτης should be read only once (as in Codd. 106, 155): (2) that ὡς ἡ ψυχή σου is an epexegesis, or the original form, of ὡς σύ: (3) that ἀδελφὸν is the correct reading, if the whole clause ἄγε αὐτὸν ὡς ἀδελφὸν be not an added paraphrase of ἔστω ὡς σὺ (ὡς ἡ ψυχή σου).

It seems also probable that the unintelligible clause ὅτι ὡς ἡ ψυχή σου ἐπιδεήσεις αὐτῷ veils a paraphrase of ἐν αἵματι ἐκτήσω αὐτόν.

xxxii. 22.

Codd. AS¹, 55, 106, 155, 157, 253, 254, 307 καὶ κρινεῖ δικαίοις καὶ ποιήσει κρίσιν: Codd. B, (23), (296) . . . . δικαίως: Cod. 248 . . . . δικαίους.

Latin: ' sed judicabit justos et faciet justitiam.'

The context clearly requires δικαίοις: cf. Is. 11. 4 κρινεῖ ταπεινῷ κρίσιν.

xxxvi. (xxxiii.) 3.

Codd. AS, 23, 55, 106, 155, (157), 248, 253, 254, 296, 307, 308 ἄνθρωπος συνετὸς ἐμπιστεύσει νόμῳ καὶ ὁ νόμος αὐτῷ πιστὸς ὡς ἐρώτημα δηλῶν [106, 307 δῆλον, 248 δήλων] ἑτοίμασον λόγον καὶ οὕτως ἀκουσθήσῃ: Codd. BC . . . . ὡς ἐρώτημα δικαιων [accent uncertain].

Latin: ' homo sensatus credit legi dei et lex illi fidelis: qui interrogationem manifestat parabit [Cod. Amiat. ' paravit'] verbum et sic deprecatus exaudietur.'

The ordinary punctuation of the passage connects ὡς ἐρώτημα δηλῶν with the preceding words: and it is possible that this punctuation is anterior to Cod. B, and accounts for the reading δικαίων (if δικαίων and not δικαιῶν be intended).

But the Latin helps to make it probable that the clauses properly run as follows:—

ἄνθρωπος συνετὸς ἐμπιστεύσει νόμῳ,
καὶ νόμος αὐτῷ πιστός·
ὡς ἐρώτημα δηλῶν, ἑτοίμασον λόγον,
καὶ οὕτως . . . . [?='deprecatus'] ἀκουσθήσῃ.

'A man of understanding will put his trust in the law,
And the law will be to him trustworthy:
Fashion thy speech, as one who states a question
And so . . . . shalt thou be listened to.'

The use of ἐρώτημα in the philosophical sense of a formal question or problem is not out of harmony with the character of the book.

xxxvi. 18.

Codd. AS, 55, 155, 253, 254 πόλιν ἁγιάσματός σου . . . . τόπον καταπαύματός σου : Codd. 23, 106, 157, 248, 296, 307 πόλιν ἁγιάσματός σου . . . . τόπον καταπαύσεώς σου : Codd. B πόλιν ἁγιάσματός σου . . . . πόλιν καταπαύματός σου. The Latin supports Cod. B : 'civitati sanctificationis tuae . . . . civitati requiei tuae.'

xxxvi. 22.

Codd. AS, 155 εἰσάκουσον κύριε δεήσεως τῶν οἰκετῶν σου : Codd. BC, 23, 55, (106), (157), (248), (253), (254), (296), (307), (308) . . . . ἱκετῶν σου. The Latin supports Codd AS : 'exaudi orationes servorum tuorum:' but in Ps. 73 (74). 23 Cod. S agrees with Cod. B in reading ἱκετῶν : (Cod. A is there deficient : and neither word is a correct translation of the Hebrew עָרַר).

xxxvi. 31 (28).

Codd. AS, 23, 55, 157, 253, 254, 296, 307 τίς γὰρ πιστεύσει εὐζώνῳ λῃστῇ ἀφαλλομένῳ ἐκ πόλεως εἰς πόλιν [296 πέδιον : so 308] : Codd. BC . . . . σφαλλομένῳ . . . . : Codd. 106, 155, 248 . . . . ἐφαλλομένῳ . . . .

Latin : ' . . . . quasi succinctus lateo exsiliens de civitate in civitatem.'

Syriac : *Pesch.* ' who would trust a youth like a goat leaping from city to city ? '

The Syriac appears to supply the missing element in the metaphor : the wifeless and homeless man, wandering from city to city is like a goat leaping from rock to rock.

xxxviii. 27.

Codd. AS, 55, 106, 155, (157), 253, 296, 307 καὶ ἡ [55, 106

omit ἡ] ἐπιμονὴ αὐτοῦ ἀλλοιῶσαι ποικιλίαν : Codd. BC, 23, (248), (254), (308) .... ἡ ὑπομονὴ ....

Latin : ' assiduitas ejus variat picturam.'

The Latin confirms ἐπιμονή, ' assiduity' or ' perseverance' as distinguished from ὑπομονή, ' moral endurance.'

xxxviii. 28.

Codd. A, (157), 307 καὶ καταμανθάνων ἔργον σιδήρου : Codd. S, 55, 106, 254, 308 .... ἔργα σιδήρου : Cod. 296 ἔργοις σιδήρου : Cod. 155 .... ἐργασίαν σιδήρου : Cod. 23 .... ἔργῳ σιδήρου : Cod. 248 ἐν ἔργῳ σιδήρου : Codd. BC .... ἀργῷ σιδήρῳ : Cod. 253 ἔργου σιδήρου.

Latin : ' considerans opus ferri.'

The reading ἀργῷ σιδήρῳ 'unwrought iron' (ἀργὸς is used of metal in this sense in Joseph. *B. J.* 7. 8. 4 ἀργός τε σίδηρος καὶ χαλκὸς ἔτι δὲ καὶ μόλιβδος, so Pausan. 3. 12. 3) is in itself possible : the smith is sitting at the anvil and looking at the glowing unwrought mass on which he is about to work : but the difficulty of the use of the dative case with καταμανθάνων seems insuperable. If the reading of Cod. A, ἔργον σιδήρου, be correct, there does not appear to be any adequate reason for the numerous variations : the Syriac translation ' implements of weight' suggests that the original reading was the comparatively rare word ἐργαλεῖα (σιδήρου), which is found only in Ex. 27. 19 : 39. 21 (40). The picture would thus be that of a smith sitting at the anvil, and scanning his implements : very soon καρδίαν δώσει εἰς συντέλειαν ἔργων, ' he will give his mind to the completing of the works.'

xxxix. 13.

Codd. ACS, 23, 106, (157), 248, 253, 296, 307, 308 βλαστήσατε ὡς ῥόδον φυόμενον ἐπὶ ῥεί'ματος ὑγροῦ : Codd. B, (55), 155, (254), ... ἐπὶ ῥεύματος ἀγροῦ.

Latin : ' quasi rosa plantata super rivos [Cod. Amiat. ' rivum '] aquarum.'

The quotation of the passage in Clem. Alex. *Paed.* 2. 8, p. 216, ὡς ῥόδον πεφυτευμένον ἐπὶ ῥευμάτων ὑδάτων βλαστήσατε, is remarkable as giving the Greek original of the Latin, and thereby showing that a recension existed which does not survive in any MS.

xlii. 5.

Codd. ACS, 155, 157, 253, 307 περὶ διαφόρου πράσεως ἐμπόρων:
Codd. 23, 106, 248, 254, 296 περὶ ἀδιαφόρου πράσεως ἐμπόρων:
Codd. B, (55), (308) περὶ ἀδιαφόρου πράσεως καὶ ἐμπόρων.

The Latin, ' de corruptione emptionis et negotiatorum,' points to a reading διαφθορᾶς for διαφόρου: probably through a misunderstanding of the meaning of διαφόρου, ' purchase-money.'

xliii. 9.

Codd. ACS², 55, 106, 155, (157), 248, 253, 254, 307 κόσμος φωτίζων ἐν ὑψίστοις κυρίου: Cod. 23 κόσμον φωτίζων ἐν ὑψίστοις κύριος: Codd. B, (296), (308) κόσμος φωτίζων ἐν ὑψίστοις κύριος.

Latin: ' mundum illuminans in excelsis dominus.'

It seems probable that Cod. 23 has preserved the right reading, and that there are four parallel clauses, each referring to the moon: that is to say, the moon is described as

κάλλος οὐρανοῦ,
δόξα ἄστρων,
κόσμον φωτίζων,
ἐν ὑψίστοις κύριος.

xliii. 25.

Codd. ACS κτῆσις κτηνῶν: Cod. 248 κρίσις κητῶν: Codd. 106, 157 κτῆσις κήτων: Codd. 254, 307 κτίσις κτηνῶν: Codd. B, (23), (55), (155), (253), (296) κτίσις (308 πτίσις) κητῶν.

The Latin, ' creatura belluarum,' makes it probable that κτίσις κτηνῶν is the true reading. But itacisms are so frequent that nothing certain can be determined from the Greek MSS.

xliv. 17.

Codd. AS², 55, 106, 155, 157, 254, 308—

Νῶε εὑρέθη τέλειος δίκαιος·
ἐν [106, 157 καὶ ἐν] καιρῷ ὀργῆς ἐγένετο ἀντάλλαγμα·
διὰ τοῦτο ἐγενήθη κατάλειμμα τῇ γῇ,
ὅτε ἐγένετο κατακλυσμός [106, 155, 157 ὁ κατ.].

Codd. 23, 248—

Νῶε εὑρέθη τέλειος δίκαιος·
ἐν καιρῷ ὀργῆς ἐγένετο ἀντάλλαγμα·
διὰ τοῦτο ἐγένετο κατακλυσμός [248 ὁ κατ.].

Codd. B, 253—

Νῶε εὑρέθη τέλειος δίκαιος·
ἐν καιρῷ ὀργῆς ἐγένετο ἀντάλλαγμα·
διὰ τοῦτο ἐγενήθη [253 ἐγένετο] κατάλειμμα τῇ γῇ
διὰ τοῦτο ἐγένετο κατακλυσμός.

Latin :

'Noe inventus est perfectus justus
et in tempore iracundiae factus est reconciliatio.'

Syriac : *Pesch.*

'Noah was found just, a peacemaker in his time :
    At the time of the flood he was appointed a ransom for
        the world,
    And for his sake was salvation made.'

It seems probable that ὅτε ἐγένετο is the true reading, and that
the phrase ὅτε ἐγένετο κατακλυσμὸς balances and explains ἐν καιρῷ
ὀργῆς. But it is also possible that the Latin preserves the original
form of the passage, and that ἐγενήθη κατάλειμμα τῇ γῇ and ὅτε ἐγένετο
κατακλυσμὸς are glosses respectively of ἐγένετο ἀντάλλαγμα and ἐν καιρῷ
ὀργῆς : this hypothesis would account for the shortened form which
is found in Codd. 23, 248.

xlv. 20.

Codd. AS, 55, 253 ἀπαρχὰς πρωτογενημάτων ἐμέρισεν αὐτῷ ἄρτον
πρώτοις ἡτοίμασεν ἐν πλησμονῇ. The variants on this text are
Cod. 248 ἀπαρχήν, Codd. 68 αὐτοῖς, Cod. 23 ἄρτοις πρώτοις,
Codd. 106, 157, (254) ἐν πρώτοις, Cod. S¹ πρῶτον γενήματος,
Cod. B αὐτοῖς and πλησμονήν, Codd. 106, 157 εἰς πλησμονήν,
Cod. 155 πλησμονῇ.

Latin : 'primitias frugum [Cod. Amiat. 'fructuum'] terrae divisit
illi : panem ipsis in primis paravit in satietatem.'

Syriac : *Pesch.* 'he made the firstfruits of the sanctuary his inheritance, and the order of the bread, for himself and for his
seed.'

The Latin suggests that the original text was .... ἐμέρισεν αὐτῷ,
ἄρτον αὐτοῖς ἐν πρώτοις ἡτοίμασεν εἰς πλησμονήν : this hypothesis will
account for the variants of Cod. B, 23, 106, 157.

xlvi. 15.

Codd. ACS, 23, 55, 106, 155, 157, 248, 253, 254, 296, 308 καὶ
ἐγνώσθη [155 ἐπεγνώσθη] ἐν ῥήμασιν [23, 55, 248, 253, 254, 296

ῥήματι] αὐτοῦ πιστὸς [23 πίστει, 253 πίστις] ὁράσεως [248 omits πιστὸς ὁράσεως]: Cod. B πίστει for ῥήμασιν (ῥήματι).

Latin: ' et cognitus est in verbis suis fidelis quia vidit Deum lucis.'

The Latin confirms the reading of the majority of MSS., and gives a remarkable gloss of ὁράσεως : 'his words showed that he was trustworthy in respect of his vision,' i.e. 'that he was to be believed when he said that he had seen the God of light.' But the phrase in c. xlviii. 22 is πιστὸς ἐν ὁράσει αὐτοῦ.

Such an examination as the preceding, since it is limited to a small number of passages, does not warrant a final induction. But inasmuch as the passages have not been chosen with a view to support any previously formed opinion, they may be taken as typical, and consequently as both suggesting provisional results and indicating the lines which further research may profitably pursue.

The points which will probably be most generally allowed to be established by the preceding examination are these :

(1) The great value of the versions in regard to the restoration of the text. The glosses and double versions which they embody frequently point to readings which have not survived in any Greek MS., but which carry with them a clear conviction of their truth.

(2) The inferior value of some of the more famous uncial MSS. as compared with some cursives. Of the uncial MSS. the Venetian MS. (H. and P. No. 23) is clearly the most trustworthy : whereas the Vatican MS. B preserves in many cases a text which is neither probable in itself nor supported by other evidence. The book affords in this respect a corroboration of the opinion that the same MSS. have different values for different books.

(3) The field which is open to conjectural emendation. There are cases in which neither MSS. nor versions have preserved an intelligible text : and since it is clear that the book has existed in more than one form, that it has passed

through the hands of scribes who did not understand it, and that there was no such reverence for it as would preserve its text from corruption, the same process may legitimately be applied to it which is applied to the fragments of Greek philosophers. In some cases such conjectures have a degree of probability which closely approximates to certainty.

INDEX OF BIBLICAL PASSAGES.

Passages treated at length or explained are marked with an asterisk after the page.